D1562270

Defensive Nationalism

*Explaining the Rise of Populism and
Fascism in the 21st Century*

B. S. RABINOWITZ

OXFORD
UNIVERSITY PRESS

OXFORD
UNIVERSITY PRESS

Oxford University Press is a department of the University of Oxford. It furthers the University's objective of excellence in research, scholarship, and education by publishing worldwide. Oxford is a registered trade mark of Oxford University Press in the UK and certain other countries.

Published in the United States of America by Oxford University Press
198 Madison Avenue, New York, NY 10016, United States of America.

Library of Congress Cataloging-in-Publication Data
Names: Rabinowitz, Beth, author.
Title: Defensive nationalism : explaining the rise of populism and fascism in the 21st century / by B. S. Rabinowitz.
Description: New York, NY : Oxford University Press, [2023] | Includes bibliographical references and index. |
Contents: The concepts : populism, nationalism, fascism and nativism— The synthesis: a new typology of nationalism—Karl Polanyi : theory & ambiguity— Joseph Schumpeter : technology and the "double movement"— The belle époque : railroads & telegraphy—The digital age : turbojets & computers— Economic reorganization & economic crises—Mass media & fake news— Mass immigration & global terrorism—From globalization to the nation— The turn inward : nativism & fascism—The concert of Europe— The Bretton Woods era—Conclusion : using history as a guide.
Identifiers: LCCN 2022054630 (print) | LCCN 2022054631 (ebook) | ISBN 9780197672044 (paperback) | ISBN 9780197672037 (hardback) | ISBN 9780197672068 (epub)
Subjects: LCSH: Nationalism—History. | Populism—History. | Fascism—History.
Classification: LCC JC311 .R212 2023 (print) | LCC JC311 (ebook) | DDC 320.54—dc23/eng/20230103
LC record available at https://lccn.loc.gov/2022054630
LC ebook record available at https://lccn.loc.gov/2022054631

DOI: 10.1093/oso/9780197672037.001.0001

Paperback printed by Marquis Book Printing, Canada
Hardback printed by Bridgeport National Bindery, Inc., United States of America

The book is dedicated to my father, Paul Rabinowitz, who died much too early but whose devoted love and intellectual curiosity have continued to guide me.

Contents

Acknowledgments

Several people have supported me in this project. Most of all I want to thank my two research assistants, Lilliana (Yanan) Li and Kathryn Jackson, whose steadfast support, diligent and careful work, and generous spirit have been invaluable to this project. Colleagues have also supported me. First is Richard Harris, who read through innumerable drafts and was always happy to engage with me in thoughtful discussions that pressed me to clarify my ideas. I am also always and forever indebted to Steven K. Vogel and Beverly Crawford, who have been mentors to me. They both kindly waded through a lengthy draft to give me incisive feedback. Among my fellow faculty, Lorraine Minette and John Wall generously read through some of the earlier formulations of my typologies and provided probing questions that helped me strengthen my arguments. Senior colleagues Paul Jarkowsky and Marie Chevrier have always been there for me to answer questions and guide me when needed. Although across a vast ocean, Catherine Boone has continued to be an inspiration and to believe in my endeavors, even though they have migrated far away from hers. Finally, I want to thank my editor, Angela Chnapko, who believed in this project from the beginning and has been supportive throughout.

Introduction

The Paradox of Modernity

Ours is an age of extreme paradoxes. Wristwatch telephones, driverless cars, and domestic robots that take care of mundane tasks like cleaning floors and shopping for groceries have become commonplace. Space travel is available to anyone who can pay for it. Soon untold innovations, like the Metaverse with its 3D virtual worlds, Artificial Intelligence programs, and perhaps even quantum computers, will transform everything from industry and finance and city planning to healthcare and education and dating. Indeed, it could be said that we are living in the science-fiction future of the 1950s. However, the threats that we face today are nothing like the Giant Insects and Alien Invaders that titillated and terrified mid-century moviegoers. Dangers to the stability of the world in the twenty-first century are less exotic and more treacherous than that. In the most advanced nations, we have witnessed the rise of anti-intellectual movements. Bizarre conspiracy theories and a broad distrust of science and expertise have taken hold across the developed world. At the same time, extreme ideologies, on both the right and the left, have gained ascendance across Europe and the United States, effectively splitting societies in two.

If ever there were a period animated by a spirit of its own, we appear to be in the midst of one. But, in fact, this is not the first time that history has witnessed an epoch of such vast contradictions. The turn of the last century was a period of great social, scientific, and technological promise. It was an age of new modes of traveling, thinking, dressing, and interacting. An age that saw the end of monarchical rule in Europe and brought into being the "New Woman." And still, despite all its hopes and prospects, the period went from the heights of science and rationality to the depths of irrationalism and hatred. The starkness of the transition is marked by the words of the prominent sociologist S. H. Swinny on the eve of World War I. In 1913, Swinny wrote, "it is in the modern world alone that we have seen the continuous development of science and the widening of the moral sphere, the recognition

Defensive Nationalism. B. S. Rabinowitz, Oxford University Press. © Oxford University Press 2023.
DOI: 10.1093/oso/9780197672037.003.0001

of the brotherhood of all mankind."[1] Only one year later the world would be consumed by one of the most destructive wars in history.

Is it possible that the explosive politics that erupted at the turn of both centuries is rooted in the very technological changes that brought mankind to its highest levels of sophistication? Might it be that mankind's greatest achievements can produce toxic political upheavals? This book maintains that such is the case. The claim will be made that the reason the present has so many corollaries with the turn of the nineteenth century is that in both eras, seemingly miraculous technological innovations connected people, products, money, and ideas in ways that could not have been imagined. These changes made life easier in many ways, but also unleashed widespread social and political disruptions. As global capitalism took possession of the world, social protections that had been established were stripped away, inequalities were exacerbated, and national economies were made defenseless against the actions of faraway bankers and speculators. The very organization of societies came under threat. With social disruptions proliferating, self-seeking politicians were able to galvanize growing fear and anxiety to launch left-wing populist and proto-fascist movements. What emerged was an era of national populism—what is labeled here an era of *defensive nationalism*.

Why Defensive Nationalism?

In the summer of 2017, a large assembly of torch-bearing protestors defiantly waving Nazi flags marched through Charleston chanting, "Jews will not replace us!" The bold-faced embrace of Nazism in the heart of the United States was a sign of how much the world had changed. It was, in fact, a symptom of something much larger. From 2008 to 2020 an explosion of populism and nativism erupted across the Global North on a scale not seen for a century. Nativist parties, which had existed on the margins of European politics, achieved significant and in some cases quite sizable representation in parliaments across Eastern and Western Europe. In Italy, Greece, Hungary, and Poland, parties unabashedly identified themselves as fascist. Even in the USA, white nationalism, which had been a small fringe movement, had edged its way into mainstream politics.

During the same period, the progressive and far left, long dormant in Europe and the United States, were in ascendance. Far-left parties gained support across Europe, from Podemos in Spain (2014), to Syriza in Greece

(2015), to the Left Bloc in Portugal (2015),[2] to the far-left *La Nouvelle Union populaire écologique et sociale* in France (2022).[3] In the United States and the United Kingdom, Bernie Sanders and Jeremy Corbyn, both self-proclaimed socialists, credibly contested the highest political office in their respective nations in the 2010s. Concurrently, progressive movements erupted across the globe, including the "Me-Too" social movement against sexual abuse, sexual harassment, and rape culture; anti-femicide marches in countries as diverse as Mexico, Italy, Turkey, and Sudan; and Black Lives Matter rallies held in the United States, Europe, and even Kenya.

In response to these world events, a deluge of scholarship followed. As varied as this literature is, a rough convergence has emerged. It is now broadly held that today's nativist and populist movements are interrelated responses to displacements created by globalization.[4] A general acceptance has also developed as to what the attributes of nativism and populism are.[5] Given the amount of ink that has been spilled on populism, nativism, and fascism, it is hard to imagine that much more can be said. But some puzzles do remain.

One rather important question that has not been fully answered is how populism connects or overlaps with nationalism. This may seem like a minor concern, but understanding how and when populism and nationalism merge is critical to explaining the rise of early twenty-first-century politics. In fact, it is at the heart of the matter. The political movements that have engulfed Europe and the United States clearly share attributes of both populism and nationalism. But neither concept fully encompasses what we are experiencing.[6] Identifying what the relationship is between the two, therefore, is central to explaining the politics of today.

The puzzling nature of the link between nationalism and populism has engendered a scholarly debate. On one side of the debate, it is asserted that populism and nationalism are quite distinct from one another and that, therefore, it is vital to analytically differentiate between the two.[7] The proponents of this idea argue that the outstanding feature of populism is championing the rights of "the people" against the corrupt elite establishment. Thus, at its core populism is a *vertically oriented* dichotomy, meaning it is an opposition between "the elite" and "the people." Nationalism, by contrast, is not concerned with how the "little guy" is being trampled by power and money. Quite the reverse, nationalism actually links "elites": to "the people" in a sense of shared group membership. Its central concern is to ensure that the rights of the "true citizens" are safeguarded against the encroachments of "outsiders." Nationalism is, thus, a *horizontally oriented* dichotomy that distinguishes between "us" and "them," or as social scientists put it, "in-groups" and "out-groups." The rebuttal[8] to this argument is that these concepts are more interrelated than this characterization suggests. At the heart of both nationalism and populism is promoting "the people's" interests. The existing gulf between nationalism and populism is not intrinsic to the concepts themselves. Rather, it is due largely to the fact that scholarship on nationalism has developed separately from studies of nativism/populism. We should thus be leery of using simple dichotomies to differentiate between them and instead work harder to understand how "the people" are constructed within and across both categories.

So how does the project of protecting "the citizenry" and safeguarding "the nation" intersect with defending "the people" against "the corrupt elite"? Can we reconcile these differences? This book argues we can; indeed, that we must if we are to better account for the movements that have swept across the Western world in the first decades of the twenty-first century. It seeks to answer these questions by presenting a new approach to the study of nationalism, which differentiates between *creative, consolidating,* and *defensive nationalism.* The central argument made is that both the turn of the twentieth and twenty-first centuries were "eras" of *defensive nationalism.* Defensive nationalism is defined here as a form of national populism that combines anti-liberalism and anti-globalization with economic nationalism, and which has both right- and left-wing expressions.[9] An era of defensive nationalism erupts when many nation-states are assaulted by global economic and demographic changes at the same time.

What follows is a study of what defensive nationalism is, why it arises, and what its political implications are. This is achieved by examining parallels across the Western world during the Second Industrial Revolution (1860–1910s) and the Digital Revolution (1960–2010s). In both periods, profound changes in communications and transportation contributed to internationally contagious economic crises, great flows of labor migration, extreme wealth inequality, and international terrorist movements that spread fear and distrust globally. In both periods, these disorienting changes brought into being a surge of right- and left-wing defensive nationalists.[10]

Comparing the centuries also suggests possible political directions we might be headed in. We certainly know how things ended a century ago. In the early twentieth century, the United States entered an era of progressive politics, while Europe fell to communism, fascism, and world wars. What does that bode for the twenty-first century? The jury is still out, but a central reason for writing this book is to consider how history might provide a template for the direction the Western world is moving toward over the next couple of decades.

Theory Behind the Model

Several scholars have examined the end of the nineteenth century to understand the rise of contemporary populist movements.[11] This book's contribution is to explore how the past might offer clues to the present by drawing on the works of two great theorists of the postwar era: Karl Polanyi and Joseph Schumpeter. Both were witnesses to the rise of communism, fascism, and world wars. Acute observers of the social world, each developed a theory to explain the extraordinary changes that occurred in his lifetime.

In 1944, Karl Polanyi published his singular work *The Great Transformation*.[12] The book offers an inspired explanation for the tragedies that befell Europe in the early twentieth century. In it, Polanyi traces the dramatic global shift from liberalism to fascism and socialism that developed roughly between 1860 and 1930. Polanyi argues that a decisive break occurred in the world order in the mid-1800s with the rise of finance capitalism. Finance capitalism was a wholly new and much more insidious form of capitalism, in which the great houses of finance came to direct everything from domestic policy to international relations. Whether the Rothschild family with their several banks across Europe, or the powerful industrialist John Pierpont Morgan in the United States, the world's financiers were able to prevent states from promulgating laws regarded as inimical to industry. National governments were also compelled to adopt the gold standard, effectively placing domestic economies at the mercy of international capital.

Thus, finance capitalism shaped a new globalized economy based on free-market values. But laissez-faire economics failed to produce the promised golden age. As market triumphalism took over, global economic downturns caused widespread suffering. Groups across Europe rose in opposition to the crushing conditions created by industrialization and finance capitalism. This ultimately led to the wholesale rejection of liberalism and the embrace of communism and fascism. For these reasons, Polanyi characterizes the late nineteenth-century period as a period of the "double movement": a period of economic liberalism accompanied by anti-liberal political responses.

In recent years, many academics have turned to Polanyi to explain today's social and political backlash. Polanyi's theory of the "double movement" offers a tantalizing means for explaining our present age. It is not a far stretch to see that much of what Polanyi describes of the "double movement" is easily ascribable to changes afoot today: from the liberalization of markets starting in the 1970s, to hyper-globalization of the turn of the century, to the recrudescence of nationalism and protectionism in recent decades. So many passages sound strikingly descriptive of our own times, it would seem that the concept of the "double movement" could explain the contagious spread of nativism and populism across the globe. It might also offer some insight into what could be in store for us in the coming decades.

However, applying Polanyi to the contemporary world poses serious difficulties. Polanyi himself does not offer a concrete means for understanding how such a cycle might re-emerge. To the contrary, Polanyi believed the period of the late nineteenth century was wholly unique; so much so that he characterizes the late nineteenth century as "sui generis." Therefore, those of us who find the "double movement" a compelling concept are left asking: What exactly is meant by the "double movement," and what conditions can be identified to explain its re-emergence?

To develop a means for analyzing how a second cycle of the "double movement" could occur, this study turns to the works of Joseph Schumpeter. As Polanyi, Schumpeter was interested in understanding how the great economic and industrial developments of the late nineteenth century put in motion the dramatic transformations that ultimately led to the rise of fascism and communism. In contradistinction to Polanyi, Schumpeter traces those changes not to finance capital and the gold standard, but to that which spurred intense financial speculation in the first place: railroadization.[13] For Schumpeter, the driving force behind the economic and political changes of the first half of the twentieth century were the new technologies developed during the nineteenth century.

Combining these two theories, this study analyzes the emergence of Polanyi's "double movement" in both eras as an outgrowth of sudden technological transformation. Indeed, the mid-1800s and the mid-1900s each mark the beginning of a dramatic period of innovation: the Second Industrial Revolution and the Digital Revolution, respectively. Both technological revolutions ushered in astonishing advances in communications and transportation that unified the world in unprecedented ways. These staggeringly rapid periods of modernization brought with them all manner of improvements for mankind; but they also produced widespread social dislocation. Eventually, the economic and social disruptions created by the new globalizing technologies engendered anti-liberal, national populist movements. In short, entrepreneurial innovations of the Second Industrial Revolution and the Digital Revolution made liberal globalization possible, which, in turn, engendered its opposite, an epoch of *defensive nationalism*—Polanyi's "double movement."

Outline of the Book

The book proceeds in five parts. In Part I, concepts and theories are contrasted and synthesized to produce a workable model for studying the "double movement." Parts II, III, and IV then apply the theoretical model developed in Part I to history (see Table I.1). Finally, Part V goes beyond the theories of Polanyi and Schumpeter, to examine the political preconditions that existed prior to the double movement. Thus, where Part I explains *how* the "double movement" can be studied, Parts II through IV illustrate *what* is similar about these two epochs and makes them analytically comparable, and Part V makes the case for *why* high liberalism and finance capitalism emerged in both periods.

Part I presents the theoretical model that will be used to analyze the two periods of historical change. Chapter 1 begins by offering some background to how nationalism, populism, fascism, and nativism have been analyzed to date, and what the challenges are to understanding how they converge and diverge from one another. Chapter 2 introduces a new tri-part typology of nationalism: *creative, consolidating,* and *defensive* nationalism. The typology synthesizes elements of existing concepts and organizes them into new categories. The chapter ends with a stylized sketch of right- and left-wing versions of defensive nationalism. Chapter 3 discusses the theoretical construct of the "double movement" in greater detail. The chapter commences with a more in-depth exploration of Polanyi's theory. It then examines the limitations inherent in Polanyi's work. Last, Chapter 4 explains how Schumpeter's theory of technology can be combined with Polanyi's to overcome some of these constraints. The chapter ends by explaining why the concept of *defensive nationalism* can provide a valuable tool for applying this combined theoretical model of the "double movement."

Table I.1 Similarities Between the Turn-of-the-Century Periods

	1860–1920	*1960–2020*
Revolution	Second Industrial	Digital
Postwar Peace	Concert of Europe	Bretton Woods
International Hegemon	Britain (post Napoleonic Wars)	USA (post world wars)
Economic Organization	Agricultural to Industrial Production	Mass Production (Fordism) to Flexible Production (Post-Fordism)
Int'l Monetary System	1870s—Bimetallism to Gold Standard	1973—Gold Standard to Fiat Money System
Transportation Innovations	Railroads/ Steam Engine	Turbojet Airplanes/ Shipping Containers
Communications Innovations	Printing Press, Paper pulp Telegraph, Ticker Tape	Solid-State Computers, Satellites, Internet, Cell Phones
Communications Interconnectivity	Popular Postal Systems Mail-order Catalog Mass newspaper/journal circulation Yellow Journalism	Email Online Shopping Cable TV, Social Media "Post-Truth"
Inequality & Wealth Concentration	Robber Barons	Big Tech/Banking
Int'l Economic Crises	Panic of 1873 Long Depression 1873–1879 1893 Depression Panic of 1901 Panic of 1907 1929 Wall Street Crash	1973, 1979 Oil Shocks 1987 Market Crash 2001 dot.com crash 2007–2008 Financial Crisis 2022 Global Recession
Global Pandemic	Spanish Flu 1918–1921	COVID-19 2019–2022
Mass Emigrations	From Ireland, Germany, Italy, Eastern Europe, China	From the Middle East, Africa, Latin America, Asia
International Terrorism	Anarchist	Islamist
Political Outcomes	Progressive Era, Fascism, Communism, world wars	???

Part II explains the rise of liberal capitalism, or the first part of Polanyi's "double movement." Separate comparative histories of these two turn-of-the-century periods are presented to illustrate the unique magnitude of interconnectivity that characterized both. This section will show that innovations in communications and transportation allowed for the globalization of finance and trade and the spread of liberal ideology. Chapter 5 examines critical aspects of the period from 1860 to 1890. The chapter traces the impact of railroads, steamships, telegraphy, paper pulp, and the printing press on multiple aspects of society and the economy. Chapter 6 offers a parallel analysis of the mid-twentieth century, paying particular attention to the combined effects of turbojets, containerships, satellites, computers, the Internet, and cell phones.

Part III and Part IV both focus on the second half of the "double movement." Part III presents a series of chapters that describe the social and economic dislocations created by globalizing liberalism, while Part IV looks at the political responses to those profoundly disorienting changes. In Part III, three separate chapters analyze some of the more consequential disruptions of the eras. Chapter 7 examines how massive reorganization of the global economy impacted existing social structures and made domestic economies extremely vulnerable to global price shocks. Chapter 8 looks at the new forms of mass media that emerged and the effects those media changes had on society and political stability. Finally, Chapter 9 outlines the ways in which mass migrations and new forms of globalized terror further destabilized the Western world. Following this, Part IV examines how political elites were able to capitalize on these social and economic dislocations, to challenge the established order and mobilize anti-liberal, anti-global, economic nationalist movements. Chapter 10 identifies the defensive national movements that took hold across Europe and the United States in both periods. It looks at what motivated these new defensive national movements, who led them, and how the right- and left-wing forms compare with one another. Chapter 11 looks more specifically at the emergence of nativism and fascism in both periods.

The final part of the book moves beyond Polanyi and Schumpeter. For it is not enough to present a practical means to identify and study the "double movement." It is also necessary to account for why it emerged, that is, what was distinctive about both periods that allowed for finance and trade to globalize to such extraordinary proportions. Accordingly, Part V provides an explanation for what precipitated the "double movement." The section argues that the critical factor that accounts for the initial rise of liberalism and globalization was an extended period of peace among the global powers of the day. In other words, the "double movement" was made possible by unique interludes of cooperation among the most economically advanced nations. Chapter 12 catalogs how the negotiated peace settlement following the Napoleonic Wars, called the "Concert of Europe," provided the space for trade and innovation to flourish. Chapter 13 will look at the how Bretton Woods accords that were reached after the two great world wars also produced a period in which finance, trade, and innovation were able to reach historic levels, setting the cycle in motion for a second time. The book concludes with a discussion of the limitations of this historical comparison, but also considers how comparing our age to these bygone years might be fruitful for thinking about possible future developments.

PART I

THEORY

Over the past two decades, talk show hosts, news pundits, academic scholars, and editorial writers have been absorbed by the rise of populism, nativism, and fascism in our times. Most present only one piece of the puzzle, whether that be the relationship between populism and nativism, or the similarity of right-wing movements across the centuries, or populism's connection to globalization. Often these discussions are also partial in that they tend to focus on radical politics, either of the right or the left, without explaining how each relates to the other. This book seeks to connect the dots across these various and sundry discourses.

The thesis of this book is that the only way to explain the fact that parallel movements on both the right and the left are forming across so many countries at the same time is that we are witnessing a generalized response to structural changes in the global system. Moreover, this response has occurred before. The turn of the nineteenth century was a period characterized by similarly puzzling dichotomies: unparalleled scientific and technological advances produced economic and social interconnectivity across the globe that was followed almost immediately by a dangerous inward turn toward nationalism. Most surprising of all, this rejection of internationalism was particularly strong among the most technologically and economically advanced nations. Put simply, both were epochs of a "double movement."

But such an assertion leaves us with a critical question: What does it mean to say, in effect, that "history is repeating itself"? Obviously, history does not literally repeat itself. Every time period is different from the one that preceded it. There has to be some kind of reasonable analytic model that can guide such a reading of history. So, the task here is to develop clearly specified guidelines for comparing these turn-of-the-century periods. Accordingly, this book takes a two-step approach. The first step is to clarify what the theoretical basis could be for making such a large claim. The second is to apply that theoretical model empirically to the two time periods.

Part I lays the analytic groundwork for the historical analysis that follows. In the four chapters that make up this section of the book, existing concepts and theories are contrasted and synthesized to produce a workable model that can be used to study the "double movement" in different time periods. Chapter One provides the foundation for this endeavor, by introducing key aspects of the concepts being investigated, namely nationalism, populism, fascism, and nativism. The chapter examines how these four discourses converge as well as where they depart from one another. Chapter Two builds upon these existing categories by presenting a new typology that organizes elements of these four concepts into novel categories of nationalism: *creative*, *consolidating*, and *defensive nationalism*. The chapter ends with a more extensive discussion of right- and left-wing versions of defensive nationalism.

Having established the foundation that lies behind the construct of defensive nationalism, the next two chapters describe critical elements of Polanyi's and Schumpeter's theories. The deeper examination of these theories is undertaken to explain how they will be amalgamated into a coherent analytic model. Chapter Three discusses in greater detail the theoretical construct of the "double movement." The chapter commences with an exploration of Polanyi's theory and then discusses the limitations inherent in it as well as the challenges of applying the "double movement" to a different period. Chapter Four surveys key aspects of Schumpeter's theory of technology and explains how it can be combined with Polanyi's concepts to overcome some of these constraints. The chapter ends by explaining why "defensive nationalism" provides a valuable tool for applying this combined theoretical model of historical change to both time periods.

1

The Concepts

Populism, Nationalism, Fascism, and Nativism

It is difficult to watch the news these days without hearing someone utter the words "white nationalism," "populism," or "fascism." We hear equally about the "radical left," "cancel culture," and "replacement theory." We understand these things are encircling us, but how best to label them is a lot less clear. Is it true that we are on the precipice of fascism? Or is that merely hyped-up rhetoric? And how does this all relate to "cancel culture" and the far left? Scholars are puzzling through a parallel series of questions. There are debates over how and when populism and nationalism overlap, and what the relationship is between nativism, neo-fascism, and fascism. The problem is that although all these concepts clearly relate to one another, they do not wholly coincide.

This book seeks to answer these questions by reorganizing concepts commonly associated with nationalism, nativism, fascism, and populism. Accordingly, what follows is a regrouping of existing taxonomies. The goal is to produce a new approach to nationalism that will better unify these various strains. To that end, this chapter outlines the concepts that will be reworked: nationalism, populism, fascism, and nativism. It presents, in short form, the basic ideas associated with each of these concepts, highlighting how they align and where they diverge. The chapter is divided into four sections, each of which introduces something of the history of each concept, as well as the approaches that scholars have taken to define each.

Nationalism

Nationalism might seem to have always existed, but it hasn't. At least not in the guise that we know it today. For most of history, "nations" were understood to be communities of shared descent with a common language, customs, and traditions, but they were not fused with a state.[1] Indeed, the compound noun "nation-state" is peculiarly modern. In ancient Rome, the

Defensive Nationalism. B. S. Rabinowitz, Oxford University Press. © Oxford University Press 2023.
DOI: 10.1093/oso/9780197672037.003.0002

root term for nation, *natio*, was contrasted with the term *civitas*, which referred to a body of citizens united under law. The schism between a legal-
political unit and a nation of shared ancestry remained throughout the
Middle Ages and into early modern times. The union of "*natio*" and "*civitas*"
only came about in the late eighteenth century, when empires were toppled,
and the sovereignty of kings was transferred to the people. Ever since states
have been equated with the populations they represent, "the nation," and it is
"the people" to which the sovereignty of the state inheres.

France's expansionism was the central catalyst behind this late eighteenth-
century political convulsion. As Napoleon marched his forces across Europe,
new leaders emerged rousing people to resist French Imperialism. The
early nationalists were "a small number of scholars, publicists, and poets."[2]
In Prussia, German philosopher Johann Gottlieb Fichte (1808/2008) made
a series of public addresses urging the Germanic-speaking youth to rise up
and fight against the French invasion. Fichte claimed that the Germanic peoples, though physically divided, were naturally a "nation" linked by their
superior language and culture. He warned that if the thirty-nine German-
speaking states did not unite into one nation-state, their Germanic heritage
could be forever lost to French *Civilisatrice*. A similar process occurred in the
areas now considered Italy. When the French invaded the "boot" of Europe,
they defeated a medley of principalities and kingdoms. Napoleon imposed
a surrogate government upon the region to rationalize the administration
of its various states. In response, the Italian journalist Giuseppe Mazzini
beseeched the Italian people to form a unified political front and resist the
French. In equally stirring speeches, Mazzini called upon the peoples of Italy
to overcome their differences and defend the "nation" God had so clearly
ordained for them by providing natural boundaries of "great rivers" and
"lofty mountains."[3]

At the end of the century, French historian and linguist Ernest Renan
argued that these definitions of nationalism were misleading and, moreover, were producing dangerous xenophobia. In his famous lecture, "What
Is a Nation?" (*Qu'est-ce qu'une nation?*), Renan showed that nationalism was
based neither on language and culture, nor geography, nor was it ancient or
God given. He explained that, in point of fact, nationalism was a relatively
recent phenomenon in human history, created through historical accident.
Modern states had developed over centuries, through conquest and assimi-
lation; their populations and borders shifting over time. Any honest look at
history would reveal that there has been no continuity:

France is Celtic, Iberian, Germanic. Germany is Germanic, Celtic, and Slavic. And in no country is ethnography more embarrassed than Italy. Gauls, Etruscans, Pélasgians, Greeks, and any number of other groups have crossed there producing an unquantifiable mixtures. The British Isles, taken together, present a mixture of Celtic and German blood the proportions of which are singularly difficult to define. The truth of the matter is that there are no pure races.[4]

To Mazzini's assertions of Italy's God-given borders, Renan replied that geography could no more determine a nation than race, for though "It is incontestable that mountains separate"[5] it is also true that some mountain ranges do not. Hence, nothing conclusive can be derived from fact that a mountain divides the land. The nation's long-historical continuity is, in truth, nothing more than a chimera built on myths of historical glory and martyred heroes. In fact, what makes nationalism possible is the forgetting of uncomfortable truths, "The act of forgetting, I would even say historical error, is an essential factor in the creation of a nation."[6] Though Renan acknowledges that myths are an essential ingredient of nationalism, he maintains that the core of nationalism is not culture but *civic belonging*. Therefore, nationalism, Renan proclaimed, was a social contract between the territorial government and its citizens, what he referred to as a "daily plebiscite."

By the mid-twentieth century, this dichotomous understanding of nationalism as an exclusive ethnic identity determined by blood or nature, versus a historically constructed identity based on legal categories, had become the bedrock of nationalism studies. In recent years, these categories have come under scrutiny. It has been argued that there is no neat dividing line that separates a-cultural, civic nationalism from exclusionary, identity-based, ethnic nationalism. In fact, civic nationalism easily shades into ethnocultural nationalism, which is why it can be difficult to parse out French or Turkish or Russian national identity from the country's culture, language, and dominant ethnicity. Nonetheless, even today, despite pleas to move beyond ethnic vs. civic nationalism,[7] the opposition arguably remains central.

In addition to defining nationalism, there is a body of scholarship dedicated to studying its *impacts*. In the late 1930s, Hans Kohn (1939) argued that nationalism was a potential force for good. That is because nationalism uniquely engenders an emotional attachment, which "is qualitatively different from the love of family or of home surroundings."[8] Kohn explains that before the "age of nationalism," "the masses never [felt] their own life,

culturally, politically, or economically, dependent upon the fate of the national group."[9] Only after nationalism did people identify "with the life
and aspirations of uncounted millions whom we shall never know, with a
territory which we shall never visit in its entirety."[10] Hence, nationalism is
singular in that it integrates masses of people into a concrete whole. Kohn
does recognize that nationalism can create a religiosity of sentiment that can
plunge mankind into catastrophe. But he holds onto the possibilities latent
in nationalism. Just as religion was once was the source of bitter wars across
Europe, "A similar depoliticization of nationality is conceivable. It may lose
its connection with political organization, and remain only as an intimate
and moving sentiment."[11] In this way, Kohn submits, the emotional affinity
that nationalism engenders could one day widen "to include supranational
areas of common interest and common sympathy."[12]

Unlike Kohn, Hannah Arendt focuses on the ills of nationalism. In her
famous treatise *On Totalitarianism* first published in 1951, Arendt examines
how the nation-system system came into being after World War I. It was only
then that each state was identified with its own unique national community.
However, in the process, millions of people were left in legal limbo. In this
new international political order "true freedom, true emancipation, and
true popular sovereignty could be attained only with full national emancipation." The unintended consequence of this was that "people without their
own national government were deprived of human rights."[13] Groups who
had long resided in former imperial territories, but who were not regarded
as members of the cultural "nation," were no longer considered rightfully
part of the state. Denied formal citizenship, they were left vulnerable to any
kind of atrocity perpetrated against them.[14] Nationalism had, thus, created
"the stateless"—a wholly new class of people "forced to live outside the
common world . . . thrown back, in the midst of civilization, on their natural givenness, on their mere differentiation."[15]Subsequently, liberal scholarship has followed Kohn in focusing on the benefits of affective national ties;[16]
while others have followed Arendt in concentrating on the danger nationalism poses to "outsider" groups.[17]

That these two interpretations of nationalism are diametrically opposed
to one another reflects the fact that nationalism itself is fundamentally
two-faced, meaning that nationalism is both liberating and exclusionary.[18]
Nationalism is liberating in that it champions the power of the people
over oppressive regimes. In the nineteenth century, nationalism was the
force through which popular movements deposed kings and emperors.

In the twentieth century, the enshrining of the "Right to National Self-Determination" in the United Nations Charter became the legal means through which colonized peoples around the world defeated their European oppressors. Indeed, before nationalism, "the Sovereign" was the king, who was the center of the political order and held to be the embodiment of the state. Luis XIV expressed this directly, famously declaring, *L'etat est moi*. With nationalism, the king's sovereignty was transferred to "the people." Formerly subjugated peoples were turned into "citizens," and the state became the embodiment of its citizenry. And yet, the very process of turning "subjects" into "citizens" is what makes nationalism exclusionary. For once the state was delimited by its national population, it became imperative to distinguish the "real people"—those who have rights, duties, and privileges as citizens within that territory—from trespassers. Exclusionary citizenship became the hallmark of the international political order.[19]

Other scholars have examined why nationalism arose in the late eighteenth century. Two of the best-known works in this vein are Ernest Gellner's *Nations and Nationalism* (2006)[20] and Benedict Anderson's *Imagined Communities* (2006).[21] For Gellner, nationalism emerged as a consequence of public education. Up through the late eighteenth century, education was largely private and restricted to the wealthy. Most people learned what they needed to know by working for their family or apprenticing with a tradesman. Uniform basic education was a product of the Industrial Revolution. Industrial societies were unique in that they required a large workforce able to speak the same language, read basic instructions, and understand rudimentary math. In response, the state developed a standardized curriculum for the masses. Through this state-led public education system, a unified sense of identity tied to the nation-state was fashioned. Thus, industry's need for standardized education "is what nationalism is about, and why we live in an age of nationalism."[22] Along similar lines, Benedict Anderson argues nationalism developed because of print capitalism. Prior to the seventeenth century, books were precious handwritten manuscripts penned in scriptural or ancient languages like Latin, Greek, Hebrew, or Aramaic. However, after the printing press made possible the wide dissemination of printed material that could be sold to a mass audience—with the introduction of products such as newspapers, journals, almanacs, and calendars—vernacular languages became standardized. In this way, print capitalism created "unified fields of exchange and communications" across the state. This was especially true with the growth of daily newspapers. By reading quotidian national news, "people gradually became aware of the hundreds of thousands of people in their particular language-field—fellow readers [whose] visible invisibility became the embryo of nationally-imagined community." In this way, "print-languages laid the basis for national consciousness."[23]

A final strain in the nationalist literature is economic nationalism. Economic nationalism refers to a set of policies favoring trade restrictions and state intervention to protect the national economy from global market forces. As a field of study, it is related to the general discourse on nationalism, but it is more applied. The central idea behind economic nationalism is that opening one's economy to the international market will have deleterious effects on domestic industries and trade. It will allow less expensive commodities to flood the domestic market, undermining national manufacturing and agriculture. It will hurt labor by forcing down wages. Finally, it will lead to the extraction of the national resources with little return to the nation. Therefore, to protect one's economy, one must put barriers to trade in the form of tariffs or regulations and bolster local industries with state funding to ensure they can compete globally. For these reasons, liberal economists commonly invoke "economic nationalism" as a catch-all for harmful, anti-liberal, protectionist policies.[24] However, that is a little bit of an oversimplification. On the positive side, economic nationalism has been advocated for as a means for underdeveloped countries to develop their fledgling industries in the face of uneven economic power relations[25] and increase their economic sovereignty.[26] On the negative side, it has been used by xenophobic jingoists to oppose immigration and international trade.

Populism

Unlike nationalism, populism has a very long history. The term "populism" actually stretches back to ancient Rome, when the *Populares* opposed the aristocratic *Optimates*. In antiquity, as today, the label "*Populare*" had a double meaning: it could indicate someone who was "either 'pleasing the populace' or [working] 'in the interests of the populace.'"[27] The former suggests that populists are self-interested politicians who manipulate the masses to gain power; the latter that they were genuinely concerned to advance the cause of the common man. Over time, several movements have been labeled "populist," most of which have had this ambiguity at their core, including the America populist parties of the late nineteenth century, fascist movements in

Italy and Germany in the early twentieth century, and socialist movements in Latin America in the mid-twentieth century.

Like the scholarship on nationalism, the literature on populism has focused on how best to categorize it, explain why it emerges, and what its effects are. However, the debates have been quite different. Unlike nationalism, twentieth-century scholarship on populism was largely centered on defining what kind of phenomenon it was. There were long debates about whether populism was an ideology, a discursive practice, a political strategy, or a style of politics.[28] Most scholars today have adopted what is termed a "minimalist definition" of populism. In this view, populism is identified by the core project of protecting "the people" from the "elite," but this dichotomy can be mapped onto different ideologies and political movements.[29] Laclau has encapsulated this best: "[Populism's] dominant leitmotiv is to situate the evils of society . . . in the abuse of power by parasitic and speculative groups which have control of political power."[30]

As with nationalism, populism has been variably characterized as a liberating force that empowers the masses, or a negative movement that promotes jingoism and xenophobia. In the early 2000s, a hot debate developed over whether populism and nativism were aspects of the same phenomenon or distinct categories. For some, populism was held to be a leftist, liberating movement; nativism a rightist, fascist movement. Over the 2010s, however, scores of content-analytic studies of political speeches, party platforms, social media, and the like conclusively found that both right- and left-wing extremist parties espouse the core populist idea of protecting "the people" from "corrupt elites." At the same time, the literature has, by and large, shown that right- and left-wing populists have different goals (albeit with some caveats). Right-wing populism is generally understood to be "identity-centered" and strongly connected to xenophobia. It is not, however, associated with any particular economic agenda. Conversely, left-wing populism is primarily "class-based," in that such movements tend to be concerned with ending unfair wealth distribution and less likely to be identity focused.[31]

Finally, there is a body of literature dedicated to explaining the genesis of twenty-first-century populism. Here there are two schools of thought. One looks at how populism is generated from below. Referred to as the "demand side" of populism, scholars who adopt this approach study populism as a movement that grows out of widespread popular dissatisfaction with the status quo. The other school of thought takes populism to be a movement that originates from above—as something orchestrated by populist leaders and parties to influence people's perceptions. This is the "supply side" of populism. In studying contemporary movements, those who look at the "demand side" of populism argue that anti-elitist, anti-establishment fervor developed either as a response to economic insecurity, particularly after the 2008 economic crisis, or as grievances and "racial animus" that has evolved in response to changing social and immigration policies. Researchers who focus on the "supply side" of populism investigate the ways in which politicians, activists, and parties have framed issues to politically mobilize followings and increase their vote share.[32]

From this cursory review, it is clear that existing theories of nationalism and populism provide little guidance for how the two converge. Both fields of study have developed vaguely similar concepts that are, nonetheless, substantively different. Like reflections in a fun-house mirror, the civic/ethnic dichotomy of nationalism is similar, yet different from the socialist/fascist dichotomy of populism. Even the liberating potential of national self-determination is similar, yet different from populism's promise of people's empowerment. I believe, we can overcome this disjuncture by reorganizing our thoughts on nationalism and, in so doing, we can explain modern-day, anti-globalization movements.

Where the two schools of study arguably come closest is in their descriptions of ethnically exclusive forms of populism and nationalism. This is precisely where we encounter nativism and fascism. Therefore, before introducing a new approach to nationalism, it is critical to identify what fascism and nativism are—and are not.

Fascism

There is a lot of misunderstanding of fascism. In common parlance, fascism is often mistakenly conflated with authoritarianism. Yet, fascism is "historically specific."[33] If nationalism is a recent historical development, fascism is even more recent. Its emergence can be dated to the early twentieth century, with the political assent of Benito Mussolini following World War I. In seeking to associate his rule with the grandeur of the Roman Empire, Mussolini adopted the symbol of the Roman state: sticks roped together (signifying Rome's unity) around an axe (signifying her power).[34] The bundle of rods or sticks was referred to in Latin as *fascio*, from whence Mussolini coined the term *fascismo*, or "fascism." Fascism was thus an epithet Mussolini chose for his new regime to convey that *Il Duce* had reunited the Italian people with the power and glory of the state.

Even with its relatively narrow temporal scope, "great difficulties arise as soon as one sets out to define fascism."[35] Some believe that fascism is best understood as a political ideology.[36] Others argue that it is a form of mass political mobilization.[37] There are also scholarly debates about its genesis. Early twentieth-century Marxist scholars argued that fascism was a tool used by the capitalist class to control the masses. Alternatively, it was argued that fascism was an organic sociopolitical response to modernization and/or capitalism.[38] Along these lines, fascism has been described as a mass psychological condition or simply a historical accident. Today, scholars question whether we are witnessing a resurgence of fascism or some kind of neo-fascism.

How and why fascism emerges may be contested, but there is a general agreement about several of its dimensions. First and foremost, almost every definition of fascism includes some reference to nationalism. It has been described as "populist ultranationalism," "revolutionary ultra-nationalism," "organic nationalism," "extreme nationalism," and "radical nationalism." Thus, Paxton underscores that fascism is always "tied to very specific national movements";[39] Payne identifies fascism as an "extreme nationalism" focused on the unique "institutional, cultural, social, and spiritual differences" of the individual country in question;[40] and Sternhell et al. assert that fascism emerged as a "new nationalism," which was in opposition to the civic nationalism of the French Revolution.[41] Even the scholar perhaps most sympathetic to fascism, A. James Gregor, emphasizes that fascism is "developmental in purpose, and regenerative in intent" and therefore closely related to developmental or economic nationalism.[42] Indeed, as with nationalism, myths of historical glory are absolutely fundamental to fascism. It has been argued that "faith in the power of myth as a motive force in history" is "key to the Fascist view of the world."[43] Payne describes how fascist leaders seek to "build a system of all-encompassing myths that would incorporate both the fascist elite and their followers and would bind together the nation in a new common faith and loyalty."[44]

Yet fascism also has elements that go far beyond the scope of nationalism. To begin with, fascism is argued to be closely associated with hypermasculinity and military virtues. It has been asserted that at the core of fascism lies "the irrational cult of war and the rejection of pacifism";[45] and that it is a form of ultranationalism that "positively values violence as end as well as means and tends to normalize war and / or the military virtues."[46] In addition to being hypermasculine and militaristic, fascism is anti-individualistic and anti-democratic. Fascists require that individual interests be subordinated to the state and propound the need for a strong totalitarian government that can exercise an extreme form of economic nationalism.[47]

Finally, many have debated how fascism relates to conservatism and socialism. Indeed, where fascism lies is difficult to parse out. Though Marxists have generally associated fascism with the right, Mussolini's "national syndicalism" and Hitler's "National Socialism" reveal that its relationship to right-wing ideology is fuzzier than that would suggest. For these reasons, Paxton argues "fascism always retained that ambiguity. [But] Fascists were clear about one thing . . . they were not in the middle."[48] In truth, fascism uncomfortably coincides with both the right and the left. Fascism overlaps with the far left in so far as it is a revolutionary ideology. Fascists seek to change "class and status relationships in society." Indeed, most definitions of fascism identify mobilization of the masses as integral to it. And yet, fascism shares many of the same precepts and goals as rightists. Like the radical right, fascists want to preserve the traditional cultural order and believe that this requires a radical form of authoritarianism. However, unlike the radical right, fascists are not committed to defending the privileges of the established elite. In other words, where fascism is revolutionary, the radical right is *anti*-revolutionary. As Payne puts it, rightist authoritarianism is "simply more rightist—that is, concerned to preserve more of the existing structure of society with as little alteration as possible, except for promoting limited new rightist elites and weakening the organized proletariat."[49]

It is in its aspiration to recruit the masses to its revolutionary cause that fascism bridges nationalism and populism. Consequently, a related bone of contention is who should be included in the pantheon of fascist leaders. Allardyce argues that true fascism only came into being in Italy and Germany when the masses were ecstatically mobilized.[50] Others count a large number of leaders and movements as fascist that have existed across the globe, even those that did not achieve mass mobilization.[51] With all these distinctions in mind, the working definition of fascism adopted here is that *fascism is an extreme form of ethnic nationalism that merges myths of an exalted national past with militarism and totalitarianism and involves the popular mobilization of the masses.*

Nativism

Of all the concepts bandied about today, nativism appears to be the most straightforward. Yet, the precise definition of the term is also highly contested. Nativism is generally understood to be related to anti-immigrant prejudice and hostility; "Beyond that, however, there is 'little consensus' with respect to what these sentiments entail and what is their scope."[52] Certainly, nativism is unthinkable without nationalism; but it encompasses a much narrower realm of phenomena. To complicate things, nativism also shares important "affinities" with populism but is more specific than populism.[53] Scholars have worked to differentiate nativism from racism, nationalism, populism, and xenophobia, as well as to understand how these various concepts interact with it.[54] Some have identified nativism as a combination of nationalism and xenophobia and others as a blend of nationalism and populism. Some see nativism as race neutral, while still others argue that it shares a blurred line with racism. There is also debate about whether it is best understood as an ideology or a discursive practice.[55]

Even though nativism shares complex affinities with nationalism and populism, the history of nativism is quite different from that of fascism. The term first entered the lexicon in the mid-1840s, with the birth of the Native American Party, more infamously known as the "Know Nothing" party (because their members purportedly answered "I know nothing" to any questions raised about the origins and goals of the political organization). The Native American Party was a single-issue party formed to oppose the large number of Catholics coming to the United States; especially Irish immigrants, who were arriving en masse to American shores to escape the punishing economic conditions caused by the Great Irish Potato Famine. The supporters of the Native American Party described their ideology as "Americanism," but their detractors labeled them bigoted nativists, from whence the term derives. As Higham explains, "The word is distinctively American, a product of a specific chain of events in eastern American cities in the late 1830's and early 1840's."[56] In the twentieth and twenty-first centuries, nativism has become largely understood to be coextensive with far-right, or "alt-right" movements and parties, especially those in Europe but increasingly in the United States as well as with anti-immigrant, conservative groups in Latin America, Africa, and Asia.

In recent years, the term "nativism" has been variably defined as "the preference for native-born people of a given society";[57] or "an intense opposition to an internal minority on the ground of its foreign" connections;[58] or as "a particular articulation of exclusionary nationalism," which leads to "a xenophobic and racist process of 'othering' against migrants and those who are perceived to not have assimilated into the nation-state."[59] In fact, specific forms of nativism can vary widely. Nonetheless, there are unifying themes that can be discerned. Through "each separate hostility runs the connecting, energizing force of modern nationalism."[60] In other words, it can be said that nativism is an extreme form of protective, xenophobic, exclusionary nationalism.

Conclusion

It is clear that nationalism, populism, fascism, and nativism are all interrelated. These connections are at times quite explicit, and yet, at other times they become very tenuous. Hence, understanding where they intersect and when they depart is critical to understanding the extreme movements developing across the world today. To explain how populism and nationalism intersect in modern-day, anti-globalization movements, the next chapter presents a new typology of nationalism. The hope is that by rethinking nationalism, we will be able to understand what it means to say that nationalism is converging with populism today, as well as how that relates to nativism and fascism.

2

The Synthesis

A New Typology of Nationalism

Whenever I teach a course on nationalism, I begin with a show of slides that present a series of contradictory notions of what nationalism is. On the Internet, one can find all sorts of quotes about nationalism. Some state that nationalism is love of one's people, or of one's homeland. Others say that nationalism is about bigotry, tribalism, idolatry, and self-deception. Some argue that it is the same thing as patriotism, others that they are opposites. Still others describe nationalism as the incubator of liberty, or a pretext for war, or a tool used by politicians to dupe the masses.

In teaching undergraduates, it is fun to begin with these kinds of discussions. But for most academics, the project of understanding nationalism is less emotionally charged and more complex. It is about analyzing how history, changing economies, social breakdowns, and the like produce movements in which this uniquely modern identity motivates people to action. Yet, even taking nationalism out of these heated emotional debates and looking at it as an object of study, it is still very difficult to zero in on what exactly it is that we are examining. There are so many approaches to studying it, so many theoretical and empirical analyses that stretch in different directions, that it is difficult to get a hold of. In short, there is nothing straightforward about nationalism.

This chapter will introduce a new way to organize the confusing potpourri of scholarly work included under the study of nationalism. The schema developed is an attempt to partially tame its octopoid nature, by subsuming its multiple offshoots under new groupings. The goal is not to offer novel interpretations of the causes or conditions associated with nationalism, nor to generate new ideas about its nature and organization. Instead, the purpose is to construct a new way of bounding the topic that can be used to analyze sociopolitical patterns across time and space.

What follows is a shuffling of concepts commonly associated with nationalism, populism, fascism, and nativism, into a new typology. Attributes

Defensive Nationalism. B. S. Rabinowitz, Oxford University Press. © Oxford University Press 2023.
DOI: 10.1093/oso/9780197672037.003.0003

long associated with nationalism are reorganized into three new distinctive categories: *creative (state-creating), consolidating (state-consolidating),* and *defensive (state-defending) nationalism.*[1] *Creative nationalism* is the study of how nations come into being. *Consolidating nationalism* is the everyday practices through which the collective sense of belonging is reinforced. Finally, *defensive nationalism* is the drive to preserve and protect an existing nation-state from global forces. By reordering the complex field of nationalism into this tri-part analytic schema, the aim is to eliminate some of the confusion associated with it as a category, and to present a more coherent way to relate the vast array of case studies developed under its domain. The broader purpose of introducing this typology is to find a means of explaining how our present age came to be stamped by anti-globalizing populism, as well as how today's movements relate to earlier manifestations of nationalism.

The next section outlines more explicitly what is encompassed in each category and suggests what scholarly literature would be associated with each. The following discussion should not be taken to be an exhaustive list of all the ways in which these forms of nationalism can be studied, but as an attempt to provide an outline of what these sub-topics cover and how they differ.

Creative Nationalism

Since the writings of Ernest Renan in the 1880s, scholars have argued that nations are not natural—they are created. In other words, nations do not simply exist, they are forged through political processes over time and in response to specific historic, social, and economic events. *Creative nationalism* is the study of how nations come into being and what those processes are.

Indeed, there have been innumerable theoretical and empirical studies of how nations have been constructed. Creative nationalism covers any study that examines the genesis of a national movement. Another way to say this is that creative nationalism has as its object of study any movement that claims there is a "nation" and seeks to define it and rally people to its cause. More often than not, the goal is to be granted statehood, but there are "nations" that do not seek statehood, such as the "Nation of Islam" or Indigenous nations that have sovereignty without full statehood. Studies included under the umbrella of creative nationalism are separatist movements, independence movements, and irredentist movements. There are many examples of separatist movements, including those that have been mounted in recent years in Catalonia, Quebec, Puerto Rico, and Scotland. This can also encompass the quest of stateless peoples to attain sovereignty, such as the struggles of the Palestinians or the Kurds. Studies of creative nationalism also cover analyses of independence movements, whether the Hattian rebellion against the French that began in 1791; or the movements that swept through Latin America between 1750 and 1914 demanding independence from Spain and Portugal; or the Serbian, Bosnian, and Irish nationalist movements of the early 1900s; or the several anti-colonial movements that shook the world in the mid-twentieth century. Finally, the process of creating a nation can be one in which it is claimed that territories separated through conquest or political processes should be unified, referred to as "irredentist" movements. Examples of irredentist movements are Argentina's claim to the Falkland archipelago, Russia's claim to Ukraine and the republic of South Ossetia in Georgia, as well as the long-standing feud between India and Pakistan over Kashmir. In a nutshell, creative nationalism encapsulates any movement directed at establishing the sovereignty of a unique national collective; independence, separatist, and irredentist movements are all examples of creative nationalism.

In studying the ways in which nations are constructed, scholars have identified several patterns that are characteristic of creative nationalist movements. The core of creative nationalism is delimiting who belongs to the national community and what makes it a cohesive unit. This begins with claims about what constitutes the national territory, the national people, and the national language. In general, such movements are inaugurated by a cluster of educated elites who rile up the masses to join in a revolutionary rebellion, persuading them of the absolute necessity of attaining territorial and/ or political recognition for their "nation." Often it involves a reimagining of the past, as well as of the present—a mythic, symbolic, aspirational vision of what the nation is. It is a depiction of the nation's core that stirs deep feelings of emotional attachment to it: the distilling of the essence of the unique collective that is mirrored in the national anthem. A central component of this process is the construction of the nation's unique history, typically focused on communal suffering, hardship, war, and national heroes. Also integral to the creative nationalist struggle is the veneration of the unique national culture, in which everything from the national food and dress to the nation's literature, religion, and art are celebrated, and with which the virtues of the national people or the national "character" are exalted.

An era of creative nationalism develops when a wave of such nation-alist movements occurs in short succession. In fact, there have arguably been three great waves of creative nationalism. The first was in the nine-teenth century, when empires and kingdoms across Europe were teetering after Napoleon's serial invasions. This led to the re-fashioning of Europe into today's modern states, including Germany, Italy, Austria, Hungary, Czechoslovakia, Yugoslavia, Poland, Finland, Estonia, and Latvia. The second wave of creative nationalism was in the mid-twentieth century after World War II had severely weakened Europe's colonial powers. Across the colonized world, independence movements gained momentum. Between 1940 and 1970, subjugated territories in the Middle East, Africa, and Asia heroically won national sovereignty. The final wave of creative nationalism came with the 1990s collapse of the Soviet Union. Out of its ashes a host of states were born or re-established from the Czech Republic and Slovenia to Croatia and Bosnia to the Caucus and Near-Eastern states.[2]

As a whole, it can be said that an era of creative nationalism develops in re-sponse to the weakening or collapse of a larger state entity. The downfall of a large imperial state, such as the former Soviet Union, frequently produces vi-olent ethnic conflicts. That is because no territory is wholly inhabited by one single ethnic/cultural/religious/racial group. Though there may be a dom-inant group, every region has a complex history of settlement. Therefore, during these periods of dramatic change, peoples who have long-lived to-gether cheek to jowl—often with a history of intermarrying—will be stirred up to fight against one another as disputes heat up over who the true citi-zens of the new nation are and what its genuine boundaries should be. This was infamously true in Bosnia and Serbia, but equally true of Buddhists and Hindus in Sri Lanka after the British ended its control over "British Ceylon," as well as the Shia and Sunni in Iraq once Saddam Hussein's brutal regime had been toppled. For these reasons, studies of creative nationalism fre-quently overlap with studies of ethnic conflict.

As an object of study, creative nationalism has two primary foci. First, scholars examine the rhetorical and strategic approaches emerging nation-alist leaders use to galvanize nationalist/separatist/irredentist movements. This could include the study of political speeches and writings, such as those of Kwame Nkrumah, the Ghanaian nationalist and first leader of an independence movement in sub-Saharan Africa; or of treatises, such as "Three Principles of the People" written by Chinese Nationalist leader Sun Yat-sen when launching the 1911 Republican Revolution that ended Qing rule of China; or an examination of the formation of a nationalist party, like John Connelly's founding of the Irish Socialist Republican Party in Dublin in 1896. Second, research on creative nationalism examines the structural conditions that produce and shape nationalist movements, which can be quite broad in scope. Examples would be a study of the relationship between the rise of nationalism and industrialization or print capitalism, such as the canonical works of Gellner (1983) and Anderson (1983).[3] Also included would be Howard's (1979) examination of how war shapes nationalism,[4] and Brubaker's (1992) analysis of how different processes of territorial integration in Germany and France shaped different conceptions of national belonging (citizenship).[5] Alternatively, structural analyses of creative nationalism can zero in on particular nationalist struggles, such as Janet Klein's (2007) study of Kurdish nationalist movements in the late Ottoman period,[6] and Prabhat Datta's (1992) study of successionist movements in Northeast India.[7]

Consolidating Nationalism

As the national community expands, the nation-state must continually rearticulate who the national people are; what the national character is; and what its culture, language, and history are. *Consolidating nationalism* comprises all the means through which the national community is stitched together, and the collective sense of belonging is reinforced; the process through which the nation-state is continually reproduced, reimagined, and reintegrated. A whole range of formal and informal practices are involved in consolidating the national identity. Informally, consolidating nationalism is essentially what we do unconsciously every time we have a barbecue on a national holiday, sing the national anthem at a ball game, or hoist the national flag in remembrance of fallen heroes. Formally, it can incorporate state actions, like changes to citizenship laws, the launching of public works, or the restructuring of national curricula. Another way to express it is consolidating nationalism is the forging of what Billig refers to as "banal nationalism": "the collection of ideological habits (including habits of practice and belief) which reproduce established nations as nations."[8]

Consolidating nationalism differs from both creative and defensive nationalism in that it is an ongoing process. It can be regarded as analogous to what evolutionary biologists describe as "static equilibrium"—the extended period after an organism is formed during which small adaptations are made but no radical change occurs. Thus, consolidating nationalism is an adaptive but equally static process in which the "organism" of the nation-state makes adjustments over an extended period of time to sustain itself in the face of incremental change. In contrast, both creative and defensive nationalism evolve quickly in response to external events; they are upheavals or reactions to what can be considered shocks to the established order from outside forces. They are, therefore, closer to what evolutionary biologists identify as "punctuated equilibrium": an interval when change happens more suddenly over a shorter period of time.[9] Consequently, creative and defensive nationalisms can manifest across many nation-states concurrently in what can be characterized as an era of nationalism because many states can be hit simultaneously by radical changes in the international order. Consolidating nationalism, by contrast, is always a process internal to a given nation-state; in other words, there cannot be an "era" of consolidating nationalism.

The study of consolidating nationalism covers topics similar to those studied under the rubric of creative nationalism, such as the development of official language policy, or national educational curriculum, or the codification of national holidays and national sports. The difference is that the study of consolidating nationalism is focused on how nationalism is solidified within an established nation-state. Hence, the purpose is not to uncover how a new state is advocated for and effectively comes into being, but rather how an existing national state is bolstered. One of the best-known studies in this vein is Eugene Weber's (1976) classic study *Peasants into Frenchmen: The Modernization of Rural France 1870–1914*. The book presents an analysis of how France established "French" as the national identity.[10] Weber explains that in the late nineteenth century, peasants living outside of Paris had little sense of "patriotism" and little knowledge of French culture or history—even of the French Revolution. In each region, whether Bretton or Alsace-Lorraine or the Pyrenees, peasants spoke different dialects, followed different customs, wore different styles of dress, and cooked different cuisines. Many were not even aware of what Napoleon's exploits had been. Weber traces how the French state turned regional "peasants" into "Frenchmen" by introducing a standardized system of modern education, enforcing military service, and instituting a national legal system across its territory.

Another such work is David Waldstreicher's *In the Midst of Perpetual Fetes: The Making of American Nationalism, 1776–1820*.[11] Waldstreicher examines how changes in popular culture, between the revolutionary period and the mid-nineteenth century, helped solidify an American national identity. By combing through late eighteenth- and early nineteenth-century almanacs, calendars, newspaper articles, printed songs, and the like, Waldstreicher pieces together the slow process through which our national holidays and festivals were established and our national heroes were sanctified. For example, Waldstreicher finds that even after the revolution several British holidays, like Guy Fawkes Day, continued to be celebrated. Nor was there any similitude in the way in which National Independence was commemorated across the territory. Over time, however, there was a codification of national holidays. His study thus traces the processes through which a shared understanding of what it meant to be "an American" was forged.

Defensive Nationalism

Finally, *defensive nationalism* is the endeavor to *preserve* and *protect* an existing nation-state. It is a sociopolitical reaction to external challenges to the sovereignty of the nation-state, whether presented by imperial powers or globalizing forces. Defensive nationalism is best understood as a particular kind of national populism, which is to say that defensive nationalism is a people's movement focused on reasserting national sovereignty and shielding the nation from external threats. Defensive nationalism is a form of populism not only because it involves the mobilization of the masses, but also because a key component is that the threats from outside are believed to be supported by the corrupt domestic establishment, who benefit from the theft from "the people" and "the nation." In this way, nationalism and populism converge. Thus, with defensive nationalism the vertical dichotomy between "*the people*" and "*the elite*" (so central to populism) is mapped onto the horizontal dichotomy of nationalism (which distinguishes between "us" and "them"), to produce an opposition between "*the nation*" and "*the globalizing enemy*" that is *simultaneously* vertical and horizontal. In short, defensive nationalism is a movement that *re-prioritizes the nation-state* and presumes international forces are hostile to it.

Like creative nationalism, defensive nationalism arises from external disturbances, or exogenous shocks created by changes to the global order. It can, therefore, spread virally across countries. Defensive nationalism can be regarded as a "demand" movement to the extent that people who feel threatened by global or neo-imperial forces become aggrieved and are thus ripe for populist mobilization. Yet, such fears are not sufficient to launch a broad defensive nationalist movement. Discontent provides the opportunity structure, but it requires a "political entrepreneur," what is referred to in common parlance as a demagogue, to mobilize that growing discontent into a national-populist movement.[12] The concept of the "political entrepreneur" comes from the literature on ethnic conflict, where scholars have explored how politicians foment conflict by manipulating and radicalizing identities for political gain.[13] As Blagojevic describes, "Rhetoric of fear, blame, and hate are used by political entrepreneurs as a tool of division and control."[14] In a parallel manner, with defensive nationalism political entrepreneurs kindle political passions over (real or manufactured) threats to the "nation" posed by malicious external forces, operating within and/or without the "nation," and with which the national elite is complicit.

Using the term "defensive nationalism" has the disadvantage of being easily conflated with nativism, but that is not the intent. Although right-wing defensive nationalism is indeed a specific form of nativism, defensive nationalism (like populism) has both right-wing and left-wing expressions. What both rightist and leftist forms share is the drive to prevent international forces from undermining "the nation"; the thread that connects the two is the desire to re-establish national sovereignty, particularly over the economy. Indeed, defensive nationalism comes closest to what has historically been studied as economic nationalism, but it encompasses more than economic concerns. Fear of foreign influences can be expressed in terms of fears of international finance, but equally in terms of the loss of sovereign control to international or intergovernmental agencies, such as the United Nations (UN), the World Trade Organization (WTO), the North Atlantic Treaty Organization (NATO), or the European Union (EU). Foreign danger can also be understood to be posed by strangers living within the nation, in the form of minority groups, migrants, or expatriate communities.

Left vs. Right Defensive Nationalism

Although the two poles of defensive nationalism converge in their desire for national sovereignty, they are not the same. Both leftist and rightest forms of defensive nationalism are premised on the need to protect the "nation-state" from the corrupting effects of the "globalizing other." However, *who* constitutes the nation and *what* comprises the malignant international power are conceived of differently. Thus, distinguishing between the two begins with an examination of how the antagonism central to national populism is developed in each—that is, how each constructs the "national people" and the "globalizing enemy."

To differentiate the two forms of defensive nationalism, the next section presents an ideal-typical representation of each. Defensive nationalism is analyzed along four dimensions: (1) construction of the national people, (2) construction of the global enemy, (3) organizing principles, and (4) policy objectives. From these dimensions, the differences between left- and right-wing versions are identified (See Table 2.1). These ideal-typical representations are meant to be neither normatively prescriptive nor exhaustive accounts of these phenomena. Similar to a grading rubric, they are used as a methodological device to provide precise parameters through which related phenomena can be studied. As Max Weber explained, the great sociologist who first conceived of this methodology, the ideal type "is not a description of reality but it aims to give unambiguous means of expression to such a description."[15]

The People

The first distinction between the two forms of defensive nationalism is whom it is *directed toward* that is, *how "the people" are constructed.*

For left-wing defensive nationalists, "the people" are understood to be coextensive with the "citizenry" defined in legal and territorial terms.[16] Left-wing defensive nationalism is thus close to Ernest Renan's "civic nationalism." As with civic nationalism, "the people" are less explicitly defined in cultural or racial terms and, therefore, national belonging is more inclusive. Hence, citizens are understood to be people born within the given territory or those who go through a process of legal naturalization. In contrast, right-wing defensive nationalism is closer to what has been described as ethnic nationalism and is best understood as a form of nativism. For the nativist, national belonging is neither a legal, nor a political construct; it is a matter of *nature*. People *naturally* belong to, and are constituted by, their "mother" or "fatherland."[17] This is generally expressed in what can be described as a myth of the *volk*.[18] The *volk* are the people of the "heartland," the "original" citizens, who make up the "genuine" national community. As with ethnic nationalism, the *volk* are identifiable by clear markers such as phenotype, dress, language, and/or religion. In this way, right-wing defensive nationalism is more exclusionary.

Table 2.1 Ideological Forms of Defensive Nationalism

Dimensions	Attributes	Left	Right
The People	Basis of Unity	**Civically based** shared history, tradition, and civic values	**Identity based** shared ethnicity, religion, language, and cultural values
	National Belonging	**Legally based** determined by law and territorial boundaries	**Identity based** determined by naturally, distinct genus of "peoples"
	Rhetorical Orientation	**Pro-urban** directed toward workers and educated leftists	**Pro-periphery** directed toward "periphery"
Global Enemy	Defining Feature	**Class based** capitalists and international corporate interests	**Ethno-Racially based** particular (outsider) ethnic groups and rival nations
Organizing Principles	Political Direction	**Progressive** seeks to expand social, economic, and political rights to historically excluded categories	**Retrogressive** the goal is to reassert the nation's "traditional culture" and "traditional values"
	Rhetorical Appeal	**Rights based** primary end is justice, fairness, equal rights, and equal access	**Fear-based** primary end is *group survival*
	Orientation	**Universalist** inherent equality of all people; equal entitlement to protections and rights	**Anti-enlightenment** rationality and universality threaten religion, tradition, and the national culture
Policy Objectives	Trade	**Economic Nationalism** ending unfair trade practices	**Economic Nationalism** ending unfair trade practices
	Jobs	**Protectionism** protection of national jobs and industries	**Protectionism** protection of national jobs and industries
	Overarching Goal	**Reducing Power of the Wealthy** creating checks on wealth accumulation by reducing corporate/oligarchic power and redistributing wealth	**National Greatness** restoring "national greatness" and "national strength" by increasing military prowess, stopping unchecked migration, and protecting national culture

Rhetorically, left-wing defensive nationalism tends to be directed toward disenfranchised workers, minorities, and those struggling to gain equal rights within the nation-state. For these reasons, it is typically better received in urban centers that have greater diversity. In contrast, right-wing defensive nationalism seeks to protect and defend the *volk* against the moneyed, urban, educated elite, whose interests and policies are believed to be exploitative of the national heartland. Urban areas are distrusted and associated with international finance, multiculturalism, immigration, and the globalizing liberal forces that endanger the existing order. Thus, although right-wing defensive nationalism can appeal to people of all classes and quite varied backgrounds, it is rhetorically peripherally based, meaning the movement's messaging is focused on the "heartland." Therefore, it tends to resonate most forcefully in areas left behind by economic transition and threatened by rapid social change.

The Global Enemy

The second distinction between the two forms of defensive nationalism is what it is *directed against* that is, *how the "global enemy" is constructed.* Both left-wing and right-wing defensive nationalism intensely distrust globalization; however, the global enemy is defined quite differently.

For the left-wing defensive nationalist, the "enemy" is thought of largely in class terms. Globalizing free trade is seen to promote corporate interests and global finance at the cost of the nation. Hence, the "enemy" is identified primarily with the monopolists and bankers who rig the game—either with individuals, like Rockefeller or Koch, or with corporations, like Shell Oil, Amazon, and Citigroup, as well as with the national politicians who aid and abet them for personal gain. As their left-wing counterparts, right-wing defensive nationalists see free trade and globalization as a smoke screen for international finance. However, these forces are understood in identity terms: the enemy is *ethnized*. On one end of the spectrum, the *volk* are threatened by miscegenation and immigration. On the other end, they are under attack from ethno-national groups dominant in finance and banking and/or from opposing nations. The common feature is that those held responsible for economic hardships are not wealthy individuals, nor even the political-economic system that created unfair advantage, but a whole class of people who, by virtue of their cultural characteristics, are regarded as avaricious and self-interested, or poor, lazy, and living off the welfare of the state.

Organizing Principles

Third, the two forms of defensive nationalism differ in the *principles around which each is organized.*

Left-wing defensive nationalism espouses universal rights and stresses the shared humanity of the nation's underclasses. The focus is on achieving equal access of opportunity for all citizens. It can, therefore, be characterized as "progressive," in that it seeks to expand rights and equalities for citizens. Right-wing defensive nationalists disavow the universalizing, rationalist assumptions of the Enlightenment; they renounce the equal rights of all men. Instead, they valorize the exceptionalism of the national culture and its people, celebrating the nation's individual greatness and superior historical achievements. Accordingly, where it can be said that left-wing defensive nationalism is progressive, right-wing defensive nationalism is retrogressive. The quest is to restore what has been lost from the past.

Policy Objectives

Finally, the two are distinguishable by the *political goals* and *economic goals* each espouses.

For left-wing defensive nationalists, the primary political goal is to *empower "the people."* This is to be achieved by reducing corporate/oligarchic power and redistributing wealth. It tends to appeal to both the educated leftist elite as well as disenfranchised groups. For right-wing defensive nationalists, the primary political end is to *restore national glory.* Right-wing nationalists fear the national culture and purity of the national "race" are in danger of being extinguished. Their desire is to ensure group survival by championing the national people's exceptionalism. Hence, right-wing nationalists are often bellicose, seeking to flaunt the nation's military might.[19] In these goals, the appeal of right-wing defensive nationalism can be far-ranging, incorporating people from different class backgrounds.

The one area where the two forms of defensive nationalism align is in their economic goals. They both champion economic nationalism—that is, protecting the economy from external forces. Both left- and right-wing defensive nationalists are concerned about international actors' control over the domestic economy as well as the loss of national jobs to overseas competition. However, even with respect to this there are distinctions. Whereas left-wing defensive nationalism is generally opposed to (neo)liberal economic policies, right-wing nationalism is not necessarily so. And though both can oppose unchecked migration, the reasoning is markedly different.

For left-wing defensive nationalists, labor migrations negatively impact both national workers and migrants. Thus, Nagle in her 2018 opinion piece argues, "open borders radicalism ultimately benefits the elites within the most powerful countries in the world, further disempowers organized labor, robs the developing world of desperately needed professionals, and turns workers against workers."[20] For the nativist, the fear of immigration goes much deeper and is much more urgent; it is nothing short of the danger of total annihilation. Nativists fear that with unchecked migration the *volk* will not only be out-voted, but out-populated and culturally eradicated by "outsider" groups.

Therefore, whereas left-wing defensive nationalists champion protectionist and isolationist policies in terms of unequal opportunity structures, right-wing defensive nationalists associate economic nationalism with group survival. And whereas left-wing defensive nationalists are not uniformly opposed to immigration, hostility to immigration is inseparable from nativism. Of course, there are many examples of groups and leaders who embody a combination of these positions. To wit, there are leftist populists who espouse racist ideas, and right-wing leaders who support rationalism and science. These ideal types represent highly abstracted concepts. Seldom, if ever, does a real-world instance correspond *exactly* to one of these "pure" constructions. As with all ideal types, be it "free-markets" or "democracy," the utility comes from assessing *where on the spectrum* a particular politician, party, or movement falls.

Spelling out the various ideal-typical permutations of defensive nationalism allows for greater clearity of what is meant by the term. For though the term has been used on occasion, its definition has remained slippery. Generally, defensive nationalism has been associated with rightist or nativist interpretations of the nation. For example, writing about Australian nationalism, Johanson and Glow (2009) distinguish between "critical" and "defensive" nationalism. In their dichotomy, defensive nationalism is explained to be the desire to protect the "true nation" and characterized by "the struggles and courage of the settler period as a means of masking Australia's racist past."[21] This is contrasted with critical nationalism, which "calls for continuous efforts on the part of citizens to identify strengths and weaknesses in national culture and to address them."[22] Hence, Johanson and Glow's term differs from the concept developed here in that it is only associated with right-wing nativism.

There are, however, those who associate defensive nationalism more broadly with a form of anti-globalization. Thus, Önis (2007), in describing Turkish nationalism, defines defensive nationalists as "inward-oriented" because they have "a negative view of globalization [and their] politics is based on fear, in the sense that they see globalization as a process leading to the erosion of national sovereignty."[23] In a similar vein, Osterhammel (2013) uses the term "defensive nationalism" to describe resistance against global capitalism, immigration, and universal liberal values.

The critical difference between these various uses of the label and the term as it is defined here is that the concept in this study is part of a clear taxonomy that fits into a broader theory of nationalism. It is thus more completely fleshed out and can therefore be used more systematically than it has been to date.[24] Indeed, with its distinctive core, defensive nationalism can be analytically differentiated from other left- and right-wing populist movements.

For example, both anarchism and communism of the late nineteenth and early twentieth centuries were leftist populist movements that swept across Europe and the United States. But, for both, nationalism was an essential part of *the problem*. Nationalist ideologies were argued to be tools "of imperialism and exploitation," used to distract "the working class from struggling against the capitalist class by spreading hatred against migrant workers and the colonies."[25] Along similar lines, the anti-globalization movements of the 1990s were leftist populist movements that were largely international in character. Whether the expanding environmental movement or anti-WTO demonstrations, the common theme was uniting people across the globe to fight global capital. The term coined was "glocal"—shorthand for "think globally, act locally"—an expression that underscored the fact that local fights were related to global struggles.

In contrast, left-wing defensive nationalists never question the givenness of "the nation"; quite the reverse, the nation is prioritized. The goal is not uniting workers internationally to fight international capitalism, but to restore economic and political sovereignty. Hence, the populist leftist struggles that emerged in Europe in the 2000s developed in opposition to the European

Union and globalization. These so-called Euroskeptic movements do not seek to unite the left across countries to fight global capital. To the contrary, they are deeply nationalist movements. Left-wing Euroskeptic parties are committed to protecting the nation from international globalization because of the harm it presents to the social-welfare system. The Latin American socialist movements of the mid-twentieth century can also be regarded as a species of defensive nationalism. Populist leaders of these mid-century movements "from Juan Domingo Perón in Argentina to Alan García in Peru, were staunchly nationalistic [and] opposed foreign investors and, in many cases, nationalized multinational firms." However, even these movements were different from today's anti-globalization movements, for they did not "decry globalization in broad terms."[26]

The same distinctions hold for right-wing defensive nationalism. Although right-wing defensive nationalists espouse ethnocentric, racialized rhetoric similar to the idioms used in other kinds of conservative and nativist movements, there are differences. For example, the Ku Klux Klan is a nativist movement that emerged in the United States during the Reconstruction era in response to the defeat of the South and the freeing of African and African American slaves. Yet, it was not directed against global capital, or even immigration but was driven by the loss of white power and white privilege. What comes closer to right-wing defensive nationalism is the brief "Know Nothing" movement that developed in the 1840s, when Irish and German immigration to the United States was surging. But even this nativist movement was focused on Catholic migrations, not globalization. In a like manner, during the mid-twentieth century political leaders as diverse as Nixon, Thatcher, Reagan, and Berlusconi were each able to generate a conservative populist movement, in part by building on fears of immigrants and minority groups. However, expansive globalization was not at the heart of their populist appeals, nor did they seek to withdraw from international alliances or vilify international trade. It was only at the end of both centuries that fears of immigration, international trade, and international finance came together to spark the formation of right-wing defensive nationalist parties. In conclusion, right-wing defensive nationalism is indeed a species of nativism, but one that is tied specifically to fears of globalization.

In summary, left-wing defensive nationalism fuses socialist goals with economic nationalism. It seeks to protect the "nation" from international interests by increasing the underclasses' access to rights and wealth and shielding them from the power and corruption of the capitalist elite.

By contrast, right-wing defensive nationalism is a proto-fascist movement that combines protectionism, xenophobia, anti-urbanism, and anti-enlightenment ideology with jingoism, traditionalism, and militarism. Indeed, right-wing defensive nationalism can easily morph into full-blown fascism. What makes defensive nationalism a proto-fascist rather than a fascist movement is the degree to which authoritarianism is embraced. Fascism is an expressly authoritarian form of ultra, ethnic nationalism, which sets itself up in opposition to democratic, civic nationalism. Right-wing defensive nationalism shares with fascism its nostalgia for a glorified mythic past, its xenophobia, and even much of its militarism and sexism. However, it is not necessarily embracing of authoritarianism. It is, nonetheless, a movement or ideology that is decisively on the road toward fascism. Indeed, some segments of today's right-wing defensive nationalist movements have crossed over to become full-blown fascist movements.

Defensive Nationalism and Polanyi's "Double Movement"

The argument developed in the rest of this work is that ours is an era of defensive nationalism. The aim is to investigate how left- and right-wing defensive nationalism came to suffuse Europe and the United States in the twenty-first century. Combining the theories of Karl Polanyi and Joseph Schumpeter, the case will be made that today's epoch of defensive nationalism is Polanyi's "double movement," and that this "double movement" was set off by the shock of rapid international integration and changes to production that developed with technological change. Furthermore, it will be argued that, to date, there have been two great waves of this form of defensive nationalism: the Second Industrial Revolution at the turn of the nineteenth century, and the Digital Revolution at the turn of the nineteenth century. Both were periods of unparalleled modernization, when nation-states were assaulted on multiple fronts: expansive immigration, globalized finance, transnational liberalism, and transnational terrorism.

No theory or analysis is born from thin air. There are always ideas that precede a scholarly work. This work is no different. There does exist a robust body of scholarship that examines how Polanyi's theory relates to nationalism, populism, and globalization. For example, the prominent Polanyian scholar, Gareth Dale, has worked to untangle the complicated ways in which Polanyi's thoughts about global capitalism relate to nationalism and protectionism.[27]

His work focuses on reconciling the difficult disconnections in Polanyian theory. Several other studies have applied Polanyi to explain the relationship between neoliberalism, globalization, and fascism;[28] or how fascism relates to internationalism, regionalism, or statism.[29] In the vast majority of this work, Polanyian concepts have been used to understand the rise of right-wing populism;[30] alternatively, when focused on left-wing politics, the object of study is generally to discover "the unfulfilled aspects" of Polanyi's thought so as to build "emancipatory or progressive visions of a fundamental reform of capitalism."[31]

This book takes a different approach. The aim here is to find a way to "operationalize" Polanyi's compelling notion of "double movement"; in other words, the goal is to provide an empirically robust way of understanding what the "double movement" is, so that it can be analytically applied to contemporary movements.[32] The concept of "defensive nationalism" is used as the means to do this. Nor is this study focused on the right or the left, but on how globalization drives the rise of both. In this, Polanyi's analysis is uniquely helpful. As Sandbrook argues, in the "Polanyian scheme, the market system wrought widespread and diverse harms. It is not only workers who are harmed, but diverse classes and groups suffering from the commodification of land and money—and today, we would want to add knowledge." Therefore, "Polanyi's refusal to reduce class or politics purely to economic interests" allows us to go beyond these confining dichotomies.[33]

There are, however, two works that do come very close to the analysis presented here, though in different ways. Andreas Novy, writing about the lessons we can take from Polanyi's *The Great Transformation*, examines today's movements in terms of the antagonism between "globalization" and what he refers to as "national capitalism." He uses the term "nationalistic capitalism" to refer to "[hostility] to supranational economic institutions like the WTO and trade and investment treaties, as well as EU bureaucracy" [that] manifests as an "anti-systemic countermovement [and] wages a cultural war against "foreign" and new modes of living."[34] "National capitalism" thus has strong parallels with *defensive nationalism* as defined here. Yet, as close as Novy comes to the concept of *defensive nationalism*, there are important distinctions. That is because for Novy anti-liberal, anti-global populism is conceived of exclusively as a right-wing phenomenon. In fact, what Novy describes as "national capitalism" is almost identical to the definition of right-wing *defensive nationalism* developed in this work. However, Novy does not touch upon left-wing *defensive nationalism*, nor does he examine how these contemporary nationalistic movements relate to other forms of nationalism. Rather, his goal is to provide the space to think about possible alternative forms of de-globalization and possible changes to "territorialized" mass politics. For these reasons, Novy's ideas complement those presented here, particularly by identifying similar tropes that align with right-wing defensive nationalism, such as anti-enlightenment, militarism, etc., without diminishing the contribution made here.

Another neo-Polanyian scholar with whom this work closely aligns is Richard Sandbrook. Sandbrook (2018) observes that technological change is a critical catalyst for today's movements. More specifically, and in a parallel fashion to the argument made in this book, Sandbrook underscores the importance of transportation and communications: "Technological change has played a key role in speeding up the pace and scope of social dislocation. Without the revolutions in transport, communications and information-processing, the complex, instantaneous world of neoliberal globalisation could not exist."[35] Indeed, it has been quite broadly accepted that globalization drives populism.[36] This study builds upon such observations in two ways: by further elaborating a theory for how this comes about, as well as by providing in-depth historical analyses to support the theory.

Ultimately, all these studies bear witness to similar phenomena. They therefore touch upon similar elements. It is in the unique synthesis of these differing elements that this book makes its contribution. The next two chapters build the theoretical model that will be used to analyze the two periods under study. The model developed is a synthesis of Polanyi's and Schumpeter's theories. In Chapter 4, Polanyi's work is discussed in greater detail. The chapter then considers several of the ambiguities that make it difficult to apply his ideas. In Chapter 5, Schumpeter's idea of innovation as the driver of social change is outlined. Finally, the chapter will account for how Schumpeter's theory can be combined with Polanyi's to create a workable model that can help us account for our period of contagious defensive nationalism.

3

Karl Polanyi

Theory and Ambiguity

From 1860 to 1914, Europe horribly morphed from a period of expanding liberalism and increased internationalism to one of fascism, communism, and world wars. In his great opus *The Great Transformation*, Karl Polanyi set out to explain how the world could have been so altered during his lifetime. He was a man born at the height of the Gilded Age, in 1886. His family, wealthy, liberal, and Jewish, were from Budapest. After serving in World War I, Polanyi went to cosmopolitan Vienna, where he became a prominent socialist journalist. However, when Austria united with Germany under Hitler, Polanyi emigrated to London. After the war, he was awarded a teaching position at Columbia University and taught there from 1946 to 1953; but his wife who had formerly been a member of the Communist Party in Europe was denied an American visa. Polanyi therefore spent his final years in Canada, where he died in 1964.

Polanyi's work provides the world with a powerful critique of market liberalism and a diagnosis of the harmful impact that laissez-faire logic can have on society. It, moreover, provides a strong model for explaining the contagious nativist and populist movements we see today, which have developed in response to globalization. The problem is that his work uses evocative metaphors that make the actual application of his theory difficult. To explore how the "double movement" can be used to analyze twenty-first-century politics, this chapter begins by tracing the contours of Polanyi's theory in more detail and then explains what the difficulties are with applying it to the present.

Theory of the "Double Movement"

Polanyi contends that the seeds of the catastrophes that befell the twentieth century were planted in the mid-1800s. The seedling—the new force that

Defensive Nationalism. B. S. Rabinowitz, Oxford University Press. © Oxford University Press 2023.
DOI: 10.1093/oso/9780197672037.003.0004

emerged in the nineteenth century—was what was commonly referred as *haute finance* (high finance), basically international finance or finance capitalism. What distinguished haute finance from other forms of capitalism is that, for first time in history, financial firms became the lynchpin of the international system.[1] With their enormous powers, the great international banking consortiums of the day reigned over countries around the world, controlling their economies and even their politics. Polanyi describes how under the regime of haute finance neither finance nor diplomacy "would consider any long-range plan, whether peaceful or warlike, without making sure of the other's goodwill."[2] In short, international finance steered politics, and politics protected international finance. The power and reach of this new form of capitalism was personified by the Rothschild family. As the bankers to Europe's monarchs, the Rothschilds had become "the only supranational link between political government and industrial effort in a swiftly growing world economy."[3]

Yet, the dramatic changes brought about by haute finance went even deeper than the fusing of international politics and finance capitalism. The rise of haute finance signifies for Polanyi the moment when social life became almost entirely consumed by market forces. Polanyi makes the case that for most of human history, trade was a minor and adjacent part of the economy. There were port cities that specialized in the trade of luxury goods; there were also local markets, to which peasants might travel for days to trade in eggs, pigs, or vegetables; there were even artisans who sold wares. But the vast majority of the world's population lived off the land and infrequently engaged in market exchanges. Not organized around trade, the economy was a function of the social order; it was there to ensure production and distribution to help maintain that social order. Whether the reciprocal trading practices of Trobriand Islanders of Western Melanesia, or the great redistributive systems of the Incas, or the elaborate hierarchy of feudal relations in Europe and Japan, the economy was embedded in the sociopolitical system that it served to sustain. Nor were people motivated by a "predilection for gainful occupations" in earlier societies.[4] To the contrary, the economic system was run by "noneconomic motivation" and functioned within "the frame of the social system as a whole."[5] Adam Smith's "*homo economicus*," the narrowly self-interested and ever-calculating individual, came into being much later in history—with the modern state. Of Smith's famous dictum that human nature is marked by the "propensity to barter, truck and exchange," Polanyi tersely remarks, "In retrospect it can be said that no misreading of the past ever proved more prophetic of the future."[6]

How then did the profit motive come to define and mediate most of our social intercourse? Polanyi argues that market ideology began in England and, because of her enormous financial powers, was spread around the world. According to Polanyi, the critical turning point came with the adoption of British poor law reforms in 1834. In fact, he states directly that "It is no exaggeration to say that the social history of the nineteenth century was determined by the logic of the market system proper after it was released by the Poor Law Reform Act of 1834."[7] To understand his claim, it is helpful to recount a short version of this history.

The Poor Laws had originally been instituted at the end of the eighteenth century, when Britain's agricultural and industrial revolutions were forcing peasants into cities, creating an alarming escalation in urban poverty. To mitigate the suffering, poor relief was established. The poor reforms, or Speenhamland Law (so named after the parish where the reforms had been conceived) mandated that "a minimum income should be assured to the poor irrespective of their earnings" by providing wage subsidies "in accordance with a scale dependent upon the price of bread."[8] Thus, the Speedham Law was effectively an early form of welfare: a government program that provided financial aid to individuals or groups who could not support themselves. However, after the Napoleonic Wars ended in 1815, Britain was saddled with enormous debt and Europe suffered from a downturn in agricultural prices. Poor relief fell out of favor. In the face of falling prices, its continuation came to be seen as "a disastrous burden."[9]

For those agitating against the Poor Laws, the theories of David Ricardo provided the ideological and moral grounds to rescind them. In 1817, Ricardo published his theory of the "Iron Law of Wages." In it, Ricardo expanded upon Adam Smith's theory of how wages were set. Ricardo argued that Adam Smith had been correct in arguing that there was a "natural price of labor," determined by the basic consumption needs necessary for the reproduction of the workforce (e.g., food, shelter, clothing). However, there was also a "market price of labor," which was regulated by the supply of laborers relative to demand. Ricardo explained that because this "market price of labor" was governed by the natural laws of the market, any government policy designed to alleviate the distress caused by the market's ebb and flow would only create greater scarcity and pain. Therefore, even though market fluctuations often hurt the weakest members of society, that pain was necessary. Ricardo concludes: "These, then, are the laws by which wages are regulated, and by which the happiness of far the greatest part of every community is governed. Like all other contracts, wages should be left to the fair and free competition of the market, and should never be controlled by the interference of the legislature."[10]

With the changing political and economic environment of the 1830s, Ricardo's theory became the basis for the Poor Law Reform Act of 1834. It was now argued that, for the greater good, the government would abandon the minimum income mandates set in the Speenhamland Law. Instead, laborers would be subject to "the inexorable laws of Nature"; and wages would be determined solely by the "ineluctable necessity" of the market.[11] Polanyi tells us, the "scientific cruelty" of this reform bill was "shocking to public sentiment."[12] "Never perhaps in all modern history has a more ruthless act of social reform been perpetrated; it crushed multitudes of lives while merely pretending to provide a criterion of genuine destitution in the workhouse test."[13] This then, the application of Ricardo's "Iron Law of Wages" to British socioeconomic policy, is when free-market ideology, or the "liberal creed" as Polanyi refers to it, was lifted from the pages of books to pervert and corrupt society at large. It was with the striking down of the Poor Laws that Adam Smith's *homo economicus* first made his appearance.

Once adopted by Britain, this market ideology was quickly spread across the globe. That was because at the time London was fast becoming "the financial center of a growing world trade."[14] As the world's creditor, Britain used her formidable powers to impose the gold standard worldwide, and with it the liberal creed exalting the primacy of markets over social protections. In this way, "the peoples of the world [became] . . . institutionally standardized to a degree unknown before."[15] Polanyi argues that by the 1880s, "the essentiality of the gold standard" had become "the one and only tenet common to men of all nations and all classes, religious denominations, and social philosophies."[16] However, this new liberal economic order brought with it dangers. With this "enforced uniformity," global finance "hovered as a permanent threat over the freedom of national development."[17] Designed to propel international commerce, the gold standard undermined national governments. States lost the power to direct their economies and prioritize national interests. Instead, "foreign trade and the gold standard had undisputed priority over the needs of domestic business."[18]

Thus, for Polanyi, the introduction of gold as the international standard of exchange marked a watershed in human history. Gold had been a medium of trade for centuries. What was momentous about the gold standard was that, for the first time, nearly all countries agreed to fix the value of their currencies to a specified amount of gold. With gold functioning as a preset, unchanging, secure vehicle for international payment, currency conversions across countries became trouble free. Soon, global trade and finance achieved historic levels. But the gold standard also allowed international finance to extend its reach, encircling national economies and choking their ability to act independently.

To compound matters, at the same time that Britain was imposing the gold standard on nations across the globe, a host of wondrous and seemingly infallible technological innovations were reshaping the world. So magical was the period, so full of art and innovation, that the French dubbed it the *belle époque*, the "Beautiful Age." Enthralled by the marvels of the age, the *belle époque* became overconfident in what the market could provide. A mystical faith in the free-market's ability to promote and preserve liberty and progress took hold. Markets ceased to be understood as the outcome of social and political processes. Like Newton's clockwork universe, it was now believed that once the market was set in motion, it proceeded mechanically with no need of human intervention. Through its own mechanical laws of supply and demand, the market was "self-adjusting" or "self-regulating." Writers like Herbert Spencer became the apostles of the theory of "self-regulating" markets. Spencer described how:

> there is in society, as in every other part of creation, *that beautiful self-adjusting principle*, which will keep all its elements in equilibrium; and, moreover, that as the interference of man in external nature often destroys the just balance, and produces greater evils than those to be remedied, so the attempt to regulate all the actions of a community by legislation, will entail little else but misery and confusion. [*emphasis mine*][19]

The mechanism of supply and demand and its corollary, "the iron law of wages," came to be understood as the best way to ensure that goods were produced, prices were reasonable, workers were employed, and society was increasingly enriched. Any attempt to curb or direct or control the market mechanism could only bring harm to the market and threaten the well-being of society. Government posed the greatest threat to the smooth functioning of the market.

> What, then, do they want a government for? Not to regulate commerce; not to educate the people; not to teach religion; not to administer charity; not to make roads and railways; but simply to defend the natural rights of man— to protect person and property—to prevent the aggressions of the powerful upon the weak—in a word, to administer justice. This is the natural, the original, office of a government. It was not intended to do less: it ought not to be allowed to do more.[20]

Thus, with the power of haute finance, politics became severed from economics. More than that, market logic was imposed on all aspects of social life. Indeed, the whole social order was reconceived and reordered. The economy was no longer embedded in society; it was no longer a function of the social order. Now society had become embedded in the market. Wendy Brown's description of neo-liberalism communicates the changes Polanyi identifies: "every human domain and endeavor, along with humans themselves, [were understood] according to a specific image of the economic. All conduct [became] economic conduct; all spheres of existence [were] framed and measured by economic terms and metrics, even when those spheres are not directly monetized."[21]

For Polanyi then, the fatal flaw of the turn of the century was that faith in progress and free trade had made people "blind to the role of government in economic life."[22] What was lost was an understanding of government's role in protecting society by "altering the rate of change, speeding it up or slowing it down as the case may be."[23] Without government as a buffer, industry and finance were able to operate without restraint. Human labor became the fodder of massive factory machines. The environment was treated as nothing more than a wellspring for industry and its dumping ground. Even the welfare of business and trade became threatened by global finance. Polanyi paints a bleak picture of what might have happened had society maintained this course and allowed itself to be fully subsumed by the market:

> Robbed of the protective covering of cultural institutions, human beings would perish from the effects of social exposure; they would

die as the victims of acute social dislocation through vice, perversion, crime, and starvation. Nature would be reduced to its elements, neighborhoods and landscapes defiled, rivers polluted, military safety jeopardized, the power to produce food and raw materials destroyed. Finally, the market administration of purchasing power would periodically liquidate business enterprise, for shortages and surfeits of money would prove as disastrous to business as floods and droughts in primitive society.[24]

This state of affairs was untenable and unsustainable. Society pushed back. In an unchoreographed reaction, "persons belonging to various economic strata unconsciously joined forces to meet the danger."[25] A series of spontaneous resistance movements sprung up, all seeking to protect the world from market forces: environmental movements, labor movements, and even businesses lobbying for trade protections. Across Europe, safeguards against the market were instituted, including "factory laws, social insurance, municipal trading, health services, public utilities, tariffs, bounties and subsidies, cartels and trusts, embargoes on immigration, on capital movements, on imports."[26] This dual movement of increasing economic liberalization imposed from above, accompanied by pressure from below for social protectionism, is what Polanyi refers to as the "double movement." He characterizes the "double movement" as the "defensive behavior of a society faced with change; it [is] a reaction against a dislocation which attacked the fabric of society."[27] Unfortunately, the cure was as bad as the disease. Society swung like a pendulum to the other extreme: the developed world was engulfed by communism and fascism. Critically for Polanyi, these extreme ideologies have to be understood in relation to the excesses of liberalism; they were all "determined by one factor: the condition of the market system."[28] As a result, "the emerging regimes of fascism, socialism, and the New Deal," although different on almost all accounts, "were similar only in discarding laissez-faire principles."[29] "Fascism, like socialism, was rooted in a market society that refused to function"; hence, the response against the international liberal regime "was worldwide, catholic in scope, universal in application."[30] For these reasons Polanyi argues "Market society was born in England— yet it was on the Continent that its weaknesses engendered the most tragic complications."[31]

Applying Polanyi: The Challenges

Several scholars find Polanyi's work to be remarkably apposite to the so-cial, economic, and political transformations we are experiencing today.[32] His concept of the "double movement" in particular has been found to be an extremely useful tool for explaining the transformation from the hey-day of market libarlism, initiated by the Reagan-Thatcher revolu-tion of the 1980s, to the rejection of globalization and populist demand to reprioritize the "nation" that has grown in strength since the turn-of-the-century. However, applying Polanyi to the contemporary world is not as clear-cut as it appears at first blush. As Dale remarks, "For Polanyians, a countermovement is the short answer, but plotting its coordinates is no simple task."[33]

In the first place, Polanyi is unclear about the mechanisms that launch the "double movement." So much so that Polanyi's work has been described as "an elegant parable."[34] Polanyi is almost purposely vague in accounting for the emergence of haute finance. He tells us that it was an institution so unique that it was "*sui generis*," in a class of its own, and "peculiar to the last third of the nineteenth and the first third of the twentieth century." And when he discusses possible explanations for its emergence, he is evasive:

> Some contended that it was merely the tool of governments; others, that the governments were the instruments of its unquenchable thirst for gain; some, that it was the sower of international discord; others, that it was the vehicle of an effeminate cosmopolitanism which sapped the strength of virile nations. None was quite mistaken.[35]

His poetic reasoning is especially pronounced in his discussion of the second half of the "double movement." Polanyi describes the response against market liberalism as "a deep-seated movement" that "sprang into being to resist the pernicious effects of a market-controlled economy." But he leaves unclear how it could be possible that "Society," presented as an undif-ferentiated whole—encompassing all classes and categories of people across all developed countries—could spontaneously organize to "[protect] itself against the perils inherent in a self-regulating market system."[36] To the con-trary, he tells us that the movement against liberalism arose "sometimes over night [sic] and without any consciousness on the part of those engaged in the process of legislative rumination."[37]

For these reasons, it has been charged that Polanyi presents society's protectionist movements as "a grab-bag" of "utterly dissimilar policies and
motives under [a] single heading." As Dale argues, "This yoking" of "various
species of protectionism" conflates such different social responses as "business protectionism or import duties" with "trade union struggles."[38] The
overdetermination of the concept has left some to contend that "the 'double
movement' concept tends to be reduced to a tautology, in that any organized
behavior that challenges unfairness or inequality in the market is included
without any further discussion."[39] This reflects what Arrighi and Silver
(2003) identify as a core ambiguity in Polanyi: his "double movement" is "an
inherently global process,"[40] yet he does not account for what force or power
enabled it to spread across the world.

Another hurdle in applying Polanyi is that, when his account is not ambiguous, it is concentrated on events that transpired in Britain in the early nineteenth century. He underscores that "Market economy, free trade, and the
gold standard were English inventions," and he states directly that "In order
to comprehend German fascism, we must revert to Ricardian England"[41] (by
which he means the period when the Poor Laws were put into effect). Given
that Polanyi's analysis of the origin of the "double movement" is so exclusively
centered on changes unique to British history, how can we use his insights to
understand the countermovement of populism and nativism today? In fact,
some have concluded that we cannot.

For several theorists the "Polanyian conceptual apparatus [has] proved
incapable of identifying the forces that led to the resurgence of economic
liberalism in the 1970s."[42] Indeed, applying Polanyi's "double movement"
to the present is questionable given the sheer magnitude of change that has
occurred since the nineteenth century. Nineteenth-century economic, political, and social development was inextricably tied to industrialization and
competing imperialist ambitions that led to the extraction of resources and
the wholesale colonial enslavement of vast parts of the globe. The trajectory of the twentieth century was shaped by very different forces: the Cold
War and the anti-colonial struggles and independence movements that
characterized the mid-twentieth century. Understanding these processes is
indispensable to a full understanding of the economic and political development of each of these eras.

Beyond this, the turn of the nineteenth century is not really comparable to
the present. Today the world is for the first time in human history more urban
than rural. Social enfranchisement movements have transformed politics

across the globe. Technologies have reached much further and had deeper impacts than ever before. The list is endless. Therefore, despite the very compelling parallels, there is a danger of committing what historians refer to as the fallacy of "presentism," that is, glossing over the innumerable, dramatic, and essential differences between periods. On a more esoteric level, using a hermeneutic understanding of the relationship between the past and the present, our current situation emanates from the historical epoch to which it is being compared. It is quite an artifice to slice and dice these two periods in such a way as to ignore the intrinsic developmental relationship between the two. All in all, the multitude of differences between the two periods makes any claim that they can be studied through the same lens rather dubious.

In addition to its historical specificity, another reason given for the inutility of using Polanyi's model is that it is based on a false dichotomy—the distinction between "embedded" and "disembedded" markets. Critics say that Polanyi "romanticizes pre-market economies, and that his work is tainted by a moralizing anti-market mentality."[43] Markets have never been free from political constraints. Therefore, it has been argued that using the concept of "embeddedness" is at the very least misleading. Dale concludes that the "double movement" is best taken to be as "a heuristic" of "the dichotomy of economy and society," but one that is limited because of its "undue emphasis upon a postulated moral distinction between" natural/embedded markets and artificial/disembedded ones.[44] In short, using the "double movement" is challenging because of the historical specificity of the original argument, the danger of "presentism," and the ambiguity of the core concepts inherent in the model.

Nonetheless, there are several counterarguments. First, it is true that the fuzziness of the distinction between "embedded" and "disembedded" markets presents difficulties for employing them. However, in this respect, the classification between "disembedded" and "embedded" markets is not really any different from many of the concepts we use to study the social world. "Embedded" and "disembedded" markets are no less clearly demarcated than other social science categories such as, "democracy," "fascism," and "communism"; or "community" and "society"; or "development" and "underdevelopment"; or even "class," "race," and "ethnicity." It arguably should not make the utility of these concepts any more or less questionable than those commonly employed in political science, economics, history, and the like.

Moreover, in point of fact, Polanyi very clearly states in several passages that the "disembodied" self-regulating market was less a reality than a driving force used to reorganize how society *should* function and *should* be measured.[45] As he puts it: "We are not dealing here, of course, with pictures of actuality, but with conceptual patterns used for the purposes of clarification. No market economy separated from the political sphere is possible; yet it was such a construction which underlay classical economics since David Ricardo and apart from which its concepts and assumptions were incomprehensible."[46] In particular, the gold standard made manifest that "the institutional separation of the political and economic spheres had never been complete, and it was precisely in the matter of currency that it was necessarily incomplete."[47] Therefore, what was pernicious was not the actual subsumption of the world under a totalizing market, but rather the increasing *tendency* toward market mechanisms. In another passage, Polanyi underscores that, though the "self-regulating market" had become the "organizing principle" of liberal society, "this is far from saying that market system and intervention are mutually exclusive terms."[48] In fact, he argues quite the reverse: "economic liberals must and will unhesitatingly call for the intervention of the state in order to establish" and maintain the self-regulated market system.[49] The truth of the matter, Polanyi tells us, is that "The accusation of interventionism on the part of liberal writers is thus an empty slogan";[50] and therefore "far from excluding intervention [. . .] liberals themselves regularly called for compulsory action on the part of the state as in the case of trade union law and anti-trust laws."[51]

Thus, despite these several critiques, a number of neo-Polanyian scholars believe the "double movement" has relevance beyond the historical circumstances for which it was developed and can be applied to current times. Recent studies have used Polanyi's theory to explain contradictory economic and political processes in the "Global South."[52] Levien and Paret (2012) construct an "embeddedness index" with World Survey data, and find evidence of a global "double movement" today.[53] Others have applied the embedded/disembedded dichotomy to prescribe ways of redressing problems caused by neo-liberalism.[54] These narrower and more prescriptive analyses are valuable applications, but they leave aside the larger questions of what steers such world-historical processes.

In a more theoretical vein, Block and Somers (2016) use the "double movement" to understand how ideas can propel a major political conversion.[55] They do so by analyzing parallels between the genesis of two welfare reform movements, the "1834 New Poor Law" in Britain and the 1996 "Personal Responsibility Opportunities Reconciliation Act" in the

United States. They find in both cases that an extraordinary national crisis allowed for the repeal of the existing welfare system. They conclude that moments of national turmoil provide the opportunity structure that makes massive ideological shifts possible. The obvious limitation of this analysis is that, although it can be applied to other national situations, it is focused on unique national crises. Hence, their approach does not clarify what accounts for the *simultaneity* and the *global scale* of the changes that Polanyi was interested in—and that we are experiencing again today. Yet, the worldwide response against liberalism is absolutely critical to Polanyi. He takes it to be inviolable evidence of the pernicious overreach of globalized market forces and emphasizes that "the universal 'collectivist' reaction against the expansion of market economy in the second half of the nineteenth century [is] conclusive proof of the peril to society inherent in the Utopian principle of a self-regulating market."[56]

There are several theories that can potentially explain how Polanyi's "double movement" could be cyclical. There is, for example, "World-Systems Theory," a strain of neo-Marxism, that explains economic patterns in terms of the global capitalist system.[57] From International Relations studies, there is "Hegemonic Stability Theory" that examines world change in terms of the rise and fall of dominate global powers (generally understood as "Western" powers, such as Portugal, Holland, France, Britain, the USA);[58] as well as "Long Cycle Theory," which analyzes war cycles in terms of the life span of economically and politically preeminent states (cycles generally posited to be around one hundred years in length).[59] For example, one of the more compelling contemporary uses of the Polanyi's theory has been developed by two World System's scholars, Beverly J. Silver and Giovanni Arrighi, who have indeed used Polanyi's "double movement" to explain our times. However, they assert that there is a central limitation in Polanyi's work that must first be overcome. For Silver and Arrighi, the problem is that Polanyi "underemphasized" the role of "unequal power relations" in "determining the historical trajectory he analyzed."[60] By putting power relations into his analysis, we can use Polanyi to account for changes happening, while at the same time keeping in mind many of the differences between these periods. Thus, Silver and Arrighi maintain that the critical link between the two turn-of-the-century periods is that, in each era a hegemonic power (Britain and the United States, respectively) was able to use its economic and military dominance to push forward an international liberal agenda. In other words, globalization "did not just happen [...]. It required considerable political stimulation without which technological and economic stimuli to increase international economic interdependence could not have taken place."[61]

This kind of World-Systems approach enables us to come much closer to explaining the re-emergence of the "double movement." In particular, the theory does a good job of accounting for the ascent of globalized liberalism in such different epochs. But it still falls a little short, for it does not fully explicate the *nationalist* responses against liberalism that developed across so many different countries. As a subset of neo-Marxist theory, World-Systems theorists understand the countermovement against liberalism primarily as a class-based struggle. Yet, nationalist movements are not class-based; people of all classes share the same national identity. Indeed, anti-globalization movements can be cross-sectional, unifying the wealthy with the working classes. Something more is still needed if we are to understand the simultaneity of these movements in the nineteenth century and in our own.

Toward a Solution

The goal of this study is to explain the rise of nativism and populism in the twenty-first century using Polanyi's compelling conception of the "double movement." To do so, some basic questions still must be addressed: How literally can we take the "double movement"? And is there a judicious way to apply the "double movement" to an alternate time in history?

I believe the answer to the latter is "Yes" and that the final passages in *The Great Transformation* provide the key to how this can be done. In his conclusion, Polanyi argues that the core problem with liberalism was that it fundamentally misunderstood how freedom is achieved in complex societies. That was because the "market view" had reduced liberty itself to nothing more than the right to make free contractual relationships. Therefore, everything had to be left to the market. This meant that under the liberal order, "The power of the state was of no account, since the less its power, the smoother the market mechanism would function." But Polanyi argues sustaining freedom in a complex society encompasses so much more. Liberty is not simply about contracts; it involves a broad spectrum of rights and opportunities. Liberty, therefore, requires a complex of institutions to safeguard it. Put simply, "rights must be enforceable under the law." Missing this basic fact, the whole international economic order came to be based upon a "Utopian fiction." Liberalism promised freedom, progress, and human perfectibility, but presumed these ideals could only be achieved in and through an economic system solely controlled by market prices. In the end, these romantic assumptions about the market "gave a false direction to our ideals." Far from freeing the world, the liberal view of markets presented "a deadly danger to the substance of society," promoting freedom "at the cost of justice and security."[62]

In a nutshell, for Polanyi the central problem with the period of market liberalism was that "Society as a whole remained invisible."[63] Hence, the "double movement"—the rejection of the market as the basis of political and economic organization—can be understood, at its core, as a rediscovery of society. But what is "society" in the modern age? What exactly was rediscovered? This is at the heart of the question.

I suggest that if the "double movement" is the rediscovery of the crucial role played by the state in providing institutional safeguards for society, the nucleus of the "double movement" is ultimately the rediscovery of the role of the *nation-state* and, by extension, a rediscovery of *nationalism*. For, in the modern world, the nation-state reigns supreme. Ever since the nineteenth century, when empires were toppled and the sovereignty of kings was transferred to "the people," states have been equated with the populations they represent ("the nation"). Today, nation-states are virtually the only political organization recognized internationally.[64] Even kingdoms and totalitarian regimes legitimate their rule by claiming to represent their national populations. In short, we live in a nation-state system. Hence, the nation-state has become the only entity that can protect society from global forces and market overreach. I therefore propose to study the second half of Polanyi's "double movement" as a surge of national populism, what I identify as an era of defensive nationalism.

Putting this all together, the aim of this work is to find a concrete way to study Polanyi's "double movement." It will do so by examining how defensive nationalism came to suffuse Europe and the United States. The rest of the book will trace how the turn of the nineteenth and the turn of the twentieth centuries were both periods of unparalleled modernization, when nation-states were assaulted on multiple fronts: expansive immigration, globalized finance, transnational liberalism, and transnational terrorism. By the end of both centuries, the ill effects of liberal market forces undermined people's initial excitement over the promise of internationalization and globalization. Protectionism, nativism, and xenophobia materialized in their stead—the second half of the "double movement."

There is, however, one more critical question remaining that Polanyi's work cannot address and that directly pertains to understanding how the "double movement" could re-emerge. And that is the following: What specific set of changes made it possible for international finance to emerge in the mid-1800s? And might there be a parallel with changes that have occurred in the twentieth century? As we know, Polanyi gives little explanation for how and why finance capitalism arose. Yet, without this piece of the puzzle, it is difficult to explain a second cycle of the "double movement." Therefore, to understand what could have set off haute finance in the nineteenth century, this study turns to the works of Schumpeter. More specifically, Schumpeter's idea of innovation as the driver of social change will be used to explain how finance capitalism and liberalism emerged in both epochs. The case will be made that technological innovation gave rise to the first half of Polanyi's "double movement."

4

Joseph Schumpeter

Technology and the "Double Movement"

A contemporary of Polanyi's, Joseph Schumpeter also sought to understand the dramatic economic and political transformations of his times. Like Polanyi, Schumpeter directly experienced the traumatic events that engulfed Europe in the early twentieth century. In fact, the two men were practically the same age. Schumpeter was born only three years before Polanyi, in 1883. Though less wealthy, he came from a well-respected, German-speaking, manufacturing family in the small town of Triesch in Habsburg Moravia (now Třešť in the Czech Republic). Their life trajectories were, moreover, very similar. Schumpeter became a professor and held a chair at the University of Bonn until the rise of the Nazis, when he chose to leave the country. He then emigrated to the United States and attained an appointment as a lecturer at Harvard University. More fortunate than Polanyi, Schumpeter was granted US citizenship in 1939 and he remained in America until his death in 1950.

Thus, both men were European émigrés, both were students of philosophy and political economy, both were consumers and critics of Marxism, and both developed novel interpretations of the relationship between capitalism and sociopolitical change. Their theories, accordingly, have important parallels but are also quite distinct from one another. Like Polanyi, Schumpeter identifies the years 1842 to 1897 as a period of momentous capitalist expansion. However, Schumpeter characterizes the mid-nineteenth century not as one marked by the emergence of haute finance, but "as the age of steam and steel."[1] In short, where Polanyi focuses on the gold standard and how its adoption changed the global economy in the mid-nineteenth century, Schumpeter traces how railroads transformed the world.

Defensive Nationalism. B. S. Rabinowitz, Oxford University Press. © Oxford University Press 2023.
DOI: 10.1093/oso/9780197672037.003.0005

Railroads and the Global Capitalism

In this lesser-known, early work, *Business Cycles: A Theoretical, Historical and Statistical Analysis of the Capitalist Process*, Schumpeter sets out to explain the rise and fall of capitalism, focusing on the same turn-of-the-century processes as Polanyi. However, unlike Polanyi, Schumpeter's project is to use theories of business cycles popular in his day to explain the extraordinary changes that took place at the end of the nineteenth century. Indeed, in the 1930s and 1940s, many economists were analyzing capitalism in terms of boom-and-bust economic cycles. As he explains in his preface, "[business] cycles are not, like tonsils, separable things that might be treated by themselves, but are, like the beat of the heart"; therefore, "Analyzing business cycles means neither more nor less than analyzing the economic process of the capitalist era."[2]

To do so, Schumpeter draws heavily from one of his contemporaries, the Russian economic theorist N. D. Kondratieff. Kondratieff sought to show that other economists were missing the mark because they were only examining short boom-and-bust cycles, which were too limited in scope. He therefore painstakingly plotted changes in interest rates, prices, trade, and production to show that cycles of prosperity and recession followed a pattern of long waves, spaced approximately fifty years apart. Importantly, Kondratieff concluded that these "long waves arise out of causes which are inherent in the essence of the capitalistic economy."[3] However, Kondratieff stopped short of saying exactly what it was within the "capitalistic economy" that might set off such cycles.

Schumpeter picks up where Kondratieff left off. Schumpeter's project is to show that cycles of prosperity begin when a significant technological innovation first appears. The logic behind his theory is that major innovations, whether railroads, electricity, or automobiles, set off "new investment opportunities [as well as] new possibilities that are created for further innovation."[4] These cumulative commercial and industrial opportunities combine to create a cycle of accelerated growth. Economic growth, in turn, drives further investment, which soars upward until the investment bubble outstrips the need for the new technologies being advanced. Each innovation-investment cycle will therefore end with a downturn. A new cycle emerges as capital finds a new, exciting innovation to begin financing, setting the whole process in motion again. Thus, each major innovation is an engine for economic growth that leaves in its wake recession or depression, until the next major innovation begins to take off. As he puts it, "every cycle [of innovation] is a historical individual."[5]

To study the rise and fall of liberal capitalism, Schumpeter focuses on three Kondratieff long waves of boom and bust, which he associates with specific innovations: (1) the "first Kondratieff," the Industrial Revolution, 1780s–1842; (2) the "second Kondratieff," the Second Industrial Revolution, 1842–1897; and (3) the "third Kondratieff," the age of electricity, 1898–1940s. It is in his analysis of the second and third Kondratieff waves that Schumpeter's theory overlaps with Polanyi's.

However, the similarities end there. Schumpeter dismisses out of hand the idea that international finance could have been the catalyst that brought the liberal order into being. To attribute such powers to haute finance is for Schumpeter backward reasoning for, as he writes, financial speculation "is nothing but adaptation to an underlying economic process." Schumpeter claims that what steers all economic processes is not global finance but "entrepreneurial activity,"[6] or what we refer to in everyday parlance as innovation. As he puts it, innovation "indirectly produces, through the process it sets going, most of those situations from which windfall gains and losses arise and in which speculative operations acquire significant scope."[7] In his schema, changes in "money and credit," and in fact, "the behavior of *all* aggregate quantities . . . constitutes the response by the system to the results of entrepreneurial activity."[8] When innovation is allowed to flourish, it attracts finance and sets economic activity in motion. Even further, innovation for Schumpeter is the essence of capitalism. Capitalism is not about supply and demand, as Adam Smith maintained. Nor is it about squeezing profit out of laborers as Karl Marx believed. Capitalism is driven by ingenious innovation. Innovation, hence, steers modern history.

Hence, for Schumpeter, to understand how the gold standard changed the world, one has to first examine the innovations of the period that gave rise to financial speculation. And for Schumpeter, the pivotal innovation that revolutionized society in the mid-nineteenth century was railroads. In short, the prime mover of change in the mid to late nineteenth century for Schumpeter was railroadization. But it was not the only innovation of import. "Railroad construction was the main but not the only factor that carried that wave of evolution."[9] Other inventions emerged, which emanated from the subterranean changes that railroad construction set off. Schumpeter notes the importance of changes that came from shipping and the development of different fuel sources. In fact, he identifies the use of petroleum for other purposes than lighting as "a 'carrying' innovation of the next Kondratieff, [which] was in the incubating stage during the second." "Gas was also a major element in the entrepreneurial activity that carried the second Kondratieff," as was "Coal mining, though perhaps to a greater degree the object of active enterprise than it was in England, was more pushed along than pushing."[10]

Though Schumpeter does not believe that global finance was the primary factor steering world developments during the belle époque, he does draw a connection between the growth of banking, speculation, and the railroads. He just reverses the causal arrow: railroadization gave rise to haute finance. For Schumpeter, Polanyi put the cart before the horse. The gold standard could not have been the critical mover of global capitalism. Instead, new forms of global finance developed as a reaction to the possibilities opened up by this all-important technology. Schumpeter explains that railroads "set off a great building boom," which created so dramatic a change that new forms of finance were required to fund these unprecedently large infrastructural projects. Credit had to be "created *ad hoc* by both the preexisting banks and the many new ones that emerged."[11] From this emerged the creation of national banking systems, "the outstanding institutional change" of the era.[12] Whether the 1847 Peel's Act in London, the German legislation of 1875 that allowed for the creation of the German Reichsbank, or the United States National Banking Act of 1863, each represented "nothing but adaptations to the situations created by our process," that is, a response to entrepreneurial innovation.[13]

The end of the Second Industrial Revolution (or the second Kondratieff wave) came after speculative bubbles caused by the railroad boom produced banking failures that ended with the Great Depression of the 1870s.[14] This also marked the beginning of the next long wave of development. As railroad construction reached a surfeit, entrepreneurial energies and finance began to be focused elsewhere. Electricity was the next great wave of innovation. Like railroads, the new technology "created new industries and commodities, new attitudes, new forms of social action and reaction." This new "carrying innovation" had such a great impact that it "changed the relative economic positions of nations, and the conditions of foreign trade."[15]

This third period in many ways corresponds to Polanyi's period of the "double movement." In fact, Schumpeter refers to it as the "Neomercantile Kondratieff," to signify that it was a period that saw the resurgence of state protectionism. During this period, Schumpeter recognizes two critical changes: "the one represented by such symptoms as the recrudescence of protection and the increase in expenditure on armaments, the other by such symptoms as the new spirit in fiscal and social legislation, the rising tide of political radicalism and socialism, the growth and changing attitudes of trade unionism, and so on."[16] Therefore, like Polanyi, Schumpeter sees this late nineteenth century move toward radicalism, socialism, and trade unionism as a response to breakdowns caused by economic and political transformations, which had begun in the mid-nineteenth century. However, Schumpeter attributes the rise of the "Neomercantile Kondratieff" not to the overreach of the market, but to sociological changes brought about by the natural development of capitalism.

According to Schumpeter, "the heroic age of industry" came to an end because prosperity and economic growth brought about the *moral degeneration of the capitalist system*: capitalists ceased "to believe in the standards and moral schemata of their own class." He explains that as capitalism took hold, one of the consequences was that traditional family ties were loosened. Yet, family had been "the center of the motivation of the businessman of old." For "Saving with a view to providing revenue for an indefinite family future" constituted "the moral scheme of life of the typical bourgeois." Not only did the middle-class bourgeoisie but also the moneyed classes lost their bearings. In fact, the moral basis of capitalism was most egregiously abandoned by the "top group" of wealthy capitalists, who absorbed "subconsciously and by an infinite number of channels, views, habits, valuations—cultural worlds— that [were] not its own." In other words, they delighted in conspicuous consumption.

Thus, by the 1910s, both the wealthy and the middle stratums had lost touch with the ethos that sustained the "bourgeois spirt"—the valuation of economic accumulation and savings. An anti-capitalist ethos of "anti-saving" took hold of society, whence it became easier to argue that "thrift is harmful to the interest of the masses always." All of this brought about "a profound change in the environment within which the capitalist engine [worked]."[17] This loss of the core values ultimately brought about the demise of capitalism.

Combining the Theories

Although Schumpeter and Polanyi cross paths in a number of ways, their analyses could not be more different. For Polanyi, the destruction of the liberal order was due to the widespread suffering liberalism wreaked on society as markets increasingly swallowed up life itself. For Schumpeter, the rise of communism and fascism after the turn of the century occurred because of a psychological and moral transformation of the capitalist class. And yet, as different as their positions are, their analyses can be combined. Moreover, by doing so, it is possible to overcome weaknesses in each of the theories. If it can be said that Polanyi has trouble concretely accounting for what propels change, Schumpeter's schema is problematic because it is contradictory; he argues that innovation drives social transformation when it works for him, and switches to a quasi-Marxist class explanation when it does not. Thus, while Polanyi is lyrically hazy about what sets off globalized liberalism, Schumpeter offers a foggy explanation for how it came to an end. Combining the two theories, therefore, can potentially provide a more thorough analysis of how the belle époque began and ended; one which can help us understand the transformations of our present age.

Bringing the strengths of these theories together, I argue that both turn-of-the-century movements were periods of the "double movement" because remarkable technological innovations in transportation and communications created "economies of speed" in addition to "economies of scale." In the Second Industrial Revolution, it was the development of railroads and steamships, modern printing technologies, and the telegraph; in the Digital Age, airplanes, computers, cell phones, and changes to shipping. In short, the reason these two periods are so similar is that both are characterized by rapid interconnectivity.

The study will empirically explore the utility of using Schumpeter's theory in conjunction with Polanyi's by examining the impact of the spectacular changes to transportation and communications that occurred during the Second Industrial Revolution (1860–1920) and the Digital Revolution (1960–2020). That these time frames are parallel is not meant to suggest that industrial, technological, or socioeconomic change necessarily occurs in hundred-year cycles. Though several scholars have made such a claim,[18] this study does not attempt to weigh in on that larger question. These periods are symmetrical not by some predetermined theoretical design, but because of careful consideration of what could be defensible criteria that can be used to isolate such moments of change. In fact, several factors formed the basis of the choice of periodicity used here.

To begin with, the focus is on periods of *modern globalization*. Different forms of globalization have arguably been around for centuries, be it the trade routes forged by the Mongols and the Romans, or the international

fairs of the twelfth and thirteenth centuries, or the expansion of transoceanic commerce in the fourteenth century. In each of these periods, peoples
and economies were interlinked and social structures were reshaped by
the spread of ideas and introduction of innovations originating in faraway
places. However, unlike other forms of globalization, modern globalization
has three characteristics peculiar to it. In the first instance, a critical marker
of modern globalization is that capital becomes highly mobile, or as Jameson
puts it, "Capital itself becomes free-floating."[19] What makes the mobility
of capital so significant is that it has the "potential to connect markets and
production in a more direct, more complex and much deeper manner than
other cross border flows" and therefore, "emerges as a more significant influence on global economic integration."[20] Once capital becomes mobile,
"Globalization [becomes] an imperative . . . requiring all nations to pursue
a common strategy," which leads to the "international integration of markets
for goods and capital (but not labor) became an end in itself, overshadowing
domestic agendas." When this happens, "Domestic economic management
[is made] subservient to international trade and finance rather than the other
way around."[21] In this way, opening up markets across the globe becomes the
"raison d'être of the global order itself."[22]

Second, modern globalization is distinct from previous forms of globalization in the magnitude of social, political, and economic interconnectivity.
It is associated with what Rodrik (2011) refers to as "hyperglobalization."[23]
A singular feature of modern globalization is the experience of extraordi-
narily abrupt shrinking of time and space. David Harvey (1989) explains how
in our modern period, the speeding-up of the pace of life and the overcoming
of spatial barriers are such "that the world sometimes seems to collapse in-
wards upon us." This experience of time-space compression "is challenging,
exciting, stressful, and sometimes deeply troubling, capable of sparking,
therefore a diversity of social and cultural political responses." Therefore, "it
is exactly at such moments [of maximal change] that major shifts in systems
of representation, cultural forms, and philosophical sentiment occur."[24]

Finally, modern globalization is inextricably linked to the development
of nationalism and political liberalism, that is, "principles and institutions,
recognizable by certain characteristics," such as "individual freedom, political participation, private property, and equality of opportunity."[25] As Sluga
observes, "[it is] difficult to think of the national and international as consec-
utive stages in the evolution of political communities."[26] Indeed, temporally,

the Second Industrial Revolution and the first era of modern globalization coincided with the rise of political liberalism and the nation-state system.

Even accepting the uniqueness of these two eras as periods of modern globalization, isolating a singular moment of historical transformation, what is referred to by scholars as a "critical juncture," obviously presents thorny problems. Clearly each historical moment is structurally dependent upon that which came before it. It is, therefore, difficult to avoid an element of arbitrariness in positing both the beginning and end points. As Capoccia and Kelemen observe, "Critical junctures and their synonyms are too often treated as bookends, or a *deus ex machina*, on otherwise carefully constructed stories of institutional development."[27] To address this problem, this study follows Schumpeter and uses statistics as an impartial guide. In fact, it is possible to isolate moments of transformation by pinpointing when dramatic changes in transportation and communication reached critical mass.

As it happens for both epochs under study, these critical transitions came at parallel moments. During both periods, the revolution in transportation began to impact the general public in the decade of the sixties (1860/1960) and reached critical mass in the seventies (1870/1970) (see Figures 5.1, 5.2, 6.1). Similarly, the communications revolution at both times had seeds in earlier innovations but began to take off in the eighties (1880s/1980s). Using criteria that is statistically defensible helps eliminate some of the ambiguity that comes with identifying a beginning point. As to the endpoint, the 1910s present an obvious breaking point from that which preceded it. Of course, 1914 was the watershed year in which World War I began. It has generally been accepted as the moment that marked the end of the period of international economic liberalism, which had dominated the preceding decades.[28] Even though there was a brief liberal resurgence in the 1920s, the general trend was away from liberalism.[29] Indeed, "From 1913 to 1950 world trade and investment stagnated, and governments reinforced this trend by building barriers to foreign goods and companies."[30] After 1918, "Tariffs, quotas, barter agreements, subsidies, and self-sufficiency programs [resulted] in a drastic decline in the volume of world trade."[31] An illustration of this is that of the fifty-one international organizations that existed in 1910, only four were still in existence by 1915.[32] The 2010s may be a less clear endpoint, but this is the era in which far-left and ultra-right national movements gained momentum across Europe and the United States, on a scale that had not been seen since the 1930s.

Addressing Objections

One objection to the proposed analysis is that focusing so exclusively on these two technological revolutions suggests a high degree of determinism. Kellner warns that technological determinism is a "one-sided optic" of globalization. It overlooks or underappreciates the fact that globalization is "a highly complex, contradictory, and thus ambiguous set of institutions and social relations, as well as one involving flows of goods, services, ideas, technologies, cultural forms, and people." In particular, "technological determinism fails to note how the new technologies [. . .] are not autonomous forces that themselves are engendering a new society and economy that breaks with the previous mode of social organization."[33]

The justification for focusing so heavily on technological change is that this study takes as its point of departure the remarkable simultaneity in the political responses we have witnessed across countries. The nativism and populism that emerged across the Global North—and even in areas in the Global South—share striking commonalities. As much as Brexit, or Donald Trump's presidency, or Gabor's "illiberal democracy" are specific to the countries in which they evolved, one can acknowledge that there is an overarching leitmotif that connects them. The only way to explain this puzzling simultaneity is to posit that some sort of macrostructural change is at the heart of it. The power of global technological forces to shape history does not negate that the actions of politicians, activists, and private citizens channel events. The degree of the response to these changes will vary in each nation. Much depends on the degree of change experienced and even more upon the political and societal leaders who emerge. Therefore, separate defensive national movements, which stem from very particular national histories and struggles, and which are led by very particular national politicians and activists, can occur in tandem to produce a "national-populist age."[34]

This line of thinking parallels Polanyi's, who underscored the commonality and simultaneity of sociopolitical movements of the late nineteenth century in so many countries "of a widely dissimilar political and ideological configuration":

> Victorian England and the Prussia of Bismarck were poles apart, and both were very much unlike the France of the Third Republic or the Empire of the Hapsburgs. Yet each of them passed through a period of free trade and laissez faire, followed by a period of anti-liberal legislation in regard to

public health, factory conditions, municipal trading, social insurance, shipping subsidies, public utilities, trade associations, and so on.[35]

Precisely because technological innovations in transportation and communications hit *people across the globe simultaneously* with *parallel forces*, multiple states experience comparable dislocations. In fact, Polanyi himself suggests that such material conditions sparked the change, "Whether the source of the change be war or trade, startling inventions or shifts in natural conditions," "the ultimate cause is set by external forces [. . .], such as a change in climate, or the yield of crops, a new foe, a new weapon used by an old foe, the emergence of new communal ends, or, for that matter, the discovery of new methods of achieving the traditional ends."[36] In another passage, Polanyi's analysis even comes very close to Schumpeter's, when he puts forth that "the establishment of market economy . . .cannot be fully grasped unless the impact of the machine on a commercial society is realized. We do not . . . assert that the machine caused that which happened, but we insist that once elaborate machines . . . were used for production in a commercial society, the idea of a self-regulating market system was bound to take shape."[37]

Another objection one might raise to this study is that there have been other periods in which revolutionary changes to communications and transportation altered social life. On what, basis then, can one claim that these periods are in fact distinctly similar? The difference in the effects of these specific periods of technological innovation can be illustrated by way of comparison to the early and mid-twentieth-century technological innovations in transportation and communications. Certainly, the telephone, television, radio, and automobiles also sped up modern life. Nonetheless, these technologies did not have the same kind of globalizing potential as did the turn-of-the-century revolutions. These technologies arguably had a greater impact on solidifying *national markets* and *national cultures*, than on facilitating international ones. For example, with the growth of the automotive industry, road systems were created that utterly transformed national landscapes. The introduction of road freight also helped increase trade. But trucking did not have an exponential impact on international trade until it was linked up with new forms of shipping and air cargo. It was not until the 1970s that the world saw exponential growth in international trade on the order that had been experienced during the belle époque. As a result, the high point in "the share of trade in output" that had been reached in 1913 "was not surpassed until the 1970s"[38] (see Figure 4.1).

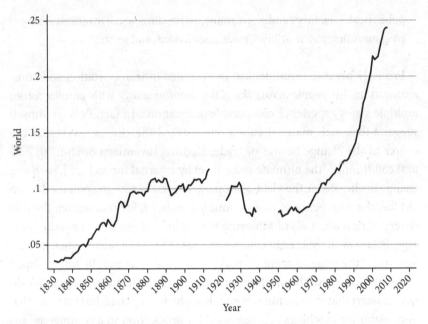

Figure 4.1 World Trade Index (Export/GDP), 1830–2014

Source: Federico, Giovanni; Tena Junguito, Antonio, 2018, "Federico-Tena World Trade Historical Database: Openness," https://doi.org/10.21950/BBZVBN, e-cienciaDatos, V1.

Similarly, the telephone dramatically transformed national infrastructure. In Europe and the United States, telephone poles dotted the countryside and wires were strung across states connecting even the most rural areas. Telephones also allowed for greater communications across borders. However, the telephone system was limited in scalability, "For each new subscriber, every telephone would have to be modified to accommodate the new number and a new cable would have to be laid to each existing subscriber."[39] Dramatic changes in global communication came only after circuit switching was adopted with the Internet. "Instead of every subscriber having a line to every other, each one just has a single line to a central switch."[40] It was therefore not until the 1970s, after packet-switching had been introduced, that the world saw an exponential change in the speed and mass of information capable of being transmitted. Once that happened, "humankind started to fulfill a long-time aspiration: a global communication network sharing, storing, and sorting the largest amount of information ever amassed."[41]

Even television and radio, though potentially international, were in relative terms limited in their impact on internationalization of the social world.

Broadcasting in the immediate postwar period was geographically limited. The transmission of broadcasting signals was blocked by large objects and blocked by the curvature of the earth. Perhaps, as a result of these geographic limitations, television programming and even radio broadcasting to a large extent were devised for and geared toward national audiences from their inception through the 1970s. Television only began to be internationalized once satellite communications developed in the 1980s, allowing signals to be transmitted across the globe.[42]

Most importantly, neither telephone, nor radio, nor television led to an exponential increase in international finance and capital mobility as the telegraph and Internet did at the turn of the centuries. Ticker tape, that quintessential late nineteenth-century innovation, remained the central medium of stock trading throughout the first half of the twentieth century. "Until as recently as the 1960s, financial information spread slowly, typically through ticker tapes. Trading was carried out almost entirely manually."[43] Dramatic change in the financial sector only began in 1980s, when the use of computer algorithms for stock trading became the norm. A strong indicator of this is that "the 1900–14 ratio of foreign investment to output in the world economy was not equaled again until 1980, but has [since] been approximately doubled"[44] (see Figure 4.1). Thus, the mid-century technologies were substantially different in their potential to augment globalization.

Perhaps the strongest objection to focusing on technological change is that it would be disingenuous to suggest that politics had nothing to do with these changes. And it absolutely would be. Politics was central. If nothing else, the hostilities among countries during the two world wars hindered international trade and finance in the early decades of the twentieth century. It would, therefore, be ludicrous to pretend that the languishing of the world economy in the early to mid-twentieth century was simply due to the technologies (or absence thereof) of the day.

In fact, in Part V it will be advanced that, though technology was the *proximate cause* of the "double movement" in these two epochs, politics was the *deeper cause*. The argument that will be put forth is that these periods were similar because, in both, a new postbellum international order had been created that made possible new forms of globalizing technology. In the early nineteenth century, the Concert of Europe delimited a new international order following the Napoleonic Wars; in the mid-twentieth century the Bretton Woods agreements shaped international relations after the two world wars. These unique periods of peace among the world's

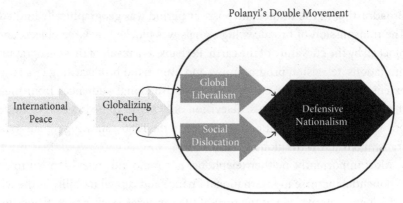

Figure 4.2 Logic of the Argument

industrial powers allowed for the rebuilding of war-torn economies, the revival of industry and innovation, and the loosening of protective trade policies. Eventually all these processes made possible the emergence of re-markable innovations in transportation and communications that ushered in technological revolutions. Thus, in both eras, extended periods of peace made it possible for technological revolutions to develop, which produced high-liberalism and hyper-interconnectivity (see Figure 4.2). Therefore, what makes these turn-of-the-century periods analogous is twofold: the ex-tended periods of peace that preceded each (the deeper political cause), as well as the globalizing effects of the new technologies that developed during the periods of technological revolution (the more proximate technological cause).

However, the primary objective of this book is to illustrate how the "double movement" can be applied to today's movements and why it is rel-evant to do so. Accordingly, the bulk of the book is focused on making the case that these two epochs actually are comparable. Parts II, III, and IV trace how innovations in communications and transportation achieved during the Second Industrial Revolution and the Digital Revolution brought into being global liberalism and anti-liberal nationalism. In contrast, the last part, Part V, examines the factors that *precipitated* the changes described in the center of the book. Thus, the logical and temporal order of the analysis is inverted. Admittedly, this is an unconventional approach. The last history chapter of the book is, if you will, a prequel to the rest of the book.

PART II

GLOBAL INTERCONNECTIVITY AND THE RISE OF THE MODERN LIBERAL ORDER

The belle époque, roughly from the 1860s to the 1910s, was a period of mind-bending innovation, rapid urbanization, and exhilarating modernization. Although the period is characterized by a multitude of astonishing advances, arguably those most responsible for the rapidity of the era's sea-changes were technological innovations in transportation (railroads and steamships), and communications (changes in printing technology and telegraphy). One hundred years later, after the end of what Schumpeter referred to as the "heroic age of industry," the world started once again down the path of globalization. In so many ways, aerospace and computer technologies were to the digital age what steamships and insulated telegraph cables had been to the belle époque. Indeed, in both epochs transportation and communications revolutions completely transformed the world. Everything was altered, from social practices to commodity production to political organization to man's relationship to his environment. The rapid-fire change also produced parallel forms of liberal internationalism, the first half of Polanyi's *double movement*.

To better understand the scope of these changes and how they came about, the next two chapters apply Schumpeter's theory of technological innovation to explain the rise of liberal capitalism. Chapter 5 will trace how new forms of transportation and communications created unparalleled interconnectivity that brought about the first modern liberal era. Chapter 6 will follow suit, examining how one hundred years later, mid-twentieth-century technologies altered man's ability to traverse time and space, producing the second era of modern liberalism.

PART II

GLOBAL INTERCONNECTIVITY AND THE RISE OF THE MODERN LIBERAL ORDER

5

The Belle Époque: Railroads and Telegraphy

The mid-nineteenth century was indeed "the age of steam and steel," and that was as true on land as it was at sea. On the land it was steam-powered railroads; on the sea it was steam-powered ships. At the same time, new printing technologies and telegraph revolutionized information flows. Together, the transportation and communications revolutions of the late nineteenth century changed interpersonal relations, international relations, and everything in between. It brought into being the first era of modern liberalism.

The Transportation Revolution

In 1800 the fastest way to go anywhere on land was to ride a horse. Local rail systems had been around for several decades, but they were primarily used to support existing canal systems. However, by the mid to late nineteenth century, steam-powered rail coaches had displaced both horse-drawn wagons and stagecoaches worldwide.

In the United States, up through the 1840s passenger rail travel was extremely limited. Indeed, the US Secretary of Interstate Commerce mused in 1895 that "As late as 1850 there seems to have been little conception of the influence which the railways were to wield in the development of the interstate traffic of this great country, and of the country itself."[1] An important milestone was the completion of the transcontinental rail line in 1869. The dream of a rail route connecting the Atlantic to the Pacific was not new, yet the costs were prohibitive and the political will had been limited. The impetus for the transcontinental railroad was the American Civil War. Abraham Lincoln understood that a railroad connecting the coasts would support communities and military outposts on the frontier, make valuable resources in the west easier to access, and unite the new territories in Oregon and California to

Defensive Nationalism. B. S. Rabinowitz, Oxford University Press. © Oxford University Press 2023.
DOI: 10.1093/oso/9780197672037.003.0006

the heart of the Union. On July 1, 1862, Lincoln signed the Pacific Railway Act. The act chartered a new railway company, the Union Pacific Railroad, that was to connect the already existing Central Pacific Railroad with the rail systems in the east to create a cross-continental railroad. Seven years later, the two rail lines were ceremoniously joined, physically linking the West to the East Coast. To commemorate the achievement, on May 10, 1869, a final golden spike was theatrically hammered into the line where the two great rail systems met at the dusty outpost of Promontory, Utah, in front of a large crowd that had been assembled to witness the historic moment

But these changes were in no way unique to the United States. A parallel development was occurring across the developed world. In fact, the first country to expand railroad usage was Britain. As early as 1844, Britain had a fully developed rail system serving just under twenty-eight million passengers. It would take the rest of Europe thirty years to catch up. It was not till the 1870s that "main lines were completed everywhere, even in countries where the start had been late."[2] The new European rail systems linked the west of Europe to its most easterly points, Constantinople, Salonica, and Vladivostok. The rapidity of the change must have been astonishing. Switzerland in 1850 had a meager thirty-four rail engines in the whole country and Austria had only 671 in 1852. By 1870 Switzerland had almost one thousand rail engines and Austria had 9,160 by 1875.[3] France, Germany, and Italy more than doubled their mileage between 1870 and 1890. Perhaps even more astoundingly, over the same period, Britain's passenger rail travel increased one hundredfold, with approximately 288 million people using the railroads in the 1870s, half of whom were traveling third-class.[4] Rail transit was, thus, particularly important for British of lesser means[5] (see Figure 5.1). Even in Latin America, a railway network had begun in Argentina as early as 1855.[6]

Nonetheless, the largest rail expansion was in the United States, where rail lines increased by a whopping 76 percent, "from 52,900 miles in 1870 to 93,200 miles in 1880"[7] (see Figure 5.2). Railroad development was so central to the growing United States economy that in the early 1880s the Pennsylvania railway was the nation's largest corporation, carrying over two million tons of industrial and consumer goods every year. An early account of what it was like to travel by passenger rail was recorded in the *New York Times* in 1869. In the article entitled "ACROSS THE CONTINENT: From the Missouri to the Pacific Ocean by Rail. The Plains, the Great American Desert,

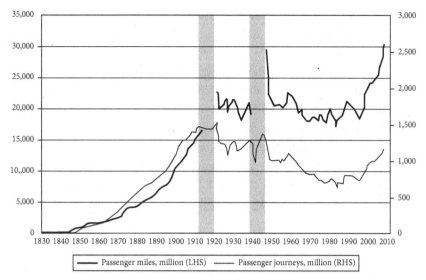

Figure 5.1 Railroad Development in Britain, Passenger Miles/Journeyed (Millions) 1830–2010

Source: https://publications.parliament.uk/pa/cm200809/cmselect/cmtran/233/233we02.htm, Contains Parliamentary information licensed under the Open Parliament Licence v3.0.

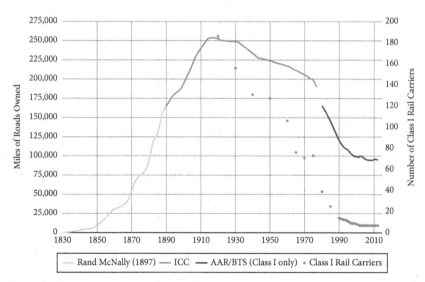

Figure 5.2 Railroad Development USA

Source: https://transportgeography.org/contents/chapter5/rail-transportation-pipelines/rail-track-mileage-united-states/.

the Rocky Mountains. One Hundred Hours from Omaha to San Francisco,"
the correspondent marveled at the wondrous change railroads had brought:

> What a contrast between then and now! The slow, toilsome, tedious jog-
> ging of the mule-drawn trains over the vast, dreary waste—a dozen or
> fifteen miles made at the end of the day—then the night bivouac, with de-
> fensive preparations against the Indians; now, whirling along at the rate of
> thirty miles an hour, with sumptuous repasts during the day and luxurious
> couches during the night! What a contrast even with the comparative ra-
> pidity of the overland mail coaches, for [one passenger] informs me that
> three years ago he was ten days and nights in making this distance we have
> just traversed in two![8]

As railroads were forever altering transcontinental travel, steamships
were transforming transoceanic travel. Steam-powered vessels had already been in use for some time and played a critical part of the First
Industrial Revolution. However, steamboat conveyance was restricted to
canals and rivers and its use was primarily limited to cargo carriage. From
the early 1800s, steam vessels were the primary means of transporting
materials, like rubber, copper, and palm oil, needed to fuel Europe's and
America's growing manufacturing industries. European colonizers used
steam-powered gunboats to access inland waterways in China, the Middle
East, and Africa. In the United States, steamboats transported trade goods
and slaves up and down the Ohio, Mississippi, and Hudson Rivers. It
was not until the 1860s that steamships capable of long sea voyages were
developed.

Although a number of improvements played a part in making steamships
seaworthy, the most important was switching from wood to coal as the primary fuel. Coal not only took up much less space than wood, it also burned
much more efficiently.[9] The critical change came in 1867 with the invention
of the convection boiler, a sophisticated marine boiler that could safely and
efficiently burn coal. Before this, marine boilers functioned more like kettles;
water was turned into steam by simply boiling it above a wood-burning fire
contained in a box. The convection boiler added a flue to the boiler through
which gas from the burning coal entered and then was transformed from
heat to steam. This was an exponential change that enabled ships to carry
enough fuel to travel across the Atlantic Ocean. A sense of the enormity of
the change is captured by the fact that in Germany alone, between 1871 and

1887, "Steamship capacity rose by about 454 percent and steamship crewmen about 226 percent."[10]

Oceanic travel advanced further with the completion of the Suez Canal in 1869. Cutting across the Suez Isthmus in Egypt at the top of the African continent, the canal connected the Mediterranean Sea to the Red Sea. Before its construction, even the new steamships with their sophisticated coal-burning boilers could not carry enough coal to circumnavigate beyond Africa. But, having a direct channel between the two seas meant that ships traveling from the North Atlantic to the Indian Ocean no longer had to traverse the length of the African coast. This reduced the distance traveled between Britain and India by some 4,500 miles. Now, for the first time in history, "steamships became a viable means of transporting goods from Europe to Asia."[11] Indeed, the Suez Canal was a monumental feat on the order of the ancient pyramids. The excavation took ten years and used state-of-the-art dredgers. It also took the lives of one hundred thousand men and boys, most of whom were peasants forced to toil in unhealthy conditions and live in dilapidated tents where cholera, smallpox, and all manner of diseases were spread.[12]

These profound changes to travel brought international trade to new heights. It is true that the First Industrial Revolution had made mass production possible, but it was only after railroads and steamships reduced distribution costs that trade became thoroughly internationalized. The new means of transportation allowed for an unprecedented volume of goods to be conveyed, at unprecedented speeds, and with greater efficiency.[13] Transatlantic trade costs fell roughly 60 percent from 1870 to 1900.[14] As a consequence, "world exports expanded by an average of 3.4 per cent annually, substantially above the 2.1 per cent annual increase in world GDP," and "the share of trade in output (or openness) rose steadily, reaching a high point in 1913, just before the First World War, which was not surpassed until the 1960s."[15]

Steamships and railroads not only transported goods; they also carried people, information, and ideas. It is estimated that in 1820 only one in every five thousand US citizens traveled abroad. A century later, an average of one in every 324 Americans was making international excursions annually. The impact on immigration was even greater. Before the nineteenth century, travel was formidable, slow, and costly, particularly across oceans. Not many people chose to emigrate to new continents. The largest transfer of peoples from one continent to another had occurred by means of brutal force, through the Atlantic slave trade. Those who willingly embarked on such an arduous journey were few, primarily merchants and "a relatively small trickle of settlers, agriculturalists, and miners to frontiers throughout the world."[16] The new transportation technologies changed all of that. By the 1880s, "intensive emigration spread south and east as far as Portugal, Russia, and Syria."[17] In fact, 1820 to 1913 witnessed one of the largest self-directed movements of people the world had ever seen: "26 million people migrated from Europe to the United States, Canada, Australia, New Zealand, Argentina and Brazil . . . An even larger number of Chinese migrated to countries around the Pacific Rim and beyond."[18]

The Communications Revolution

While transportation was transforming the world, communications were revolutionizing society at as rapid of a pace. Change began with new innovations in printing. At the beginning of the nineteenth century, printing was an artisan's practice. It involved multiple steps all performed by hand, from inking the plate to stacking the sheets. Changes that revolutionized the industry began in the 1860s.

In 1863, the first automatic rotary-fed printing press was developed. The automatic press consisted of a cylinder around which text and images were curved and then rotated by a drum to spin out printed sheets. Whereas before the rotary press, two men manually operating a wooden screw press might complete a maximum of 3,500 sheets in a day, with the rotary press it was possible to produce 8,000 sheets *per hour*.[19] Other innovations came soon after, including monotype and linotype setting, which allowed printers to set an entire line of type at once.[20] Simultaneous developments were being made in paper production. Before the 1860s, paper was made from cotton, literally from cotton rags, a very labor-intensive process. The introduction of paper pulp dramatically cut manufacturing costs. Because wood could be pulped in a mill in large quantities, the commercial production of paper was now possible on a scale never before achieved.[21] Combined, these various innovations made the quick and easy production of bulk print products feasible. With the reduction in printing costs not only inexpensive books, "pulp fiction," but also large batches of newspapers, whether broadsheets or journals or small dailies, could be produced cheaply. It was the birth of mass media.

The new rail systems contributed to the rapid sharing of information among private individuals as well. Prior to the 1860s, the post was extremely slow and so costly it was used almost exclusively for commercial purposes. An attempt to improve the speed of mail carriage was made in the United States with the introduction of the Pony Express in 1860. But the Pony Express was not much more affordable and remained in operation for a little over a year. Once railroads became viable, it was quickly eclipsed. The expansion of rail systems reduced inland transport costs "by over 90 per cent between 1800 and 1910."[22] These changes had an enormous impact on personal communications. For example, in 1850 Americans received five letters a year on average. By 1900, that number had increased to approximately ninety-four pieces of mail per person.[23] As a measure of this rapid growth, the number of United States post offices almost tripled from around 28,500 in 1860 to just short of 77,000 in 1901.[24]

Low-cost printing and rapid rail distribution also meant companies could now sell their wares directly to people living in small towns and remote rural areas. A new commercial industry came into being—the mail-order catalog. The famous Parisian department store Au Bon Marché introduced its mail-order service in 1871. One year later, in August 1872, Montgomery Ward published the world's first general merchandise mail-order catalog. Several other enterprising retailers followed suit, including Rowland Macy in 1874, John Wanamaker in 1876, Hammacher Schlemmer in 1881, Richard Sears in 1886, and Alvah C. Roebuck in 1896. Sears was one of the most stunning success stories of the mail-order business. His first small mailer for watches in 1886 ballooned into a 786-page catalog in only one year's time! In fact, so profitable was the mail-order business that Montgomery Ward and Sears eventually had two of the largest business enterprises in the United States.[25]

Even more significant to the revolution in communications was the astonishing development of telegraphy. As Lew and Carter observe, "The telegraph was the first mode of communication to virtually eliminate the effect of distance, allowing for near instantaneous communication."[26] The first intercontinental telegraph wire was laid in 1858, connecting North America to Europe. Before the cable was laid, news from Europe had typically taken over six weeks to reach the United States.[27] After the transcontinental cable, "information flowed across the Atlantic at the speed of an electrical impulse."[28] The change was dizzying. Soon, "New cables were being laid all over the world . . . Malta had been linked to Alexandria in 1868, and a direct cable was laid from France to Newfoundland in 1869. Cables reached India, Hong

Kong, China and Japan in 1870; Australia was connected in 1871, and South America in 1874."[29]

Telegraphy transformed business almost overnight. Prior to the telegraph, New York merchants trading with England typically received updates from their foreign associates once or twice a month and the information received was usually several weeks old by the time it arrived. But, with the telegraph, "traders in virtually every major center gained more and better access to vital information about harvest prospects and about prices in both the grain exporting and importing regions."[30] "Suddenly the price of goods and the speed with which they could be delivered became more important than their geographic location."[31] To stay competitive, businesses had to adapt to the new technology. "The result was an irreversible acceleration in the pace of business life."[32]

Telegraphy impacted commercial trade in other ways as well. The telegraph "allowed shipping companies to redirect ships in response to changing opportunities," and enabled railroads to lower costs by helping them better "utilise their track and avoid double-tracking."[33] Everything from the military to corporate organizations to newsgathering came to rely on the telegraph for communication and coordination.[34] Indeed, the telegraph changed businesses large and small, whether "the processing of tobacco, grains, whiskey, sugar, vegetable oil and other foods . . . [or] the refining of oil and the making of metals and materials . . . glass, abrasives, and other materials."[35] One of the most critical changes was that trade in commodities became global as prices for everything from cotton to corn could be reliably communicated instantaneously. Diverse industries became global businesses, such as "Metal markets, ship brokering, and insurance."[36]

Changes to Finance

With the miraculous innovations in transportation and communications, finance capital was able to take flight. This was in part because accompanying the telegraph was another noteworthy innovation, the ticker tape. Ticker tape "provided brokers across the country with a printed transcript of trades on exchange floors almost immediately after they had happened." This meant that, for the first time, traders had access to "up-to-the-minute stock, gold, grain, cotton, and oil quotations as well as general financial and political news."[37] Together, telegraphy and ticker stock provided the foundation for new forms of finance. They opened up futures trading, and greatly facilitated "arbitraging differences in securities prices across markets."[38] By the 1880s, several thousand bankers and brokers across the United States subscribed to Western Union's ticker service.[39]

Of course, new forms of capital finance also developed at this time. Schumpeter rightly recognized that the great national banking institutions of the mid-nineteenth century were developed largely in response to investment opportunities presented by railroads. Arguably, the globalization of haute finance itself can be dated to 1852 with the establishment of *Crédit Mobilier*. The new form of investment banking is deemed by some to be as profound a financial innovation as the creation of the joint-stock companies in the Middle Ages. *Credit Mobilier* was founded in Paris by the Péreire brothers to compete with the Rothschild Banks' lucrative monopoly in industrial finance. However, the Rothschild Banks had a weakness: they only offered short-term capital loans. The innovation introduced by the Péreire brothers was to provide financing for long-run investment needs. *Credit Mobilier* was, thus, the first bank to issue long-term bonds; and they did so primarily for the construction and acquisition of railroads across Europe and the United States. *Credit Mobilier* did not solely fund railroads, but it was their bread and butter. Even the initial capital for *Credit Mobilier* had come from railroads. The Péreire brothers had been the central bankers for the French rail industry before branching in this new direction. With *Crédit Mobilier,* the brothers extended their ventures abroad, widening the scope of their investments.

The United States was where the largest rail projects were attracting capital investments, but the brothers funded rail systems in Austria, France, Spain, and beyond.[40] So great was the change made to industrial banking that *Credit Mobilier* sparked a "financial revolution that rapidly diffused throughout the continent."[41] "The difference between banks of the credit-mobilier type and commercial banks in the advanced industrial country of the time (England) was absolute . . . there was a complete gulf."[42] As Gerschenkron explains:

> The number of banks in various countries shaped upon the image of the Péreire bank was considerable. But more important than their slavish imitations was the creative adaptation of the basic idea of the Péreires and its incorporation in the new type of bank, the universal bank, which . . . successfully combined the basic idea of the credit mobilier with the short-term activities of commercial banks.[43]

In response, "A network of affiliated investment banks was set up in England (International Financial Society Limited), Spain (*Credito Mobiliario Espanol*), Germany (*Darmstadter Bank*), Italy (*Credito Mobiliaire Italiano*), and Holland (*Credit Neerlandais*)."[44] "All these new institutes were big joint-stock banks, with huge amounts of share capital, whose charters tended to very much resemble those of the Crédit Mobilier."[45] Thus, finance actually began to globalize *before* the wide adoption of the gold standard in 1870, as Polanyi dated it, and, moreover, it developed largely in response to the investment opportunities opened up by the mid-century explosion of railroad construction.

The coalescence of all these technological innovations brought into being international liberal trade.[46] Between 1870 and 1911, "a truly global economy was forged for the first time, extending from the core of Western European industrializers to late-comers in Eastern Europe to raw material suppliers on the periphery."[47] Many scholars date the beginning of the new globalized trade regime to 1860, the year that Britain and France came to a comprehensive trade agreement. The "Cobden-Chevalier agreement," so named after the two principal negotiators, was historic because it included the world's first "Most-Favored-Nations" clause. The clause guaranteed any tariff concessions granted by either of the signatory states would be extended to a third trading partner. The Most-Favored-Nations clause, hence, created a powerful incentive for other nations to follow suit and was quickly picked up across Europe. After the "Cobden-Chevalier agreement," "France concluded a treaty with Belgium in 1861, followed in quick succession by agreements with the German Zollverein in 1862, Italy in 1863, Switzerland in 1864, Sweden, Norway and the Netherlands in 1865, and Austria in 1866."[48] Thus, the new treaty helped expand trading opportunity among states, making the spread of free trade much easier[49] (see Chapter 12).

New International Fora

The growth of liberal trade required more than most-favored-nations treaties. Indeed, several international organizations were established to support the international character of the miraculous technological changes that were developed during the Second Industrial Revolution. One of the first international institutions established was the International Union for Weights and Measures (1857). Everything from ohms to volts to amperes to watts, and joules were standardized across nations. This was followed by a series of other organizations, including the International Telegraphic Union (1865), the Universal Postal Union (1874), and the International Union of Custom Tariffs (1890). In 1884, a Prime Meridian Conference was held in Washington, which with that achieved the standardization to time across the globe for the first time in history.[50] Other forms of standardization were also introduced, such as standardized settings for railway gauges.

Perhaps most important of all the forms of standardization developed during this period, as Polanyi contends, was the adoption of the world's first international monetary system, initially based on gold and silver, and then only on gold. Gold had, of course, been a medium of exchange for eons. But the international gold standard was something entirely new. For the first time in history, each country agreed to exchange a unit of its domestic currency for a fixed quantity of gold. This meant that any currency could be freely convertible, whether at home or abroad, because exchange rates between countries were fixed. In other words, by establishing the value of a unit of currency in almost every state to a predetermined quantity of gold, there now existed a uniform and regulated medium of international payments.

Remarkably, by the 1880s, "International gold and silver standards became nearly universal . . . [having been embraced in] North and South America, Europe, Russia, Japan, China, as well as other European colonies and independent countries. By 1908 roughly 89 percent of the world's population lived in countries with convertible currencies under the gold or silver standard."[51] The momentousness of this change is perhaps better grasped when one considers that into the early decades of the nineteenth century, the various states in the USA had different currencies and banking regimes. It took approximately half a century to create a standardized national US currency—and that was within only one country. The immensity of creating a fixed exchange rate across the globe was thus considerable and is widely held to have facilitated a dramatic increase in trade volume. One measure of how much the gold standard impacted trade is that, under the gold regime, the ratio of GDP to international trade in Europe "increased from 29.9 to 36.9%."[52]

The internationalization of foreign trade and investment after the 1870s was made possible not only because of the gold standard but also through imperial conquest. With colonization, European powers were able to plunder resources from the lands they had colonized to meet their industrial needs. They were also able to expand their industrial production because they now had new captive markets. These intentions were made unabashedly transparent in an astonishingly honest remark attributed to the British imperialist and founder of the former territory of Rhodesia, Cecil Rhodes. In this frequently referred to quote, Rhodes reputedly stated:

> We must find new lands from which we can easily obtain raw materials and at the same time exploit the cheap slave labor that is available from the natives of the colonies. The colonies would also provide a dumping ground for the surplus goods produced in our factories.

In fact, both haute finance and railroads were central to the success of these colonial enterprises. Polanyi describes how the "tentacles of haute finance" were used for "The epic of the building of railways in the Balkans, in Anatolia, Syria, Persia, Egypt, Morocco, and China."[53] Railroads were built across Africa, the Middle East, and Asia to more cost effectively transport tons of raw material to the colonial ports. Gains from these new rail systems were enormous. In the 1930s, one investigator in Britain's overseas territories estimated that "human porters could carry a maximum of 1,450 ton-miles of freight per annum; heavy animals, 3,600; 'horsed wagons,' 118,800; [and] tractor trains, 1,000,000"; in contrast, broad-gauge railways could carry 3,613,50 ton-miles of freight per annum, a dramatic increase.[54] In a similar fashion, the United Fruit Company first gained a foothold in Central America by financing railroads in Costa Rica and Honduras at the turn of the century. The company later became a central instrument of US imperialism in Latin America.

The New Internationalism

But it was not only trade, finance, and control over the world's resources that were internationalized at this time. The telegraph also helped create a modern sense of global interconnectivity. Many people became "fervent believers in the peacemaking potential of the telegraph."[55] One commenter expressed how, "In a very remarkable degree, the telegraph confederated human sympathies and elevated the connection of human brotherhood. By it the peoples of the world were made to stand closer together."[56] In fact, the term *du jour* was "Internationalism."

Though attributed to Jeremy Bentham in the previous century, by the nineteenth century "internationalism" had come to describe a new mode of being in the world.[57] Internationalism was used to express people's enormous sense of optimism about the modern era. J. A. Hobson famously described the sense of the miraculous transformation to society that this one word encapsulated, in an address to the Society for Ethical Culture of Philadelphia titled "The Ethics of Internationalism":

> It is through the facilitation of news, through the press and the telegraph service, that we are brought to-day into ever closer, more immediate and sympathetic contact with the whole world. Everyone, to-day, as we say familiarly, lives at the end of a telegraph line, which means not merely that all the great and significant happenings in the world are brought to his attention in a way which was impossible a generation or two ago, but that they are brought at once and simultaneously to the attention of great masses of people, so that anything happening in the most remote part of the world makes its immediate impression upon the society of nations. The whole world is made cognizant of it, and the immediate and simultaneous sympathy it arouses brings a new element of sociality into the world. In this sense we may say that the world has been recently discovered for the mass of civilized mankind.[58]

Perhaps the best known expression of this is John Maynard Keynes's oft-quoted passage, depicting how quotidian this new mode of being had become:

> The inhabitant of London could order by telephone, sipping his morning tea in bed, the various products of the whole earth, in such quantity as he might see fit, and reasonably expect their early delivery upon his doorstep . . . he could decide to couple the security of his fortunes with the good faith of the townspeople of any substantial municipality in any content that fancy or information might recommend. He could secure forthwith, if he wished it, cheap and comfortable means of transit to any country or climate without passport or other formality . . . and could then proceed abroad to foreign quarters, without knowledge of their religion, language, or customs, bearing coined wealth upon his person, and would consider himself greatly aggrieved and much surprised at the least interference.[59]

In step with this optimism, a multitude of international nongovernmental organizations came into being. Indeed, nonprofit international organizations increased by an average of ten organizations a year during the 1890s, reaching a peak in 1910 with fifty-one organizations operating in multiple countries.[60] Among the international nonprofits founded at this time, many remain till this day hallmarks of the positive side of the international sphere, including the Red Cross (1863), the First International Congress of Women's Rights (1878), the modern Olympics (1896), the Nobel Prize (1901), and the Salvation Army. In fact, the Salvation Army had been founded as a modest organization in Britain, but by 1910 it was represented in more than thirty states.[61] One of the most self-conscious expressions of the new internationalism was the advent of World's Fairs. Each fair served as a platform for states to showcase themselves. Over twenty countries participated, presenting exhibits of their industrial and scientific achievements, or cultural uniqueness. The precursor to these World's Fairs was "the Great Exhibition of the Works of Industry of All Nations" organized by Prince Albert and held at London's the Crystal Palace (for which occasion the breathtaking glass and metal structure was built in 1851). It was such a success that it was followed by the world expositions in New York in 1853, London in 1862, Philadelphia in 1876, Paris in 1889, Chicago in 1893, Brussels in 1897, Paris in 1900, Buffalo in 1901, St. Louis in 1904, San Francisco in 1915, and Chicago in 1933–34. Indeed, the period from the late 1800s to the early 1900s is regarded as "the golden age" of World's Fairs.

Conclusion

Altogether, the novel forms of transportation and communications of the mid-nineteenth century linked people in ways inconceivable a decade earlier. The modern turn-of-the-century world was one in which people, goods, and ideas could be carried at previously unimaginable speeds, across large expanses of space—even oceans. Every part of social life was transformed, from media, to shopping, to trade and finance. Railroads, steamships, printing technologies, and the telegraph represented the triumphal spirit of the new age. Through them a new cult had taken shape, whose sacred pillars were modernization, progress, and expansionary growth.

6

The Digital Age: Turbojets and Computers

A century after the "age of steam and steel," history seemed to begin to repeat itself. Turbojets and containerships revolutionized twentieth-century
transportation in much the same way as railroads and steamships had one
hundred years before. And just as the speed at which information was shared
and disseminated in the 1880s and 1890s was transformed by the new communications technologies, in a remarkably analogous manner three parallel
innovations utterly revolutionized communications at the end of the twentieth century: (1) solid-state electrification, which made possible microproc-
essing and portable computers; (2) packet switching, which made possible
the Internet; and (3) satellites, which made possible instantaneous global information exchange. All three were developed in tandem and brought about
the Digital Revolution.

The Transportation Revolution

As with railroads, air travel had been possible since the early part of the century. Nonetheless, it was not until mid-century that air travel really took
off. Indeed, up to the 1950s, passenger flights had been limited, and cargo
flights nonexistent. In the second half of the twentieth century, both rapidly
increased. Writing in the 1950s when air travel was just beginning to expand,
one student of transportation history recognized the parallels to the previous
century:

> History repeats itself . . . If we substitute a modern date, airlines for railways,
> and railways for waterways and canals, we have something of the general
> view which today is taken of the possibilities of air cargo.[1]

Whereas in the 1950s, the average traveler voyaged overseas by ocean liner, by
the 1960s aircraft had become the primary means of transcontinental travel.[2]
The extraordinary mid-century growth in the passenger airline industry was

Defensive Nationalism. B. S. Rabinowitz, Oxford University Press. © Oxford University Press 2023.
DOI: 10.1093/oso/9780197672037.003.0007

due to several innovations, including the introduction of turbo-propeller air-craft in the early 1950s, transatlantic jets in 1958, and finally the 1969 debut of the revolutionary Boeing 747—the first wide-bodied aircraft. With these serial changes, between the 1950s to 1970s "the cost of jet travel [decreased] by an average of over 5% a year"[3] (see Figure 6.1). What had been regarded as a glamorous means for the rich and famous to voyage around the world had become available to the average person. In fact, from 1950 to 1970, the period that came to be known as "the jet age," passenger flights grew tenfold.[4]

Airfreight "represented yet another major transportation breakthrough."[5] Airmail had begun in the 1910s and was in usage throughout the 1920s. But air cargo did not come into its own as a separate industry until the 1970s, when a young Yale graduate decided to implement ideas that he had devel-oped for one of his economics assignments. Fredrick Smith had received a "C" for his term paper in which he had argued that in the computerized age there was a need for reliable overnight delivery. Undeterred by his professor's rebuff, Smith launched FedEx in 1973, the world's first business dedicated to next-day delivery. Before FedEx, next-day delivery was rare and extremely costly. In general, air cargo was transported in the holds of passenger air-craft and had limited integration with ground transport. Smith created the first airline wholly devoted to cargo flights. Moreover, the airline was supported by a global logistics network based on the "hub and spoke" model

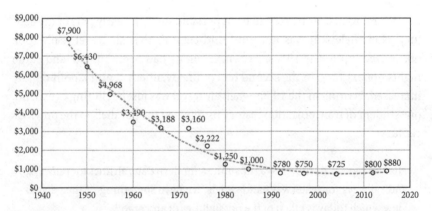

Figure 6.1 Average Airfare between New York and London, 1946–2015 (in 2012 dollars)

Source: Expanded from Bowen, J. (2004), "World-Shapers: The Geographical Implications of Several Influential Jet Aircraft," paper presented at the 2004 Conference of the American Association of Geographers. Note: In 2012 dollars. Round trip. https://transportgeography.org/contents/chapter5/air-transport/air-fare-new-york-london/.

that coordinated ground delivery with the routing of cargo flights.[6] With its promise of next-day delivery, the industry grew exponentially. Both the volume and number of products expanded massively, as did the distances covered.[7] "By 1980, the real costs of airfreight had fallen to about a quarter of its level at the beginning of the Second World War."[8] As a result, "Between 1975 and 2004, air tonnages grew at 7.4 percent per annum, much faster than both ocean tonnage and the value of world trade in manufactures in this period."[9]

During the same period that air cargo was being modernized, an equally impactful revolution was taking place in shipping: containerization. The container may seem to be a humble invention, but it was actually quite revolutionary. Standardized containers allowed cargo to be loaded, unloaded, and stacked using cranes and special forklift trucks. This made transferring goods from ships to rail flatcars and then to semitrailer trucks exponentially easier and faster. Prior to containers, shipping was an elaborate and extremely costly process. In addition to the expense of crating, insuring, and storing products, the basic process of loading and unloading ships was a hugely complex and time-consuming task. Levinson describes some of what was involved:

> the cargo that crossed the docks was a jumble. Consumer goods might come packed in paperboard cartons. Heavier industrial goods, such as machinery and auto parts, were encased in custom-made wooden crates. Barrels of olives, bags of coffee, and coils of steel might all be part of the same load of "general cargo." An incoming truck or railcar brought hundreds or thousands of such items, each of which had to be unloaded and stored in a transit shed, a warehouse adjacent to the dock. When a ship was ready to load, each item was counted by a checker and hauled on to the dock.[10]

Containers automated the labor-intensive processes of opening, sorting, repacking, and hauling. This mechanization dramatically cut shipping costs and radically improved the speed and efficiency with which goods were transported. For all these reasons, "The container represented a radical advance in transportation [. . . similar to those of] the steamship, the canal, the railroad, and other technologies that brought economic transformation in their wake."[11]

Though quantifying the absolute gains in world trade and economic growth to containerization is difficult (and is in some dispute),[12] it is clear that containerization made a substantial impact. "In 1970, container ships comprised only 2 percent of the world shipping tonnage available to carry general cargoes. By 1996, that total had grown to nearly a third, with tonnage carried equal to 55 percent of general cargo trade."[13] In fact, the decade after air cargo and containerization were introduced, "the volume of international trade in manufactured goods grew more than twice as fast as the volume of global manufacturing production, and two and a half times as fast as global economic output."[14] In other words, trade was being driven by something other than changes in production. As Levinson observes, "Something was accelerating the growth of trade even though the economic expansion that normally stimulates trade was weak."[15] The dramatic lowering of freight costs from both air cargo and but even more so from containerization are prime candidates.

The Communications Revolution

Along with these radical changes in transportation were concomitant transformations to communications. It could be said that the Digital Revolution is very much a legacy of the Second World War. Even more specifically, that it was "largely [the] unintended outcome of military procurement decisions made by the United States Defense Department."[16] And if one were to pinpoint a date when it all commenced, the case could be made that it all began with the Soviet launch of Sputnik on October 4, 1957.

The launching of Sputnik shocked the world; shock quickly turned to fear. Few in the United States government or military had anticipated the Soviets would have such spectacular space capabilities so soon. US policymakers, fearful of falling behind, quickly sought to accelerate their space and weapons programs. One of the most consequential changes was the formation of a new defense agency dedicated to winning the space race. In 1958, shortly after the Soviet success with Sputnik, the US Department of Defense formed the Advanced Research Projects Agency (ARPA). ARPA poured money into the research and development of several space and communications innovations they hoped would surpass those of the Soviets. By the 1990s, the cross-fertilization of the fruits of these various endeavors had blossomed into what would be dubbed "The Information Age."[17] Thus, the "information revolution" largely originated in the United States and from there spread through much of the industrialized world.[18]

Among the innovations fostered under this new defense program were silicon chips, which made modern computers possible. Computers existed in the mid-twentieth century, but they were nothing like the everyday-use computers of the twenty-first century. In fact, it is not much of an exaggeration to say that early twentieth century computers are to today's computers what giant fossilized dinosaur skeletons are to the hummingbird. The first fully programmable electronic computer ever built was unveiled in 1944, during World War II at Massachusetts Institute of Technology (MIT). The groundbreaking "Electronic Numerical Integrator and Computer" (ENIAC), as it was named, weighed 30 tons, was 1,000 square feet, and used about 18,000 vacuum tubes. As late as the mid-1970s, "personal computers were more of a dream than a reality."[19]

The innovation that allowed the computer to be transformed from a room-sized machine to a pocket-sized smartphone was the silicon chip.[20] Before the silicon chip, electrical receivers were made up of several moving elements, all packaged together in fragile heated vacuum tubes. Unlike these bulky vacuum tube transistors, silicon allowed engineers to design streamlined, monolithic integrated circuits. That is because silicon is a semi-conducting material, which means simply that silicon can be made to conduct electricity (allowing electrons to freely float, as copper wires do), or to insulate electricity (preventing electrons from freely moving along the surface, as rubber does). Silicon could therefore be sculpted into small, flat, multilayered pieces, each layer with a different electrical property. Because semiconducting material eliminated the need for separate component parts and wires, it came to be referred to as "solid-state" technology. Solid-state technology was to become the "technological architecture [that] enabled the dawning of the 'Computer Age.' "[21]

The first silicon chip was developed in 1961. Remarkably it was alighted upon by two engineers at the same time, working independently of one another, Jack Kilby and Robert Noyce. Perhaps less coincidentally, both were working for companies receiving US defense funds. Robert Noyce would go on to co-found the first company to revolutionize computer design, Intel Electronics. In 1973, Intel produced the first programmable processor, which, with only 4 bits, was powerful enough and yet small enough to make desktop computers feasible. By 1991, the 64-bit microprocessor had been manufactured. Containing 500 million transistors, these powerful but tiny processors made portable computers and cell phones possible.

It was the genesis of the modern communications age.[22] Like the telegraph, computers transformed business as usual. Computer systems allowed for better tracking of merchandise. Firms could know more precisely where goods were en route and could project when they would arrive. In fact, the combination of containerization and computers was so revolutionary that it helped bring into being an entirely new form of economic organization: flexible production.

Up through the 1970s, industrial production was still largely based on the model that Henry Ford had pioneered in the 1910s. In the "Fordist" model of production, one company controlled all aspects of production—from research and development to building all the parts and bits to assembling the final products and preparing them for bulk shipment—all of which was housed in a giant factory plant or industrial complex. But with the enormous reduction in transportation costs made by computers and containers, "Sprawling industrial complexes where armies of thousands manufactured products from start to finish gave way to smaller, more specialized plants that shipped components and half-finished goods to one another in ever lengthening supply chains."[23] Computers and containers had so increased the efficiency of handling and tracking merchandise, companies were freed from having to have factories located near a port. As a consequence, "the cost of bringing raw materials in and sending finished goods out had dropped like a stone," altering the whole relationship between production and distribution. Multinational manufacturers could now "choose the cheapest location in which to make a particular item.'" Small towns, even those located far away from ports and population centers, "'could entice large companies to take advantage of their cheap land and low wages.'"[24] Within a couple of decades, companies were transformed into networks of suppliers and assembly plants that spanned the globe. Off-shoring became the new paradigm for industry. A whole new model of development, based on global supply chains, would change the lives of people around the globe: flexible production.

In addition to the silicon chip, US Defense Department's ARAP funded research on another innovation that was critical to the digital age, the Internet. In the throes of the Cold War, a central goal of the United States Defense Department was to find ways to covertly pass data from one agency to another. Therefore, while ARAP was supporting engineers developing computers with solid-state circuits, they were also funding others who were working on how data could be securely transmitted.

In 1967, the agency launched a project they awkwardly dubbed "Advanced Research Projects Agency Network," or ARPANET. ARPANET engaged with several universities that had engineering research centers, charging them to construct "a cooperative network of time-sharing computers."[25] To head the "Command and Control" of this new communications project, ARAP appointed in 1962 a former MIT computer engineer, J. C. R. Licklider, who was researching the possibility of constructing a global computer network. His 1960 paper, "Man-Computer Symbiosis,"[26] spelled out many of the features of the contemporary Internet.[27]

The central innovation underlying the new communications technology that was to make the Internet possible is packet-switching technology. Licklider, known as "Lick," had long been interested in the "effects of interrupting speech waves—turning them on and off intermittently or masking them with intermittent noise—upon their intelligibility."[28] With packet switching, data is broken into small pieces of variable length, called a "packet." To send a message, a number of small packets are transmitted, each of which is formatted independently of one another, and then reassembled at the destination into one file. Because the packets are formatted separately, they do not have to be transmitted in order to be correctly received. This was advantageous because anyone intercepting the message would not know how to assemble the packets properly, rendering the message indecipherable.[29] Another advantage of packet switching was that, unlike telephone transmission which requires each user to be individually connected to a particular telephone line, with packet switching bits of data could be sent across any number of different lines at any time, making it both harder to trace as well as easier to transmit large amounts of information.

The first indication that a computing network would be viable came in 1969, when four "computer nodes" at four research institutions—UCLA, Stanford, UC-Santa Barbara and University of Utah—sent messages to one another. The "Inter-net," shorthand for interconnected computer networks, had been born. From this modest start, the vast potential of the "Internet" was immediately recognized. However, it first had to be made accessible to the average person. Over the course of the 1980s, several companies created systems with this goal in mind, among them Archie, Gopher, WAIS, and the World Wide Web. But it was the simple point-and-click mechanism of the Web that won the day.[30] The critical turning point came in 1990, when Sir Tim Berners-Lee, a British computer scientist working at the European Organization for Nuclear Research (CERN), made public the codes he had innovated for the Web—Hyper Text Markup Language (HTML), Uniform Resource Identifier (URL), and Hyper Text Transfer Protocol (HTTP). The Internet was now available to anyone with a computer and a phone line. Internet use "took off like a rocket."[31] "The arrival of the Web in 1990 was to the internet like the arrival of the international combustion engine to the country lane."[32] In 1993, there were approximately 130 active websites, by 1995 according to some estimates the number of sites had increased almost 100 fold to 15,768.[33] By 2005, the Internet had over a billion users worldwide.[34]

Another innovation critical to US strategic military interests and central to the dawning of the Information Age is satellite technology. Shortly after the Soviets sent the beach-ball-sized Sputnik into orbit in 1957, the United States launched its own satellite, Echo 1. It did not take long for the commercial potential of satellite communications to be capitalized upon. The first satellite capable of two-way communications was developed by AT&T in partnership with NASA as well as with the governments of France and the United Kingdom. Telstar 1 was fired into orbit in 1962.[35] It was the first satellite to transmit live images to both sides of the Atlantic, by receiving microwave transmissions and redirecting them to the earth. Telstar 1's success signaled the birth of a new global communications industry. Only two years later, eleven countries signed an agreement to operate satellite communications conjointly—Austria, Canada, Japan, the Netherlands, Norway, Spain, Switzerland, the United Kingdom, the United States, the Vatican, and West Germany. They formed the International Telecommunications Satellite Organization (Intelsat), whose goal was to develop a global satellite communications system. In 1965, the consortium sent its own satellite into orbit, Intelsat I. It was, in fact, Intelsat 1's transmission of scratchy black-and-white images of the Apollo 11 lunar landing that held the world spellbound in 1969.

Just as the telegraph had made possible the first period of modern mass communications, satellites brought cable television into being. Soon after the launch of Intelsat, terrestrial cables were developed to facilitate the delivery of satellite content to individual homes. An entirely new form of accessing information and entertainment was born. Cable television utterly transformed mass media. The change began incrementally but quickly picked up steam. In 1973, the Canadian Broadcasting Corporation began distributing its video programming to Canadian customers using Telesat's Anik A satellite. HBO followed suit in 1975, distributing video programming to US customers by satellite. The commercial and technical success of these ventures led to greater use and acceptance of satellite broadcasting. By the mid-1980s, there was an explosion of live reporting via satellite. Cable Networks were established worldwide. A decade later, satellite communications had become the primary means of distributing television programming around the world.

Even though these new communications technologies were being developed in the 1960s and 1970s, the "Internet Age" did not really come into being until 1991. That was the year that AOL, the first popularized email service provider, was launched. When email was introduced to the world in the 1960s (yet another offspring of ARAP), its use was largely restricted to university research centers. Very few people knew what it was or how it worked. It took the development of accessible software products in the early 1990s, such as America Online (AOL), Hotmail, and Yahoo, for email usage to blow up. The radicalness of the change was akin to the expansion of the post in the latter half of the nineteenth century. Individuals could share information more quickly than ever imagined. To mark the change, the term "snail mail" briefly entered the lexicon, a disparaging contrast between the traditional postal system and the rapidity of personal communication that email provided.

During the same period, cell phone usage was inaugurated that would a few decades later remake society in its own image. If computers were a rare commodity in the 1960s, portable cell phones were nonexistent. Although car phones were around as early as the 1930s, these early phones were too large and cumbersome to carry around in a pocket or purse. Motorola introduced the first handheld phone model in 1973. An indication of its size is that the first "portable" phone was dubbed the "brick." Ten years later, an updated commercial version of the "brick" was rolled out. With a sale price set at US$ 4,000, the Motorola DynaTAC 8000X was almost exclusively used by business executives. It was also extremely cumbersome. Approximately 9 inches long, weighing in at 2.5 pounds, and with a battery life of less than half an hour, it was neither compact nor easily transported. Truly portable phones that were available to the general public did not appear until the late 1990s, when the first pocketable flip-phone came on the market. From then on, changes to cell phone technology came fast and furiously. In 2000, smartphones enabled users to access email and the Internet wirelessly. By 2019, a Pew study found that more than five billion people owned cell phones worldwide, approximately half of which were smartphones.[36]

Perhaps, the greatest impact of these communications technologies was not in highly industrialized countries, but rather in the "Global South." Prior to the 1990s, much of the developing world was cut off from daily communications. For many countries, constructing national phone cables and wiring homes individually was simply too costly. Satellites offered direct connectivity at a fraction of the cost. With just a few communications towers, areas formerly off the grid could be connected to the wider world. By the 2010s, satellites had made it possible for populations living in remote parts of Bolivia, faraway Polynesian Islands, and the Saharan desert to have access to Google and Facebook.[37]

The impact of satellites, however, went far beyond changes in information sharing and entertainment media. To begin with, like the telegraph, satellites had an immediate impact on international trade. With the efficiency and speed of information, "Advances in telecommunications greatly reduced the cost of international commerce and so expanded the scope of global financial markets."[38] According to WTO trade statistics, "the value of world merchandise exports rose from US$ 2.03 trillion in 1980 to US$ 18.26 trillion in 2011, which is equivalent to 7.3 per cent growth per year on average in current dollar terms" and when considering the degree of change in volume terms, "world merchandise trade recorded a more than four-fold increase between 1980 and 2011."[39]

It was not long before the Internet itself became a medium of trade, further revolutionizing retail. Just as the railroads and low-cost printing had opened up the possibility for mail-order catalogs, at the turn of the twentieth century, computers, satellites, and the Internet brought "e-commerce" into being. In 1994, a small start-up company, Amazon, launched the first online bookselling site. At the time, the idea of shopping on the Internet was foreign to most people. Within a few years, Amazon had begun to undermine brick-and-mortar titans of the book trade, such as Barnes and Nobles, Waldenbooks, and Crown Books.[40] One year after Amazon made its debut, eBay founder Pierre Omidyar introduced the first virtual Auction Web "dedicated to bringing together buyers and sellers in an honest and open marketplace."[41] Over the next ten years, online shopping took the world by storm and by 2017 Internet commerce was fully globalized.

Changes to Finance

Just as happened with telegraphy, the enhanced speed of information sharing brought about by the Internet altered almost every sector of the economy, but most especially international finance. As late as the 1960s, financial trading was carried out using the same technology that had been established in the 1870s: ticker tape! This meant trading continued to be conducted manually.[42] After the 1970s, traders were able to place orders for financial products over a computer network. Systems quickly evolved that allowed for the almost instantaneous execution of trades. So much so that by the 2010s fortunes could be gained or lost through High-Frequency Trading in just *milliseconds*.

Computerization of financial markets began in the early 1970s, when the New York Stock Exchange introduced the "Designated Order Turnaround" system (DOT). The following year, the National Association of Securities Dealers Automated Quotations, better known as NASDAQ, was rolled out. NASDAQ used cutting-edge information-systems technology to create a completely digital trading arena. Other automated trading platforms followed. The first fully automated futures exchange was launched in 1988, Swiss Options and Financial Futures Exchange (SOFFEX). Even the great old man of trading—the Chicago Mercantile Exchange (CME), established in 1848—had a role in creating the world's first electronic trading platform in 1992. CME Globex provided users twenty-four-hour access to global markets. Over the course of the early 2000s, the proliferation of platforms dedicated to online trade continued worldwide.

As in the previous century, the new technologies tranmogrified the entire structure of the global financial system. Clear boundaries that had existed between "distinctive functions like banking, brokerage, financial services, housing finance, consumer credit, and the like" became "increasingly porous."[43] Indeed, "Whole sectors that were once non-traded (and thus impervious to foreign competition)—such as banking, retail, medicine or education—[were] rapidly transforming through e-banking, e-commerce, e-medicine or e-learning into some of the most globally tradable sectors."[44] At the same time, wholly new markets in commodities, stocks, currencies, and debt futures sprung up.[45] Soon, the global financial system had become "so complicated that it [surpassed] most people's understanding."[46] In a *Financial Times* article from 1987, the author's expression of awe inspired by the dramatic changes occurring at the end of the twentieth century mirrored the wonderment John Maynard Keynes expressed a century earlier:

> "Banking," said the *Financial Times* (8 May 1987), "is rapidly becoming indifferent to the constraints of time, place and currency." It is now the case that "an English buyer can get a Japanese mortgage, an American can tap

his New York bank account through a cash machine in Hong Kong and a Japanese investor can buy shares in a London-based Scandinavian bank whose stock is denominated in sterling, dollars, Deutsche Marks and Swiss francs."[47]

New International Fora

Like the end of the nineteenth century, the rapid expansion of trade and finance also led to the formation of new international fora. In 1971, the World Economic Forum was created in Geneva, Switzerland. Better known as Davos, after the location of its first conference in 1973, the forum was created to be a platform through which "the world's leading companies" could come together "to shape a better future."[48] A year later, in 1972, the first International Conference on Computer Communications (ICCC) was held in Washington, DC. The organization would ultimately produce the Transfer Control Protocol/Internet Protocol (TCP/IP) we use today. In the same year, 1972, The United Nations held its first conference on the Human Environment in Stockholm, Sweden. It was to be the genesis of modern international environmental conventions. Not long after, the first world conference on women was held in Mexico City in 1975, with representatives from 133 governments and 6,000 NGOs.

However, arguably the most transformative international body created in response to the fundamental changes occurring in the global economy during the second half of the twentieth century was the Word Trade Organization (WTO). The impact of the WTO on global trade was similar to the effect of the "Cobden-Chevalier agreement" at the end of the nineteenth century. Founded during talks held in Uruguay at the 1990 General Agreement on Tariffs and Trade (GATT) meeting (subsequently referred to as the "Uruguay Round"), the WTO was a game changer—and purposely so. The new system was designed to open countries to the market as much as possible. In fact, the WTO was created to supplant the trading order that had guided world affairs since the 1940s, when the Bretton Woods agreements were established after World War II.

In the postwar era, the architects of the Bretton Woods had tried to devise an international system that could balance the need to promote international trade against the importance of protecting domestic economies. Accordingly, the Bretton Woods agreements included provisions that

would give participating states some flexibility in instituting protective social policies or trade tariffs if they deemed them critical for their national
economies (see Chapter 13). But the WTO marked a dramatic conversion
in the international trade regime. The organization set out to greatly limit
the ability of domestic governments to interfere with the market in any
way, whether by imposing tariffs to protect their labor markets, or shielding
their environments from industrial development. To do so, a new legal and
normative framework that restricted state-led protectionist measures was
inaugurated. Even today, the organization's "overriding purpose is to help
trade flow as freely as possible" by lowering trade barriers that include "customs duties (or tariffs) and measures such as import bans or quotas that
restrict quantities selectively."[49] The WTO also empowered large global business concerns to devise and enforce an expansive liberal agenda across the
globe. Its imposition of free-market liberalism was, thus, even more comprehensive than the British gold standard in the 1870s. The era of neo-liberalism
had commenced.

Globalization

The establishment of the WTO marked the beginning of the neo-liberal era.
However, there were other ways in which the new forms of interconnectivity
were changing people's conception of the world. Just as "Internationalism"
came to signify new forms of progress and liberal ideals, so too did the term
"Globalization" at the end of the twentieth century. And, just as a century
earlier the telegraph symbolized for J. A. Hobson and his contemporaries the
new internationalism, the World Wide Web became synonymous with this
new form of interconnectivity. In the 1990s, there was talk of the Internet
having spawned a new "global village" and "global civil society."[50] The great
potential of the Web was particularly feted by leftist intellectuals, who celebrated the Internet for its transformative powers. The Internet was held to
be revolutionary because it was an "inherently international medium"[51] that
was "constructed collectively" with "no central authority to determine its
overall structure" and for which "the barriers to creating material [were] relatively low."[52] Many proclaimed that the Internet was paving the way for "new
forms of democratic political agency."[53] Academics wrote of how the Web
was helping to forge a "sphere of ideas, values, institutions, organizations,
networks, and individuals . . . operating beyond the confines of national

societies, polities, and economies."[54] It could be said that the Internet was believed to hold the promise of fulfilling the long-wished-for leftist vision of people's empowerment enshrined in the anthem of the Communist Internationale: "Let us gather together, and tomorrow/The Internationale/Will be the human race."

The hoopla surrounding the emancipating potential of the Internet and globalization prompted Ronaldo Munck to write somewhat derisively about the "GCS [Global Civil Society] myth."[55] Yet, it was true, at least in part. As the century came to a close, the unifying potential of the Internet seemed to be coming to fruition. The new technologies made possible a proliferation of nonprofit international organizations that rivaled those of the belle époque. Over a decade, International Nongovernmental Organizations (INGOS) multiplied at an astonishing rate, from around 6,000 in 1990 to approximately 25,540, in 2000.[56] Moreover, the new INGOS were unifying people around the world. Peoples from Europe, the Americas, Asia, the Middle East, and Africa were able to join forces to fight for everything from human rights and the environment to fair trade practices, Indigenous rights, and fair labor standards.[57]

Conclusion

All in all, the technologies of the 1960s and 1970s—from airplanes and containers, to satellites, computers, the Internet, and cell phones—revolutionized travel and communications worldwide. Commerce, finance, individual intercourse, and mass media were forever transformed as global communications became exponentially faster and the barrier of physical distance was eroded. People's very understanding of their place in the world and their relation to one another would never be the same.

The parallel transformations that occurred in the second half of both centuries are striking: from mail to email, mail order to e-commerce, mass newspapers to satellite news, and ticker tape to automated trading. Not least of which was the analogous rise in global trade and the dramatic push toward economic liberalism. For the second time in history, the compression of time and space radically altered the very texture of human life. And once again, these dramatic changes in interconnectivity seemed to be ushering in a new era of global cooperation and coordination.

But sadly, unbeknownst to the people living in the last decade of both centuries, there was a sinister side to the marvels of these new eras. The promise of progress and peaceful interconnectivity would in both epochs lead to something much bleaker. Within a couple of decades, countries with advanced economies would be plagued by spectacular wealth inequalities. Dramatic shifts in production would strike the "heartland" much harder than the urban centers. Changing opportunities would draw migrants to developed countries, just when global economic shocks were beginning to hit their national economies. Global finance's control over national economic agendas would only magnify the pain caused by all these changes. Collectively, these displacements set off the second half of Polanyi's "double movement."

PART III

THE DARK SIDE
OF GLOBALIZATION

The decade before the dawning of the new century, mankind's triumphant advances seemed to signal that the world was headed toward a new, modern era of peace and global prosperity. It was believed our shared humanity would triumph and that the modern world's unrivaled levels of internationalism would increase understanding and extend compassion to peoples across the globe. But this liberal vision was soon overshadowed by a series of darkening clouds. The ill effects of liberal market forces undercut people's initial excitement over the promise of internationalism. Protectionism, nativism, and xenophobia materialized in their stead.

Schumpeter's schema is valuable for understanding the rise of hyperglobalization and the spread of liberalism in each epoch. His theory can be applied to illustrate how, during both the Second Industrial Revolution and the Digital Revolution, new innovations in transportation and communications made possible the internationalization of finance, the opening of markets, and the flow of people and products at an unprecedented level. Yet, his analysis is a much weaker tool for interpreting the responses against globalization and liberalism.

In contrast, Polanyi is hazy about the mechanisms that unleashed the double movement, but he explains much better than Schumpeter why liberalism produced anti-liberal responses. Polanyi helps us understand how in the late nineteenth century, laissez-faire policies were spread across the world, threatening existing forms of social organization. He describes how institutions that had formerly protected people began to erode as economic changes were challenging people's livelihoods. Market mechanisms were unable to protect society from the pain and suffering caused by these transformations. All of this provided fertile ground for anti-liberal movements. Hence, Polanyi's theory offers a much more coherent explanation for the rise of anti-global, national populism.

The following chapters will examine the kinds of changes Polanyi centers on to show that they were present in both epochs. Although it is not feasible to present historical examples of all the socioeconomic shifts that materialized in response to globalizing technological revolutions, it is possible to illustrate some of the more consequential ones. The following exposition will focus on the interconnections among these radical changes and how they helped foster social distress. Chapter 7 will examine how revolutionary technologies destroyed traditional forms of economic organization. The uprooting of people's livelihoods occurred at the same time as increased dependence upon trade and finance made national economies vulnerable to international price shocks. Eventually, this led to globally contagious economic crises. Chapter 8 explores how the communications revolutions in both periods introduced new forms of mass media. The manner and speed with which information was able to flow presented society with newfound opportunities, but also presented grave dangers. Finally, Chapter 9 will look at how mass immigration evolved in tandem with never-before-seen modes of globalized terrorism, sparking fear across the developed world and provoking an anti-immigrant backlash at the close of both centuries.

7

Economic Vulnerability: Productive Reorganization and Financial Crises

During both the Second Industrial Revolution and the Information Age, new technologies brought about a wrenching reorganization of the means of production. This produced a period of extraordinary flux. Traditional jobs and social structures were undermined. Compounding the magnitude of these changes was the fact that domestic economies were becoming increasingly vulnerable to the complex and highly integrated structure of the emerging liberal international economy. In both periods, these combined forces produced contagious economic crises that hit the peripheral regions hardest, creating a political rift between the "heartland" and the privileged urban centers.

Nineteenth Century

Economic and Demographic Uprooting

It would be an understatement to say that the Second Industrial Revolution transformed society. So monumental were the changes that Henry George, a prominent politician and theorist of the day, described the period as having "clothed mankind with powers of which a century ago the boldest imagination could not have dreamed."[1] Everything was impacted, including "Traditional family, rural social organization, religious beliefs, and systems of government, both local and national."[2] One of the most profound shifts produced was the dramatic migration of peoples—both internally and externally. As Hobsbawm observed, "The nineteenth century was a gigantic machine for uprooting countrymen."[3]

Cities across Europe and the United States had largely stagnated during the eighteenth and into the early decades of the nineteenth century. But the Second Industrial Revolution's insatiable demand for labor rapidly

Defensive Nationalism. B. S. Rabinowitz, Oxford University Press. © Oxford University Press 2023.
DOI: 10.1093/oso/9780197672037.003.0008

accelerated urbanization. After the 1860s, peasants began to pour into the expanding urban centers. In Germany, there were large-scale migrations from the countryside to the growing industrial regions, particularly to the larger cities. According to one estimate, "by 1907 only about half (31.4 million) of the total German population of 60.4 million continued to live in their place of birth."[4] In Spain, regions near ports that were connected to the early railway network experienced the greatest rural-to-urban migration, such as Barcelona, Bilbao, Valladolid, Alicante, and Gijón.[5] Up until 1860, "the bulk of Americans were still rural . . . only 16 per cent lived in cities of eight thousand or more inhabitants."[6] Within two decades, that had dramatically changed.

In the more advanced economies, like the United States, Germany, and France, most rural migrants made their way to the rapidly industrializing cities in their respective countries. However, in less-developed countries, peasants were forced to cross the seas. With lower-cost steamship and rail travel, from 1870 and 1900 thousands of people journeyed abroad looking for a better future.[7] Between 1880 and 1900 alone, European emigration jumped from approximately 800,000 to 1.4 million annually.[8] Immigrants were coming from "south and east as far as Portugal, Russia, and Syria."[9] One of the countries that contributed the most to this movement of peoples was Italy. By the late nineteenth century, mechanization and changes to production had begun to force Italian peasants off their land. Farmers faced severe conditions: insufficiently arable land, overpopulation, and unemployment.[10] Virtually every region suffered population losses. But Italian industrialization was still in its infancy. The urban and industrial regions were, therefore, unable to absorb the influx. A large portion of the rural population was forced to leave the country. "The majority of these emigrants went to other European countries and to the Americas." Net emigration from Italy reached an astounding five million between 1871 and 1921.[11] This was equally true of other, less-developed countries. For example, in Finland the railways and industrialization had been introduced in the late 1800s, but they had developed at a slow pace. In the last decades of the nineteenth century, industry only made up 5 percent of gainful employment. For the bulk of the Finnish population, agriculture was still the primary livelihood. Some peasants migrated to the more populous southern parts of Finland, but the vast majority of migrations were to the United States and Canada.[12]

Thus, by the latter part of the century, the world's cities were grappling with an unprecedented concentration of people. So dramatic and sudden was this demographic shift that no nation was prepared for the upheaval. Across Europe and the United States, cities felt the "pressure on existing institutions and services, especially the provision of education, health education, transport and power."[13] However, it was not only cities that were affected; even the stability of agrarian society was profoundly shaken. The growth of the global market economy was forcing agriculture into the new industrial world order.

For centuries, agriculture had been dominated by family-run farms that sold their produce to local and regional markets. But as railroads and steamships made it possible to transport bulk produce over long distances, regions that had been "hitherto unexploitable" were brought "within the range of the world market."[14] At the same time, industrialization was creating new demands for agricultural products. Rapidly enlarging cities had a growing work force to feed. Expanding industries required an ever-increasing supply of raw materials. In country after country, farms were turned into large-scale commercial enterprises. "Sweden more than doubled its crop area between 1840 and 1880, Italy and Denmark expanded it by more than half, Russia, Germany and Hungary by about a third."[15] Even in the United States, agricultural exports rose twentyfold, from approximately five million hectoliters to more than one hundred million between the 1840s to the end of the 1870s.[16]

New Economic Vulnerabilities

The extraordinary modernization of the productive base of the economy "could not but undermine" the social organization of the agrarian world. On the one hand, commercial agriculture "loosened the traditional ties of men to the land of their forefathers."[17] On the other hand, agricultural producers became highly susceptible to the vicissitudes of the market. Ironically, the sheer size of the new commercial farms made them vulnerable to international shocks. Traditionally, farmers had produced perishable foodstuffs that could not be transported over long distances, like dairy products, eggs, vegetables, or fruit for local markets. Hence, they had greater immunity to fluctuations in the world economy. That was not so for commercial exporters.

Agriculture's newfound exposure to global trade led to tragedy in the 1870s, when a glut of American wheat on the world market caused the price of wheat to drop precipitously. A global agrarian depression hit. A number of things contributed to the global decline in wheat prices, but the major contributor was the end of the American Civil War. With the wars' end, the combination of increased manpower from demobilized Civil War troops, and a wartime accumulation of money capital enabled American farmers to make the most of new mechanized farm machinery. At the same time, the rail networks built during the Civil War made it possible to transport wheat in far greater quantities than had been possible using the old canal system. Steam transportation technologies, furthermore, allowed the cheaper American grain to be more readily distributed to European consumers, undercutting European farmers.[18] Hence, with the rise in global trade, markets around the world became flooded with American wheat and the price of this world staple crashed. The ensuing economic downturn came to be referred to as "the Long Depression."

The Long Depression of the 1870s and 1880s was an economic crisis like none that preceded it. It was, in truth, the world's first global economic crisis.[19] That was because, although the Long Depression was caused by a wheat price shock, the scale and scope of the crisis were a direct consequence of the structure of the global economy. The deeply intricate and multilay-ered liaisons among banking houses and national industries had integrated independent state economies to an unprecedented degree. In fact, the Long Depression reached the proportions it did because multiple economies had been made vulnerable by the bursting of an international speculative bubble in railroad construction that had been evolving since the 1850s. Governments and banks around the world, from the United States to Turkey to South America to Austria, had accumulated vast amounts of debt to fund large-scale railroad projects. But, after a couple of decades of feverish railroad speculation, the number of railroad projects undertaken outpaced demand. Thus, economies around the globe were impacted as retracting credit and plummeting wheat prices produced stock market crashes across Continental Europe and the United States.

The first European market crash occurred in 1873 in Vienna, when European investors rushed to divest their holdings in American railroad se-curities. This had a domino effect. "With the first scare, commodity prices fell, bonds went into default, over-extended bankers failed, and credit began to contract."[20] Once begun, the downward spiral worsened. Divestments depressed the market, further lowering stock and bond prices. Pressure on teetering railroad firms intensified. As debts came due, many railroad firms had to default on their bank loans. Banking across Europe imploded. At roughly the same time, pandemonium broke out on Wall Street when news spread that the well-respected New York merchant banking house, Jay Cooke and Co., had been forced to close its doors. Across the United States, "Stock prices tumbled, followed by a veritable wave of insolvencies, including more than thirty brokerage houses."[21]

The financial panic of 1873 was followed by a second panic only two decades later that hit the United States particularly hard. In the United States, the period from 1897 to 1899 came to be referred to as "the Great Depression." Once again, the crisis had its origins in international finance. This time, however, the problem began with inflated investments in Argentinian infrastructure. In the 1890s, the great banks were heavily invested in what was seen as an up-and-coming economy. However, when the country's wheat crop failed, Argentina was forced to default on its loans. In response, investors quickly pulled out, sending the banks spinning.

The Argentinian crisis was compounded by a decline in gold production, which was brought about in part because of the international adoption of the Gold Standard.[22] By the 1870s, gold had been officially adopted as the international currency against which national reserves were held. But within a little more than a decade, gold supply was not able to keep up with the growing demand for the universal medium of exchange. Thus, from 1856 to 1860, "the annual average production of gold in the world had been worth $134,000,000, in the period 1881–5, it had sunk below $100,000,000."[23] Panic broke out when it was announced that the gold reserve in the United States Treasury "fell below a hundred million dollars, the amount set by law and tradition as a safe fund for the redemption of the outstanding paper currency."[24] As the news spread, there was a run on gold in the United States. The panic turned into a severe depression. In the United States, "Hundreds of thousands of workers lost jobs, and by 1894 about 4,000,000 were unemployed."[25] President Grover Cleveland was forced to borrow $65 million in gold from Wall Street banker J. P. Morgan and the Rothschild banking family of England to save the economy.

Thus, the advances of the 1870s and 1880s, from railroads and steam-operated machinery to the gold standard, ironically brought about these serial catastrophes. The global depressions of the late nineteenth century stemmed from the high levels of monetary interconnectivity these new technologies had created. And both depressions produced economically disastrous consequences that destabilized already floundering social structures, paving the way for the reactionary politics that was to develop at the turn of the century.

Twentieth Century

Changes to the Economic and Social Order

An equally enormous transformation in the productive base of the economy occurred during the Digital Age, producing similar effects. The new forms of production and interconnectivity, made possible by modern transportation and communications technologies, transformed everything from migration patterns to banking. The paradigm of economic organization that had characterized the Industrial Age began to teeter. By the 1980s, a new era of capitalist development emerged; and as one hundred years earlier, these cumulative changes produced a series of global economic panics.

Among the factors that contributed to the dramatic shift in economic organization of the developed world was the combination of containerization and computers. Together, containers and computers made shipping so much more efficient that companies no longer needed to locate their factories near a port. They could "choose the cheapest location in which to make a particular item."[26] As a result, the Fordist model of production that had been the hallmark of twentieth-century industrialization was made obsolete. Vertically integrated firms, in which everything from parts to packaging to assembly was done in-house, was rapidly coming to an end. The system that was emerging in its place was characterized by a much greater flexibility of supply chains, personnel, and products.[27] In the new mode of production, which was to be dubbed "flexible accumulation," everything became organized globally. In effect, small countries were turned into suppliers for wealthy countries and subcontracting and consultancy were internationalized. The change turned small and large industries upside-down. Even multinational corporations, which had already achieved global distribution, were dramatically impacted. Now, not only their distribution of goods but their very organization had to be internationalized.

All this rapid-fire change allowed for an explosion of new products and services. Where the Industrial Revolution had produced phones, cars, and other devices available in a few colors and styles, the Digital Revolution was technicolored. Everything from lattes to search engines could be personalized to meet the needs of individual users. An indication of the dramatic changes occurring in the structure of the economy was the rise of the service sector. In the early 1990s almost "50 percent of the global stock of FDI [foreign direct investment] was in services activities."[28] In the United States alone, employment in services, which had traditionally accounted for 56 percent of workforce employment, jumped to approximately 73 percent by the 1990s.[29]

The shift was not only from goods to services. The "acceleration in the rate of technological change" made technology itself "the most crucial factor in economic growth and international competitiveness."[30] "Information" became one of the most dynamic and profitable commodities of the world economy.[31] Firms from all sectors, whether manufacturing or marketing, came to rely on technological innovation for their competitiveness. Corporations that could "produce knowledge, respond to knowledge, generate brands and market them" were able to "establish breathtaking market power."[32] "Fortunes [came to] rest on the prospect of inventing, selling, and competing with new ideas and creative products."[33] To put it simply, where the Fordist model of production was based on productive integration, flexible accumulation was made possible by instantaneous, globalized information.

There were other ways that technology was transforming the organization of production. The increased flexibility in operations spelled doom for many traditionally organized businesses. As market access and integration were internationalized, firms were no longer tied to domestic funding, domestic labor, or even domestic consumers. There followed "a wave of bankruptcies, plant closures, [and] deindustrialization."[34] By the 1990s, even white-collar workers were finding that their pensions were no longer guaranteed, and their secure jobs had become endangered. The hardest hit were the regions associated with heavy-industry or resource-based industries like coal. Indeed, in "the 23 most advanced economies, employment in manufacturing declined from about 28 percent of the workforce in 1970 to about 18 percent in 1994."[35] One of the more dramatic consequences was that labor unions began to steadily lose power. "Faced with strong market volatility, heightened competition, and narrowing profit margins, employers . . . [pushed] for much more flexible work regimes and labour contracts."[36]

In the process, once-thriving industrial centers were transformed into peripheral cul-de-sacs "suffering from loss of infrastructure, disappearance of jobs, erosion of skills, increasing inequality of income and sheer human misery."[37] Whole communities in Europe and the United States became exiled from the new economy. In the United Kingdom, it was the West Midland, the North West, Yorkshire-Humberside, the North, Wales, Scotland, and Northern Ireland that suffered most from manufacturing decline; in Germany it was the older, resource-based industrial heartland such as Nordrhein-Westfalen; in France, the formerly prosperous industrial northeast; in Italy, de-industrialization hit both new and old industrial regions in the North, from Veneto, Emilia Romagna, Liguria, to Peimente, Lombardia, and Toscana.[38] No industrial region was left unscathed.

New Economic Vulnerabilities

As a century earlier, the rapid globalization of finance and radical restructuring of the productive organization of the advanced industrial nations produced a number of economic crises. One of the worst came in 2008. And once again, the United States was at the root of it all. As was true in the previous era, the genesis of the 2008 financial crisis was a American speculative bubble—this time a housing bubble driven by exceedingly lax mortgage lending policies. With the unfettered expansion of global finance, the American banking crisis impacted the world, weakening domestic economies and furthering tensions between urban and peripheral areas.

It all began in the 2000s, when American banks, having too much cash on hand (too much liquidity), began to look for ways to move their money so they could earn interest on it. The banks began to issue "subprime mortgage loans," offering people, who under normal circumstances would not have been regarded as a viable credit risk, variable low-interest or no-interest loans. Once banks began implementing these subprime lending policies, shady actors quickly realized they could make a killing by preying on people who did not understand the complexity of the loans. An ever-increasing number of unsuspecting victims fell into the hands of pop-up mortgage companies, who roped in people with limited funds to take out loans, not explaining that having a variable mortgage meant their zero-percent mortgage rate could be inflated overnight. The subprime lending market ballooned.

The coming storm was compounded by the fact that in the 1980s, with the neo-liberal turn, the United States had loosened regulations on banking. One of the most consequential changes was the relaxation of the Federal Reserve's monitoring of investment banks' reserve funds. Regulatory laws, some dating back to the 1800s,[39] mandated that banks keep a percentage of the capital they had as reserves, rather than using it for lending or investment, in case of market volatility. These regulatory laws were put in place to protect bank depositors from losing everything in the event that there was a run on the banks, as happened so spectacularly in 1929. But, in the 1980s, government regulations were relaxed across the board. Through the 1990s the policy environment continued to soften.

Taking advantage of the loose regulatory environment, in 1997 J. P. Morgan Chase introduced a strange financial entity they called "Credit Default Swaps" (CDS). These were financial derivatives[40] that allowed an investor to "swap" or "offset" their credit risk by selling them to someone else. Worse still, these CDSs were "off-balance sheet affiliated entities." In other words, these financial instruments[41] were off the books (hence the name "off-balance sheet"), so they were not subject to the normal rules. The seller of a swap—unlike a normal bank, or even an insurance company—was not required to maintain a specific level of reserves in the event that there was a default. The risk was therefore much greater.

Using these questionable accounting practices, in the 2000s the banks were able to make high-risk, high-return investments in worthless subprime mortgages, with no capital reserves to back them. Using credit default swaps, "bundles" of risky subprime mortgages were sold. In other words, the banks holding these risky mortgages sold them to speculators who were hoping to make money on the lucrative housing bubble, but who were also promised that if sometime in the future the loans went into default, the bank or financial company selling the loan would pay the buyer a previously determined sum. As a Brookings Institute report explains, these "new financial innovations thrived in an environment of easy monetary policy by the Federal Reserve and poor regulatory oversight."[42] In no time, Wall Street jumped on the subprime lending bandwagon. After 2000, they began promoting and channeling institutional investments into subprime-mortgage markets. As bad mortgages were bundled together and repackaged as credit default swaps products, and then pushed by rapacious traders to investors across the board, trade in Credit Default Swabs grew into a trillion-dollar market.

In the process, financial institutions took on trillions of dollars of worthless, unbacked subprime-mortgage securities. When the speculative bubble burst and the housing market came crashing down, so too did Wall Street and several American banks. The spectacular banking failure in the United States reverberated across the world. The fall of so many American financial institutions produced a liquidity crisis that impacted global money markets. Soon the crisis hit Europe as well.

Making the situation more combustible, across the United States and Europe the financial crisis destabilized depressed rural areas and small cities and towns already reeling from the broader changes to production.

The growing rift between peripheralized communities in decline and the thriving metropolitan areas, where technology and service-oriented firms had agglomerated, was widened. Thus, once again in history, changes to the global economic system of production in conjunction with higher levels of financial integration compounded already widening social dislocations. All of this was to fuel the anti-liberal, anti-globalization movements of the 2010s.

Conclusion

Comparing these turn of the century periods, it is clear that parallel displacements transformed societies across the developed world. In both epochs, globalizing technological revolutions destroyed traditional forms of economic organization and made national economies extremely vulnerable to international speculation. As a result, within a few decades contagious economic crises hit Europe and the US. The impact on the rural and peripheral areas was particularly catastrophic. All of this set the stage for the anti-international, defensive nationalist movements that would envelop the developed world in the new century.

8

Information Overload: Mass Media and Fake News

Another hallmark of both turn-of-the-century periods was radically new forms of mass media that led to a period of "fake news" at the century's close. The phenomenon of media misinformation is not unique to these periods. "Fake news" has a long history; some trace it back to the mid-fourteenth century, others as far back as the ancient Romans.[1] In fact, arguably the period in media history that is most distinct is the one in which *objectivity* became the norm—the mid-twentieth century. Nonetheless, the late nineteenth-century period of Yellow Journalism and the twenty-first-century era of "post-truth" signify something wholly different from the periods that preceded them. What was different was the scale of media reach and the immediacy of its impact. Therefore, the magnitude of the harm posed by misinformation in both time periods was critically different from anything hitherto experienced.

Nineteenth Century

Modern Journalism Is Born

The 1890s saw the birth of the first era of modern journalism. The new technologies of the Second Industrial Revolution had made mass media possible for the first time in history. Improvements in print technology, such as fast cylinder presses, new typesetting machines, and cheap wood-pulp newsprint, revolutionized the production of newsprint. "Instead of 1,000 copies daily, the horizontal cylinder of the rotary Hoe press turned out 20,000 an hour."[2] Telegraphy also dramatically altered news coverage. The telegraph conducted information more rapidly giving rise to wire services that made syndication possible.[3]

In the eighteenth and early nineteenth centuries, overseas information traveled slowly. Correspondence between the United States and Britain

Defensive Nationalism. B. S. Rabinowitz, Oxford University Press. © Oxford University Press 2023.
DOI: 10.1093/oso/9780197672037.003.0009

could take up to two months. International news and even foreign intelligence were generally acquired through the foreign press, which printed government press releases verbatim. But once the telegraph linked cities across the world, people could get up-to-the-moment reports from faraway places. Even news from Africa came within reach. In the early 1870s, people in the United States and Britain were transfixed by Henry Morton Stanley's cabled dispatches of Dr. Livingston's exploits across the continent.[4] Immediate access to Information from overseas meant that editors, no longer dependent upon government releases, could develop their own news corps stationed abroad. The foreign press service was consummated.

Across the Western world, domestic news industries were altered as well. Rail transportation in combination with innovations in printing technologies reduced distribution costs. In response, newspaper publishers slashed retail prices. Sales soared. In Canada, circulation of "the Toronto *Telegram* went from 5,000 in 1878 to almost 25,000 by 1889 and 94,000 by 1920."[5] A surge in publications also swept across Europe. In Britain, "it was calculated that the number of newspapers [in 1861] had virtually doubled from 562 to 1,102, although it was conceded that a substantial portion of these titles were very short-lived."[6] By 1896, *Lloyd's Weekly News* of London reached a million readers. In France, national press circulation expanded more than eight times as the real cost of Parisian newspapers dropped over 50 percent.[7]

In the United States the media boom was also prodigious. News readership increased spectacularly, "from 3.5 million daily newspaper readers in 1880 to 33 million in 1920."[8] In fact, "So great was the demand by 1870 that no self-respecting city paper limited itself to one appearance a day."[9] Local news also proliferated. "Any place with more than five thousand people could support a daily, and many supported two or more: one for Democrats, the other for Republicans."[10] Lower distribution costs also unleashed "what one contemporary called 'a mania of magazine-starting.'"[11] Before 1850, "Few magazines circulated far from their places of publication; no general magazine reached a truly national audience."[12] By 1900, magazines were commonplace in homes throughout the United States. "The number of periodicals increased more than fourfold, from 700 in 1865 to 3,300 in 1885, in those two decades. By 1900 there were no fewer than fifty national magazines, some of them with circulations of more than 100,000."[13]

The new mass media had two opposing effects. On one hand, information was decentralized. Lower printing costs had made it feasible for papers to cultivate a consumer base focused on particular issues. The period saw a proliferation of media outlets. There were papers published by the Suffragettes promoting women's voting rights, Labor Union Weeklies advocating for improved working conditions, and anarchist rags calling for the radical restructuring of society. In the United States, by 1870 there were over five thousand different newspapers and periodicals, one-tenth of which were published daily.[14] A host of "ethnic presses" also grew in distribution, which combined social activism with social and cultural matters of concern to their specific populations. In New York, one could find multiple Jewish presses, in San Francisco Chinese-language newspapers took off, in Oklahoma it was the Native American newspapers, and African American papers circulated across several states.[15] "By 1914, there would be 1,264 foreign-language newspapers, which garnered about a fifth of the total advertising dollars in the United States."[16]

Ironically, however, the same technologies that paved the way for specialized media markets also allowed for the monopolization of news. Up until the early nineteenth century, newspapers were family-owned enterprises and readership was relatively small, restricted largely to the literate intelligentsia. But, by the end of the century, the efficiency of rail transportation had made it possible to dramatically increase circulation. The lower cost of large-scale printing and the capacity for larger circulation enabled publishers to lower the selling price. The "Penny Press" came into being. News was now accessible to the masses.

The new mass media changed the business of news publishing. "Newspapers had become big businesses by the 1880s, with towering downtown buildings, [and] scores of reporters."[17] With all these changes to the publishing business, there also emerged a new historical persona: the media mogul. The new media moguls wielded "the power of large corporations, [using] the resources at their disposal to sell newspapers and influence politics."[18] This was in part because, even though the cost of large-scale news production had dropped, the initial costs of launching and running a national newspaper had jumped by leaps and bounds. The "Rising costs, particularly in relation to new printing technology, distribution and the larger staff needed to compile bigger newspapers, made it more difficult for newcomers to enter the industry."[19] "Consolidation and chain ownership exploded in the first decades of the 1900s, as market changes made taking over rival papers more lucrative and increased barriers of entries for new papers."[20] Over time, the "big newspapers had to take on the characteristics of corporations just to carry on their business."[21]

One of the more consequential changes to the industry was that advertising came to surpass subscription fees as the primary source of revenue. In the United States, this fundamentally altered the very character of the news. It is not often remembered now, but American newspapers had traditionally been funded by political parties.[22] Editors were closely associated with parties for which they largely functioned as mouthpieces. "Making good Democrats or Republicans mattered more than making a good profit."[23] Newspapers unabashedly and "publicly pledged their allegiance to either the Democrats or their nineteenth-century opponents, be it Whig or Republican," which was seen to be "natural and proper," for "newspapers were esteemed on the basis of their 'influence'—their persuasiveness and political authority.' "[24]

This all changed when "higher profits from advertising allowed newspapers to break their affiliation with political parties and to declare themselves independent."[25] Moreover, papers which could afford national advertising were able to lower their prices even further without sacrificing the profitability of the business. Soon, the "straightforward control or patronage of the press by political parties was replaced by the modern machinery of media management."[26] New intermediary industries of advertising and public relations blossomed. Information syndicates, such as the Associated Press, United Press, and Reuters were developed to minimize the costs of news collection and make information more uniform.

The First Era of Mass Fake News

In this new media world, monopolized by large news outlets and controlled by media moguls, newspapers began to compete for market share. It now became critical to reach new audiences. Before 1880, "the newspapers had not yet begun to break into the tenements."[27] This was in large part because readership was limited by low levels of literacy. But with the rising number of factory jobs created during the Second Industrial Revolution, national public education systems were created.[28] For the large newspaper consortiums this spelled dollar signs. Improvements in literacy and reduced production costs meant newspapers could now reach a vast and previously untapped market: the working and middle classes.[29]

To capture this expansive audience, a new form of journalism materialized, Yellow Journalism. Whereas traditional journalism had been rooted in ideological frameworks, focused on propounding political positions, and targeted to a relatively small and elitist part of society,[30] the "new" journalism catered to the needs of this much larger audience by appealing to "fundamental passions."[31] They "adopted varying proportions of sensationalism, populism, and socialism to address the interests of new, urban, working-class, and immigrant readers."[32]

In fact, it was the bitter rivalry between two major American newspaper titans of the age, Joseph Pulitzer and William Randolph Hearst, that set Yellow Journalism in motion. To outsell the other, each introduced sensational media content. Pulitzer's *New York World* and Hearst's the *New York Journal* redesigned news to shock, entertain, and titillate urban working-class readers.[33] A new formula for the news was pioneered: "love and romance for the women; sport and politics for the men,"[34] all headed by sensational crime coverage. "The effect of the application of this formula was to enormously increase the circulation of the newspapers, not only in the great cities, but all over the country."[35]

To make the news more alluring to their new customer base, the two publishing barons innovated several cutting-edge techniques. They introduced scare headlines printed with larger and bolder typeface to attract readers. Shocking or scandalous headers were accompanied by illustrations that bore little resemblance to reality, simply to add zest to the emotional impact.[36] After photomechanical reproduction became possible, "up-to-the-minute sensationalistic pictorial storytelling" was added to enhance the lurid news copy.[37] Another successful innovation was the comic strip. In fact, the term "Yellow Journalism" was derived from the *Yellow Kid*, the first comic strip that ever appeared in newsprint, created by Richard Outcault for Pulitzer's *World*. Not to be outdone, in 1897 Hearst introduced Rudolph Dirks's strip "Katzenjammer Kids" in his *Journal*.[38]

The "new journalism" with its bold headlines, exaggerated content, and new forms of imagery, began in the United States but spread within a decade to France and then to England. In England, Alfred Harmsworth (better known under his later title, Lord Northcliffe) was to become the archetypal press baron. He launched the *Daily Mail* in 1896, which became the market leader in London and paved the way for other mass-marketed newspapers. In fact, the *Daily Mirror* pioneered the model of popular journalism that still shapes English newspapers today. Northcliffe understood the new working-class readership. He rejected the long-winded Victorian style of news telling and adopted practices pioneered in the United States and France. His paper focused "on short, sharp and snappy stories and use of headings and subheadings."[39] To build circulation, Northcliffe used publicity stunts and public competitions. One such competition was to guess how much gold the

Bank of England would have on December 4, 1889. The winner was promised £1 a week for life. The gambit was so successful that "250,000 copies of the edition which announced the result were sold."[40] The *Mirror* was also an important pioneer of photojournalism. "Mirror photographers went to great lengths, and at great personal risk, to produce eye-catching photographs, including photographing the interior of Vesuvius, climbing Mont Blanc and crossing the Alps in a balloon."[41,42]

Contradictory Effects

Mass media's effects on society were both salutary and destabilizing. The most immediate transformation was in the very concept of "news" itself. "Journalism had to essentially redefine itself, to remain economically viable, find audiences, and establish a position in what could be labeled a 'democratic market society.'"[43] The new journalism renounced the political and social aims of the editors of old. No longer the champions of popular causes, these modern editors regarded themselves, first and foremost, as "news gatherers."[44] It was Pulitzer who recognized that the best way to fight popular causes "was not to advocate them on the editorial page but to . . . write them up—in the news columns."[45] His paper introduced the precursor to our contemporary investigative reporting, "muckraking." The muckrakers were known for their detailed, accurate journalistic accounts. They focused on social issues and particularly on exposing political and economic corruption of the new industrialists and mega-banking institutions.

Beyond that, the new media was transforming the way the social world was represented and even the way in which power was exercised across society. The Yellow Press extended the habit of reading news to the masses, including women and immigrants. By disseminating information and ideas to a much wider population of readers, it became an agent of change[46] and helped democratize both political and cultural authority.[47] Thus, by the late 1880s, it was clear to many contemporary observers that a new information order had come into being.

However, the new media had a number of pernicious effects as well. The insatiable drive for readership and increased commercialization of the industry had carried journalism to extremes. Emphasis on sensationalism rather than facts introduced new social dangers. The critiques of William Randolph Hearst and his *New York Journal* were particularly heated. It was charged that by repeatedly featuring articles that claimed European immigrants spread diseases, his paper was heightening anti-immigrant sentiment. Hearst's incessant attacks on President McKinley and the oft-printed cartoon depictions of the president as the puppet of great business trusts and wealthy financiers were believed by many to have fomented the anarchist assassination that felled the president.

Most infamous of all was Hearst's stretching of the truth to propel America into the Cuban-Spanish conflict. In February 1898, Hearst's *New York Journal* published a series of articles claiming to present evidence that the warship, the USS *Maine*, had been intentionally destroyed by a Spanish explosive device. The *Journal* characterized the sinking of the *Maine* as an act of war against the United States. Later, it was determined that there had been no conclusive evidence of Spanish sabotage. But the damage had been done. American sentiment had been inflamed. Soon after these spurious accusations had been published, McKinley, with the American public behind him, was able to launch the Spanish-American War, America's first imperial war fought in Cuba and the Philippines.[48] Undeterred by his critics, Hearst continued to support the war effort, sending *Journal* reporters "small cameras on the battlefront to bring the war home to newspaper subscribers."[49]

Nineteenth-century scholars tried to grapple with how to classify the enormous shift in the organization and representation of social knowledge and what it all meant for the future. However, characterizing the change and its potential effects proved to be as elusive as it was fascinating. In England, worries were expressed about the influence these new forms of print communication could exert on society. Elites had trepidation about the larger social and political effects of the rapid expansion of readership, which had been made possible by cheap newspapers. Commentators were troubled by the fact that "The technology of speed in composing, printing and distribution" was allowing print "to permeate all realms of society."[50] For some, "Newspapers appeared to be changing everything, from the appearance of city streets to the ways in which the English language was written and spoken."[51]

In the United States, concerns were raised that Yellow Journalism's blurring of fact and fiction, its penchant for hyperbole and sensationalism, and its emphasis on antisocial behavior would undermine essential institutions. Just as damning was the concern that journalism had become a commodity. As late as 1920, Arthur Baumann lamented that, "The ownership of a newspaper [has become] a commercial organisation for the purpose of getting money, its one business is to sell news, not ideas."[52] Thus, whereas in the

1880s commentators held optimistic views of the liberating possibilities of the press, as the century drew to a close the news media came to be seen as a nefarious force in society.

Twentieth Century

In the twentieth century, all around the globe, in every nation, national communications systems were developed. However, by the twenty-first century, these national media markets had fragmented, and mass production of information had fallen by the wayside. As in the turn of the nineteenth century, this brought into being a period paradoxically characterized by both the centralization and decentralization of media. And as in that earlier period, the new media's effects on society were both constructive and destructive.

A New Era of Mass Media

Twentieth-century "Mass production was not confined to automobiles; there was mass production in news and ideas as well."[53] The communications innovations of the belle époque had produced the possibility of a national media market. Changes, however, began to take shape in the 1980s, when satellite television and broadband cables exponentially increased the number of available channels. In no time, individuals were even able to record televised content. These innovations bequeathed much more power to end users than had been conceivable in the mid-twentieth century. No longer dependent upon a handful of television channels, customers could choose what to watch and when. Soon after, Internet platforms completely altered the transmission of information. At the turn of the century, the democratizing potential of the Internet seemed indisputable. Internet pages, which were originally only produced by people with technical knowledge, could now be made by anyone. Especially after Facebook emerged in 2004, people were able to create and pass on information at will. By the 2010s, Web content could be generated by anyone.

Another dramatic change developed in the financing of media. If the late nineteenth century was marked by the birth of the advertising industry, the turn of-the twentieth century was characterized by its slow demise. An early 1990 prophecy that "the last vestiges of traditional mass advertising will disappear"[54] has largely come to pass. Instead of mass marketing, companies have developed "adaptive marketing," where product offerings are made at the micro level and continually adjusted to satisfy individual customer demands.[55] In the 1990s, it was assumed that this process would increase the power of consumers: "The information superhighway will become the global electronic supermarket of the 90s, uniting producers and consumers directly, instantly, and interactively."[56] What was not understood at the end of the twentieth century was the degree to which "control over data [would become] a key resource for political and economic power."[57] Given the voluminous amounts of data generated every millisecond on the Web, only large-scale institutions were able to manage its storage and collection. This helped strengthen the power of the state and private industry. By the 2010s, "Big Data collection and storage [was] managed in a highly centralized fashion, resulting in privacy-intrusion, surveillance actions, discriminatory and segregation social phenomena."[58] Consequently, in this data-driven world, "the internet, despite its countless founding techno-utopias about its subversive and democratic potential,"[59] has, to the contrary, provided both governments and corporations unforeseen powers.

Even worse, to improve individualized user experiences, media platforms created automated systems that could recognize what people's interests were. This led to the development of proprietary technologies capable of tracking people's desires, and even coding people's relationships to one another. Social media platforms such as Instagram and Twitter and most especially Facebook continued to champion the liberating and democratizing potential of their platforms. But, all the while, they were quickly centralizing control over data to commodify it.[60] In this brave new world, privacy was to become something of a quaint notion of a bygone world. By the 2010s, "data protection had become increasingly linked to Internet firms" and the Internet itself transformed into a "web of corporations."[61] Thus, whereas user-generated content dominated the Web in the first decade of the twentieth first century, by the second decade, Internet platforms were progressively shaping politics; economics; and, indeed, all social interaction.

Contradictory Effects

All of this dramatically altered the way in which people accessed news and information. The new communications technologies both empowered individuals, allowing them to directly connect with one another across vast distances, and disempowered them by facilitating the strategic spread of misinformation. Just as the mass communications technologies of the nineteenth century led to the production of Yellow Journalism, the Digital Age has given birth to what has been coined the "post-truth" era. The label gained so much traction that in 2016 that it was added to the Oxford Dictionary, where it was defined as: "relating to or denoting circumstances in which objective facts are less influential in shaping public opinion than appeals to emotion and personal belief."[62] Resembling the bold scare headlines developed during the period of Yellow Journalism, in the "post-truth" era, online platforms use techniques designed to elicit emotional responses, like boldly printed, clickbait headlines that entice people to click on a site and read more. It didn't take long for bad actors to figure out that such techniques were a perfect way to disseminate false information. Fake, emotive news stories began to proliferate across the Internet. False information was used to rile up people's emotions, encourage support for extremist ideologies, and change the outcomes of elections in advanced democracies like Britain and the United States, as well as less-developed ones like Guyana and Kenya.

As mass-market newspapers had a century before, the Internet changed the media industry. Print newspapers began a precipitous decline. In the United States, between 1990 and 2008, a quarter of all American newspaper jobs disappeared.[63] Even before the pandemic of 2019, newspapers were closing their doors at an alarming average rate of two per week. It was reported in 2022 that "Over one-fifth of Americans now live in [a place with limited access to local news], or in a place that is at risk of becoming one."[64] Similar problems have begun to plague the news industry in Europe. In a policy paper for the European Union put out in December 2020, it was found that the European news sector had made a significant shift to digital media. Although paid subscriptions remained the major source of income in the European media market, digital advertising was "quickly becoming the main source of revenues for both news broadcasters and publishers." The report found further that "Between 2014 and 2017, the turnover of the European written press subsector declined at a [compound annual growth rate] of 0.33% leading to a turnover of EUR 73,275 million in 2017."[65]

To make matters worse, by the early 2000s, trust in print media had plummeted in the United States. In its stead, an increasing number of people, particularly young people, turned to Internet bloggers, amateur YouTube videographers, and TikTok aficionados for critical information about the world. Indeed, according to the article, "'Abandoning the News,' published by the Carnegie Corporation, thirty-nine per cent of respondents under the age of thirty-five told researchers that they expected to use the Internet in the future for news purposes; just eight per cent said that they would rely on a newspaper."[66] Confidence in news media also eroded across Europe, particularly after the advent of the Coronavirus pandemic. In one survey conducted by the Edelman Trust,[67] which collected data about how opinions were shaped by the epidemic in Brazil, Canada, France, Germany, Italy, Japan, South Africa, South Korea, the United Kingdom, and the United States, it was found that "Only 43% [of respondents] consider[ed] the media trustworthy on Covid-19, making journalists less trusted than coworkers, NGO representatives, politicians, and 'a person like yourself.'" This trend has been particularly apparent in Italy, Spain, and especially France, where "2019 Digital News Report by the Reuters Institute ranked France last among European countries in terms of public confidence in the media."[68]

Furthermore, just as the cost of entry into mass media markets increased in the nineteenth century, so too in the twenty-first century newcomers have been squeezed out. The early entrants into the Internet, like Google, Facebook, and Amazon, have not only amassed breathtaking fortunes, they have also been able to solidify their dominant position on the Web. Laissez-faire policies adopted in the United States aided the monopolizing power of these companies, where most of the large tech companies have been located. Regulations on media mergers put in place in the 1960s and 1970s, to ensure that a diversity of voices and opinions could be heard on the air or in print, began to be repealed in the 1980s. With these changes the 1990s witnessed Sony's union with Columbia Pictures and AT&T's acquisition of NCR. Mergers and acquisitions of large media conglomerates have continued through the twenty-first century.

Nor has there been the political will to control the monopolistic practices of large Web companies. This has allowed the twenty-first century media moguls, like their earlier counterparts, to assume fearsome powers. Where men like Pulitzer, Hearst, and Norcliffe could manipulate mass public perceptions, in the early twenty-first century Mark Zuckerberg the CEO of Facebook, and Jack Dorsey the CEO of Twitter, had the potential to change the outcome of national elections, promote or militate against ethnic cleansing, and even possibly determine the fate of liberal democracy.

Conclusion

Ironically, just as in the previous century, the more the new digital media decentralized information, the more monopolized it became. Internet companies have been able to consolidate power over how information is distributed and used. As media platforms increased their ability to filter, rank, and recommend information, the algorithms they had created began to mediate social, economic, and, perhaps most ominously, political interactions.[69] These twin processes have led to a paradoxical outcome: information has been increasingly directed by individuals, at the same time that it has been increasingly manipulated, constrained, and influenced by governments and monopolist corporations.

The consequences of these changes have been quite weighty. Digital media and cable television produced an upside-down, "through-the-looking-glass" world, in which a significant portion of the world's population held more faith in information provided by disgruntled individuals blogging in their basements, than in established media organizations with procedures in place to vet and triangulate information. The new forms of mass media, moreover, undermined people's trust in established institutions, taking a great toll on the very mechanisms that keep liberal democracies functioning. Together, the new world of mass communications helped propel anti-liberal populism and neo-fascist movements of the 2010s.

9

Foreign Fears: Immigration and Global Terror

In both eras, these same technological innovations brought into being something else the world had never seen before: an era of international terrorism. At the turn of the nineteenth century, a relatively small group of radical anarchists wreaked havoc across Europe and the United States. In the twentieth century, the same thing occurred with Islamist terrorists. In both epochs, the new transportation and communication technologies provided the tools to conduct these new forms of coordinated internationalized destruction, as well as the means to broadcast the news of the events across the world in real time.

Compounding these developments, immigration increased exponentially just when national communities had begun to struggle from the impacts of a global economy in transition. Fear that foreigners were taking away jobs and introducing dangers to the nation became intensified by new forms of sensationalized media. As tensions developed between immigrant groups and host-country citizens, anti-immigrant backlashes came to permeate politics and feed nascent *defensive nationalism* across the Global North.

Nineteenth Century

Global Terror

In 1893, during a performance of Rossini's opera *William Tell*, a bomb was hurled into the Barcelona Opera House. Thirty or more people were killed. Again, on February 12, 1894, a young man threw a bomb into a café near the Gare Saint-Lazare in Paris. For the belle époque, the randomness of these bombings was an unfamiliar horror. There had been acts of public violence before, but the targets had all been state officials—tsars, unpopular politicians, or perhaps a group of soldiers or policemen. Now, for the first

Defensive Nationalism. B. S. Rabinowitz, Oxford University Press. © Oxford University Press 2023.
DOI: 10.1093/oso/9780197672037.003.0010

time, the targets were "innocent people who just happened to be in the wrong place at the wrong time."[1] "In an age unaccustomed to terrorist attacks on women and children, the shocking spectacle of their murder at the hands of anarchists drove many observers into a frenzy."[2]

The attacks were conducted by anarchist extremists. Though small in number, they were empowered by a new deadly technology: dynamite. Alfred Nobel's 1866 invention proved to be the ideal delivery system for a poorly funded, anti-establishment movement. Explosive devices could be hurled anywhere by anyone—into crowded cafés, religious processions, and operatic performances. For the first time in history, lone actors could easily target large numbers of civilians. The new forms of violence were terrifying, not only for their arbitrary lethality but also their global scale. The violence was not restricted to any one country. Nor was it restricted to the European continent. Anarchist terrorism first appeared in the United States in 1886 with the bombing of a labor rally in Haymarket Square in Chicago. The bombing shocked the nation. Seven police officers and at least four civilians were killed, and dozens were injured. Fifteen years later, an anarchist assassinated President William McKinley in 1901. Even more deadly was the 1920 bombing of Wall Street, which left 30 people dead and 143 seriously injured.

The internationalization of these terrorist attacks, and the fact that "the dynamiting and assassinations often took place in several countries simultaneously . . . magnified their psychological impact and made them seem part of one vast terrorist conspiracy."[3] The sense of alarm was further intensified by "the fact that the blasts seemed linked together in chain reactions of violence that were impervious to police efforts at prevention."[4] For example, "Between March 1892 and June 1894 eleven dynamite explosions rocked Paris and killed nine people. In Spain, bombs hurled at a Corpus Christi procession and at a theatre audience in Barcelona caused deaths by the score."[5] The years 1892 to 1901 came to be known as the "Decade of Regicide." More monarchs, presidents, and prime ministers of major world powers were assassinated than at any other time in history. Among those assassinated were President Sadi Carnot of France in 1894, Prime Minister Antonio Cánovas of Spain in 1897, the Empress Elizabeth of Austria in 1898, and King Humbert of Italy in 1900. "Never before had European statesmen and monarchs been assassinated in such rapid succession."[6]

The new internationalism provided the means for anarchist violence to spread across borders. It is also what motivated it. Anarchist terror was launched as a desperate attempt to stop global capitalism. The assassin who shot McKinley, "When asked later why he had shot the president, Czolgosz replied, 'McKinley was going around the country shouting about prosperity when there was no prosperity for the poor man.'"[7] Indeed, a founding premise of anarchist theory was that capitalist society was a place of constant violence; it was embodied in "every law, every church, every paycheck was based on force."[8]

Yet, anarchists initially did not set out to target civilians. The turn to terror came after some true believers, frustrated by the fact that the masses had not risen up in revolt, felt that impassioned speeches and mass-produced tracks had been too paltry an approach. Other means would be required to awaken the proletariat to the dangers of capitalism's destructive force. It was argued that "In such a world, to do nothing, to stand idly by while millions suffered, was itself to commit an act of violence."[9] For a handful of the most radical anarchists, this not only necessitated that capitalism be opposed with equal ferocity, but it also justified terrorist acts against the general public. The solution was what was called "propaganda of the deed." No longer would their message be communicated through public speeches and media—it would be transmitted through violent acts: assassinations and bombings across bourgeois society. As Emma Goldman explained, anarchist violence was an unavoidable response to "capital [which comes], like a vampire, to suck the last drop of blood of the unfortunate." She described how there were "millions of unfortunates who die in the factories, the mines, and wherever the grinding power of capital is felt" and concluded that therefore, "Compared with the wholesale violence of capital and government, political acts of violence are but a drop in the ocean."[10]

Threats from Immigration

During the same period, waves of immigrants were coming to England and the "New World," especially from Italy, Germany, and China. The migrations, which largely occurred in response to the agrarian depressions of the 1870s and 1890s, produced fear in receiving countries that were also trying to cope with the economic instability. The most immediate fear was that this massive influx of people would put downward pressure on unskilled wages. In several countries there was an anti-immigrant backlash. Advanced nations shifted away from open immigration. In the anglophone countries, United States, Canada, and Australia, the first restrictive immigration laws were adopted in the 1880s. But it was not only the anglophone countries. Immigration restrictions were set in Denmark and Germany. Even Argentina and Brazil reversed their open-door policies in the 1880s.[11]

Initially, anti-immigrant legislation enacted in Canada, Australia, and the United States was targeted specifically against Asians. In the United States, bans on Chinese immigration began in 1888 and were strengthened over the next three decades. By 1891, the ban had been extended to "the immigration of persons likely 'to become public charges' as well as those 'assisted' in passage."[12] Australia hardened its immigration laws between 1890 and 1930. Like the United States, Australia's policy was predominantly an anti-Asian immigration policy. "Australia maintained a strict policy aimed at keeping the country one of British and Irish descent, while avoiding persons of 'yellow' skin."[13]

If Asians were feared for job competition, European immigrants were feared for posing an economic as well as a security threat. As the anarchist threat intensified, anti-immigration sentiment became increasingly focused on European émigrés. Although anarchists came from all classes of the population, in the public imagination it was the migrants from Italy, Germany, Eastern Europe, and Ireland that were behind all the problems caused by radical labor "degeneracy," and terrorism. Indeed, anarchist ideology was burgeoning among the new proletariat, many of whom had emigrated from those countries. Working in miserable factory conditions and living in urban squalor, it is not surprising that a portion of these recent settlers became radicalized and joined labor movements as well as anarchist causes.

The scope and visibility of anarchist terrorism helped advance the mounting nativist backlash in Europe and the USA. In addition to being subject to increased surveillance and arrest, immigrant groups across Europe became subject to mob violence. Jensen describes how:

Mobs sacked the homes and schools of immigrant Italian workers and other Italian-speakers residing in the Austrian Empire. In Trieste, they wrecked Italian cafes and a gymnastic center; in Linz and Budapest, employers summarily fired Italian workers. Hundreds of Italians fled back to Italy . . . On the outskirts of Berlin a mob burned down a slum-dwelling housing fifty itinerant Italian workers.[14]

The same was true in the United States, where a popular backlash against immigrants exploded:

> Anarchists lost their jobs and had their possessions confiscated; on occasion they were beat up. Anarchists were arrested simply because they were anarchists. In Rochester a grand jury was asked to indict the city's 100 anarchists on the charge of conspiracy to overthrow the government, although eventually it refused to do so for lack of evidence . . . More than fifty suspected anarchists, including Emma Goldman were arrested in Chicago and held without bail for seventeen days on suspicion of involvement with the assassination.[15]

The fact that "the Age of Anarchist Terrorism" coincided with the beginning of the "Age of Mass Journalism" only helped intensify these fears.[16] Sensationalism sold copy. And little was more sensational than terrorist bombings. The papers exploited and exaggerated the danger anarchists presented to society. One Italian journalist described anarchism as "the most important ethical deviation that may ever have disturbed the world."[17] The new mass journalism, thus, escalated fears of migrants. Even though only a handful of individuals on the fringes of society were engaged in violent acts, the press painted them as part of an organized league of international anarchists who sought to undermine world security. In 1908, Frank Harris captured the impact the media had had on Americans' perception of the danger posed by the anarchists. He describes how:

> the whole American population was scared out of its wits by the Haymarket bomb. Every day the Chicago police found a new bomb. I thought they had started a special manufactory for them, till I read in the *Leader* of New York that the same piece of gas-piping had already served as a new bomb on seven different occasions . . . Everyday there were illegal arrests by the hundred; every day hundreds of innocent persons were thrown into prison without a shadow of evidence; the policemen who could denounce and arrest the greatest number of people got the quickest advancement. The whole town was frightened to idiocy.[18]

Frank Harris also describes the hysteria that developed after one of the men accused of the Haymarket bombing, Luis Lingg, blew himself up in his prison cell before he could be executed:

The city seemed to go mad; from one end of the town to the other men began to arm themselves, and the wildest tales were current. There were bombs everywhere. The nervous strain upon the public had become intolerable. The stories circulated and believed that afternoon and night seem now, as one observer said, to belong to the literature of Bedlam. The truth was that the bombs found in Lingg's cell and his desperate self-murder had frightened the good Chicagoans out of their wits. One report had it that there were twenty thousand armed and desperate anarchists in Chicago who had planned an assault upon the jail for the following morning. The newspaper offices, the banks, the Board of Trade building, the Town Hall, were guarded night and day. Every citizen carried weapons openly. One paper published the fact that at ten o'clock on that Thursday night a gun store was still open in Madison Street, and crowded with men buying revolvers. The spectacle did not strike any one as in the least strange, but natural, laudable. The dread of some catastrophe was not only in the air, but in men's talk, in their faces.[19]

Twentieth Century

Global Terror

The turn of the twentieth century also witnessed the birth of a new form of international terrorism—Islamic jihadism. As in the century before, the globalization of terror was both enabled by and a response to hyper-globalization.

Islamic terrorism had existed in the 1960s and 1970s, but it took a fundamental turn in the 1980s. The ideology of the global *ummah*, or Pan-Islamism, dates back to the late nineteenth century, when European empires ruled the majority of the world's Muslims. Pan-Islamism holds that Muslims are one nation, or *umma*, which must be united to meet the challenges of the modern world. However, with the creation of independent national states across the Muslim world in the early twentieth century, the focus of political Islam shifted away from the goal of uniting the *ummah*, to one focused on gaining political representation of Islamic parties within individual nation-states. There were Muslim groups that used violent tactics in the mid-twentieth century, like the Egyptian Muslim Brotherhood and the secular Palestinian Liberation Organization; but mid-century hijackings, bombings, and assassinations were carried out with the goal of forcing the international community to take action on specific national issues.

It wasn't until the 1980s and 1990s that the ideology of the global *ummah* was revived. The revival developed in response to the ever-increasing imposition of American imperialism, the capitulation of corrupt and oppressive Middle Eastern governments, as well as to what was perceived to be the West's general hostility to the interests of the Muslim and Arab worlds. In short, the revived Pan-Islamist ideology was "based on the view that the umma [was] being systematically oppressed by outside forces, and that all Muslims [had] a responsibility to help other Muslims in need."[20] What emerged was a new form of Pan-Islamism, which "represented a macro-nationalism [that] transcended the nation-states."[21]

Osama bin Laden is the personage perhaps most closely associated with this movement. In the 1990s, bin Laden was the figurehead of the first Islamic terrorist network, al-Qaida. Al-Qaida, which translates as "The Base" or "The Foundation," had humble beginnings. It began as a military operation organized to support the Afghan fight against the invading Soviet army, in what was then referred to as the Afghan "holy war." Focused as it was on stopping the tide of Soviet expansionism, bin Laden's multinational, Sunni Islamist fighting organization was cultivated and supported by the US government. Following the ancient proverb "The enemy of my enemy is my friend," bin Laden's forces received seed funds and training that was directed by the United States and delivered to the rag tag group of fighters sequestered in the Afghan mountains with the help of the Saudi Arabian and Pakistani governments.

In 1989, bin Laden began focusing his animus on the Saudi/United States alliance. By 1992, the mission of al-Qaida had been established: they would now target the United States and her allies. When, in 1995, the United States stationed some 550,000 coalition troops in the Saudi desert during the prosecution of the 1991 Gulf War, bin Laden was so enraged by what he believed was an affront to Saudi Arabia's sovereignty that he wrote an open letter to the Saudi king, in which he "declared war on the United States and called for a guerrilla campaign to oust US forces from Saudi Arabia."[22] Over the next five years, al-Qaida developed into a streamlined training center. By the turn of the century, bin Laden had created a sophisticated operations center in Afghanistan that processed thousands of recruits and was capable of launching large-scale campaigns across the globe, while being virtually unassailable in its rough mountain refuge.

Thereafter, Islamic terrorism spread rapidly. In the early 2000s, the world saw a proliferation of global jihadist movements from the Islamic State (IS) to Boko Haram to smaller extremist movements linked to al-Qaida. The broad appeal of these globalized Islamist movements was "growing resentment" among people across the Muslim and Arab world "over conspicuous wealth, accumulation, the increasing gap between rich and poor, an awareness of structural exclusion on a global scale, and the erosion of time-honoured approaches to social welfare" as the market demands cuts or the abolition of transfer payments.[23] Islam promised to be the antidote to the neo-liberal American order. Islamists scorned the secularism of advanced capitalist economies that extolled "the cult of individualism" above the community and separated duties to the state from religious observance. Their goal was, hence, to stop the spread of American capitalism and militarism that was enslaving the world. Indeed, the attack that brought al-Qaida to world attention and came to represent this new form of Islamic threat, the 2001 bombing in New York City, had as its target the building most symbolic of United States' hegemony over global finance—the World Trade Center.

The reach of new technologies was as critical to the genesis of these new forms of violence as was the changing global order. Of course, none of this would have been thinkable without jet-propelled airplanes. Jets had made intercontinental travel accessible. It also made it exponentially more lethal. Whereas the anarchists had used dynamite to bomb cafés, the 9/11 World Trade Center bombing made use of a large jet plane carrying tons of fuel to blow up two of the tallest buildings in the world. The catastrophic power of an airplane bomb introduced the world to a whole new order of terrorism.

Changes in communication also played a vital role. Cell phones and "social networking media, such as Facebook, Twitter, YouTube, Flickr and blogging platforms"[24] enabled terrorist groups to develop a global following. The Internet was used by tech-savvy terrorists to spread jihadist propaganda and recruit followers from all over the globe. With their agile use of the new technologies not only could jihadist groups find converts from all corners of the globe, they were also able to internationalize their targets. Cell phones and the Internet enabled an individual or a relatively small group of Islamists working remotely from any strategic compound to terrorize people virtually anywhere.

The new technologies facilitated the development of "an entirely new pattern of attacks, namely 'globalized suicide attacks,'" that were markedly "distinct from the traditional, localized pattern of suicide attacks" used by national groups in the 1970s, such as the Lebanese Shiite political party and militant group Hezbollah; and the Kurdish separatist movement in Turkey, the PKK.[25] The 1990s saw "a rise in the number of suicide attacks, the number of countries targeted by suicide attacks, and the number of organizations that plan and execute suicide attacks."[26] The "unprecedented numerical rise, geographic spread, growing lethality and marked increase in the number of groups employing suicide missions every year" had "amounted to nothing less than a full-scale globalisation of this tactic."[27]

As with anarchist terrorism, the unpredictability of the location of these acts and, in some cases, the synchronization of terrorist attacks across countries added to the fear they produced. In 2014 alone, there were Islamic terrorist attacks in Afghanistan, Iraq, Pakistan, Nigeria, Denmark, Tunisia, Yemen, Libya, Kenya, Saudi Arabia, Somalia, the United States, Turkey, Kuwait, Tunisia, Cameroon, India, Bangladesh, Australia, Bangladesh, Somalia, Chad, Niger, Egypt, Philippines, Bosnia and Herzegovina, and Russia. And the list goes on. The randomness of the targets was equally terrifying. Included were bombings of tourist beaches in Bali, Indonesia, and Egypt; attacks to the financial capital of India; a bomb planted at the Boston Marathon; a savage attack on people shopping at a mall in Nairobi; and the beheading of cartoonists working for the French satirical newspaper *Charlie Hebdo* in Paris.

Finally, to amplify the effects of their actions, Islamist groups used shocking means of violence. They employed visually arresting methods, such as beheadings of kidnapped journalists filmed and posted to the Internet, explosions in holy places while innocent people gathered to pray, and machine gun attacks on harmless revelers at a concert. It was the ruthlessness in addition to the randomness of this new form of terrorism that induced horror and panic across the world.

As had happened a century earlier, Islamist terrorism of the late twentieth century was made global as much by the spread of liberal imperialism as by the modern technologies that made it feasible. In reaction to US expansionism, radical Islam jumped "from a desperate national struggle into identification with the global ummah."[28] Al-Qaida's targets were even similar to those of the anarchist terrorists who preceded it: "US imperialism, [and] symbols of globalization."[29] Each was in its essence a "fight against the global order."[30]

Immigration Threats

The late twentieth century has been characterized by some as the second "age of migration." Although the total numbers of immigrants moving globally across borders may not be as statistically significant as that would suggest,[31] there were important ways in which migrations did increase, particularly to the countries with advanced economies.

It was in Northern America and Western Europe that very high rates of migration were experienced from 1965 to 1990. One estimate suggests that by 1999, "one in every 13 persons living in the West [was] an international migrant."[32] Salt and Clarke (2000) found that by 1992 in Western Europe "total numbers of recorded foreign workers . . . had risen by 23.1% to 7.3 million," up from 5.9 million only four years earlier, and that these "increases in Western Europe's recorded foreign workers occurred almost entirely in the late 1980s and early 1990s."[33] One of the contributing factors to this surge in migration was greater access to passenger air travel. The development of the air passenger industry allowed the period from the late 1980s to the early 1990s to become a time of "unprecedented migration."[34] Another contributor was the "global trend toward *laissez-faire* economic policies," which not only lifted barriers for trade and capital flows but also increased migration flows: a trend that "further accelerated after the fall of the Berlin Wall in 1989, heralding an age of 'market triumphalism.' "[35] In fact, starting in the 1960s, several countries relaxed their immigration laws.[36]

By the turn of the century, this influx of foreigners had begun to create serious tensions, particularly in communities already reeling from the loss of industrial jobs who were fearful of job competition. At the same time, international terrorism was on the rise, and it was associated with immigrant groups—this time Muslims. The high visibility of the Islamic terrorist attacks helped produce a backlash against Muslims, what most academics today refer to as "Islamophobia." Fear of Muslims was not, of course, wholly new, but it did dramatically escalate after the spectacular obliteration of the World Trade Center buildings. "Prejudice against Muslims in Western countries preceded the 9/11 attacks in the United States, but those events and other acts of violence by terrorists since that time have created a climate for increasing anti-Muslim attitudes in many countries."[37]

In the United States, the terrorist attacks of September 11, 2001, "prompted the profound realignment of the US immigration system from increased surveillance and data tracking" to changes in intelligence agencies and local law enforcement.[38] Immediately after the attacks, hate crimes against Muslims peaked.[39] Sensationalized news fanned the flames of this anti-immigrant sentiment. As in the preceding century, rising migration and Islamist terror came at the same time as the emergence of twenty-four-hour cable news. Fear of foreigners was intensified by the new forms of media that exploited the emotional force of anti-immigrant stories. Sensationalism, characteristic of the period of Yellow Journalism, came to be the currency of the new cable networks. No matter that those perpetrating terror represented a small fraction of followers of Islam, scare headlines, "breaking news" segments, and editorial commentary contributed to the increased fear and distrust of Muslims as a whole, as well as foreigners more generally. "One American media outlet, Fox News, was especially given to sensationalism following the events of 9/11."[40] Indeed, studies have found that regularly watching Fox News is correlated with holding negative attitudes about Muslims.[41]

Donald Trump's presidency also appears to have inflamed anti-Muslim sentiment. His rhetoric against Muslims heated up the issue of Muslim immigrants, as did his "Muslim Ban," an executive order he issued one year after taking office that prohibited entry to the United States of people from six predominantly Muslim countries. In fact, the year Trump came to power, anti-Muslim attacks, which had been in abeyance after the dramatic uptick following the 9/11 attacks, increased by 44 percent.[42]

Fear of Muslims went far beyond the shores of America. Across Europe anti-Muslim sentiment had begun to fester during the 1990s. Several right-wing parties were established. But Islamophobia had remained largely on the fringes of the political scene up until the bombing of the World Trade Center. After that horrific attack, anti-Muslim sentiment came raging to the fore. Attacks of foreign residents increased, and extremist parties gained powers even they could not have even dreamt would be possible a decade earlier.

In many ways, the Islamophobia that gripped Europe in the early twenty-first century was not dissimilar from the panic that took hold of Europe in the nineteenth century over the "Jewish Question." In Sweden, the far-right party, the Sweden Democrats, "focused [on] anti-Islam narrative . . . identifying Islam as public enemy number one."[43] The Danish People's Party (DPP) described Islam as an "anti-modern, anti-democratic, patriarchal, violent dogmatic religion belonging to a lower level of civilization." In Holland, the now defunct LPF (*Lijst Pim Fortuyn*), formed in the aftermath of the 9/11 attack, "called for a stop to all Muslim immigration."[44] And when the far-right Polish party Law and Justice, came to power in 2015, not only did acts of hatred and xenophobia become more frequent, but the government "refused to take in non-Christian refugees as part of an EU relocation plan, citing security concerns."[45]

Aside from trying to curtail Muslim immigrations and painting Muslims essentially as the anti-Christ, a series of anti-Islamic reforms were introduced across Europe, some more successful than others. For example, in 2004, France banned young girls from wearing veils in state schools and then passed an even more controversial law in 2011 that banned the wearing of a niqāb (the face covering that only leaves the eyes visible) in public places.[46] Belgium's lower parliamentary house voted to ban all face coverings in public the year before. In Switzerland in 2009, "a thin majority of voters 'supported a proposal to ban the construction of minarets throughout the country.'"[47] One of the leaders of the anti-minaret campaign charged that the structures served as 'beacons of Jihad' and landmarks of an intolerant culture, which puts its God-given, Islamic law over the law of the country."[48] The building of a mosque also became a lightning rod in Poland when, in 2010, 150 people protested at thesite, chanting "Blind tolerance kills common sense."[49]

Conclusion

In both periods, the dislocations caused by economic change were magnified by the dramatic movement of peoples and the emergence of violent terrorist movements dedicated to the destruction of the liberal political order. In response, economic nationalism came to be merged with a generalized fear of international forces. The world was poised for an era of defensive nationalism.

PART IV

ANTI-GLOBALIZATION

In the latter decades of both centuries, there was still some faith in internationalism. The general narrative of the benefits of liberal trade was still dominant. Even social movements, labor unions, and environmental activists still believed in working across borders for a larger cause. However, by the early part of the new century, internationalism had almost entirely receded. The faith in economic progress and interstate cooperation had been replaced by anti-liberal movements, in which right- and left-wing politicians propagated defensive nationalist discourses.

This section will show how the golden age of international commerce produced reactionary defensive nationalism. This is what Polanyi describes as "spontaneous" forms of resistance against transnational liberalism. But Polanyi's language is too indefinite and elusive to pin down precisely what he means by this, or how his conceptual framework can be used methodologically. The following two chapters examine how "society"—understood as a wide swath of classes and interests—resisted internationalism and battled to protect itself from the dislocations created by hyper-globalization. It will do so by examining left- and right-wing defensive nationalist movements that arose in both epochs.

The analysis of defensive nationalism is divided into two parts. Chapter 10 will trace the birth of defensive nationalism on the right and the left in both periods. It will cover three key aspects. The first section will analyze the genesis of these movements in the United States and Europe. It will identify what factions of society headed the movements and what the rhetorical differences were in the way "the people" and "the nation" were defined by the right and the left. The second section will examine the rise of economic nationalism in the guise of state protectionism. The third section traces how growing wealth disparities shaped the way in which the global enemy was defined on both the right and the left. In Chapter 11, the focus will be on the turn toward nativism and fascism in both periods. The first section will examine how anti-immigrant backlashes manifest as nativism, and the different forms that took. The final section will discuss the rise of anti-liberalism and anti-rationalism that came to characterize the right-wing movements in both periods (see Table 10.1).

10

From Globalization to the Nation

The technological revolutions of the turn of the last two centuries created peculiarly modern forms of interconnectivity that produced peculiarly modern forms of social dislocation. They also engendered equally modern political responses. This chapter will look at how right-wing and left-wing formulations of who "the people" and "the nation" were developed, how economic nationalism became dominant, and lastly how each side of the political spectrum defined the international forces that were threatening the nation.

"The People" and "The Nation"

Nineteenth Century

In the 1880s and 1890s, something new was brewing around the world. The rapid rise in immigration, coupled with economic distress and international terrorism, galvanized people in a whole new way. The period was to witness the materialization of an entirely new form of struggle. Across the advanced world, defensive nationalism took hold. This uniquely modern crusade became the dominant political movement of the era.

The irony was, as Polanyi underscores, that the anti-liberal response began as soon as the gold standard had been accepted as the international medium of exchange. Indeed, "the heyday of elite cultural globalization was before 1870. Nationalist cultural identities gained in importance in the latter decades of the nineteenth century."[1] On both sides of the Atlantic, nativist, populist, anti-international movements sprung up. Each side, however, followed a different trajectory. In Europe, defensive nationalism was spearheaded by the nobility and industrialists who were hit hardest by changes to agriculture and trade. By contrast, in the United States, with no history of feudalism, the impact of the economic changes was felt most severely by farmers, particularly grain farmers across the Midwest. They were the ones to mobilize and

Defensive Nationalism. B. S. Rabinowitz, Oxford University Press. © Oxford University Press 2023.
DOI: 10.1093/oso/9780197672037.003.0011

Table 10.1 Ideological Forms of Defensive Nationalism

	Left-Wing Defensive Nationalism	Right-Wing Defensive Nationalism
Basis ("the people")	Class-based	Nativist
Nemesis ("global enemy")	International capital	Foreign penetration
Constituency	Predominantly urban based	Predominantly peripherally based
Orientation	Forward-looking, Progressive	Backward-looking, Retrogressive
Goals	Equality of opportunity	Restoration of traditional (religious) order
Rhetoric	Rights-based/Equity	Fear-based/Group Survival
Protection For	Economically disadvantaged and less privileged	Heartland "natives," traditional family and patriarchy
Economic Policy Objectives	Checks on wealth accumulation Reduction of corporate power Unfair trade deals Protection of national jobs	Unfair trade practices Unchecked migration Unfair trade deals Protection of national jobs

to define the populist understanding of the battle between "the people" and "the enemy."

American Defensive Nationalism

In the United States, the global panic of 1893 was the defining moment that ushered in this new form of political mobilization. The panic began when gold mining in the United States failed to keep up with supply, resulting in a run on gold. The "Great Depression" that followed was the worst financial crisis the United States had experienced hitherto (see Chapter 7). The situation eventually grew so bad that, "During the winter of 1893–94, charities were strained to the breaking point. Long lines appeared at the soup kitchens."[2]

The misery experienced by the working classes prompted the first popular protest rally in Washington DC. The DC rally was the brainchild of Jacob S. Coxey, an Ohio businessman, aspiring politician, and astute publicist. Coxey, long interested in reform, had co-authored the "Good Roads Bill," which he presented to Congress. The bill proposed a public roads program to aid the unemployed. After introducing his bill to Congress, Coxey looked for a way to drum up support for it. He alighted upon a novel promotional strategy. To make the scope of the problem of unemployment visible to the nation, Coxey organized "an army of laborers" to descend upon DC. On March 25, 1894, a great mass of unemployed workers, hobos, and tramps, from as far away as Oregon, began to make their way to the Capitol for what was announced to be a "petition in boots."[3]

Although unemployed laborers formed the greater part of "Coxey's army," it was the farmers who came to form the central nexus of the American left-wing defensive nationalist movement. Farmers were hit especially hard by the drop in the gold supply because it occurred in tandem with falling farm prices. The fall in farm prices was quite sharp. From 1864 to 1896, "the price of farm products fell by over sixty percent"; farmers "felt the squeeze of falling prices and feared they might lose their independence."[4] Many farmers also had a heavy debt burden, which the currency crisis only magnified. To bolster agricultural prices, farmers advocated for a system of "bimetallism." Their goal was to increase the availability of money by pegging silver to gold. The "free-silver" movement (as it came to be labeled) pitted farmers against "pro-gold" advocates. The latter included those who headed financial establishments in the Northeast, railroad barons, and large industrialists, all of whom benefited from the rise in trade and financing that the gold standard had facilitated.

In fact, this political battle has been immortalized in the childhood classic *The Wizard of Oz* based upon the first of a series of books written by L. Frank Baum.[5] Although there is debate about whether the story was intentionally written as an allegory,[6] all its components work to illustrate the free-silver movement of the period. The story begins in the heartland of the United States, Kansas. Its protagonist is Dorothy, an average, young farm-fed girl. In fact, the center of the free-silver movement was Kansas, and it was made up of farmers like Dorothy's family and neighbors. The yellow brick road that Dorothy walks down symbolizes gold bullion, the contested national monetary standard. The "Wonderful Wizard of Oz" represents the federal government, which could decide by fiat (through wizardry) what metal, silver or gold, (oz. being the abbreviation for ounce) would be the center of the economy. In the original version, Dorothy's slippers were not ruby but silver symbolic of midwestern farmers' aspiration for a silver standard. Along the way, Dorothy encounters munchkins (the American population), a brainless scarecrow (farmers), a heartless tinman (industry), and a cowardly lion (politicians). Finally, the Wicked Witch in the story represents powerful individuals aligned against silver. Some have suggested that the character represents President Grover Cleveland, who worked hard to oppose the silver movement.[7] However, another possible candidate for who the Wicked Witch signifies is J. P. Morgan.

John Pierpont Morgan was arguably the person who best exemplified the "pro-gold" camp. Morgan was the richest man in the world. During the Great Depression, while the rest of the country suffered, Morgan's companies thrived. Although he came from a wealthy banking family, J. P. Morgan made his spectacular fortune in railroads. Yet, Morgan did not build railroads; he took over or consolidated failing railroads under his control. These hostile takeovers even came to be referred to as "Morganization" (reputedly also the original inspiration for the game Monopoly).[8] In 1901, Morgan switched his focus to steel, forming US Steel—the first billion-dollar corporation in the world.[9] Public resentment grew against the railroad magnate, especially among farmers who were heavily affected by Morgan's monopolistic control of rail freight prices. J. P. Morgan became the symbol of all that was wrong with American politics, the quintessential "Wicked Witch." The magnitude of opprobrium felt toward the great railroad magnate is palpable even a century later. A contemporary wrote: "No other system of taxation has borne as heavily on the people as those extortions and inequalities of railroad charges which caused the granger outburst in the West, and the recent uprising in New York."[10]

Thus, the battle over gold versus bimetallism produced a self-identified populist movement, particularly in the West, where farmers blamed the greed of eastern bankers and industrialists for the depressed state of the economy. The American populist parties of the 1890s drew their largest followings from the central farmland states of Omaha and Kansas. The cardinal goal of the movement, summed up in the Omaha Chapter of the People's Party platform, was "to restore the government of the Republic to the hands of 'the plain people,'" "the urban workman," and "pauperized labor" who were "denied the right to organize for self-protection."[11] A critical figure at the time was Mary Elizabeth Lease, a riveting orator who helped found the Kansas People's Party. Lease was also politically savvy. By organizing a slate of populist candidates to run for the Kansas legislative election, her Kansas People's Party won control of the legislature with ninety-one seats. The success of the populists in Kansas boosted other populist movements across the country.

Whereas the People's Parties were strong in the Midwest and to a lesser extent in the South, in the East it was labor unionists and socialists who gained left-wing populist support. One individual who gathered a significant following was a radical reformer who ran for mayor of New York in 1896, Henry George. George had developed a unique economic theory, which came to be known as "Georgism." The central tenet of Georgism was that the root of all economic crises was inflated property values. The logic was that as property values rise, they inevitably produce irresponsible speculative bubbles, which inevitably burst. Hence, private property is the source of economic dislocations. George's solution was to effectively eliminate private property by placing a high tax on it and at the same to cease taxing labor. George published his theory in an eloquently written book *Progress and Poverty* (1879).[12] The book, with its scathing critiques of the extreme greed of the idle wealthy, gained popularity and Georgism briefly took hold as a political movement in the East.

But it was William Jennings Bryan who became the standard bearer of the burgeoning left-wing defensive nationalist movement. A congressman from Nebraska from 1890 until 1895, Bryan was considered the national leader of the Free Silver Movement. Bryan's superior oratory skills had unexpectedly won him the Democratic nomination for the presidency in 1896. At the Democratic Convention, Bryan made a stirring speech in defense of the free-silver platform. Later dubbed the "Cross of Gold Speech," Bryan galvanized the auditorium with his famous closing words: "You shall not press down upon the brow of labor this crown of thorns, you shall not crucify mankind upon a cross of gold." So rousing was the speech that the next day the *Atlanta Constitution* reported that "Deafening cheers rent the air and articles of every description were thrown high above the surging sea of humanity."[13]

European Defensive Nationalism

In Europe, the emergence of defensive nationalist movements followed a very different trajectory. In the late nineteenth century, international anarchist and communist movements formed the core of European left-wing, anti-liberal movements. Their goal was to defeat global capitalism by uniting workers across what they regarded as artificial national boundaries. But after the turn of the century, they too had become nationalist.

In 1864, the Communist International was established at a meeting in London attended by labor leaders and radical nationalists from France, Italy, Germany, and London. The most famous delegate in attendance was Karl

Marx, who represented Germany. The Comintern, as it came to be known, held three important conferences. Over time, however, founding members of the Comintern came to support nationalist policies. Indeed, "the tension between national sentiment and internationalist aspiration was never resolved in socialist theory or practice and was to haunt all three Internationals."[14] This is illustrated by Vladimir Lenin's political transformation. Lenin had vehemently argued that "democracy and nationalism were little more than deceptions used by the bourgeoisie to divert the working class from revolution."[15] However, facing the stark circumstances in which the Soviet Union found itself at the tail end of World War I, Lenin was compelled to place national interests and state economic development ahead of international revolution. In 1917, he instituted what he labeled "War Communism"; in reality, it was economic nationalism. The policy agenda focused on industrializing the Soviet economy and advancing the languishing Soviet State. Thus, even at the center of the international communist movement, defensive nationalism took hold.

Although left-wing defensive nationalism evolved more slowly in Europe than in the United States, strong right-wing defensive nationalist movements developed very early on. These right-wing defensive nationalist movements were led by members of the elite classes: the nobility, as well as members of the bourgeoisie and industrialists hurt by open trade policies. They spoke to the same fears of globalization and threats to "the nation" as their left-wing counterparts, but they used very different idioms. For conservative nationalists, "the nation" that was under attack was not the average worker or laborer being crushed by the actions of powerful railroad magnates. "The people" were those who lived in the rural "heartland" and made up the heart and soul of the nation: the *volk*.

One of the first writers to connect national revival with protecting the "heartland" was a French aristocrat, Arthur de Gobineau. Gobineau's theories were related to a larger movement developing across Europe at the time, especially in the arts, Romanticism. The Romantics were on a "quest for authenticity," which they expressed through the "spiritual and artistic identification with the local and national way of life in the countryside." The fascination with the peasantry came from the idea that "the local and national way of life in the countryside" represented "the 'incorruptible' nation." Unlike urbane civilization, "Nature" was "the true source of life, dignity and sanctity." As Anthony Smith explains, "this turn towards rural labour [betokened] a deeper self-identification with the peasantry" and a "general expansion of national sentiment," which identified " 'the land and its people' as emblems of national authenticity." Thus, the Romantic movement was characterized by a "turning away from the sophisticated but often corrosive lifestyles of the city," to embrace "the deeper, more permanent, sacred truths of human life, which could be appreciated and embodied most faithfully in the simple life, the labour and the customs of 'the people,' the rural poor."[16]

Gobineau built on this romantic tradition, combining notions of racial purity with the peasantry. In his treatise, "*Essai sur l'inégalité des races humaines*" ("Essay on the Inequality of Human Races") published between 1853 and 1855, Gobineau idealized agrarian society and disparaged the modern city as a giant cesspool of unrooted people undermining the purity of the French nation. By the latter part of the century, Gobineau's ideas had become increasingly popularized. In Wilhelmine, Germany, Gobineau's theories found fertile ground. Indeed, Gobineau's essay was translated into German in 1874, where a Gobineau Society was set up to propagate his ideas.[17] Soon after, the early German nationalist Konstatin Frantz published a political treatise in 1879, *Der Untergang der alten Parteien und die Parteien der Zukunft*, in which he directly echoed Gobineau's themes:

> What does the peasant care whether they have the same laws a day's journey from his village as at his home? But he must desire all the more to keep to his traditional law with which all the habits of his life are entwined. Similarly, what does the petty burgher, whose business transactions do not extend beyond his immediate neighbourhood, care? So that exactly those elements who form the stable basis of a nation, not only have no interest in a general and uniform civil code, they are decidedly harmed by being required to fit themselves into the new legal provisions. Only the mobile section of the population is at all interested in it, i.e., those who have no fixed abode, or who travel frequently, or whose business activities result in far-flung connections. Hence it is at merchants and manufacturers and most to fall pure speculators, that opportunity will henceforth smile: to start form one point and everywhere set up business, everywhere speculate in land and buy up estates, because the legal forms and conditions of such transactions are everywhere the same. So it is for the purpose of providing elbow-room for this mobile element that we have shaken the solid foundations.[18]

More generally, among conservative German circles, agriculture was exalted "as a symbol of the fatherland and a nursery of national strength and energy."[19] Conservatives declared that the contempt for the peasants of the land was the chief cause of the moral, material, and intellectual decline of Germany. In a publication of the day, the *Konservative Korrespondenz*, it was proclaimed that the rural population "forms an irreplaceable basis not only for our German army but for the entire national power of the *Volk*."[20] These ideas were later propagated by Hitler, who described his fight for Germany as a defense of the German peasantry against the urban centers: "When I fight for the future of Germany peasantry against the urban, I must fight for German soil and I must fight for the German peasant. He renews us, he gives us the people in the cities, he has been the everlasting source for millenniums, and his existence must be secured."[21]

Such sentiments were in no way restricted to Germany. Across Europe, and to a lesser extent the United States, national public figures were promoting extreme nationalism. These late nineteenth-century romantic nationalists exalted "the nation and tradition . . . as the sole moral creative forces, the only ones able to prevent decadence."[22] The reactionary movement was typified by the writings of several intellectuals of the day, from George Sorel, the revolutionary syndicalist in France; to Enrico Corradini, the Italian novelist, essayist, journalist, and political figure. The new breed of conservative intellectuals embraced an ideology that combined myth and nationalism with anti-liberalism. However, there were also differences among them. For proto-fascist thinkers like Sorel and Corradini, the *volk* were not the peasantry. Their brand of anti-democratic, racialized nationalism was blended with Marxism and anarchism. They believed the heart of the nation lay with the working proletariat. Thus, Sorel advocated "anarcho-syndicalism" and Corradini "national-syndicalism," both revolutionary philosophies that held that the workers should combine forces to overturn the liberal-capitalist, democratic, state through industrial unionism, or syndicalism. Many of these nationalists were also heavily influenced by Social Darwinism and "appropriated biological language," which they "applied to politics and all human relations."[23] For example, Alfredo Rocco, a conservative Italian nationalist, saw history as "a perpetual, quasi-Darwinian struggle among nations, with each nation understood as a distinct biological organism."[24]

These ideologies were, thus, the precursors to fascism that would be adopted a few decades later. The revolutionary mobilization of the masses and the quasi-mystical exaltation of the nation would then fully be actualized under the strict guidance of an authoritarian leader.

Twenty-first Century

As in the preceding century, job displacement and economic insecurity led to the defensive nationalist movements of the twenty-first century. There had been a series of financial panics in the 1990s, mostly felt in Latin America and Asia. But it was not until the financial crisis of 2008 that the precariousness of global financial speculation hit Europe and the United States directly. After 2008, a series of Eurosceptic and populist movements gained large followings.

As in the earlier period, the core of the late twentieth-century left-wing movements were internationally organized. One of the more consequential leftist crusades was the "global justice movement" that emerged in the 1990s. It had developed largely in response to the increasing power the World Trade Organization (WTO) was exercising on states' domestic affairs. The WTO had obligated governments around the globe to eliminate protective regulations and tariffs. In Polanyian terms, it was a process of dis-embedding the market from measures established under the Bretton Woods framework.[25] In practical terms, it meant that laborers, farmers, and Indigenous people had no one to protect them from plundering multinational corporations that were swooping in to extract labor and resources. In response, activists in the Global North joined in solidarity with activists in the Global South to force the WTO and its state sponsors to respect national trade unions, environmental laws, and Indigenous rights.

But the global justice movement was surprisingly short-lived. Even before the global economic crisis in 2008, the movement had begun to wane. Arguably, the apex of the global justice movement was the protests held during the 1999 round of WTO negotiations in Seattle. Fifty thousand protestors took to the streets. The "Battle in Seattle" united a diverse collection of civil-society actors: "Environmentalists clad in turtle costumes marched alongside Teamsters, black-clad anarchists alongside the Raging Grannies."[26] The Seattle protests also brought the WTO to the attention of the general public. In fact, after Seattle there was "a wave of other mass protests at meetings of multilateral economic organizations—including the International Monetary Fund (IMF), the World Bank, the World Economic Forum, and the G20—at different sites around the world."[27] And yet, at the next series of WTO negotiations held in Doha in 2001, protests were comparatively anemic. States and civil society groups had already begun focusing on their specific interests. In general, by the early 2000s, internationalism was on the way out, setting the stage for the national populism that was to emerge. The final spur was the 2008 economic crisis. After the global economic crisis had hit, incipient anti-liberal, anti-globalization movements began to develop both in Europe and the United States.

In the United States, the first social protest movements that emerged in the wake of the 2008 economic crisis were not expressly organized against globalization; but they were forerunners to the defensive nationalist movements that came into being a few years later. Anger came to a pitch when, rather than prosecute the top banking executives behind the financial crisis, the United States government bailed out the banks and allowed the company heads to resume control of the same corporate banking conglomerations that had so spectacularly failed under their watch. To add insult to injury, while the country was reeling from the fall-out of the crisis and thousands of Americans were losing their homes, it was reported that these CEOs gave themselves large bonuses a year after their banks failed. Their bonuses had effectively been paid for with taxpayer money, that is through government bail-out funds. This had taken things too far. People took to the streets.

In 2011, the "Occupy-Wall-Street" movement took shape. Its goal was to target the established elite and international finance. Several demonstrators set up camp in Wall Street's Zuccotti Park, which they renamed Liberty Plaza (emulating the successful Egyptian occupation of Tahrir Square that had brought down Hosni Mubarak's government earlier that year). The right also began to mobilize. After the 2008 election of the first African American President, Barack Obama, closely followed by major Republican losses in both houses, a new crop of organizers led an insurgent "Tea Party" movement (so named to connect their movement with the protests on tea taxes that had set off the American Revolution). Like the left-wing Occupy movement, the Tea Party was angered by Wall Street and the political elite's complicit support of these powerful financiers. But reactions on the right included something else in addition: racial animus. Many were galvanized by the false notion that Obama was not an American citizen. The "Birther" movement was indeed central to the Tea Party. At Tea Party protests, it was not uncommon to find protestors carrying placards with racist depictions of the president.

Four years later, during the lead-up to the 2016 presidential election, the scales had fully tipped. Public sentiment had had time to stew and all the themes that had emerged with the Occupy and Tea Party movements came to a head. A palpable disgust with the political establishment had combined with the fear that globalization had run amuck. Populism ran so high that two outsider candidates had unparalleled success: each representing different polls of the defensive nationalist fervor that was beginning to take hold globally. On the left was Bernie Sanders, a long-established socialist who campaigned on the Democratic ticket against the corrupt party establishment, corporate greed, and for returning the power to the people. On the right, the man who had been a central propagator of the myth of "birtherism" and who had little support within the Republican Party establishment, Donald Trump, who proclaimed it was time to "drain the swamp" in Washington, DC.

In Europe, the process was different but parallel. Right-wing nativist parties had been on the upswing since the 1990s. In 1994, Hagtvet described "the spectre of nationalism, re-emerging and attended by a flurry of right-wing extremist behaviour" across Europe.[28] But that proved to be just the beginning. After the 2008 global economic crisis, a large number of populist politicians across Europe were able to expand their base, and in some cases form new parties. In this way, "Parties that were inexistent or largely unknown prior to 2008 were propelled into the political mainstream."[29] In less than two decades, European support for both far-right and far-left parties more than doubled, from 15 percent to in 1992 to almost 35 percent, after 2015.[30] Many of the far-leaning parties were later labeled "Eurosceptic" parties because their supporters were galvanized by their opposition to the Eurozone.

These twenty-first-century defensive nationalist movements were mobilized by similar kinds of rhetoric as their nineteenth-century counterparts. On the left, "the people" were identified primarily as the average worker who had become a pawn in the hands of the wealthy. For example, Alexis Tsipras, the leader of the "Coalition of the Radical Left" party (Syriza), won the Greek Prime Ministership in a major upset in 2012 by declaring: "On one side there are workers and a majority of people and on the other are global capitalists, bankers, profiteers on stock exchanges, the big funds. It's a war between peoples and capitalism."[31] Similarly, Jeremy Corbyn, the socialist who had upset the apple cart in Britain by becoming the leader of the Labour Party in 2015, galvanized the left by campaigning to protect the average man: "Pensioners anxious about health and social care, public servants trying to keep services together. Low and middle earners, self-employed and employed, facing insecurity and squeezed living standards."[32] In the United States, Bernie Sanders, also a socialist running on a major party ticket, emphasized that the body politic was made up of diverse working people and celebrated that diversity during his 2016 presidential campaign:

> our diversity is one of our greatest strengths. Yes, we become stronger when black and whites, Latino, Asian American, Native American, when all of us stand together. Yes, we become stronger when men and women, young and old, gay and straight, native-born and immigrant fight together to create the kind of country we all know we can become.[33]

The rhetoric used by those on the right also paralleled the earlier defensive nationalist movements. As their nineteenth-century counterparts, they too defined the "nation" in terms of "the heartland," or the *volk*. However, the *volk* of today are more likely to be portrayed as the people who live on the periphery of cosmopolitan urban centers (rather than as rural farmers or the "proletariat" per se), particularly people who live in areas that have fared the worst from international trade competition. On both sides of the Atlantic, these peripheral regions had suffered from a "decline in manufacturing employment [that] initiated the deterioration of social and economic conditions . . . exacerbating inequalities between depressed rural areas and small cities and towns, on the one hand, and thriving cities, on the other."[34] In small towns and rural communities across Europe and the United States, a bitterness took hold against urban areas, where finance and the new service industries benefited most from globalization. Those living in the areas blighted by deindustrialization became especially ripe for political mobilization. As Voss explains, "the likelihood for a rise of rightwing populism depends on the relative number of marginalised working-class voters as a result of widened labour market segregation, their mobilising capacity, and above all the generalisability of their experience of socioeconomic decline."[35]

Politicians who were willingly to use divisive language and hate to drum up support quickly recognized they could profit from the situation. New political entrepreneurs emerged who conjured up all kinds of dangers posed by invading hordes of immigrants to the "true" citizenry, the *volk*. Britain's right-wing white-supremacist party, *The National Front*, pronounced on their home page that "National Front represents the indigenous peoples of the United Kingdom,"[36] by which they meant white, Anglo-Saxons. In a 2016 interview, Frauke Petry, a co-chair of the racist and xenophobic right-wing party, Alternative for Germany (AfD), openly called for revaluing the term "*völkisch*." Treating such a term neutrally was seen by most Germans as outrageous. The adjective had no active meaning apart from the late nineteenth-century movement that was "chauvinistically nationalist, anti-democratic, authoritarian, anti-Semitic, militaristic and racist."[37] This claim was therefore shocking to the larger society in Germany, where for half a century people had taken great pains to condemn Nazism. In a 2010 speech, Geert Wilders, the leader of the radical-right Party for Freedom (PVV) in the Netherlands, contrasted the liberal establishment's support of Islamic migration with the needs of the true Dutch, "What this cabinet was especially good at was ramping up mass immigration, the support of Islamisation and hollowing out the Dutch character of the Netherlands."[38] Similar pronouncements were made by nativist leaders across Europe, from Italy, France, Hungary, and Spain, as well as others.

Less directly, but with equal force, Trump in his inauguration speech at the 2015 Republican Convention invoked the plight of the *volk* when he spoke of "the forgotten men and women of our country"; the "wounded American families [who] have been alone." These "forgotten country-men" Trump described as "the laid-off factory workers, and the communities crushed by our horrible and unfair trade deals . . . People who work hard but no longer have a voice." Trump contrasted the "forgotten Americans" victimized by globalizing forces, with inner-city populations. The latter he portrayed as willfully idle, the "58% of African American youth are not employed. 2 million more Latinos are in poverty today than when the [Barak Obama] took his oath of office less than eight years ago. Another 14 million people have left the workforce entirely."[39] In other words, Trump made clear who the true American *volk* were, as well as who they were threatened by.

In general, nativist rhetoric became more commonplace during the 2010s. Extreme ideologies no longer had to hide in dark, faraway corners. The small, isolated far-right factions of the 1990s had grown in numbers, gained in political strength, and were now able to come out in full daylight and be accepted into the mainstream.

State Protectionism

The rediscovery of national society was as much a state process as it was a civil society movement. As Polanyi observed, one of the first manifestations of the "double movement" was protectionist policies. In both periods, protectionism materialized just when international integration and the new global economy were beginning to emerge. In fact, they came in tandem.

Nineteenth Century

It did not take long to recognize that global liberalism posed a threat to industry, farmers, and workers. Almost as soon as international trade had been liberalized, anti-trade tariffs, particularly of grain, were instituted across Europe in the late 1870s and 1880s.[40] By 1890, even the United States had adopted stringent protectionist policies.

In Europe, open trade was especially harmful to the interests of the landed nobility and large industrialists who were powerful enough to pressure their governments to enact legislative protections. Two of the first countries to erect trade barriers had actually been early adopters of the new free-trade agreements: Germany and Italy. As early as 1851, the Piedmontese government in Italy began to lower tariffs and liberalize their trade policies. By 1863 the kingdom had even signed a free-trade agreement with France.[41] Similarly, in the early 1870s, Otto von Bismarck established the new German Reich "on free trade principles and low tariffs."[42]

However, the "grain invasion" from the United States provoked a reversion to protectionism. As Rodrik explains:

> The transport revolutions and tariffs resulted in an influx of grains from the New World and sharply lower prices. Everywhere on the Continent agricultural interests clamored for protection, often making common cause with industrialists who were reeling under competition from the more advanced British producers (and increasingly from American exporters too) onward.[43]

By 1878 and 1879, Italy and Germany, respectively, adopted tariffs to protect their landed nobility and industrialists. In Germany, the flood of American wheat on the global market hastened the end of the "golden age of German agriculture, which began in the 1830s."[44] "Stagnating production, high costs, and declining prices produced an agrarian crisis in Germany of serious proportions."[45] The *junkers*, Germany's landed elite and the industrialists began to clamor for something to be done. Bismark, who had never been ideologically committed to open trade, reversed himself. Germany abandoned free trade and introduced tariffs on grain, pig iron, and livestock.[46] Thus, by the end of the seventies, "the chancellor Otto von Bismarck shifted to an authoritarian and protectionist domestic policy, which was heralded by the Anti-Socialist Law of 1878 and the tariff act of 1879."[47]

The Italian government faced similar forms of destabilization as wheat prices dropped. In the 1880s, tariffs were dramatically increased on grain. So devoted were they to these protectionist policies that by 1913 the Italian government was levying a "roughly 40% ad valorem tariff on wheat."[48] In fact, comparable protectionist responses to laissez-faire trade were embraced across Europe. France and Sweden reimposed tariffs in the 1880s; Russia increased grain protections in 1877 and again in the mid-1880s; and Austria-Hungary and Spain adopted protectionist policies in the 1870s and 1880s.[49] "Of the major Western European powers, only Britain adhered to free trade principles."[50,51]

In the United States, "economic nationalism [also] prevailed."[52] In the initial period after the Civil War, the United States had fully embraced the new laissez-faire ideology. Successive governments looked beyond the home market to export the country's growing agricultural and manufacturing surpluses. However, as the deleterious effects of international capitalism became more pronounced, pressure mounted for the government to institute tariff reforms. After a decade of debates, "economic nationalism visibly manifested itself in 1890 with the passage of the highly protective McKinley Tariff."[53] The McKinley Tariff was "the era's highest tariff."[54] The Act mandated that tariffs be placed on most imports, some as high as 49.5 percent. The passage of the Act "sent political–economic shockwaves throughout the globe, from England to Australia, and sparked corresponding global demands for protectionist retaliation."[55] Even in Britain, the center of the "liberal creed," "the McKinley Tariff's policies helped to call into question Britain's liberal, free trade, global empire by drumming up support for an imperial, protectionist, preferential Greater Britain."[56]

Twentieth Century

A similar process evolved in the twentieth century. Almost as soon as globalization began, protectionism emerged. Economic interdependence and expanding financial speculation left national economies vulnerable. These processes caused major economic crises, from the oil shocks of the 1970s to the nearly ruinous financial crisis of 2008. Facing increased political pressure, even the most dogmatic supporters of free trade adopted protectionist policies.

During the postwar era, laissez-faire economics was largely considered a discredited theory of bygone years. After the terrible market crash of 1929, the dominant economic model was that of the prominent British economist John Maynard Keynes. Keynes had argued that markets were not perfectly self-adjusting and that, therefore, governments had to invest in the economy to ensure full employment and to buffer society from inevitable market downturns. But the global economic recession in the 1970s eroded trust in government's ability to repair the economy. Keynesianism lost favor in many circles. A new liberal ideology, neo-liberalism, that had been on the periphery of the academic world gathered an increasing number of adherents. The followers of this new brand of liberalism held an even more stringent conception of free-market liberalism. Laissez-faire capitalism was deemed to be inextricably linked to political freedom and economic individualism. This strain of liberalism was exemplified by the writings of staunch anti-communists, such as Josef Hayek's treatise on economic theory, *The Road to Serfdom*;[57] and Ayn Rand's novel, *Atlas Shrugged*.[58]

Thus, by the late 1980s a new liberal economic order had come into being. For the second time in history, there was a broad consensus in favor of freer trade. Using arguments that strongly echoed Herbert Spencer's in the nineteenth century (see Chapter 3), the proponents of the new economic theory depicted globalization "as a spontaneous and agentless economic process, propelled by the ingenuity of markets and the magic of the invisible hand."[59] International integration of markets for goods and capital was promoted as an end in itself. The United States was "the primary driver of neoliberal economic order restructuring the economy globally."[60] With the political and economic might of America and to a lesser extent the European Union, "Domestic economic management was to become subservient to international trade and finance rather than the other way around."[61] By the 1990s, the WTO had reintroduced "a significant expansion in supranational authority."[62]

Yet, just as global finance was beginning to overshadow domestic agendas, several countries instituted protectionist tariffs. In fact, "the 'deep integration' bargain reflected in WTO treaties came into question almost as soon as the ink was dry."[63] It became rapidly apparent to those involved in major exporting industries—from automobiles to steel and rubber to machinery—that they were facing much more competition in both inter-national and domestic markets. Almost as quickly as free-trade treaties had been agreed upon, both labor and capital "switched to protectionism." Thus, along with the "enthusiasm toward a deepening of international economic integration," there developed the fear "that economic integration had gone quite far enough."[64]

Hence, during the 1980s, "the GATT regime underwent a metamorphosis which cannot be simply understood as an evolution of the regime within the embedded liberal normative texture."[65] As Rodrik explains, "GATT's purpose was never to maximize free trade. It was to achieve the maximum amount of trade compatible with different nations doing their own thing."[66] The upshot was twofold. On the one hand, weak, developing countries were forced to radically liberalize their struggling economies. They were directed to elim-inate any and all labor and environmental protections, open themselves to foreign direct investment, sell off government owned industries (including public utilities) to private owners, and even roll back government-funded education and healthcare. On the other hand, governments in the advanced nations hypocritically evaded opening their own markets and built bulwarks against facing risks from international competition.[67]

America, the country that perhaps more than any other pushed for de-veloping countries to open their markets, was among those that fought the hardest to protect its steel, textiles, footwear, and clothing producers.[68] This protectionist posture even seeped into popular culture. As early as 1975, the American International Ladies Garment Workers Union (ILGU) launched a television campaign that resuscitated the old union jingle "Look for the Union Label" to promote the purchasing of products made by American union workers rather than cheaper goods made over-seas. Competition from Japanese automobile manufacturers, who were producing cheaper, fuel-efficient cars, brought into being a new phase of Japan bashing. American politicians vilified Japanese manufactures and exhorted Americans to buy products made in the United States. Anti-Japanese sentiment reached such a pitch that in 1983 two white auto workers who mistook a young man out celebrating his birthday, Vincent Chin, for being Japanese, savagely beat him to death. When the attackers pled guilty to Chin's murder, the judge only sentenced them to serve three years' probation and ordered them to pay a $3,000 fine. They were given no jail time. This incident proved to be a portent of the nativism that was to be widely embraced a few decades later.

Inequality and the Global Enemy

During both these periods, the dominant economic power of the day, Britain in the nineteenth century and the United States in the twentieth, promoted a liberal economic agenda that maximized gains to the wealthy. As a consequence, in both periods of modern globalization, inequality grew sharply. Increasing inequities fueled growing defensive nationalist movements. Left- and right-wing defensive nationalists charged that the painful restructuring of the economy was guided by nefarious global financial forces working in cahoots with corrupt domestic elites. However, each side characterized these global players differently. For leftists, the sinister global force was high finance, industry, and billionaire capitalists; for the nativists, the malevolent power was particular ethnic groups, especially those associated with finance or opposing nations.

Nineteenth Century

The nineteenth century infamously came to be known as the age of the "Robber Barons." Indeed, wealth concentration spiked between 1870 and 1900 (see Figure 10.1). While an increasing number of workers were forced into punishing factory jobs and miserable slums. the great captains of industry, like Carnegie and Rockefeller, and their financiers, such as the Rothschilds in London, the Périere brothers in France, and J. P. Morgan in the United States, accumulated spectacular fortunes. Henry George, the popular economist of the day, described the duality of the age:

> the tendency of what we call material progress is in nowise to improve the condition of the lowest class in the essentials of healthy, happy human life. Nay, more, that it is still further to depress the condition of the lowest class . . . between top and bottom. It is as though an immense wedge were being forced, not underneath society, but through society. Those who are above the point of separation are elevated, but those who are below are crushed down.[69]

In reaction, left-wing defensive nationalist movements of the era emphasized the predatory nature of international capitalism. Mary Elizabeth Lease, who helped organize the Kansas People's Party, the first populist party

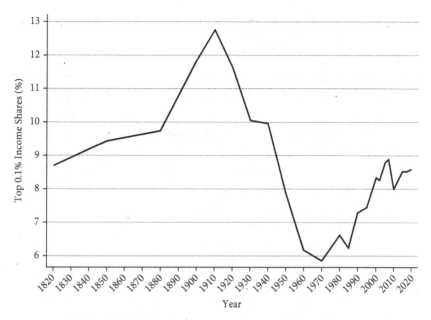

Figure 10.1 Top 0.1 percent Income Shares (%), 1820–2020

Source: "Global Income Inequality 1820–2020: The Persistence and Mutation of Extreme Inequality,"
Lucas Chancel and Thomas Piketty (2021), July 5, 2021, wid.world/longrun.

in the United States, declared that "Wall Street owns the country. It is no
longer a government of the people, by the people, and for the people, but
a government of Wall Street, by Wall Street, and for Wall Street. The great
common people of this country are slaves, and monopoly is the master."[70]
Similarly, the Omaha Platform of the People's Party argued that railroad
magnates and great industrialists were the enemies of the people, whose
ability to steal the "fruits of the toil of millions" had bred "two great classes—
tramps and millionaires."[71] William Jennings Bryan in his celebrated Cross
of Gold Speech proclaimed, "What we need is an Andrew Jackson to stand,
as Jackson stood, against the encroachments of organized wealth."[72] He
described the populists as in a battle waged between "the idle holders of
idle capital" and "the struggling masses, who produce the wealth and pay
the taxes of the country."[73] A few decades later, Teddy Roosevelt, adopting
some of the positions outlined by the populist parties, made a speech on
"New Nationalism" in 1910. The speech centered on the need to free government "from the sinister influence or control of special interests" and to
overcome the "unfair money-getting [that] has tended to create a small class

of enormously wealthy and economically powerful men, whose chief object is to hold and increase their power."[74]

In contrast, right-wing defensive nationalism defined the problem in terms of outsider ethnic groups. In the late nineteenth century, this manifest as a deep-seated anti-Semitism that took hold of Europe. Jews became the embodiment of every evil associated with modernity, especially the modern economy in which wealth in money had superseded wealth based on land ownership. Jews had long been viewed "contemptuously as the personification of the money-grubbing bourgeois, petty, cowardly, selfish, and materialistic," but as nationalism gained prominence, anti-Semitism became "infused with the more traditional nationalist criticism that Jews were prime exponents of internationalism. Because Jews were scattered throughout the world and supposedly gave primary allegiance to their religion which transcended individual nation-states, they could never be considered loyal citizens of a single state."[75]

This intensified fear of the threat the Jewish populations posed to European nations manifested in hundreds of pamphlets, newspaper articles, books, and treatises all weighing in on the "Jewish Question." The Jewish Question was a debate over how to handle these rootless strangers threatening Europe. People debated about whether the Jewish population should be resettled, deported, or assimilated. The Jewish Question became a hallmark of the politics of the age and reflected in literary circles. In the 1850s, the great German composer Richard Wagner carped that "According to the present constitution of this world, the Jew in truth is already more than emancipate: he rules, and will rule, so long as Money remains the power before which all our doings and our dealings lose their force."[76] A couple of decades later, Houston Stewart Chamberlain, the British proto-fascist living in Germany, warned that the ultimate aim of the Jew was to create a situation where "there would be in Europe only a single people of pure race, the Jews, all the rest would be a herd of pseudo-Hebraic mestizos, a people beyond all doubt degenerate physically, mentally and morally."[77]

These reactionary, racialized sentiments propelled right-wing defensive nationalist movements. In France, the "Antisemitic League of France" (*Ligue antisémitique de France*) was founded in 1889. The league soon modified its name to National Antisemitic League of France (*Ligue nationale antisémitique de France*), clearly indicating its nationalist aspirations. The league spread anti-Semitic propaganda as well as diatribes against Masons and Communists (international organizations that it was believed the Jews were running). They became particularly active during the Dreyfus Affair. In Germany, the *Alldeutscher Verband* (Pan-German Party) formed in 1891. Along with its opposition to liberalism and social democracy, the party assailed "Jewish capitalism."

Such anti-Semitic diatribes stand in contrast to left-wing movements that focused on the evils of the *capitalist class*. William Jennings Bryan actually took pains to underscore that "We are not attacking a race, we are attacking greed and avarice, which know neither race nor religion. I do not know of any class of our people who, by reason of their history, can better sympathize with the struggling masses in this campaign than can the Hebrew race."[78] And yet, these right/left-wing distinctions are not hard and fast. Some American populists also blended anti-Semitism with their attacks on global capital. "Several prominent Populist authors named the House of Rothschild as the reason for agrarian misery. Still others told of scheming, devious, in-bred, commercial Jews. Mary E. Lease labeled President Grover Cleveland 'the agent of Jewish bankers and British gold.'"[79]

Twentieth Century

In the second period of modern globalization, wealth concentration and in-equality returned to levels not seen since the late nineteenth century.[80] Neo-liberal policies were at the heart of the change. The policies championed in the 1980s were designed to remove any regulatory framework that could hinder business. They also worked to undermine the social welfare systems that had been put in place in most countries following World War II. One of the central effects of the neo-liberal turn was a dramatic upsurge in wealth inequality across the advanced economies, and most particularly in the United States.

By the 2010s, wealth concentration, measured as the ratio of private wealth to national income, returned "to the high values observed in the late-nineteenth century, which were as high as 600–700%"[81] (see Figure 10.2). Like the Robber Barons who preceded them, most of this wealth was amassed by the new captains of industry—founders of today's tech giants. Indeed, ac-cording to *Forbes Magazine*'s 2021 rankings, eight of today's top ten richest people were owners of mega-tech companies—Jeff Bezos, Bill Gates, Mark Zuckerberg, Larry Elson, Steve Ballmer, Elon Musk, Larry Page, and Sergey Brin.[82]

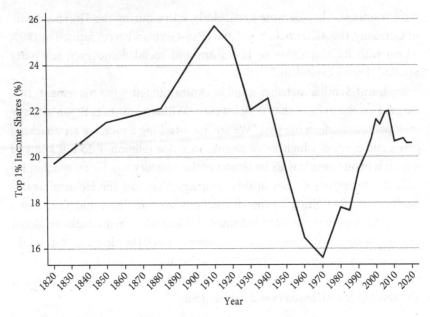

Figure 10.2 Top 1 percent Income Shares (%), 1820–2020
Source: "Global income inequality 1820–2020: The Persistence and Mutation of Extreme Inequality," Lucas Chancel and Thomas Piketty (2021), July 5, 2021, wid.world/longrun.

Twenty-first-century formulations of left-wing defensive nationalism echoed those of the earlier American populists. Like their earlier counterparts, leftists put the blame for economic dysfunctions on powerful corporate concerns and global finance. Bernie Sanders in a 2016 speech declared, "Our trade deals were written by large multinational corporations for multinational corporations. Trade is a good thing. But we need a trade policy that works for working families, not just large corporations."[83] A centerpiece of Jeremy Corbyn's Labour Party manifesto, issued in November 2019, was ending the "tax and cheat" culture of multinational corporations: "Huge multinational companies often act as if the rules we all live by don't apply to them. They use loopholes to claim they don't owe tax and cynically push their workers to the limit."[84] The socialist candidate in the French 2012 presidential election put it most succinctly, "*Mon véritable adversaire, c'est le monde de la finance.*"[85]

For the left, nefarious global capitalism was also associated with particular individuals who control inordinate amounts of wealth and corporate power. Just as J. P. Morgan came to symbolize ill-gotten gain for leftists during the *fin de siècle*, Jeremy Corbyn declared that "the system is rigged for the rich. So

thanks for making that clear, Mr Murdoch."[86] In his General Election campaign speech on May 9, 2017, Corbyn focused on the fact that "In the last year,
Britain's 1,000 richest people have seen their wealth rise by 14 per cent to £658
billion—that's nearly six times the budget of our NHS."[87] In the same vein,
Bernie Sanders in a 2016 speech declared that "it is not acceptable, and it is not
sustainable that the top 1/10th of 1 percent now owns almost as much wealth
as the bottom 90 percent. Or that the top 1 percent in recent years has earned
85 percent of all new income. That is unacceptable. That must change."[88]

For those on the right, however, like late nineteenth-century defensive
nationalists, the global enemy was neither global capital, nor industry, nor
wealthy individuals but specific *ethno-national* groups who menace the nation. The enemy was *embodied* in an opposing national/cultural group.
Victor Orbán, the Hungarian prime minister since 2010 and former president of the conservative party Fidesz, spread "imagery of powerful Jewish
financiers scheming to control the world."[89] In Italy, Elio Lannutti, a Five
Star senator, "suggested on twitter in January [2019] that Jews controlled the
world banking system, and quoted the anti-Semitic 'Protocols of the Elders of
Zion.' "[90] Yet, cultural classifications of the global enemy also manifested more
subtlety. The far-right leader of Hungary, Gabor explained that the Hungarian
nativist party, "The Movement for a Better Hungary" (*Jobbik)*, opposed global
capitalism, "and its three main representatives—the USA, the EU and Israel—
from the pedestal of universal human values."[91] And whereas Sanders and
Corbyn saw multinational corporations as the malign international influence
undermining the economy and working people, President Trump presented
China as the nemesis hurting Americans, whether through "their devastating
currency manipulation,"[92] or their pernicious spread of the Coronavirus.[93]

However, just as a century ago, these left/right distinctions do not always
hold. For example, anti-Semitism has been on the rise with left-wing defensive nationalist leaders as well. An infamous example is Gerard Filoche, a
member of France's Socialist Party national bureau, who was expelled from
the party in 2017 for tweeting an image with anti-Semitic overtones.[94]

Conclusion

The paralellels between the two periods are striking. In both eras, economic,
demographic, and political changes ushered in a period of national populist
fervor, which expressed itself on both ends of the political spectrum.

In the late nineteenth century, leftist-populist parties in America responded to radical displacements by rallying honest farmers and workers, "the people," to fight against the machinations of heartless bankers and industrialists who were privileging international finance over the national economy. In Europe, the dislocations caused by modernity produced an extreme form of nativism. Fear and hatred was targeted primarily against ethnic-others who were believed to have invaded and polluted the "heartland" and who it was feared were poised to overtake it.

In the twenty-first century, the problems caused by globalization once againg engendered a national populist backlash. On the left, national populists oppose the established system, be it establishment parties or international organizations, which are seen to be nothing more than the mouth pieces of the wealthy and multinational corporations. On the right, the fear of changing times has merged with a nativist fear of white genocide and the danger of immigrant hordes.

Thus, in both periods, people threatened by social and economic displacements seemed to have spontaneously moved in parallel directions. In the United States and Europe, citizens on both the right and the left banned together to shield their ways of life from the ravages the liberal order had set into motion. It could be said that national societies rediscovered themselves in their opposition to globalization. Across the developed world, economic nationalism took center stage.

Yet, along with economic nationalism, the rhetoric of defensive nationalism pushed some on the right closer and closer towards fascism. In both eras, the emergence of proto-fascist movements began to menace the very nations they were striving to save.

11

The Turn Inward

Nativism and Fascism

At the turn of the century in both epochs, societies were facing a maelstrom of change. In this period of extraordinary transition, political entrepreneurs, or "demagogues," were able to capitalize on escalating anti-immigration sentiment, angst caused by international terrorist violence, and fear of economic decline. Nativism became widespread in right-wing circles, but also gained ground within some segments of the left. The fomenting jingoism resonated most especially with people who were not benefiting from the modern economy and whose standard of living was most in jeopardy.

At the same time, right-wing political leaders and activists were able to foment anger over changes occurring more broadly in society. In both eras, political liberalism had been gaining ground and secularism was on the rise. Liberal social movements were winning political rights for marginalized groups and working to end gender discrimination. However, these liberal reforms were not embraced by all. Among certain segments of the population, there developed a growing resentment over what many experienced as an assault on the traditional family order and an encroachment on long-accepted customs of their communities. For some, only a complete rejection of political liberalism and an embrace of authoritarian nationalism could save the nation from what they perceived to be its catastrophic decline. The world was witnessing the early signs of fascism.

Anti-Immigrant Backlash

Nineteenth Century

In the latter decades of the nineteenth century, amid global economic crises, unpredictable anarchist bombings, serial assassinations of heads of states, and with an unprecedented number of immigrants converging on overcrowded

Defensive Nationalism. B. S. Rabinowitz, Oxford University Press. © Oxford University Press 2023.
DOI: 10.1093/oso/9780197672037.003.0012

cities, there developed anti-immigrant backlashes across Europe and the United States. Prejudicial policies and vitriolic rhetoric spiked. Nativism had arrived.

While European socialists were broadly supportive of workers of all stripes, the left-wing People's Parties in the United States, which were concentrated in the Midwest and the South and were predominantly concerned with protecting the agrarian economy, vociferously opposed immigration. At their first national convention, the Omaha People's Party drew up their party platform. In it, they condemned "the fallacy of protecting American labor under the present system, which opens our ports to the pauper and criminal classes of the world and crowds out our wage-earners." The platform went on to demand that "all lands now owned by aliens should be reclaimed by the government and held for actual settlers only."[1]

In the West, the "army" of unemployed workers that Coxey had raised to march on Washington shared the same vision. They were as supportive of the silver movement as they were of anti-Chinese and anti-Japanese immigration laws. In an 1894 interview with a laid-off laborer in Portland who was a member of the "Coxey Army," Adjutant R. M. Weed, made these sentiments clear: "We shall ask Congress to coin the silver seigniorage in the United States Treasury; to enact a law restricting all foreign immigration for the period of 10 years at least, and to furnish the unemployed labor on public works."[2] The anti-immigrant strain ran so deep within the American radical left that as late as 1915, Lenin denounced the "jingo-socialism" championed by "the opportunist leaders of the S.P. [Socialist Party] in America, who are in favor of restrictions of the immigration of Chinese and Japanese workers."[3]

The response against foreign penetration was even more virulent for those on the right. Where on the left, anti-immigration demands were largely framed in terms of economic competition, on the right, alien populations were opposed because the danger they presented was seen to be nothing short of the destruction of the national race. The core of these fears was directed against Jewish populations across Europe.

In the 1850s, Gobineau had ascribed "the degeneration of a society to the dilution by intermarriage and ensuing degradation of the pure blood of its founders."[4] These concerns took political form in 1890s with the Antisemitic League of France and the Pan-German League *Alldeutscher Verband* (ADV). The latter openly called for prohibitions against breeding with "inferior races" like the Jews and Slavs to ensure German racial hygiene. This ideology reached its apotheosis in the German *völkisch* movement. The *völkisch* movement propagated a bio-mystical version of racial nationalism. "Rootedness" was an essential component of their ideology, which asserted that there was an eternal national connection between the people, the land, and the individual. This rootedness was symbolized by the union of "blood and soil" and represented the organic connection between the body of the people and the native land. Anti-Semitism was also at the core of this movement. For, "with its metaphysics of eternal national rootedness, its symbolism of blood and soil, its antiurban, antiliberal bias . . . who better fitted the requisite negative stereotype of rootlessness and alienness, of liberalism, socialism and capitalism"[5] than the Jew.

The movement against the Jews was not restricted to Germany and France. In Romania, over two hundred anti-Semitic laws were passed between 1879 and 1913. In addition to legally excluding Jews from rights and privileges of the state, the Romanian government conducted a series of expulsions of Jews in 1881, particularly journalists or intellectuals critical of the government. This treatment culminated in the mass emigration of Romanian Jewry.[6] More infamously, in Russia, following the assassination of Tzar Alexander II by "socialist terrorists," anti-Jewish "pogroms" (organized ethnic massacres) spread like an epidemic from one village to another, in a manner never before seen.[7] In general, even where actions against Jewish populations did not include such devastating violence, the alienness of "the Jew" became a central trope in defensive nationalist discourses of the era.

Twenty-first Century

As in the preceding century, the turn of the twentieth century was a time of high migration and anti-immigrant backlashes. Sensationalized news, global terror threats, and an increasing sense of economic scarcity worked together to stoke the fires of nativism.

In the 2010s, immigration pressures intensified across Europe. With war raging in Syria, Iraq, and Afghanistan, the European migrant crisis came to a zenith in 2015: 1.3 million people streamed into Europe requesting asylum. To give a sense of the magnitude of the migrations, the number of asylum seekers who applied in that one year accounted for about one-tenth of all applications that had been received by EU countries as well as Norway and Switzerland for the past thirty years![8] Euroskeptic parties exploited the fear that these migrations engendered, helping them to achieve previously unimaginable gains. In some instances, the increase in support for far-right and far-left Euroskeptic parties was quite astounding. For example, the far-right wing "Danish People's Party" jumped from 13.8 percent in 2007 to a commanding 21.1 percent in 2015; the Polish "Law and Justice" party garnered a walloping 37.6 of the vote share.[9] The Swedish Democrats, which "before 2006 . . . was more or less out of public view and perceived as a small movement with neo-Nazi flourishes," but over the next decade the party's popularity "surged both in Riksdag seats and in public opinion polls" and by 2014, they were "the third largest party in parliament."[10]

Exploiting xenophobic prejudices and resentments became a fundamental tool for almost all radical right-wing political organizations. Across the far right, "nativist parties, such as France's Front National, the British National Party, the Dutch Freedom Party, Sweden's Democrats, and Greece's Golden Dawn, place immigration and immigrants in the focus of their political narrative."[11] Similarly, Trump, in his 2016 acceptance speech at the Republican Convention recounted stories of "children [who] were killed by illegal immigrants" and warning about the "violence spilling across our border"[12] to galvanize political support. In Hungary, the far-right party, *Jobbik*, capitalized "on the widespread discontent at the presence of the ethnic Roma populations."[13] The party went so far as to "set up the Hungarian Guard," whose members dressed in Nazi-like uniforms and marched in villages and towns containing a relatively high ethnic Roma population."[14]

Fear of specific immigrant groups was often expressed in very concrete terms. One could say that the embodiment of the enemy had been accompanied by the embodiment of the threat. Donald Trump infamously referred to illegal immigrants as rapists and murders.[15] The same rhetoric was used by right-wing leaders across Europe. In 2017, the Swedish far-right party distributed a leaflet claiming that decades of mass immigration had brought to Sweden all kinds of illegal, violent problems, "Due to decades of mass immigration, our previously safe country is not safe any more [sic]. Not only do we have a very high number of shootings and gang-related violence . . . but Sweden now has the second highest number of rape reports in the entire world."[16] In like manner, in February 2017, the former leader of the Swedish far-right party *Ukip*, Nigel Farage, claimed in a radio interview that since large numbers of refugees arrived in Sweden, the country had seen a "dramatic rise in sexual crime and its southern port city of Malmo—the third largest city in the country—had become Europe's and possibly the world's 'rape capital.' "[17] The leader of Italy's Fascist Party, the Leg, explained in a television interview that "For me, the problem is the thousands of illegal immigrants stealing, raping and dealing drugs."[18]

But for the nativist, the danger posed by immigration goes far beyond economic and social disruptions. The core fear is nothing short of group extinction. Fear of miscegenation and white genocide once again became a rallying cry for right-wing nativists, echoing the racist xenophobia of the late nineteenth century. David Duke warned in 2004 that because of the "relentless and systematic destruction of the European genotype," the white race "faces a world-wide genetic catastrophe. There is only one word that can describe it: genocide."[19] The extreme right-wing party in England, the British National Front, before being forced to take down their website, asserted that "Multiracialism has been a disaster for Britain—only a policy that enforces a total ban on immigration and the humane repatriation of all immigrants and their descendants to their ancestral homelands can save this country from chaos."[20] The German right-wing party, the AfD, portrayed the influx of refugees after September 2015, "as an 'invasion' meant to destroy Germany."[21] And the leader of the radical-right Party for Freedom (PVV) in the Netherlands, Geert Wilders, underscored that "Our history compels us to fight a battle that is not an option but a necessity. After all this is a battle for the [. . .] survival of the Netherlands as a recognisable nation."[22]

By 2022, concerns about white genocide had actually become mainstream in American politics, when the Republican Party openly embraced the "Great Replacement" theory. The Great Replacement theory holds that white people are being replaced by immigrants, Muslims, and other people of color in their "home" countries, and often blames Jews for orchestrating these demographic changes. As the Southern Poverty Law Center explains, "paranoid narratives of 'white extinction' have appeared to exist only on a radical fringe of racist political movements," but it is only in recent times that elected officials in high office overtly propagate such messages.[23] In its themes, the Great Replacement Theory echoes the sentiments of the proto-fascists in Europe who believed the Jews to be behind "the disintegrating forces of modern materialism, libertarianism, and internationalism," threatening the very existence of Europe.[24]

However, the contemporary relationship with anti-Semitism and white nationalism is one that has become complicated in the twenty-first century. While many white nationalists believe in conspiracy theories about "international Jewry," as was witnessed in the Charlotte March of 2017 when it was chanted "Jews will not replace us," far-right parties have also sought to join forces with far-right Israeli leaders, in their fight against Muslims and immigrants. Georgetown University's fact sheet on the Swedish far-right party, The Sweden Democrats, explains this complicated relationship:

> The Sweden Democrats are informally connected with other far-right European parties. In December 2010, SD co-signed the "Jerusalem Declaration" along with the Austrian Freedom Party (Freiheitliche Partei Österreichs, FPÖ), Belgium's Flemish Interest (Vlaams Belang, VB), and Germany's Freedom Party (Die Freiheit), as part of a pan-European, far-right delegation to Israel. An example of far-right parties in Europe attempting to rebrand their Nazi and anti-Semitic origins while adopting anti-Muslim and anti-immigration rhetoric and policies, the delegation met with other far-right Israeli politicians to defend "Western civilization" and "Judeo-Christian cultural values" from "a new global totalitarian threat: fundamentalist Islam."[25]

For left-wing defensive nationalists, even though they almost uniformly denounce xenophobic depictions of foreigners, the goal of protecting national workers has made unchecked immigration an issue for several. Jeremy Corbyn in 2017 opposed "the wholesale importation of underpaid workers from central Europe in order to destroy [British labor] conditions."[26] Bernie Sanders fought the 2007 guest-worker bill, arguing that bringing "many hundreds of thousands of lower-wage workers into this country will only make a bad situation even worse."[27] And in 2019, Prime Minister Mette Frederiksen, leader of Denmark's Social Democrats, ran on a leftist/anti-immigration platform. She won mass support by asserting that "the price of unregulated globalisation, mass immigration and the free movement of labour is paid for by the lower classes."[28]

Anti-Liberalism and Anti-Rationalism

Finally, in both turn-of-the-century eras, it was not anticipated that the extension of rights, equality, and secularism would threaten traditional, religious communities so much that it would produce a reactionary crusade against political liberalism. But that is just what happened. The cosmopolitan view of an increasingly mobile and culturally blended world was feared by many and easily used by right-wing defensive nationalist leaders to inculcate a sense of siege among the *volk*.

Nineteenth Century

In the nineteenth century, a revolutionary intellectual movement was gestating that was the antithesis of liberalism and individualism. It was an ideological "rebellion against 'the rationalist individualism of liberal society' and the new industrial society."[29] Its followers decried social mobility and democratic equality. They craved the simplicity of the traditional agrarian world, exalting "the nation" over cosmopolitan society. This Counter Enlightenment movement had begun earlier, in the late eighteenth century. Perhaps the best-known reactionary conservative is Edmund Burke, who wrote one of the most famous treatises against the French Revolution, *Reflections on the Revolution*, published in 1790. Burke's critiques were adopted by conservative groups across Europe over the course of the next century. But it was not until the 1870s that "a new antipositivist, antirationalist culture" emerged.[30] Thereafter, "the rejection of the Enlightenment and the French Revolution exploded."[31]

The anti-liberal movement of the late 1800s built off the ideas of Romanticism developed in the first half of the century. Romantic poets, novelists, and painters of the early nineteenth century had sought to reinvest the world with a sense of "awe" for the natural world and an appreciation for the beauty of the irrationality of love. Against the cold scientific rationalism of the Enlightenment, they called for a "return to Nature" and propagated a "cult of authenticity."[32] By the 1870s, the rejection of Enlightenment rationalism and embrace of nature had morphed into a deeply conservative, *political* movement. Conservative romantics rejected the notion that people were abstractly equal. In nature, there was no such thing as abstract humanity and, therefore, no such thing as the universal Rights of Man as had been proclaimed by the French. It was contrary to nature to hold that everyone was equal and, therefore, it would be unethical to decree that everyone had equal rights. People were naturally divided by their place in society, whether peasants and the aristocracy, or women and men. Every society had a traditional, natural order; and each nation was a unique cultural collective that had to be celebrated and preserved as one would an endangered species. Romantic conservatism was thus an expressly cultural nationalist movement.

This ideological rebellion was largely an elitist movement shaped by right-wing intellectuals. The new right-wing elites were "nationalist, populist and anti-democratic"; they "legitimized and gave respectability to the violent downfall of the liberal order, as well as supplying the conceptual framework for the take off of fascism."[33] Peter Pulzer encapsulates the views held by these late-century anti-enlightenment groups:

> the later Romantic despised Rationalism and the Enlightenment. He detected the sin of intellectual arrogance in it. He championed intuition against analysis, imagination against empiricism, faith against the intellect, and history against science. He rejected the individualism and cosmopolitanism of the preceding generation which seemed to overemphasize the happiness of the individual.[34]

The *völkisch* movements that developed in Germany at the end of the nineteenth century were among those expressly positioned in opposition to France's proclamation of the rights of man. These "Anti-Revolutionaries" fought "against the spirt of the French Revolution with its radical-democratic ideas about the sovereignty of the people."[35] What mattered was not "abstract" or "artificial" legal citizenship but rather biology and race.[36] Disdaining Enlightenment rationalism, they embraced mysticism and cultural truths. George Mosse explains that "The basic mood of the ideology is well summarized by the distinction between Culture and Civilization ... The acceptance of Culture and the rejection of Civilization meant for many people an end to alienation from their society."[37] Yet, those who advocated for a return to culture and the authentic peasant life, "did not come for the lower classes of the population. On the contrary, they were men and women who wanted to maintain their property and their superior status."[38]

Similar conservative Romantic movements were stirring across Europe. In France, in 1871, Ernest Renan wrote his *Reforme intellectuelle et morale de la France*, "a pamphlet violently attacking the French Enlightenment," in which he argued that the French Revolution and democracy were "responsible for the French decadence."[39] Other leading French rightists, such as "[Maurice] Barrès, [Georges] Sorel, [and Gustave] Le Bon, wrote diatribes against 'the rationalist individualism of liberal society' and the new industrial society."[40] Using the same lexicon, Italian conservatives "wrote against the postulates upon which liberalism and democracy were based."[41] The Italian nationalist political figure Enrico Corradini "opposed all facets of Enlightenment culture."[42] This new school of Italian thought was typified by the writings of Gaetano Mosca, who is credited with originating the Theory of Elitism, which posited that elites were naturally superior. Even in the Netherlands, the Anti-Revolutionary Party (*Anti-Revolutionaire Partij*, ARP), was founded in 1879 as a way to combat liberal democracy. Rejecting notions of equality and rights, they sought to restore religion and monarchy, and reaffirm tradition and patriarchy.[43]

Some of these new nationalists also embraced a masculinist vision of war as heroic and a sign of a country's virility. Italian nationalists Alfredo Rocco and Enrico Corradini believed war and imperialism were valiant national struggles. Corradini feared that the Italian people had become effete because the "pious bourgeois platitudes about universal peace and brother-hood [had] corrupted the class from which Italy's leaders came." He lamented that "A new stage in the history of imperialism was about to begin, but tragically for Italy the Italians had no sense of the occasion."[44] Rocco believed nations were in a constant struggle for survival of the fittest, and that the heroic fight was essential to national survival.[45] Corradini and Rocco's ideas of martial heroism, individual sacrifice, the need for discipline and obedience, and the grandeur of Rome were early expressions of the fascist ideology that would take over Italy a few decades later. For these reasons, one of the most respected historians of fascism, Zeev Sternhell, argues that the origin of fascist ideology has to be dated back to the end of the nineteenth century.[46]

Twenty-first Century

Like the century that proceeded it, between 1990 and 2010 there was a 180-degree change in society's understanding of liberalism and its relationship to globalization. A growing number of far-right groups began to disavow enlightenment values. Gábor Vona, former president of the Hungarian far-right party "Movement for Hungary" (*Jobbik Magyarorsz.gért Mozgalom*), expressed his rejection of the Enlightenment very directly: "If we identify modernity, which ranges from the Renaissance to the Enlightenment to global capitalism, with the left, then we are certainly right-wing."[47]

In today's world, the term "enlightenment" is not often evoked; but anti-science, anti-expertise, and anti-intellectualism have become all too familiar. A 2020 article in *Scientific American* exclaimed, "Antiscience has emerged as a dominant and highly lethal force, and one that threatens global security, as much as do terrorism and nuclear proliferation."[48] The *Boston Review* declared, "Science is under fire as never before in the United States."[49] Moreover, the spread of these ideologies has been far and wide. "Scientific denial is a practice that [has been] largely intertwined with far-right movements, which have expanded across Europe, with emphasis on Hungary, Austria, Italy, France and Germany and several countries in Latin America, including Brazil and the United States of America, during Donald Trump's presidential term."[50] In trying to grapple with this unnerving movement, Cristóbal Bellolio identifies three key aspects of this twenty-first century populist *zeit geist*:

> populist actors worldwide have grounded their scepticism, distrust, or hostility to scientific inputs, to the extent that they are relevant for political action: (1) they raise a moral objection against scientists who have been allegedly corrupted by foreign interests turning them into enemies of the people; (2) they present a democratic objection against the technocratic claim that scientific experts should rule regardless of the popular will; and (3) they employ an epistemic argument against scientific reasoning, which is said to be inferior to common-sense and folk wisdom, and antithetical to the immediateness of political action.[51]

Tom Nichols in his 2017 book *The Death of Expertise* has summed up the irony of the age best: "These are dangerous times. Never have so many people had so much access to so much knowledge and yet have been so resistant to learning anything."[52]

There are, however, critical differences between today's anti-rationalism and that of the last century. The rejection of science and rationalism in the twenty-first century has been driven more by political figures than intellectuals. It has also been less ideological and more self-serving. Anti-rationalist proclamations are frequently made by politicians when it will help them gain an advantage. For example, the prime minster of Hungary, Viktor 'Orban, refused to attend policy-specific debates in the last two Hungarian elections, since, in his mindset, "what needs to be done is obvious; no debate about values or weighting of empirical evidence is required."[53] Trump repeatedly dismissed the overwhelming evidence that he lost the 2020 election.[54] Beyond that, Trump and his allies intentionally conducted a misinformation campaign, spreading the false allegation that his opponent had stolen the election through fraud. Along similar lines, Putin, when launching his invasion of Ukraine, "used a barrage of increasingly outlandish falsehoods to prop up its overarching claim that the invasion of Ukraine is justified." In this instrumental version of anti-rationalism, it is not surprising to see that today's populist leaders do not reject all scientists—only those whose views threaten their power. The scientists they are willing to endorse are those whose claims support their personal endeavors. As Szabados rightly recognizes, what has emerged is a form of "patronage" science.[55]

One reason these kinds of outright lies have been accepted by significant portions of the population is that distrust of expertise and journalism has been cultivated, often by the very politicians who have the most to gain by discrediting factual reports. Trump began his 2015 presidential campaign slandering the professional journalists both individually as well as respected newspapers, charging that all they produced was "Fake News." His former presidential counselor, Kellyanne Conway, infamously coined the term "alternative facts" as a way to promote false ideas. The right-wing party Five Star in Italy, which achieved representation in the Italian parliament from 2014 to 2017, "like other populist parties in Europe, attacks the press as a matter of routine, often for publishing 'fake news.'"[56] In Russia, since Putin gained almost complete control over the Russian media, it has become the president's mouthpiece, regularly demonstrating "a shameless willingness to disseminate partial truths or outright fictions."[57]

By 2020, the rhetoric of individual politicians had been internalized by many—so much so that it had morphed into a generalized distrust of all institutional sources of information. What has emerged is essentially "a worldview" in which "the good is found in the common wisdom of the people rather than the pretensions of the expert," and in which any claims to expertise are regarded with apprehension and suspicion.[58] One cannot help but hear the echoes of Peter Pulzer's description of the figure of the late nineteenth-century Romantic, who "despised Rationalism" because he "detected the sin of intellectual arrogance."[59] Indeed these sentiments reflect the appeal to the primordial vitality of the people in opposition to the effete rationalism of the Enlightenment that characterized rightist ideologies of the nineteenth century. As Sternhell et al. explain:

in order to ensure the welfare of the nation, one had to turn to the people and exalt the primitive force, vigor, and vitality that emanated from the people, uncontaminated by the rationalist and individualist virus. For the revolutionary Right of 1890 as for that of 1930, the incomparable merit of popular opinion was its unreflecting spontaneity, springing from the depths of the unconscious.[60]

Today we see the same celebration of "spontaneity" of popular opinion. This has come particularly clear with the triumph of the QAnon movement. Like the *völkisch* movements in Germany, QAnon has emerged as a mystical, nationalist movement that gained traction in the United States as well as among some of the more extreme groups in Europe. The Internet-led conspiracy movement espouses ideas that come very close to a form of White Christian Nationalism.[61] Indeed, although people from many different walks of life have been ensnared by QAnon, in the United States it has been particularly resonant with evangelical Christians. QAnon seems to be especially compelling to people who, like the artisans and bourgeoisie in Germany at the turn of the century, feel they "are rapidly sinking to [a lower] class status and who [feel] themselves isolated."[62]

Like the proto-fascist ideologies of the late nineteenth century, QAnon followers reject rationalism or at least of the idea that knowledge comes from formal study. They eschew "expert opinions" as patently false manipulation of the "deep state," and believe that only by piecing together obscure clues through their own powers of intuition can they alight upon the Truth. To paraphrase Pulzer once again, QAnon followers embrace intuition over analysis, imagination over empiricism, faith over the intellect, and history over science. Moreover, QAnon shares with the *völkisch* movements of the late nineteenth century the deep desire for a connection with a traditional past and an emotional way out of the troubling displacements created by the modern economy. Its followers have faith in its vision of an apocalyptic future, in which evil elites will be washed away in a deluge of biblical proportions and replaced by rightful leaders.[63]

Interestingly, a parallel movement has been sweeping across Italy. Italians on the far right have been mobilized by, of all things, the fantasy world created by J. R. Tolkien. Tolkien's "agrarian universe, full of virtuous good guys defending their idyllic, wooded kingdoms from hordes of dark and violent orcs" has become a pillar for the hard-right's reconstruction of "a traditionalist mythic age [full of] symbols, heroes and creation myths."[64] Indeed, for thousands of Italians, "hobbits are the symbol of a radical movement to reimagine fascism and restore far-right movements to glory."[65] The fascist embrace of Tolkien actually began in 1977, when far-right party and youth leaders organized the first "Hobbit Camp," hoping to invest youth with "Traditionalism" and bypass the stigma associated with fascism. Other Hobbit Camps followed, but the movement remained on the fringes of Italian society for decades. By the early 2010s, this right-wing fantasy-fiction movement had picked up steam.[66] So much so, that by 2022 Giorgia Meloni, the first women to be elected to the office of the prime minister (and who had attended Hobbit Camps as a child), openly proclaimed that she regarded *The Lord of the Rings* not as fantasy, but as a "sacred text."[67]

There can be no doubt that we are witnessing a contemporary neo-Romantic movement, on par with those that characterized the end of nineteenth century. The growing popularity of QAnon and the political appropriation of Tolkien's fantasy world can only be understood as harkening the return of fascism.

Attacks on Religion and the Family

The virulence of anti-enlightenment movements in both eras were not only fomented by the fear of demographic displacement. These reactionary movements were also born in response to a perceived liberal attack on the traditional family and traditional religious order. And, in fact, in both eras political liberalism had chipped away at the patriarchal, religious, family order.

An indication of the degree to which liberal values were internationalized is the success of gender equality movements in both epochs. Golding (1980) describes the period from 1870 to 1920 in the United States as "the era of single women."[68] The "New Woman" was characterized as a young, single woman who had migrated to the urban center for work. In the American media, "the New Woman" was ever present. She was the subject of a "proliferation of articles, books, pamphlets, satirical verse and cartoons."[69] The concurrent emergence of the bicycle became almost synonymous with this new historical figure. These new peddle-powered machines were radical because they afforded young women an ease of movement in the urban terrain. Yet, women's advances were not limited to bicycling. A much more profound political shift was also taking place. From Albania to Iceland, Azerbaijan to Slovakia, women's suffrage became a reality. Between 1907 and 1921, women won the right to vote in twenty-two countries sequentially (see Table 11.1).

Nineteenth-century right-wing defensive nationalists were threatened by this historic movement for gender equality. Their goal was to reassert the nation's "traditional culture" and "traditional values." In Italy, proto-fascists

Table 11.1 Women's Suffrage

Albania (1920)	Georgia (1918)	Poland (1918)
Austria (1918)	Germany (118)	Russia (1918)
Azerbaijan (1921)	Hungary (1918)	Slovakia (1920)
Belarus (1919)	Iceland (1915)	Sweden (1919)
Czech Republic (1920)	Latvia (1918)	Ukraine (1919)
Denmark (1915)	Luxembourg (1919)	United Kingdom (1918)
Estonia (1918)	Netherlands (1919)	
Finland (1906)	Norway (1907)	

Source: Women's Suffrage and Beyond, *http://womensuffrage.org/?page_id=97*, accessed March 17, 2017.

considered women in the public sphere "a threat to the Italian race. The prevailing attitude was that women were meant to be procreators; outside the home they risked sexual degeneration, and the loss of their maternal nature was believed to imperil the future of the race."[70] Even the humble bicycle became a target of those who feared the changes these New Women would bring to the established patriarchal and religious order. In Edwardian England, it became commonplace to see postcards showing young women smoking or getting onto a bicycle juxtaposed against neglected children in a dirty home with slogans like "The Way It's Going" or "The New Woman."[71] In the United States, "Traditionalists decried the woman cyclist, who no longer had a chaperone to protect her from a stranger's advances."[72] For them, the bicycle was a symbol of "moral transgression . . . sometimes regarded as the yardstick for female respectability."[73]

In the twenty-first century, right-wing parties have been highly threatened by women's increased empowerment. Indeed, while opposition to liberal ideals of equality under the law lies at the heart of right-wing extremism,[74] the reactionary response to gender equality movements has been especially virulent. In the United States, the Southern Poverty Law Center's describes how many right-wing extremist groups use "hyper-masculine imagery" that "reinforces misogyny and traditional gender roles," where "degradation and disrespect of women [is] often couched in a cherishing of women as the keepers of the home."[75] The Spanish right-wing party, *Vox*, even sought to repeal laws against gender violence.

At the same time, between 2000 and 2016, twenty-three countries legalized gay marriage (see Table 11.2). The marriage equality movement has been

Table 11.2 Passage of Gay Marriage

Argentina (2010)	France (2013)	Scotland (2014)
Belgium (2003)	Greenland (2015)	South Africa (2006)
Brazil (2013)	Iceland (2010)	Spain (2005)
Canada (2005)	Ireland (2015)	Spain (2005)
Colombia (2016)	Luxembourg (2014)	Sweden (2009)
Denmark (2012)	New Zealand (2013)	The Netherlands (2000)
England / Wales (2013)	Norway (2009)	United States (2015)
Finland (2015)	Norway (2009)	Uruguay (2013)

Source: Pew Research Center *http://www.pewforum.org/2015/06/26/gay-marriage-around-the-world-2013/*, accessed March 17, 2017.

particularly threatening to traditional, religious communities and has helped fuel the reactionary rejection of universal rights and equality embedded in political liberalism. With gay marriage laws passing in country after country, opposition to gay rights became strident on both sides of the Atlantic—and even beyond, in countries like Brazil. As Fukuyma has observed, "Religious conservative thinkers decry the 'moral laxity' of liberalism" and embrace "overt authoritarian governance to restore 'religiously-rooted' standards of behavior."[76]

This is especially so in Eastern Europe, where there have been strong traditionalist reactions to gender equality movements. Conservative traditionalist parties, from Estonia's Conservative People's Party of Estonia (EKRE) to Poland's Law and Justice Party to Hungary's *Fidesz* (Hungarian Civic Alliance) to Putin's United Russia Party, have all positioned themselves as Christian bulwarks against the destruction of society and the vile attacks on the family that gay marriage poses.[77] Anti-gay sentiment was expressed more crassly by the British *National Front*, which posted on their former web page that "Very many of 'our' MPs are placemen, foreigners and queers with no interest in the future of our nation."[78]

It is, thus, clear that nativism and fascism are prevalent today. This is neither partisan rhetoric nor hype. Right-wing defensive nationalism is indeed proto-fascist, meaning that it is a movement that incorporates nativism and anti-liberalism, with masculinist ideologies and militarism. Of course, not all right-wing defensive nationalist groups are the same. Some are nativist and militaristic without being anti-liberal. Others have fully embraced fascism. The latter are the movements that, in addition to espousing nativist, anti-liberal, militarist, sexist ideologies, propound the idea that revolutionary authoritarianism is the only way to cleanse society of its ills.

Right-wing defensive nationalism, therefore, has to be understood as a very real threat to the political order. It is undeniable how much the anti-rationalist, anti-enlightenment, anti-equality movements of today mirror their late-nineteenth century counterparts. As unimaginable as it was twenty years ago, it would seem that history has begun to repeat itself.

Conclusion

Surveying these different movements across different time periods provides answers to the questions with which this book began. By comparing the similarities across these two remarkable periods, we can ascertain very clear patterns; patterns that help make sense of the populist and nativist movements that spread so unexpectedly in the first decades of the twenty-first century.

What we have learned is that the rediscovery of society that emerged at the dawning of the twentieth and twenty-first centuries can be read as a resurrection of nationalism one in which populism and nationalism combined to produce an epoch of defensive nationalism. The case studies show that, in both periods, separate left-wing and right-wing defensive national movements appeared simultaneously across multiple countries, each of which was concentrated on reasserting economic sovereignty, addressing the inequities that had developed from extreme wealth concentration, and stamping down the dangers believed to be posed by mass immigrations and threats to the traditional family.

The histories traced here have also shown, as Polanyi rightly understood, that in our complex modern world the nation-state was then, is now, and will likely remain, the only entity that can protect society from international predation and market extremism. Therefore, case studies also illustrate that it is possible to account for the emergence of a second double movement, without succumbing to historicism, by examining anti-liberalism as a socio-political response to vast social and economic displacements that come from great technological change. Innovative global technologies are central to this process because they bring about astounding changes that effectively shorten time and flatten space (to paraphrase Tom Friedman),[79] and because they change every imaginable level of human intercourse.

In the final analysis, it can therefore be said that it does appear to be true that man's highest technological achievements can sadly also act as conduits for dangerous political movements. Technological revolutions produce magical innovations that symbolize the greatest potential of humankind. But the upheaval and flux that follows in their wake, like the dangerous trail of burning rocket exhaust, can leave exposed the fiercist and basest parts of our nature.

PART V

POSTWAR PEACE

In many ways, arguing that the double movement developed in both epochs raises as many questions as it answers. For it does not fully explain why there should have been a confluence of so many similar things at the same time in both periods. If technological revolution explains hyper-globalization and hyper-liberalism, what explains the explosion of innovation that produced those revolutions? And how exactly are these tied to the adoption of a new form of international exchange? To understand how the modern global order first emerged and then re-emerged, the next two chapters will examine the prelude to these two periods of hyper-globalization.

In fact, the rise of the liberal order in both eras materialized out of the ashes of major power conflict. From 1793 to 1815, Europe was under the constant threat of Napoleon's annexation of Europe. Similarly, from 1914 to 1917, and again from 1934 to 1945, Europe was besieged by Germany's expansionary designs. Both periods of interstate war involved all the powerful states of the day.[1] At the end of both conflicts, the major powers came together to forge a new international order that they hoped would allow peace to endure; and so it did. As Kevin O'Rourke observes, "the wars of 1793–1815 were such a traumatic event that they produced a surprisingly durable peace settlement—resembling, from this point of view, the war of 1939–45."[2] The peace among the world's industrializing nations required an unprecedented level of international cooperation. One consequence of this sustained peace was that it provided the space needed for innovation to flourish and international commerce to blossom.

The importance of the long-standing peace that followed the Napoleonic Wars was not lost on Polanyi. It was, in fact, his starting point. The initial puzzle Polanyi poses is: what held peace among these formerly belligerent powers for 100 years? This is a curious puzzle, because the agreements hammered out from 1815 to 1817, referred to as the Concert of Europe, were rather flimsy. There were neither strong international organizations nor clear mechanisms that could hold different actors accountable. Polanyi notes that the Concert of Europe "amounted at the best to a loose federation."[3] For these reasons, Polanyi is highly skeptical that such insubstantial accords could actually have held the peace for one hundred years. As he explains,

> International disequilibrium may occur for innumerable reasons—from a dynastic love affair to the silting of an estuary, from a theological controversy to a technological invention. The mere growth of wealth and population, or their decrease, is bound to set political forces in motion; and the external balance will invariably reflect the internal. . . . Once the imbalance has gathered momentum only force can set it right.[4]

He therefore concludes that the Concert of Europe might be regarded as an expression of a "revived peace interest"; but, as he colorfully retorts, interests "remain platonic unless they are translated into politics by the means of some social instrumentality."[5] It is here that Polanyi contends that there had to have been another force, something unique to the nineteenth century, that explains how peace among the rival powers was maintained. And that, he claims, was *haute finance*. Polanyi dismisses the relevance of the post-Napoleonic international order because he believes it does not account for why peace was maintained. But it might account for how finance became globalized in tandem with global trade.

The next two chapters will make the case that four critical outcomes from the postwar period in both epochs help explain the rise of global trade, finance capitalism, and with that hyper-liberalism. First, trade and industry were able to ramp up; second, a new center of finance and economic power emerged that could impose a liberal agenda; third, mounting pressures from trade forced the adoption of a new international monetary system; and fourth, these combined processes provoked a global economic crisis, which provided the political impetus to dismantle what remained of the earlier protective order. The combined effect of all of these outcomes was that capital became mobile, laissez-faire trade globalized, and the "liberal creed" internationally disseminated. All of this set the stage for the double movement in the latter part of both centuries. Chapter 12 will examine these changes in terms of the early nineteenth century, and Chapter 13 will look at the same processes in the mid-twentieth century.

12

The Concert of Europe

Prior to the nineteenth century, European interstate relationships were described as "balance of power" politics; a system in which the continent's various kings, queens, and princes sought to protect themselves from one another by matching their power with that of their potential adversary. It was, thus, a system characterized by the constant jockeying for control over resources, territory, and political influence, with no one state emerging triumphant. Even the wars conducted against Napoleon were fought by a series of unstable alliances. Seven successive coalitions were raised to counter France's occupation. By the war's end, the trauma of the two-decades-long conflict brought with it a realization on the part of Europe's monarchs that they could not return to the former status quo. Balance-of-power politics, with its unremitting struggle for dominion, had "generated intolerable international tensions, produced increasingly serious armed conflicts, and inspired progressively extravagant plans of aggression."[1] Moreover, Napoleon had threatened the political existence of all of Europe's monarchs. If Europe was to maintain peace and sovereign leaders preserve their dominions, something new and altogether different would have to be devised. From 1814 to 1815, representatives from over two hundred European polities came together. Led by the Allied powers—Great Britain, Prussia, Russia, and Austria—the first European Congress was held in Vienna.

By 1817, after a subsequent series of congresses, the "Concert of Europe" was in place: a set of multilateral agreements that laid the foundation for "a functioning and promising system of international relations" radically different from the balance of power system it replaced.[2] The new order was based on "a principle of general union, uniting the states collectively with a federative bond, under the guidance of the principal Powers."[3] Indeed, the Concert of Europe marked a new world order, one that was unique in European history. It was a period of sustained peace. From 1814 to the outbreak of the First World War in 1914, there were, of course, a small number of wars in Europe, but they were relatively limited in impact and duration and involved only a handful of states.[4] Although there is debate about the accuracy of Polanyi's

Defensive Nationalism. B. S. Rabinowitz, Oxford University Press. © Oxford University Press 2023.
DOI: 10.1093/oso/9780197672037.003.0013

characterization of this period as the "Hundred Years Peace," in terms of average battle durations, battle deaths per year, and a host of other statistical criteria, nineteenth-century Europe was far less war-ridden and militaristic than it had been in the eighteenth century or was to become in the twentieth century. In fact, "During the 17th and 18th centuries, the Great Powers were involved in war 94% and 78% of the time, respectively, compared to 40% of the time in the nineteenth century."[5]

Two major components of the New World order helped secure the peace. First, a framework was created to ensure that peace would be the common responsibility of the major five powers—the four Allied powers plus France (after the Bourbon King had been restored to the throne). To achieve this end, the negotiating powers devised "a loose mechanism for consultation and dispute resolution through periodic great-power meetings."[6] Meetings of the sovereigns or their respective ministers were scheduled to be held at fixed periods, "for the purpose of consulting upon their common interests, and for consideration of the measures which at each of those periods shall be considered the most salutary for the repose and prosperity of Nations and for the maintenance of the Peace of Europe."[7] But perhaps even more importantly, the great powers redrew the map of Europe. Territorial rights of large and small states alike were agreed upon. This included the guaranteed independence of Switzerland and Spain; Holland's restoration; the formation of a confederated Germany; the division of Italy and restoration of papal states to Rome, as well as agreements over contested territories between Portugal and Spain, Norway and Sweden, and Russia and Prussia.

Settled boundaries put an end to destabilizing large-scale conflicts among the largest powers on European soil. Conflicts did continue to be staged between Europe's dominant powers but, for the most part, hostilities among the most powerful nations were moved offshore. No longer competing for territories in Europe, "wars in the periphery of the system" took on far "greater significance."[8] Rivalries over the control of resources and markets were waged in far-flung territories, like the Levant, the Sudan, and Afghanistan. "The post-Napoleonic period was to be a period of unparalleled colonial expansion. During the last three decades of the nineteenth-century, 'extra-state wars' peaked.[9] The forums developed in the Concert of Europe were even used to negotiate settlements over how to carve up the entire African continent among the European powers. Through these mechanisms, "the map of domination of the world's spaces changed out of all recognition between 1850 and 1914," [10] furthering economic development of the Western economies.

Peace Accords and the Expansion of Trade and Industry

The end of power politics had also brought to a close "the era of great European trading monopolies" and "non-tariff barriers which had distinguished the eighteenth century."[11] Although certain sectors of trade and industry would continue to be protected,[12] by and large, the peace marked the demise of mercantilism as it had been practiced for centuries. Therefore, another consequence of the Concert of Europe was that the new order "had profound and long-lasting effects on international trade worldwide."[13] Indeed, the "world's trade between 1800 and 1840 [almost] doubled."[14]

Change in trade protectionism did not happen in one fell swoop. The Napoleonic Wars had been long and severe. Directly after the decades-long conflict, the continent was exhausted, trade and industry were depressed, and governments were encumbered with debt. Added to these woes, "In 1816 there was a disastrous harvest all over Europe. The price of all provisions rose while the prices of all other commodities continued to fall."[15] Even when new innovations in farming were able to produce record harvests,[16] without the high government demand that had existed during the war, agricultural prices plummeted.[17] Given how large a portion of Europe's population was engaged in agriculture, these price fluctuations had an enormous impact. Clapham ventures that, in England, despite having the continent's strongest economy, "the years from 1815 to 1820 were, both economically and politically, probably the most wretched, difficult, and dangerous in modern English history."[18] The depression in England was so deep that it "continued almost unabated until 1833, when importation of foreign fertilizers greatly reduced production costs."[19] The "great agricultural depression of the period after the Napoleonic wars," thus, prompted a "clamor for protection to agriculture."[20]

And yet, there were rays of hope. At the same time that agriculture was languishing, industry was slowly rallying. Between 1819 and 1825 manufacturing began to recover.[21] England experienced "a building boom" before 1825, which produced a "general increase of physical production ... in cotton textiles, coal and iron, and transportation."[22] Ironically, the resurgence of industry was due in large part to the same cessation of war demand. Whereas agricultural prices were negatively impacted, the dramatic change in demand "caused dislocation and unemployment on a vast scale."[23] This, counterintuitively, spelled good fortune for the industrialists, because "ample labour supplies" were "moving into the market," rendering the price of labor relatively cheap. The cumulative effects amplified over time, so that between 1853 and 1855, industrial "employment grew by leaps and bounds" both in Europe and overseas, "whither men and women now migrated in enormous numbers."[24] Everything from British cotton exports to Belgian iron exports just about doubled between 1850 and 1860.[25] Even in Prussia, 115 companies, not counting the ubiquitous railway companies, were established: "almost all of them in the euphoric years between 1852 and 1857."[26]

The recovery of industry was also made possible because a surge of investment, which, in spite of all the difficulties of the postwar period, was considerable. Though the long war hurt farmers and agriculturalists, "large Government borrowings had created a new class—the Fund holders." These financiers "benefited from the falling prices; [and] the system of taxation tended to favour them at the expense of other classes, they, therefore, continued to have a substantial surplus to invest."[27] With this rise in investment and industry, trade barriers were slowly peeled away. "Prohibition of export of raw silk was withdrawn in Piedmont, Lombardy and Venetia in the 1830s, freedom to export coal from Britain enacted in the 1840s."[28] In France, "tariffs were adjusted downward, in coal, iron, copper, nitrates, machinery, horses," after "Industries complained of the burden of the tariff on their purchases of inputs, and especially on the excess protections accorded to iron."[29] By the end of the 1840s, a movement towards free trade was underway across Europe:

> The Swiss constitution of 1848 called for a tariff for revenue only and protective duties were reduced progressively from 1851 to 1885. Netherlands removed a tariff on ship imports and prohibitions against nationalization of forcing ships. Belgium plugged gap after gap in its protective system in the early 1850s . . . Piedmont . . . and Spain, Portugal, Norway and Sweden (after 1857) undertook to dismantle their protective prohibitive restrictions.[30]

The definitive turning point came in 1860, when France and Great Britain signed a free trade agreement (see Chapter 5). The treaty ended tariffs on main items of trade between the two countries, such as wine, brandy, and silk goods from France; and coal, iron, and industrial goods from Britain. But the effects of the treaty went far beyond these two nations. As Kindleberger writes, "with the Anglo-French treaty the trickle [of free-trade] became a flood."[31] This set the stage for the dramatic upsurge in a liberal trade in the mid-century, when "Between 1850 and 1870 it increased by 260 percent."[32]

Predominant Economic Power

Polanyi observed that after the Napoleonic Wars, "London had become the financial center of a growing world trade."[33] One reason for London's ascent was that the war had undermined the eighteenth-century seats of finance, Amsterdam, and Paris. "Amsterdam's relative position would deteriorate during the Napoleonic Wars and never fully recover. Paris, too, was hard hit by France's defeat."[34] The defeat of France further enhanced the position of London's financiers because debts incurred by Napoleon's campaigns, particularly the disastrous Russian campaign, were enormous. With the added burden of war reparations, "The restored [French] monarchy remained very weak and was only rescued by a series of new loans in 1817."[35] It was the London-based bank Baring Brothers that provided the funds. Thus, "The financing of France's war debt was a clear sign of London's ascendance as the leading financial centre." Indeed, "By 1815, Barings had become the largest bank in Europe."[36] Within a decade, however, Barings was overshadowed by another British banking family, the financial behemoth run by the Rothschild family, who had also made their fortune financing Great Britain's war effort during the Napoleonic Wars. Between the Baring Brothers Bank and the Rothschilds', Britain became "the world centre for the issuing of foreign loans. Countries such as Prussia, Austria, Russia, Belgium, Spain, Brazil, and Argentina took out loans in the British capital."[37] The cumulative result was that by 1875, London was "supreme in cosmopolitan and domestic money markets alike."[38]

Britain's uncontested control over finance is also attributable to its industrial and imperial expansion during the Napoleonic Wars. During the war effort, the British army and navy funded improvements in steam engines as well as critical innovations in iron and related trades—including iron railways and iron ships. In this way, the "seat and backbone of the nineteenth-century British capital goods industry" were developed through wartime spending, which bolstered the subsequent phases of the Industrial Revolution.[39] All the while, "imperial tribute extracted from the colonies into capital invested all over the world enhanced London's comparative advantage as world financial center vis-à-vis competing centers such as Amsterdam and Paris."[40] As a result, "By the end of the Napoleonic Wars, Britain was in a unique position relative to other European states. It was the only industrial power. It had the only naval force that was truly global. And its empire far surpassed in geographic scope that of any other European power."[41] The combined effect was that London was set to become "the natural home of *haute finance*."

Once established, British banking remained the center of global finance. Throughout the nineteenth century, Britain "enjoyed relative economic pre-eminence, the deepest financial markets, and the largest creditor position."[42] Their worldwide financial networks and dominant position in trade had forced countries to be dependent upon the kingdom and maintain allegiance to Britain. The global networks of the "closely knit body of cosmopolitan financiers" became a central "instrument of British governance of the inter-state system."[43] Indeed, for most of the century, the United Kingdom was able "to govern the interstate system as effectively as a world empire."[44]

With its economic and military might, Britain became the world leader—the taste- and change-maker of the day. Given her inordinate powers, Britain was able to foist her ideology of free markets upon the world. As Polanyi argues, "The nineteenth century, as cannot be overemphasized, was England's century. The Industrial Revolution was an English event. Market economy, free trade, and the gold standard were English inventions."[45] British predominance was, thus, a critical means through which economic liberalism became internationalized.

New Medium of International Exchange

In the 1860s, only two countries were on the gold standard: Great Britain and Portugal. Most countries used some form of bimetallism. There were countries that adopted both silver and gold as legal tender, as had been done initially in the United States. Others designated silver as their national currency and issued a parallel gold currency for international trade.[46] However, after 1870, an increasing share of the world economy came into the orbit of the classical gold standard.[47] By 1885, "So complete was this transformation" that "there was no longer a single mint open to the unlimited coinage of silver in either Europe or the U.S."[48] In fact, within five years of the network of free-trade agreements that had begun with the Cobden-Chevalier Treaty, Europe had begun to move toward the unification of their monetary systems.

A few factors helped promote the adoption of a unified system of exchange. At the most basic level, gold is an ideal medium for high-volume trading. In fact, "the value per bulk of gold was roughly 15 times greater than that of silver;" therefore, it has been argued that "gold would naturally become more important as a medium of exchange in the environments where the size and frequency of transactions and incomes were growing."[49] But the major impetus behind adopting a unified currency was that Europe was rapidly becoming a "single market" system. The dramatic growth in international commerce had brought into being "a climate favourable to the simplification of commercial practices."[50] As early as 1851, discussions began about standardizing the means of trade. The reason that year is notable is that representatives from around the world came to London for "The Great Exhibition of Works of Industry of All Nations." The event was basically the first of a series of World's Fairs, at which countries from around the world could display their achievements in special exhibitions. Given the opportunity, the participants of the Great Exhibit were able to discuss trade relations. They quickly recognized that the existing system of trade was anachronistic. The problem was that goods measured and priced in units that differed from country to country was impeding trade.[51]

Initially, France played a central role in this process. In fact, as early as 1850, France, Belgium, Switzerland, and Piedmont were unofficially using a common currency.[52] In December 1865, this group of countries, under the direction of Napoleon III, formally rationalized the exchange system and adopted the Latin Monetary Union (LMU). In addition to adopting a single currency—the franc (which was the first official international monetary system ever established), France, Belgium, Italy, and Switzerland also agreed upon a unified system of weights and measures—grams, meters, the decimal systems.[53] But France did not stop there. Once the LMU was ratified in 1866, the French Ministry of Foreign Affairs sent out a letter to diplomatic agents across Europe, as well as in Russia, the Ottoman Empire, and the USA, inviting all the advanced nations to either join the LMU and adopt the French coinage, or at the very least to participate in a conference that would be organized to create a new monetary union.[54]

Even so, as important as France was to the rationalization of European exchange, it is difficult to take the enormous economic and political power of Britain out of the equation. Britain may not have had "hegemonic" control over the global economy, as many have argued,[55] but her power and influence were undeniably critical in shaping the adoption of the gold standard. The first sign of British influence came immediately after the LMU was established. Though several countries were supportive of France's proposed convention, the British Foreign Secretary "declined the offer to join the Convention," explaining that the agreement would require that they "alter very materially the existing monetary system of this country."[56] Without British support, the French program for a unified coinage was dead by 1871.[57] In its stead, Britain backed its own international gold standard.

The regime of the classical gold-standard superintended by the British was distinct from what France had proposed in the 1860s. The international gold standard, as it came to be implemented, was integrally connected to the "liberal creed." Unlike the proposed French system, the British gold standard would not be monitored or regulated through political collaboration. It would work automatically, steered by the inviolable mechanism of the market.[58] It therefore very much reflected the values of the British establishment. British liberals, "such as Mill and Cobden, saw free trade primarily as a tool to strengthen a peaceful cosmopolitan world society. Free trade would foster peace, they argued, by creating ties of interdependence and spreading 'civilization.'"[59] They therefore asserted that, by itself "the gold standard would maintain international equilibrium, discipline government policy, and foster international trade and finance by providing a common monetary standard. And it would accomplish these goals automatically through market forces with a minimum of discretionary government involvement in the monetary sector."[60]

There were some dissenting voices, even in Britain. Nationalists feared that the gold standard would overpower national economic interests. German economist Friedrich List famously criticized liberals for seeing "individuals as mere producers and consumers, not as citizens of states or members of nations"; and argued that in contradistinction to the liberal notions of cosmopolitanism, "As the individual chiefly obtains by means of the nation and in the nation mental culture, power of production, security, and prosperity, so is the civilisation of the human race only conceivable and possible by means of the civilisation and development of the individual nations."[61] In the end, however, the tide had already turned. Opposing voices were drowned out by the drumbeat of *haute finance*.

Britain's ability to compel other countries to adopt this liberalized version of the gold standard was due to her predominance on the world stage. As global capital markets became progressively centered in London, gold gained ascendency. Some have argued that "the status of gold derived disproportionately from the British example";[62] in other words, that it was due to England's soft power. Certainly, by mid-century Britain had become the model of progress and success. Great Britain was the "undisputed technological leader, [...] the largest exporter and importer in the world and possessed the largest commercial fleet."[63] Nonetheless, London's coercive power was clearly central. London's financial markets had become the lynchpin of international finance and commercial trade, all of which were aligned with the gold standard. With the British pound functioning as "the world's currency for international transactions,"[64] Britain could impose her will on the world.

The impact of the gold standard on trade and finance was almost immediate. "From the 1870s on, the widespread adoption of the gold standard enabled capital to move internationally without fear of arbitrary changes in currency values or other financial hiccups."[65] With this surge in capital mobility, "The globalization experienced by the world economy in the decades before World War I was nothing short of extraordinary."[66] However, the gold standard enabled something else as well—increased economic instability. Domestic currencies increasingly became the handmaiden of international capital markets. Tying one's currency to gold stockpiles made it difficult for countries to adjust their own monetary policies in response to changes in economic conditions. Thus, the gold standard and capital mobility created the conditions that would, in the not-too-distant future, bring about the demise of the new monetary regime. In particular, countries now faced the risk of suffering the consequences of a run on gold during periods of economic hardship. That is precisely what occurred in the 1870s and 1890s. Consequently, the period of formal adherence to the gold standard was short-lived: only from "1862–1866, 1883, and then again between 1924 and 1932 (when exchange controls were introduced)."[67]

Economic Crisis

For the first half of the nineteenth century, free-market liberalism was more of a theory than an actual practice. The fact is that guilds still controlled pricing and labor and governments continued to maintain controls over trade and moneylending. This was true even in the birthplace of laissez-faire ideology, Britain. Polanyi put great stock in the 1834 repeal of the Poor Laws, identifying this as the moment that the "liberal creed" was put into public policy. But Britain remained protectionist for another decade. In fact, most protectionist policies in Britain were not ended until after 1846. Arguably, the more significant moment for liberalism was the repeal of the "Corn Laws." The Corn Laws had been instituted during the great agricultural depression following the Napoleonic Wars to protect farmers from the terrible price fluctuations of the period. With the defeat of the Corn Laws in 1846, the bourgeoisie won the day over feudal landlords and free markets won the day over protectionist trade laws. This laissez-faire victory was to be brought continent-wide in 1848.

The coming world-historic change was precipitated by an agrarian recession, in which a European-wide economic crisis was sparked. It began in 1846 when a major harvest failure in Ireland and England created a shortage of domestic food supplies. The food shortages in the United Kingdom had a domino effect. It produced "price increases and trade deficits" that were so severe that they led to "an external drain of bullion from the Bank of England."[68] To make matters worse, the banking crisis was magnified by a speculative bubble. Between the 1820s and the 1840s, there had been "a vast expansion of credit, particularly through speculative investment centered in projects for railway construction."[69] With the retrenchment of the British economy, railroad investments now "exceeded the limits of the capital resources of the nation."[70] In short, the agrarian recession burst the European "railroad bubble." "Credit money in effect came crashing down, leaving a shortage of 'real money' and specie in 1847–8."[71]

The credit crunch was felt across the entire European continent. The problem was that "the whole continent [had become] vulnerable to simultaneous" economic calamities, as Europe became "more and more unified precisely because of the internationalism of money power."[72] A witness to these events, John Stewart Mill, described how the crisis spread:

> This combination of a fresh demand for loans, with curtailment of the capital disposable for them, raised the rate of interest, and made it impossible to borrow except on the very best security. Some firms . . . stopped payment: their failure involved more or less deeply many other firms which had trusted them; and, as usual in such cases, the general distrust, commonly called a panic, began to set in.[73]

The social and political impact of the economic crisis was enormous. It did not only impact banks and speculators. The agrarian crisis "undermined the already low living standards of peasants, workers and the petit bourgeoisie, . . . [and] led to an increase in strikes, demonstrations, food riots and increased criminality."[74] France was particularly hard hit. "Runs on banks resulted in many failures in the provinces and affected even the Bank of France, which saw its deposits reduced from 320 million in June 1845 to

57 million in January 1847."[75] The lapse in confidence, thus, "produced a liquidity crunch at just that moment when calls for the unpaid balance on railway shares found French capitalists dangerously overextended."[76] From the banks and the capitalists, the effects of the credit crunch cascaded across society in a descending spiral:

> Once the crisis began seriously to impinge on the financial sector, it was inevitable that it should also affect industry. In rural areas, grain shortages translated into a reduction in cash income because none but the richest peasants disposed of a sufficient surplus to take advantage of high prices. The result was a decrease in rural purchasing power and demand for urban goods. The diminished need for agricultural labor also accelerated the migration of landless peasants toward the cities. This growing urban working class was particularly hard hit, because its greater market dependence left it highly vulnerable to economic fluctuations.[77]

In fact, the banking crisis so destabilized Europe that it precipitated a year of revolution. In 1848, "Revolution triumphed through the great central core of the continent."[78] In countries across Europe, the radical lower middle-classes banded together with discontented artisans and small shopkeepers, to demand a new order based on the liberal principles of civil rights and parliamentary governments. Between February and April of that year, Europe's monarchies were overthrown in succession. The "revolutionary zone" stretched west from France, north to the German Confederation, south to Italy, and east to the Austro-Hungarian Empire. Developed and underdeveloped countries were equally vulnerable, with anti-monarchical zeal hitting regions as "backward" as Calabria and Transylvania, as "advanced" as Rhineland and Saxony, as literate as Prussia, and as illiterate as Sicily.[79]

In the end, the liberal moment did not last. By the end of 1849, "all the revolutions had collapsed and the short and violent European experiment in liberal (and, in some countries, democratic) politics was over."[80] Yet, the impacts of 1848 were long lasting. Europe's traditional order never fully recovered. After the revolutions of 1848, sovereigns across Europe were forced to adopt liberal changes. "Even the most arch-reactionary Prussian junkers discovered during that year that they required a newspaper capable of influencing 'public opinion'—in itself a concept linked with liberalism and incompatible with traditional hierarchy."[81] "Most important of all was the emancipation of hundreds of thousands of peasants, religious minorities and colonial slaves."[82]

The credit crisis of 1847–48 had, thus, upset the footing upon which the old order had stood. As national banks fell like dominoes, trust in a state-led economic order was eroded. The crisis sparked an "overwhelming consensus among economists or indeed among intelligent politicians and administrators" that the antidote to the economic woes of the mid-1840s was economic liberalism.[83] After 1849, all existing "institutional barriers to the free movement of the factors of production, to free enterprise and to anything which could conceivably hamper its profitable operation, fell before a world-wide onslaught."[84] Across the continent, guild laws that prohibited artisans' freedom to practice whatever trade they wanted were abolished, the laws against usury were disbanded, and governments loosened their control over mining. "Even establishing joint-stock companies with limited liability became both considerably easier and independent of bureaucratic control."[85]

The remnants of the medieval mercantilist economy were finally and forever liquidated. A new consensus was now in place that would allow capitalism to reign. In Polanyian terms, the credit crisis of 1847–48 was the catalyst that allowed the liberal creed to flourish and disembedded markets to spread internationally.

13

The Bretton Woods Era

After the utter devastation of World War II, in the last year of the war, the Allied powers met in the picturesque New Hampshire town Bretton Woods, to outline the contours of a new international economic order. Just as the world powers dedicated themselves at the Congress of Vienna to creating a new international system that would preclude devastating conflicts, with the Bretton Woods agreements, "an attempt to rebuild the global economy took shape."[1]

As with the Concert of Europe, boundaries among former belligerents were agreed upon. And, as in the preceding century, territorial, military, and economic agreements among powerful nations pushed competition over resources largely onto foreign shores. Superpower rivalries were fought in regions remote from the industrialized centers. Proxy wars were battled in Asia, Africa, and Latin America. The 1890s had had the dubious distinction of being the most war-prone decade, but that record was surpassed during the 1970s.[2] Once again, the expansion of military power served as an engine of economic growth, as did control over foreign markets. And once again, "extra-state" conflicts kept the carnage and destruction of war in distant lands, allowing trade among the world's wealthiest nations to advance. In this way, the new international political and economic order created a space for the resurrection of the world economy.

Postbellum Peace and Trade Resurgence

The peace accords allowed for the rebuilding of war-torn economies and the revival of industry. Both the vanquished and the victors were able to reconstruct their infrastructure and manufacturing sectors. They were not only able to rebuild their industrial facilities; they were also able to incorporate new technologies such as the moving assembly line, which was adopted in Europe in the 1940s. Perhaps more critically, synthetic fibers

Defensive Nationalism. B. S. Rabinowitz, Oxford University Press. © Oxford University Press 2023.
DOI: 10.1093/oso/9780197672037.003.0014

and petrochemicals reached Europe and Japan in the 1950s. Once these technologies were adopted, European and Japanese manufacturers were able to introduce new products. With their industries growing, Western Europe and Japan embarked upon successful export drives, contributing to a surge in trade. "Production of new chemicals, automobiles, television sets, and synthetics such as nylon grew at two or three times the American rate in the 1950s and 1960s."[3] "Japan was the most dramatic success story," where Japanese exports were one-twelfth those of the United States in 1950, by 1973 they were more than one-half.[4] In fact, "Postwar economic growth was extraordinary everywhere," and particularly in the advanced capitalist nations, which, as a whole, "grew three times as fast as in the interwar years and twice as fast as before World War One."[5]

As in the previous century, expanding trade over time led to the loosening of protective measures. One of the critical mechanisms was the General Tariffs and Trade agreement (GATT). GATT was to become "a pillar of the Bretton Woods institutional order."[6] Unlike the World Bank or the IMF, GATT was not an organization. It was a periodically scheduled forum—similar in this respect to the Concert of Europe—at which countries met to negotiate tariffs and trade barriers. The first GATT agreements took place over a six-month period in 1947. The talks encompassed "more than forty-five thousand tariffs that covered about half of the world market."[7] Like the trade agreements that started with the Anglo-Franco Cobden-Chevalier Treaty, GATT was made up of a series of bilateral trade agreements, the centerpiece of which was the Most-Favored-Nation clause. This meant that each agreement signed between two countries (be it over automotive parts or shoes), would be automatically extended to all the other participants. GATT "allowed a gradual and general reduction in trade barriers" across countries and industries. So much so that by 1967 average tariffs on nonagricultural goods were the lowest they had been since the mid-nineteenth century.[8]

With all these cumulative changes, the 1960s was to become "the golden era of Bretton Woods."[9] It was a decade in which industry multiplied and world trade exploded. "Exports grew more than twice as rapidly in the economy, 8.6 per cent a year."[10] Indeed, "By 1973 international trade was two or three times as important to every OECD economy as it had been in 1950, more important than during the decades before World War One."[11]

Predominant Economic Power

Just as Britain dominated the world economy in the nineteenth century, the twentieth century was marked by "a new world order centered on and organized by the United States."[12] And like Britain before it, the United States—now the world's banker, industrial leader, and military might—was able to spread its liberal agenda even more forcefully than the British had before them.

The United States had emerged from World War I with the world's strongest and most vibrant economy. The war had done a good deal to further the United States' position. World War I had severely "disrupted European financial markets and reduced the supply of trade credit offered by European banks," all of which provided American banks with a critical opening.[13] Yet, even before World War I, "American and German enterprises quickly began to drive British rivals out of international markets and even out of Britain's domestic market."[14] By the outbreak of war, Germany was dominant in the production of chemicals and pharmaceuticals and the United States outpaced the world in producing "light, volume-produced machinery, firms like Singer and United Shoe Machinery in sewing machines, International Harvester and John Deere in agricultural machines, and Remington Typewriter, National Cash Register, Burroughs Adding Machine, and Computing-Tabulating-Recording (whose name was soon changed to International Business Machines—IBM) in office equipment)."[15] Therefore, although the British pound continued to account for a significant portion of foreign trade holdings in central banks, by the end of the 1920s, a substantial share of international trade was financed by dollar-denominated exchanges.[16]

After World War II, US industrial dominance was solidified. As the only major industrial power not to have been heavily bombed during the six years of carnage, and having been able to grow industries exponentially by producing war supplies, the United States became "the undisputed political and economic leader."[17] Indeed, World War II impelled the growth of US industry, not only because "industrial output greatly increased," but also because "wartime needs . . . created new technologies that transformed industrial products and processes."[18] For example, part of the United States' new supremacy came from her dominion over the modern aircraft industry, which had increased by leaps and bounds with the wartime effort. In 1939, the first year of World War II, the United States produced only 5,865 planes; during the penultimate war year, she produced 95,272.[19]

Thus, by 1945, America had become the preeminent financial and industrial power as Britain before her, with New York the financial center. "With such a level of industry, supported by huge gold reserves, the dollar was king."[20] The United States' dominant position was further consolidated by the enormous reach of American companies. As the world recovered from World War II and the global political situation stabilized, the largest American corporations, which had flourished in response to war spending, began to look for new investment opportunities abroad. "A new wave of US multinational companies spent $5.4 billion in direct capital investment between 1950 and 1954. Among these were the likes of General Electric, Standard Oil, and IBM, all based in New York."[21] Before World War II, "the typical international investor was a bondholder or banker who lent money to foreign governments and corporations. In the Bretton Woods era, the typical international investor was a corporation that built factories in foreign nations."[22] Consequently, between 1945 and the mid-1960s, the United States accounted for the vast majority of all new FDI flows.[23] In raw numbers, investments made in Europe and Japan by American firms grew twenty times, from two billion dollars in 1950 to forty-one billion in 1973.[24]

In this way, American multinationals "had a formidable impact on globalization." They integrated "the world economy in a manner that differs from trade, finance, migration, or technology transfer."[25] American corporations even introduced a "structure that [would come to serve] as a framework for interchanges and relationships, including further mobilization of investments, exports and imports, technology, knowledge, general information transfers, and, most important, management itself."[26] In fact, foreign direct investment made by American multinationals "succeeded in tying the industrialized world together more tightly than it had been since 1914."[27] Ultimately, the global economic liberalization of the latter half of the twentieth century would be part and parcel with American supremacy.

New Medium of International Exchange

As had happened in the nineteenth century, the expansion of trade led to the creation of an entirely new monetary order: the fiat system. Once again, the unified field of exchange would facilitate global trade and global finance, setting the stage for the second double movement. The new monetary system was developed in response to failures in the economic order that had taken shape during the postbellum period. In many ways, the postwar trade system became a victim of its own success.

At the war's end, the world depression of the 1930s still loomed large in the thinking of policymakers and the general public. Finance and global capital were regarded as dangerous forces that had to be contained.[28] Accordingly, a top priority of the architects of Bretton Woods was to ensure that an international economic collapse of the magnitude of the 1929 crash be made impossible, or at least very difficult. It was regarded of paramount importance to prohibit speculation on "hot money," money that is regularly moved in and out of currency markets for short-term gain.[29] But at the same time that the Bretton Woods negotiators sought to constrain irresponsible capital flows that could undermine domestic economies, they did not want to discourage companies from investing internationally or from borrowing from one another, especially when so many countries were in desperate need of economic support. The solution was to develop a middle ground "between gold standard rigidity and inter-war insecurity."[30]

The middle ground adopted was the "dollar-backed gold standard." As cumbersome as this appellation is, the principle behind the system was fairly straightforward. In the new system, United States dollars, not gold, would be the anchor for international money exchange. In other words, dollars would be the world's reserve currency. This would be achieved by fixing the value of the dollar to gold. It was decided that the value of one ounce of gold would be set as equal to US$ 35. Fixing the dollar, it was hoped, would curtail destabilizing currency speculation and "hot money." The flexibility would come by allowing all other currencies to be adjusted as needed.[31] In addition, governments were required to maintain capital controls, that is, taxes or prohibitions on moving money across borders for speculative purposes.

From 1950 to 1970, the industrialized world "navigated" this "middle road." The system based on this "monetary compromise" has been described by some in Polanyian terms as a period of "embedded-liberalism."[32] It was liberal because it was not based on protectionism. Participating countries did not have to cloister themselves off from international trade and finance, as communist regimes did. It was embedded in the sense that governments were able to insulate their markets against the most pernicious effects of free-market liberalism. Pro-business policies could be implemented along with substantial government involvement in the economy. This enabled governments to engage in extensive trade, while still providing social safety nets and buffering themselves from wild international speculative bubbles. It was the beginning of what would be termed "the Welfare State."

For a couple of decades, the compromise was successful. Currency values were kept stable and currency markets were left open to encourage trade and long-term investment, while risky financial flows were kept in check. Indeed, the system achieved its twin goals: it curbed short-term capital flows and was still able to facilitate long-term investment. In fact, the Bretton Woods economic order allowed for the steady reconstruction of industry and the re-emergence of global trade without the kind of capital mobility that had been so damaging before World War II. However, as trade and investment were restored, a fatal flaw in the dollar-backed gold standard was revealed. The system placed too much pressure on the United States' gold stock.[33]

Troubles began when the United States lost its overarching economic position. In 1946, the United States had been the supreme manufacturer and exporter, producing 50 percent of the world's industrial output.[34] But by the 1960s, as the world economy was restored and commerce and industry were resuscitated globally, Western Europe and Japan had taken over a significant share of international trade. "International competition thereafter intensified as Western Europe and Japan, joined by a whole host of newly industrializing countries, challenged the United States . . . to the point where the Bretton Woods agreement cracked and the dollar was devalued."[35] With a decreasing share of the world market, American goods became more costly, which meant the dollar's purchasing power diminished. But, because the gold-dollar ratio was fixed, the dollar's *official* value remained constant. The truth was that, with its purchasing power reduced, the dollar was no longer as strong as the fixed ratio to gold would suggest. The dollar's strength was nothing more than an artifice, an illusion. It did not take long for investors and overseas banks to recognize the dollar's weakness. Fearful of the underlying instability of US currency, dollars began to be cashed in for gold.

The world economy was now under threat. For, "There was not enough gold in the world, let alone in American reserves, to buy up all the world's dollars. Eventually the United States would run out of gold, and the promise that the dollar was as good as gold would not be honored."[36] The world risked the very thing the architects of Bretton Woods had tried to avoid: a run on gold. The whole edifice created in 1945 was in danger of coming crashing down. The critical turning point came in 1971 when Nixon took the dollar off the gold standard. If the United States had been willing to decrease its domestic spending or raise interest rates, it might have restored the dollar to the value it was supposed to hold. But President Nixon was facing re-election and was not willing to institute politically costly policies. Instead, Nixon announced to the nation, on August 15, 1971, that the gold window would be closed. Foreign governments could no longer exchange their dollars for gold. Now all currencies would float. The "fiat system" had come into being.

The 1971 "Nixon shock" signaled the end for the Bretton Woods system. "In the realm of international monetary relations, the closest approximation might be a whirlwind: fixed exchange rates came flying apart."[37] The finishing blow was the Nixon administration's devaluation of the dollar in 1973 in response to massive speculative currency movements against the dollar. At IMF headquarters, an obituary was circulated for Bretton Woods:

> R.I.P. We regretfully announce the not unexpected passing away after a long illness of Bretton Woods, at 9 P.M. last Sunday. Bretton was born in New Hampshire in 1944 and died a few days after his 27th birthday [...] The fatal stroke occurred this month when parasites called speculators inflated his most important member and caused a rupture of his vital element, dollar-gold convertibility.[38]

The end of the Bretton Woods compromise symbolized the closure of the period of "embedded liberalism." Embedded liberalism required that domestic economies be insulated from the pressures of laissez-faire capitalism. Trade could flow but not unrestrictedly; and international investment could be encouraged but with some controls. The system had worked before the Nixon shocks because controls ensured that "Capital flows were minimal."[39] However, once the fiat system was adopted, world financial markets were set free. The sleeping goliath had been released from its dormant state. International speculators could once again "move money in response to differences in national monetary conditions and could threaten the independence of national macroeconomic policy."[40] "The rupture . . . was permanent; . . . the early 1970s marks a caesura in the way the industrial West conducts its business."[41] The global economy went from "a pre-1970 world of limited capital mobility to a post-1980 world of relatively high capital mobility."[42] "Floating and often highly volatile exchange rates thereafter replaced the fixed exchange rates of the postwar boom."[43] Subsequently, there was an ever-greater geographical mobility of capital.[44]

With the introduction of the fiat system, the seeds were sown for the re-birth of finance capital and its twin, the liberal creed. Certainly, there were differences between the development of the gold standard and the fiat system. For one thing, the United States was not committed to unbounded free trade as Britain had been. The monetary system established at Bretton Woods was one in which production "of world money was taken over by a network of governmental organizations motivated primarily by considerations of welfare, security, and power."[45] This hybrid system was quite different from the British gold standard, in which "the circuits and networks of high finance had been firmly in the hands of private bankers and financiers who organized and managed them with a view to making a profit."[46] Nonetheless, in both epochs a novel international monetary order was called into existence by the exigencies of expanding trade. And the impact of the introduction of both monetary systems was very similar. In both periods, high levels of capital mobility forced governments all over the world to remove or reduce taxation and develop policies that would be supportive of international capital. The foundations for high liberalism were put into place.

Economic Crises

What finally tipped the scales away from the social and economic protections baked into the Bretton Woods system was the 1970s oil crises. Not only did these crises mark the end of the post-World War II economic boom, but they also set off a slow but steady ideological turn away from the welfare state and embedded liberalism. Thus, the economic and political balance of the mid-century boom was upended by a contagious economic recession that impacted the world economy in ways that parallel the 1846–47 agrarian recession.

The economic crisis was driven by two oil-price shocks, one in 1973 followed by a second in 1979. The first oil shock occurred when the United States decided to support the Israeli military during the 1973 Yom Kippur War. In retaliation, members of the Organization of Arab Petroleum Exporting Countries (OAPEC) proclaimed an oil embargo. The embargo lasted until March 1974. At the time, the United States, Canada, Western Europe, Australia, and New Zealand relied heavily on crude oil, and OPEC was their major supplier. Western countries, hence, faced substantial petroleum shortages. As oil prices skyrocketed, all sectors of the economy were affected. Thus began the global recession. A second oil shock occurred in 1979 when oil supply was again curtailed, this time because of the Iranian Revolution.

Like the aftermath of the 1846–47 economic crisis, the global recession of the 1970s produced a shift away from "embedded capitalism" and toward the wide adoption of laissez-faire fundamentalism. That was because the oil crisis hit the two most advanced liberal economies, the United States and Britain, particularly hard. Both countries experienced a period of "stagflation": a period of high inflation accompanied by high unemployment. Government was quickly blamed for the recession. With low job creation and escalating consumer prices, it was argued that excessive government spending and highly inflated labor prices created by unions had brought the crisis about. Constraints placed on market freedoms that had long been accepted as necessary state prerogatives were discredited. Markets, it was now argued, could better allocate funds and shift investment in ways that would be profitable to enterprises, regions, and economic sectors.

The 1980s became a period of economic and political restructuring, as the "pressure for financial deregulation gathered pace" and "the attack upon the real wage and organized union power, that began as an economic necessity in the crisis of 1973–5, were simply turned by the neo-conservatives into a governmental virtue."[47] In 1980, this shift would be solemnized as the birth of the Reagan-Thatcher revolution, when "Nineteenth-century beliefs in the 'self-regulating market'—in Polanyi's sense—became the official ideology of the US government."[48] Under the tutelage of the two leaders of "the free world," the four-decades-old Progressive Era regime was abandoned.

When Margaret Thatcher came to power in 1979, Britain had had a relatively socialized economy. There was widespread government ownership of industries and trade unions were very powerful.[49] However, in the 1970s, the economy suffered a severe setback. By "1975, inflation hit twenty-five per cent. The next year, Britain became the first developed country to receive an I.M.F. bailout."[50] Thatcher believed Britain's Keynesian economic policies, which gave government the power to intercede in the economy to keep employment levels high and reduce the harm that market forces could produce, were the problem. Thatcher set out to free the economy from such undue restraints. She privatized the major government-owned industries and sold government-owned housing to tenants. As Thatcher, when Regan assumed office in 1981, the American economy was also experiencing a severe downturn. Political crises in the 1970s had gravely reduced world oil production.

The price of gas at the pump increased exponentially. Even worse, the scarcity of oil was such that gas had to be rationed across the United States. With gas prices skyrocketing, the price of all goods rose. Regan was elected on a platform to "make America great again." He argued that the problem with the American economy was the "nanny" welfare state, which had allowed the federal government to balloon and hampered business. To reduce inflation and improve job creation, Regan set out to restructure the economy. His "trickle down" economic theory was based on the assumption that when industry leaders prospered, the rest of the country would prosper. He, therefore, introduced policies designed to end constraints on trade and industry. He undermined the power of labor unions, retrenched government regulations, and lowered tax rates.

The "Reagan-Thatcher Revolution" marked the rebirth of the "liberal creed," of laissez-faire economics. Because of the inordinate power of the United States, especially after the establishment of GATT and the WTO, "austerity, fiscal retrenchment, and erosion of the social compromise between big labour and big government became the watchwords in every state in the advanced capitalist world."[51] By 1986, some version of the neo-liberal mantra of free markets and preventing government excess was being intoned in financial centers around the globe. For the second time in history, the world would be subject to the unstable flux of mobile capital, almost wholly freed from political restraints.

But just as Polanyi describes the hypocrisy of nineteenth-century free-trader ideologues, in the twentieth century, governments that most loudly championed non-intervention and fiscal conservatism became more, rather than less, interventionist. The difference was that now the interventions were designed to protect capital and industry, not the weakest members of society. The "modalities, targets of, as well as the capacity for, state intervention" was changed, but this did not mean that state interventionism decreased; to the contrary "in some respects—particularly regarding labour control—state intervention [became] more crucial."[52] What was true of this second period of disembedded markets was that government was now working to protect capital interests rather than society. Above all, the liberal creed had once again triumphed. Social protections that had been the anchor of the Bretton Woods system had been eliminated. High liberalism was on the move and society was once again being steamrolled by global capital. The double movement had been set in motion.

Conclusion

Just as the post-Napoleonic War period, the post-World War II period was a novel interlude of sustained accords among the major powers. The prolonged peace in both epochs allowed for investment in industry, the flourishing of innovative technologies, and the resurgence of international commerce. As world trade steadily rose, there developed a demand for a new monetary system that gave capital enhanced mobility. Expanding trade and capital mobility greased the wheels that produced global economic shocks. The remnants of the protectionist order crumbled and liberalism triumphed over social protections. The world was poised for an era of globalization and the double movement.

In the final analysis, the postbellum periods provided the space among the advanced industrial countries that would allow for a confluence of global trade and global finance. Schumpeter was arguably correct that technological innovation set in motion the extraordinary modernization of the late nineteenth and twentieth centuries. Revolutions in transportation and communications collapsed time and space, forever altering social, political, and economic relations. But the reason technology reached such zeniths was because an extended period of peace among the most advanced nations allowed innovation and international commerce to soar. If technological revolutions created the unfathomable level of global interconnectivity that set off the double movement, it was the politics that preceded it, the sustained period of international stability, which created the possibility for those revolutions to unfold.

Conclusion

Using History as a Guide

We have arrived in the twenty-first century to a world in which democracy has been threatened in the very nation that regards itself as her beacon. Medieval-like conspiracy theories of Satanic rituals and lizards hiding under human form have taken hold in some of the most advanced countries in the world. This is certainly not what was envisioned by the likes of Stanley Kubrick and Arthur C. Clarke, the futurists of the twentieth century. How can we make sense of all this? How did we get here?

At the very least, if we were not aware of it before, we should have learned by now that history does not soar upward in a straight arrow toward liberty, reason, and freedom. Nor does it repeat itself. It is neither linear, nor circular. Perhaps it is better understood as a wobbly spherical ellipsis of sorts. As the dictum goes, history does not repeat itself, but it does rhythm. The Gilded Age certainly does rhythm with today's Digital Age. Like our own moment in history, it was a period dominated by the ideal of individualism, colored by an almost religious belief in the power of markets, and marked by the rise of a small group of super-rich entrepreneurs and bankers. It was also an era of profound incongruities. On one side, there was the liberal triumph of women's enfranchisement, remarkable strides in fighting disease, and the miraculous introduction of the electric light, the phonograph, and the telephone. On the other side, the working poor were left to suffer in "the deepest poverty, the sharpest struggle for existence, and the most of enforced idleness."[1]

The numerous parallels with our own times suggest that using such a historical comparison can provide insight into how we got to where we are and, perhaps, even offer a glimpse of what is to come. Yet, there are such dramatic differences between the periods being compared. Given that this is so, to what extent can history be a guide?

Arguably, there are some valuable lessons from the previous century that can direct our thinking about the future. One such lesson is offered

Defensive Nationalism. B. S. Rabinowitz, Oxford University Press. © Oxford University Press 2023.
DOI: 10.1093/oso/9780197672037.003.0015

by parallels in the evolution of mass media in both eras. At the last turn of the century, for the first time in history, new forms of communication and transportation created the possibility of disseminating news to a mass audience. The Broadsheet and Penny Newspaper were to the Gilded Age what the Internet and social media are to the Digital Age. At first, this led to a race to the bottom. Sensationalism sold copy. But Yellow Journalism did come to an end. Change began with campaigns against the printing of dangerous advertisements made by "nostrum manufacturers" that falsely claimed their products were "medicinal" cures. The newspapers for a long time were able to hide behind a *caveat emptor* policy, claiming that it was the responsibility of news readers to determine the veracity of advertisements, not the news publishers. In response, independent journalists, called "muckrakers," put unceasing pressure on the news industry to adopt an ethical posture. At the same time, the large news outlets were becoming dependent upon advertising dollars to stay in print. The industry began to recognize both the importance of fostering a politically heterogeneous readership and protecting itself from potential legal sanctions. Newspapers began to police themselves. "Objectivity and professionalism became a buffer, helping commercial newspaper companies stake a claim to their legitimacy as they monopolized local markets and as daily newspapers not owned by wealthy individuals or corporations began to disappear."[2] By 1923, the American Society of News Editors issued its "Canons of Ethics," the first standards for ethics in journalism. This was the beginning of responsible journalism.

We may be undergoing a similar process today. In June 2020, increasing public disaffection with Facebook's handling of hate speech and misinformation prompted large corporate advertisers, like Coca-Cola, Verizon, Levi Strauss, and Unilever, to threaten to pause advertising on the social network. The heat was also felt by Twitter, Reddit, and YouTube. Social media platforms began to take action. Some accounts were taken down. Some warning messages were put up. Thus, public discontent influenced powerful advertisers to push these large tech giants to start policing themselves. The momentum increased after the January 2021 storming of the Capitol in the United States. Facebook, Twitter, and others banned Donald Trump from using their platforms. Like the American Society of News Editors who banded together to develop standards for ethical journalism, Facebook launched its own Oversight Board. Designed to be independent, the board was tasked with developing a set of policies and principles to govern decisions on digital content and the company's governance. It therefore appears that we may be moving toward a new era of media control in which freedom of speech will be better balanced against the need to protect society from dangerous, incendiary rhetoric. As in the last century, it is likely that the media's self-policing will not be enough. We will probably need to develop a new legal structure to address the communications world of today. But looking to history does offer a hint of how that might come to pass.

That said, there are also critical differences between the two eras. In the early twentieth century, the tragedy of World War I and the severity of the Great Depression wreaked havoc across Europe and the United States. Although the combination of the COVID-19 pandemic and the oil crisis set off by Russia's invasion of Ukraine have undermined sociopolitical structures and national economies, the suffering experienced in Europe and America during the first decades of the twentieth century was arguably on a whole order of magnitude more intense than the displacements experienced across the developed world in the early 2020s (with the exception of Ukraine). Additionally, as polarized as we are in the developed world, we are nowhere near as divided as the advanced nations were in the 1910s and 1920s when communists and fascists faced off against one another. Although alt-right movements of today strongly resemble the fascist movements of yesteryear, communism remains a discredited alternative. As much as conservatives might try to paint social welfare policies as communist, they are not. Thus, the poles themselves are not as dichotomous.

Another crucial difference is that democratic institutions are more deeply rooted than they were at the naissance of the last century. With the exceptions of Britain and the United States, modern democratic systems in the early twentieth century had either not yet been instituted or were quite new and fragile. Even though we have seen the radical right make steady gains across Western Europe and the United States, those gains have continued to be reined in by liberal political institutions. It is true the United States has faced serious threats to her democratic system and witnessed the undoing of liberal social policies once thought sacrosanct. Yet, the political system has, thus far, been able to hold the most serious of these anti-democratic forces at bay. Where fascism has been able to take greater hold, democracy is as new and vulnerable as it was in Western Europe at the turn of the century. Countries in the former Eastern bloc, such as Hungary, Poland, and Russia, have gone the furthest in rolling back democratic reforms.

Moreover, unlike people living a century ago, we have a recorded history of the tragic effects of fascism and communism. Presumably, more people are concerned to guard against such occurrences than were at the turn of the nineteenth century. Evidence of this is that by spring of 2021, much of the hot air had gone out of several white supremacist/neo-fascist movements. The leaders of the Golden Dawn in Greece were behind bars. The website of the British National Front had been permanently removed. Even Donald Trump had been banned from Facebook. There are therefore indications that we could be moving away from the worst outcomes of the last century.

Also, the world is far more urban and mobile than it was one hundred years ago. Across advanced economies, urban areas have consistently been more liberal and tolerant and supportive of the kind of social welfare systems that so effectively stabilized the world economy after World War II. All these factors combined could provide the space for a new "Bretton Woods compromise." The double movement of today could well produce a new form of "embedded liberalism," in which national economic sovereignty would be better balanced against global finance, and political freedoms would coexist with greater social protections.

On the other hand, there are many disconcerting differences. Although the falsities of the period of Yellow Journalism have strong parallels to our era of "post-truth," today's fake news is arguably more pernicious. This is, in part, because the speed with which disinformation can be spread has been amplified by modern technologies. Emotionally charged posts, with carefully chosen words and images, can be quickly passed along social media platforms by trusted friends. In this way, social networks spread dangerously false content across the Internet at lightning speed. Equally worrying is the fact that information is not dispersed evenly. The algorithms that media platforms have developed to personalize information for individuals has meant that like groups see the same things, but unalike groups do not. As a result, even when a controversial claim can be adequately "fact-checked," it may have already sowed so much outrage or confusion that any appeal to facts is rendered ineffectual. Even more disconcerting is that the motivation of bad actors on the Internet is less to spread propaganda or even misinformation, as much as to create a "topsy-turvy, disorienting reality" in which "fake news mislabels real news as fake," so that "truth feels unknowable."[3] These effects are accentuated by the fact that media platforms use "proprietary 'black box' technologies, including opaque filtering, ranking, and recommendation algorithms [that] mediate access to information," and which undermine "organizational credibility and reputational trust."[4] In this way, social networks have produced information silos that divide populations, leaving little possibility for consensus and undermining democratic processes.

Indeed, our established democracies do not seem to be as immune to authoritarianism as we once presumed them to be. Liberal values can no longer be taken for granted. In one country after another, the center has been hollowed out, democratic institutions have come under fire, and right-wing populists and demagogues still hold sway over significant portions of the population. Donald Trump's presidency revealed how vulnerable even a seemingly well-established democracy can be. So many tacit norms were violated that had never been questioned. Liberal democratic governments are vulnerable precisely because they play by the rules and respect conventional codes of behavior and decorum. But outsider populists may not. Trump was able to work within the letter of the law to bend the laws and undermine the republican structure of the government. It is possible that a future political leader could take things even further.

Across Europe and the United States, radical white-nationalist organizations, with strong ties to the military and security forces, have been coordinating and sharing tactics. In the United States, various militia groups have been stockpiling weapons for decades hoping to initiate a great "Race War." In Germany, neo-Nazi movements, with ties to groups in Switzerland and Austria, have been strengthening since 2015 and preparing for the moment when the democratic order falls and their forces can march in and assume power—what they refer to as "Day X."[5] This may sound like disillusioned posturing, but the threat should not be dismissed. In December of 2022, twenty-five people were arrested for plotting to storm the German Capitol, arrest lawmakers, execute the chancellor, and place a man descended from German nobility as the head of state. A member of the intelligence oversight committee in the German parliament explained to the New York Times that "This is not the first case of a cell like this planning for Day X." Adding that, "The number of these cases are piling up and the question is to what extent are they connected."[6] And it is not just Germany. In 2021, the Italian police foiled an extremist right-wing plot to bomb a NATO military base.[7] Even the Finnish Security and Intelligence Service reported in 2021 that right-wing extremist groups posed a growing danger to national security.[8]

There are ominous international signs as well. Over the past couple of decades, the balance of power among the global titans has become more precarious. The rise of China and Russia has eaten away at the unipolar order established after the fall of the Soviet Union. As before World War I, competing powers are increasingly vying against one another for regional control and world influence. Distrust of international fora has further weakened the foundations of an already shaky international order. Indeed, a hallmark of defensive nationalism—the combination of distrust of globalism and the move toward protectionism—is increased bellicosity. It may be that we are at the end of our cycle of one-hundred-years-peace that commenced with the Paris Peace Conference. Political spheres of influence established in the 1940s seem to be fraying at their outer limits. Ukraine, Taiwan, islands in the South China seas, and even the airspace above North Korea have become potential flash points that could set off some kind of international conflagration. What that would look like and how it would manifest remains unclear, but Russia's invasion of Ukraine in 2022 might indeed be a foreshadowing of things to come.

For these reasons, it is worth remembering the sobering example of Sir Ralph Norman Angell, turn-of-the-century lecturer, journalist, and Member of British Parliament. In his book *The Great Illusion*, published in 1910, Angell argued that industrialized countries had become so economically intertwined that a European war had become highly unlikely. Angell boldly proclaimed in his prologue that "society is classifying itself by [economic] interests rather than by State divisions; that the modern State is losing its homogeneity; and that all these multiple factors are making rapidly for the disappearances of State rivalries."[9] Angell's assurances of the power of economic interests to steady the international arena were published only four years before the outbreak of World War I! Angell is now best known for these sanguine liberal assumptions on the eve of mass destruction.

In contrast to Angell's optimistic prognosis, a contemporary of his, S.H. Swinny, proved to be much more prescient:

> Modern science, if it is the great bond of human unity, the destroyer of old divisions and animosities, the necessary basis of a human ethnic common to all peoples, is also a powerful weapon of destruction and exploitation. Unenlightened sentiment may easily be turned to evil, the spread of civilization or the protection of the weak becoming the cloak of many crimes. What could be a more dangerous situation than that in which a body of men, with large interests in the exploitation of a backward people or their land, and with the means of enlisting capable advocates in the Press, can persuade their fellow countrymen that the prosperity and power of their

own country, and the happiness and progress of the weaker race, will both be enhanced by a policy of aggression?[10]

It is unclear which of these worlds we are closer to today—Angell's ruled by a liberal ethos, or Swinny's led by unenlightened sentiment. It is even less clear in which world we will be tomorrow. What we do know, however, is that history does rhythm, and that the cacophonous sounds of defensive nationalism can produce atonal, chaotic noise that can undermine world harmony and liberal democracies. It would therefore be wise to remain ever vigilant.

Notes

Introduction

1. S. H. Swinny, "Rationalism and International Righteousness," in *Essays Towards Peace*, ed. John M. Robertson et al. (London: Watts & Co., 1913), 77.

2. Democratic Audit UK, "Understanding the 'Rise' of the Radical Left in Europe: It's Not Just the Economy, Stupid," July 12, 2018, https://www.democraticaudit.com/2018/07/12/understanding-the-rise-of-the-radical-left-in-europe-its-not-just-the-economy-stupid/.

3. Roger Cohen and Aurelien Breeden, "Pro-Macron Forces Expected to Prevail but Face Left-Wing Challenge," *The New York Times*, June 12, 2022, https://www.nytimes.com/2022/06/12/world/europe/france-elections-macron.html?campaign_id=2&emc=edit_th_20220612&instance_id=63888&nl=todaysheadlines&regi_id=51583210&segment_id=94977&user_id=13ff8d54cbf7af799d623a24b55951c7.

4. Helen V. Milner, "Voting for Populism in Europe: Globalization, Technological Change, and the Extreme Right," *Comparative Political Studies* 54, no. 13 (2021): 2286–320; Dani Rodrik, "Why Does Globalization Fuel Populism? Economics, Culture, and the Rise of Right-Wing Populism," *Annual Review of Economics* 13 (2020): 133–70; Rogers Brubaker, "Populism and Nationalism," *Nations and Nationalism* 26, no. 1 (2020): 44–66; Broz J. Lawrence, Jeffry Frieden, and Stephen Weymouth, "Populism in Place: The Economic Geography of the Globalization Backlash," *International Organization* 75, no. 2 (2021): 464–94; Michael Cox, "The Rise of Populism and the Crisis of Globalisation: Brexit, Trump and Beyond," *Irish Studies in International Affairs 28*, no. 1 (2017): 9–17.

5. Michael Hameleers and Rens Vliegenthart, "The Rise of a Populist Zeitgeist? A Content Analysis of Populist Media Coverage in Newspapers Published between 1990 and 2017," *Journalism Studies* 21, no. 1 (2020): 19–36; Alexandros Kioupkiolis and Giorgos Katsambekis, "Radical Left Populism from the Margins to the Mainstream: A Comparison of Syriza and Podemos," in *Podemos and the New Political Cycle*, ed. Óscar García Agustín and Marco Briziarelli (London: Palgrave Macmillan, 2018), 201–26; Nicole Ernst, Sven Engesser, Florin Buchel, Sina Blassnig, and Frank Esser, "Extreme Parties and Populism: An Analysis of Facebook and Twitter across Six Countries," *Information, Communication & Society* 20, no. 9 (2017): 1347–64; Maurits J. Meijers, "Radical Right and Radical Left Euroscepticism. A Dynamic Phenomenon," *Notre Europe Policy Paper* 191 (2017); Yannis Stavrakakis and Giorgos Katsambekis, "Left-Wing Populism in the European Periphery: The Case of SYRIZA," *Journal of Political Ideologies* 19, no. 2 (2014): 119–42.

6. Bart Bonikowski, Daphne Halikiopoulou, Eric Kaufmann, and Matthijs Rooduijn, "Populism and Nationalism in a Comparative Perspective: A Scholarly Exchange," *Nations and Nationalism* 25, no.1 (2019): 58–81.

7. Benjamin De Cleen and Yannis Stavrakakis, "How Should We Analyze the Connections between Populism and Nationalism: A Response to Rogers Brubaker," *Nations and Nationalism* 26, no. 2 (2020): 314–22.

8. Brubaker, "Populism and Nationalism."

9. As will be discussed in Chapter 1, *defensive nationalism* is not the same as nativism; though nativism is the right-wing expression of it, it represents only half of the concept.

10. There are of course comparable movements occurring in other parts of the world, but the scope of this project is so large that some limitations had to be put in place. Only the United States and Europe are examined.

11. See Barry J. Eichengreen, *The Populist Temptation: Economic Grievance and Political Reaction in the Modern Era* (New York: Oxford University Press, 2018); John B. Judis, *The Populist Explosion: How the Great Recession Transformed American and European Politics* (New York: Columbia Global Reports, 2016); Beverly J. Silver and Giovanni Arrighi, "Polanyi's "Double Movement": The Belle Époques of British and US Hegemony Compared," *Politics & Society* 31, no. 2 (2003): 325–55.

12. Karl Polanyi, *The Great Transformation: The Political and Economic Origins of Our Time* (Boston: Beacon Press, 2001).

13. Joseph A. Schumpeter, *Business Cycles: A Theoretical, Historical, and Statistical Analysis of the Capitalist Process, Volumes I & II* (New York: McGraw-Hill Book Company, 1923).

Chapter 1

1. Jürgen Habermas, "The European Nation-State: On the Past and Future of Sovereignty and Citizenship," trans. Ciaran Cronin, *Public Culture* 10, no. 2 (1998): 401.

2. Ibid., 402.

3. Giuseppe Mazzini, *The Duties of Man and Other Essays [by] Joseph Mazzini* (England: J.M. Dent & sons, ltd.; E.P. Dutton & co., inc., 1915), 52.

4. Ernest Renan, "What Is a Nation?" (Qu'est-Ce Qu'une Nation?, 1882)," in *What Is a Nation? And Other Political Writings*, trans. M. F. N. Giglioli (New York: Columbia University Press, 2018), 255. http://www.jstor.org/stable/10.7312/rena17430.15.

5. Ibid., 260.

6. Ibid., 251.

7. Rogers Brubaker, "The Manichean Myth: Rethinking the Distinction between 'Civic' and 'Ethnic' Nationalism," *Nation and National Identity: The European Experience in Perspective* (1999): 55–71.

8. Hans Kohn, "The Nature of Nationalism," *American Political Science Review* 33, no. 6 (1939): 1006.

9. Ibid., 1014.
10. Ibid., 1006.
11. Ibid., 1021.
12. Ibid., 1019.
13. Hannah Arendt, *The Origins of Totalitarianism* (New York: Harcourt, Brace, 1951), 271.
14. Arendt explains this in the following passage: "Denationalization became a powerful weapon of totalitarian politics, and the constitutional inability of European nation-states to guarantee human rights to those who had lost nationally guaranteed rights, made it possible for the persecuting governments to impose their standard of values even upon their opponents. Those whom the persecutor had singled out as scum of the earth—Jews, Trotskyites, etc.—actually were received as scum of the earth everywhere; those whom persecution had called undesirable became the indesirables of Europe . . . The very phrase "human rights" became for all concerned—victims, persecutors, and onlookers alike—the evidence of hopeless idealism or fumbling feeble-minded hypocrisy." [Hannah Arendt, *The Origins of Totalitarianism* (New York: Harcourt, Brace, 1951), 269]
15. Ibid., 302.
16. Yael Tamir, *Liberal Nationalism* (Princeton, NJ: Princeton University Press, 1993); David Miller, *On Nationality* (Oxford: Clarendon, 1997); David Miller, *On Nationality* (Oxford: Clarendon, 1997); Chaim Gans, *The Limits of Nationalism* (Cambridge: Cambridge University Press, 2003.
17. Eric Kaufmann, "Ethno-traditional Nationalism and the Challenge of Immigration," *Nations and Nationalism* 25, no. 2 (2019): 435–48; George L. Mosse, "Racism and Nationalism," *Nations and Nationalism* 1, no. 2 (1995): 163173.
18. Jürgen Habermas and Ciaran Cronin, "The European Nation-State: On the Past and Future of Sovereignty and Citizenship," *Public Culture* 10, no. 2 (1998): 397–416.
19. Rogers Brubaker, "Migrations of Ethnic Unmixing in the 'New Europe,' " *International Migration Review* 32, no. 4 (1998): 1047–65.
20. Ernest Gellner, *Nations and Nationalism* (Ithaca, NY: Cornell University Press, 2006), 35.
21. Benedict Anderson, *Imagined Communities: Reflections on the Origin and Spread of Nationalism* (New York: Verso Books, 2006) 46.
22. Gellner, *Nations and Nationalism*, 35.
23. Anderson, *Imagined Communities*, 46.
24. David Levi-Faur, "Economic Nationalism: From Friedrich List to Robert Reich." *Review of International Studies* 23, no. 3 (1997): 359–70.
25. Walt Whitman Rostow, "The Problem of Achieving and Maintaining a High Rate of Economic Growth: A Historian's View," *The American Economic Review* 50, no. 2 (1960): 106–18 .W. Arthur Lewis, "Some Reflections on Economic Development," *Economic Digest* 3, no. 4 (1960): 3–8; Alexander Gerschenkron, *Economic Backwardness in Historical Perspective* (Cambridge, MA: Belknap Press of Harvard University Press, 1962).

26. Andre Gunder Frank, *Latin America: Underdevelopment and Revolution* (New York: Monthly Review Press, 1969); Fernando Henrique Cardoso and Enzo Faletto, *Dependency and Development in Latin America* (Berkeley: University of California Press, 1979).

27. Nicola Mackie, "'Popularis' Ideology and Popular Politics at Rome in the First Century B.C.," *Rheinisches Museum für Philologie* 135, no. 1 (1992): 51.

28. Benjamin Moffitt, *The Global Rise of Populism: Performance, Political Style, and Representation* (Palo Alto, CA: Stanford University Press, 2016), 16–27.

29. See Rogers Brubaker, "Populism and Nationalism," *Nations and Nationalism* 26, no. 1 (2020): 44–66; Chantal Mouffe, *For a Left Populism* (London; Verso, 2018); C. Mudde, "An Ideational Approach," in *The Oxford Handbook of Populism*, ed. Cristóbal Rovira Kaltwasser, Paul A. Taggart, Paulina Ochoa Espejo, and Pierre Ostiguy (Oxford: Oxford University Press, 2017); Moffit, *The Global Rise of Populism*; Bart Bonikowski, "Nationalism in Settled Times," *Annual Review of Sociology* 42, no. 1 (2016): 427–49; Slovj Žižek, "Against the Populist Temptation," *Critical Inquiry* 32, no. 3 (2006): 551–74.

30. Ernesto Laclau, quoted in Žižek, "Against the Populist Temptation," 555.

31. See Michael Hameleers and Rens Vliegenthart, "The Rise of a Populist Zeitgeist? A Content Analysis of Populist Media Coverage in Newspapers Published between 1990 and 2017," *Journalism Studies* 21, no. 1 (2020): 19–36; Alexandros Kioupkiolis and Giorgos Katsambekis, "Radical Left Populism from the Margins to the Mainstream: A Comparison of Syriza and Podemos," in *Podemos and the New Political Cycle*, ed. Óscar García Agustín and Marco Briziarelli (London: Palgrave Macmillan, 2018), 201–26; Nicole Ernst, Sven Engesser, Florin Buchel, Sina Blassnig, and Frank Esser, "Extreme Parties and Populism: An Analysis of Facebook and Twitter Across Six Countries," *Information, Communication & Society* 20, no. 9 (2017): 1347–64; Maurits J. Meijers, "Radical Right and Radical Left Euroscepticism. A Dynamic Phenomenon," *Notre Europe Policy Paper* 191 (2017); Yannis Stavrakakis and Giorgos Katsambekis, "Left-Wing Populism in the European Periphery: The Case of SYRIZA," *Journal of Political Ideologies* 19, no. 2 (2014): 119–42.

32. Sheri Berman, "The Causes of Populism in the West," *Annual Review of Political Science* 24 (2021): 71–88; Dani Rodrik, "Why Does Globalization Fuel Populism? Economics, Culture, and the Rise of Right-Wing Populism," *Annual Review of Economics* 13 (2020): 133–170; Luigi Guiso, Helios Herrera, Massimo Morelli, and Tommaso Sonno, *Demand and Supply of Populism* (London: Centre for Economic Policy Research, 2017).

33. Mabel Berezin, "Fascism and Populism: Are They Useful Categories for Comparative Sociological Analysis?," *Annual Review of Sociology* 45, no. 1 (2019): 349.

34. Robert O. Paxton, *The Anatomy of Fascism* (New York: Knopf, 2004), 4.

35. Robert O. Paxton, "The Five Stages of Fascism," *The Journal of Modern History* 70, no. 1 (1998): 1.

36. Zeev Sternhell, "How to Think about Fascism and Its Ideology," *Constellations* 15, no. 3 (2008): 280–90; Roger Eatwell, "The Esoteric Ideology of the National Front

in the 1980s," in *The Failure of British Fascism: the Far Right and the Fight for Political Recognition*, ed. Mike Cronin (London: Palgrave Macmillan, 1996), 99–117.

37. Paxton, "The Five Stages of Fascism," 4.

38. Gilbert Allardyce, "What Fascism Is Not: Thoughts on the Deflation of a Concept," *The American Historical Review* 84, no. 2 (1979): 374.

39. Paxton, "The Five Stages of Fascism," 5.

40. Stanley G. Payne, *Fascism: Comparison and Definition* (Madison: University of Wisconsin Press, 1983), 198.

41. Zeev Sternhell, Mario Sznajder, and Maia Ashéri, *The Birth of Fascist Ideology: From Cultural Rebellion to Political Revolution* (Princeton: Princeton University Press, 1994), 10.

42. A. James Gregor, *Interpretations of Fascism* (New York: Routledge, 2017), xxviii.

43. Sternhell et al., *The Birth of Fascist Ideology*, 231.

44. Stanley G. Payne, *History of Fascism, 1914–1945* (Madison: University of Wisconsin Press, 1996), 9.

45. Jason Stanley, *How Fascism Works: The Politics of Us and Them* (New York: Random House, 2020), 122.

46. Payne, *History of Fascism, 1914–1945*, 14.

47. Sternhell et al., *The Birth of Fascist Ideology*.

48. Paxton, *The Anatomy of Fascism*, 11.

49. Ibid.

50. Allardyce, "What Fascism Is Not: Thoughts on the Deflation of a Concept," 376.

51. Payne, *Fascism: Comparison and Definition*.

52. Hans-Georg Betz, "Nativism Across Time and Space," *Swiss Political Science Review* 23, no. 4 (2017): 336.

53. Betz, "Nativism Across Time and Space," 337.

54. Theresa Davidson and Karlye Burson, "Keep Those Kids Out: Nativism and Attitudes toward Access to Public Education for the Children of Undocumented Immigrants," *Journal of Latinos and Education* 16, no. 1 (2017): 41–50; Cameron D. Lippard, "Racist Nativism in the 21st Century," *Sociology Compass* 5, no. 7 (2011): 591–606; George J. Sánchez, "Face the Nation: Race, Immigration, and the Rise of Nativism in Late Twentieth Century America," *International Migration Review* 31, no. 4 (1997): 1009–30; Tyler Anbinder, *Nativism and Slavery: The Northern Know Nothings and the Politics of the 1850's* (New York: Oxford University Press, 1992).

55. George Newth, "Populism and Nativism in Contemporary Regionalist and Nationalist Politics: A Minimalist Framework for Ideologically Opposed Parties," *Politics* (2021): 3–5.

56. John Higham, *Strangers in the Land: Patterns of American Nativism, 1860–1925* (New Brunswick, NJ: Rutgers University Press, 2002), 3.

57. Lilia Fernandez, "Nativism and Xenophobia," *The Encyclopedia of Global Human Migration* (2013): 1.

58. John Higham, *Strangers in the Land Patterns of American Nativism, 1860–1925* (New Brunswick, NJ: Rutgers University Press, 2002). 4.

59. Newth, "Populism and Nativism in Contemporary Regionalist and Nationalist Politics," 15.
60. Ibid., 4.

Chapter 2

1. See Beth Rabinowitz, "Defensive Nationalism: Where Populism Meets Nationalism," *Nationalism and Ethnic Politics* 28, no. 2 (2022): 143–64.
2. For a thorough exploration of this process, see Ronald Grigor Suny, *The Revenge of the Past: Nationalism, Revolution, and the Collapse of the Soviet Union* (Stanford University Press, 1993).
3. Ernest Gellner, *Nations and Nationalism* (Ithaca, NY: Cornell University Press, 2006); Benedict Anderson, *Imagined Communities: Reflections on the Origin and Spread of Nationalism* (New York: Verso Books, 2006).
4. Michael Howard, "War and the Nation-State," *Daedalus* (1979): 101–10.
5. Rogers Brubaker, *Citizenship and Nationhood in France and Germany* (Cambridge, MA: Harvard University Press, 1992).
6. Janet Klein, "Kurdish Nationalists and Nonnationalist Kurdists: Rethinking Minority Nationalism and the Dissolution of the Ottoman Empire, 1908–1909," *Nations and Nationalism* 13, no. 1 (2007): 135–53.
7. Prabhat Datta, "Secessionist Movements in North East India," *The Indian Journal of Political Science* 53, no. 4 (Oct.–Dec. 1992): 536–58.
8. Michael Billig, *Banal Nationalism* (London: SAGE, 1995), 5.
9. Carl Gans, "Punctuated Equilibria and Political Science: A Neontological View," *Politics and the Life Sciences* 5, no. 2 (1987): 220–27.
10. Eugen Weber, *Peasants into Frenchmen: The Modernization of Rural France, 1870–1914* (Stanford, CA: Stanford University Press, 1976).
11. David Waldstreicher, *In the Midst of Perpetual Fetes: the Making of American Nationalism, 1776–1820* (Chapel Hill: Published for the Omohundro Institute of Early American History and Culture, Williamsburg, Virginia, by the University of North Carolina Press, 1997).
12. See Steven M. Van Hauwaert, "Thinking Outside the Box: The Political Process Model and Far Right Party Emergence," *Journal of Contemporary European Studies* 29, no. 1 (2021): 84–98; Daphne Halikiopoulou and Tim Vlandas, "What Is New and What Is Nationalist about Europe's New Nationalism? Explaining the Rise of the Far Right in Europe," *Nations and Nationalism* 25, no. 2 (2019): 409–34; Manuela Caiani, "The Populist Parties and Their Electoral Success: Different Causes behind Different Populisms? The Case of the Five-star Movement and the League," *Contemporary Italian Politics* 11, no. 3 (2019): 236–50; Geertje Lucassen and Marcel Lubbers, "Who Fears What? Explaining Far-Right-Wing Preference in Europe by Distinguishing Perceived Cultural and Economic Ethnic Threats," *Comparative Political Studies* 45, no. 5 (2012): 547–574.

13. See Beverly Crawford, "Theory and Arguments: The Causes of Cultural Conflict: An Institutional Approach," in *The Myth of 'Ethnic Conflict': Politics, Economics, and 'Cultural' Violence* (University of California, Berkeley: Institute for International Studies, 1998), https://escholarship.org/uc/item/7hc733q3. Philip G. Roeder, "Liberalization and Ethnic Entrepreneurs in the Soviet Successor States," in *The Myth of "Ethnic Conflict": Politics, Economics and "Cultural" Violence*, ed. Beverly Crawford and Ronnie D. Lipschutz (University of California, Berkeley: Institute for International Studies, 1998); Chaim Kaufmann, "Possible and Impossible Solutions to Ethnic Civil Wars." *International Security* 20, no. 4 (1996): 136–75.

14. Bojana Blagojevic, "Causes of Ethnic Conflict: A Conceptual Framework," *Journal of Global Change & Governance* 3, no. 1 (2010): 10.

15. Max Weber quoted in Uta Gerhardt, "The Use of Weberian Ideal-Type Methodology in Qualitative Data Interpretation: An Outline for Ideal-Type Analysis," *Bulletin of Sociological Methodology/Bulletin de Méthodologie Sociologique* 45, no. 1 (1994): 79.

16. This civic notion of the national belonging can even be expanded to incorporate noncitizens who reside in the territory.

17. Rafal Soborski, "National Populism and Fascism: Blood and Soil against Globalization," in *Ideology in a Global Age*, ed. Rafal Soborski, 107–139 (London: Palgrave Macmillan, 2013).

18. The term "*volk*" is used as a shorthand. However, normally it more narrowly refers to a concept from nineteenth-century German "*völkisch*" movements and their contemporary "*neo-völkisch*" counterparts.

19. For a similar characterization of the right, see also Andreas Novy, "The Political Trilemma of Contemporary Social-Ecological Transformation–Lessons from Karl Polanyi's The Great Transformation," *Globalizations* 19, no. 1 (2022): 59–80.

20. Angela Nagle, "The Left Case against Open Borders," *American Affairs* 2, no. 4 (2018), https://americanaffairsjournal.org/2018/11/the-left-case-against-open-borders/.

21. Katya Johanson and Hilary Glow, "Honour Bound in Australia: From Defensive Nationalism to Critical Nationalism," *National Identities* 11, no. 4 (2009): 386.

22. Ibid., 388.

23. Ziya Öniş, "Conservative Globalists versus Defensive Nationalists: Political Parties and Paradoxes of Europeanization in Turkey," *Journal of Southern Europe and the Balkans* 9, no. 3 (2007): 247–61.

24. This also distinguishes the concept from Novy's "nationalistic capitalism," which is only focused on right-wing responses.

25. Christian Fuchs, *Nationalism on the Internet: Critical Theory and Ideology in the Age of Social Media and Fake News* (Milton: Routledge, 2020), 240–41.

26. Sebastian Edwards, "On Latin American Populism, and Its Echoes Around the World," *Journal of Economic Perspectives* 33, no. 4 (2019): 76–99.

27. Gareth Dale, *Karl Polanyi: A Life on the Left* (New York: Columbia University Press, 2016); Gareth Dale, "Karl Polanyi's the Great Transformation: Perverse Effects, Protectionism and Gemeinschaft," *Economy and Society* 37, no. 4 (2008): 495–524.

28. See Richard Sandbrook, "Polanyi's Double Movement and Capitalism Today," *Development and Change* 53, no. 3 (2022): 647–75; Hans-Jürgen Bieling, "Aufstieg

des Rechtspopulismus im heutigen Europa–Umrisse einer gesellschaftstheoretischen Erklärung," *WSI Mitteilungen* 8 (2017): 557–565; Claus Thomasberger and Michael Brie, "Karl Polanyi's Search for Freedom in a Complex Society," *Österreichische Zeitschrift für Soziologie* 44, no. 2 (2019): 169–182; Klaus Dörre, "Take Back Control!," *Österreichische Zeitschrift für Soziologie* 44, no. 2 (2019): 225–43; Robert Kuttner, *Can Democracy Survive Global Capitalism?* (New York: WW Norton & Company, 2018); Dale, *Karl Polanyi: A Life on the Left*; Dale, "Karl Polanyi's the Great Transformation."

29. See Dale, *Karl Polanyi: A Life on the Left*; Dale, "Karl Polanyi's the Great Transformation"; Gareth Dale and Mathieu Desan, "Fascism," in *Karl Polanyi's Political and Economic Thought: A Critical Guide*, ed. Gareth Dale, Christopher Holmes, and Maria Markantonatou, 151–170 (Newcastle, UK: Agenda Publishing, 2019); Sang Hun Lim, "Look Up Rather Than Down: Karl Polanyi's Fascism and Radical Right-Wing 'Populism.'" *Current Sociology* (2021), 00113921211015715.

30. See Sang Hun Lim, "'Look Up Rather Than Down': Karl Polanyi's Fascism and Radical Right-Wing 'Populism.'" *Current Sociology* (2021): 00113921211015715; Kris Millett, "On the Meaning and Contemporary Significance of Fascism in the writings of Karl Polanyi," *Theory and Society* 50, no. 3 (2021): 463–487. Dani Rodrik, "What's Driving Populism?," *Project Syndicate* 9 (2019); Karina Becker and Klaus Dörre, "Völkisch Populism: A Polanyian-Type Movement?," in *Capitalism in Transformation*, ed. Roland Atzmüller, Brigitte Aulenbacher, Ulrich Brand, Fabienne Décieux, Karin Fischer, and Birgit Sauer (Cheltenham, UK: Edward Elgar Publishing, 2019), 152–68; Brigitte Aulenbacher, Richard Bärnthaler, and Andreas Novy, "Karl Polanyi, The Great Transformation, and Contemporary Capitalism," *Österreichische Zeitschrift für Soziologie* 44, no. 2 (2019): 105–113; Dörre, "Take Back Control!"; Dale, "Karl Polanyi's the Great Transformation"; Dale and Desan, "Fascism"; Lim, "Look Up Rather Than Down."

31. See Michael Brie, ed. *Karl Polanyi's Vision of a Socialist Transformation* (Black Rose Books Ltd., 2019); Roland Atzmüller, Brigitte Aulenbacher, Ulrich Brand, Fabienne Décieux, Karin Fischer, and Birgit Sauer, eds., *Capitalism in Transformation* (Edward Elgar Publishing, 2019); Richard Bärnthaler, Andreas Novy, and Basil Stadelmann, "A Polanyi-Inspired Perspective on Social-Ecological Transformations of Cities," *Journal of Urban Affairs* (2020): 1–25; Michael Brie, "Karl Polanyi and Discussions on a Renewed Socialism," *Culture, Practice & Europeanization* 4, no. 1 (2019): 116–134; Klaus Dörre, "Landnahme: un concepto para el análisis de la dinámica capitalista, o: superando a Polanyi con Polanyi," *Política. Revista de Ciencia Política* 54, no. 2 (2016): 13–48; Axel Honneth, *The Idea of Socialism: Towards a Renewal* (Montreal, Quebec: John Wiley & Sons, 2016); Brigitte Aulenbacher, Fabienne Décieux, and Birgit Riegraf, "The Economic Shift and Beyond: Care as a Contested Terrain in Contemporary Capitalism," *Current Sociology* 66, no. 4 (2018): 517–30.

32. Sandbrook has also examined how scholars might use Polanyi to analyze the double movement today by comparing the 1830s–1931 with the neoliberal phase of the late 1970s until today. But his analysis is much looser and does not offer a schematic model such as the one presented here. See Richard Sandbrook, "Polanyi's Double Movement and Capitalism Today," *Development and Change* 53, no. 3 (2022): 647–75.

33. Richard Sandbrook, "Karl Polanyi and the Formation of This Generation's New Left," *IPPR Progressive Review* 25, no. 1 (2018): 81.

34. Andreas Novy, "The Political Trilemma of Contemporary Social-Ecological Transformation—Lessons from Karl Polanyi's *The Great Transformation*," *Globalizations* 19, no. 1 (2022): 72.

35. Sandbrook, "Karl Polanyi and the Formation of this Generation's New Left," 86.

36. Helen V. Milner, "Voting for Populism in Europe: Globalization, Technological Change, and the Extreme Right," *Comparative Political Studies* 54, no. 13 (2021): 2286–2320; Dani Rodrik, "Why Does Globalization Fuel Populism? Economics, Culture, and the Rise of Right-Wing Populism," *Annual Review of Economics* 13 (2020): 133–170; Rogers Brubaker, "Populism and Nationalism," *Nations and Nationalism* 26, no. 1 (2020): 44–66; Broz J. Lawrence, Jeffry Frieden, and Stephen Weymouth, "Populism in Place: The Economic Geography of the Globalization Backlash," *International Organization* 75, no. 2 (2021): 464–94.; Michael Cox, "The Rise of Populism and the Crisis of Globalisation: Brexit, Trump and Beyond," *Irish Studies in International Affairs* 28, no. 1 (2017): 9–17.

Chapter 3

1. See also Helen V. Milner and Keohane Robert, *Internationalization and Domestic Politics* (Cambridge: Cambridge University, 1996), 257.

2. Karl Polanyi, *The Great Transformation* (Boston: Beacon Press, 1944), 10.

3. Ibid., 10.

4. Ibid., 43.

5. Ibid., 48.

6. Ibid., 45.

7. Ibid., 88.

8. Ibid., 82.

9. M. C. Buer, "The Trade Depression Following the Napoleonic Wars," *Economica* 2 (1921): 169.

10. David Ricardo, *On the Principles of Political Economy and Taxation* (London: John Murray, 1821), 60.

11. Polanyi, *The Great Transformation*, 131–32.

12. Ibid., 86.

13. Ibid.

14. Ibid., 202.

15. Ibid., 261.

16. Ibid., 26.

17. Ibid., 262.

18. Ibid., 203.

19. Herbert Spencer, *The Proper Sphere of Government: A Reprint of a Series of Letters, Originally Published in "The Nonconformist"* (London: W. Brittain, 1843), 60.

20. Ibid., 187.
21. Polanyi, *The Great Transformation*, 10.
22. Ibid., 39.
23. Ibid.
24. Ibid., 73.
25. Ibid., 162.
26. Ibid., 151.
27. Ibid., 136.
28. Ibid., 250.
29. Ibid. 252.
30. Ibid., 248.
31. Ibid., 32.
32. See, for example, Christopher Holmes, *Polanyi in Times of Populism: Vision and Contradiction in the History of Economic Ideas* (London: Routledge, 2018); Martijn Konings, *The Emotional Logic of Capitalism: What Progressives Have Missed* (Stanford, CA: Stanford University Press, 2015); Fred Block and Margaret R. Somers, *The Power of Market Fundamentalism* (Cambridge, MA: Harvard University Press, 2014); Gareth Dale, *Polanyi: The Limits of the Market* (Cambridge, Ma: Polity Books, 2013); Richard Sandbrook, "Polanyi and Post-neoliberalism in the Global South: Dilemmas of Re-embedding the Economy," *New Political Economy* 16, no. 4 (2011): pp. 415–43; Beverly J. Silver and Giovanni Arrighi, "Polanyi's "Double Movement": The Belle Époques of British and US Hegemony Compared," *Politics & Society* 31, no. 2 (2003): 325–355; Ronaldo Munck, "Globalization and Contestation: A Polanyian Problematic," *Globalizations* 3, no. 2(2006): 175–186.
33. Gareth Dale, "Double Movements and Pendular Forces: Polanyian Perspectives on the Neoliberal Age," *Current Sociology* 60, no. 1 (2012): 12.
34. Quinn Slobodian, *Globalists: The End of Empire and the Birth of Neoliberalism* (Cambridge, MA: Harvard University Press, 2018).
35. Ibid.
36. Ibid., 80.
37. Ibid., 153.
38. Dale, "Polanyi: The Limits of the Market," 86.
39. Ibid., 78.
40. Silver and Arrighi, "Polanyi's 'Double Movement,'" 329.
41. Polanyi, *The Great Transformation*, 32.
42. Dale, "Double Movements and Pendular Forces," 11.
43. Gunnar Olofsson, "Embeddedness and Integration," *Capitalism and Social Cohesion* (London: Palgrave Macmillan, 1999), 38.
44. Dale, "Double Movements and Pendular Forces," 20–21.
45. Several Polanyian scholars have worked to reconcile the ambiguities of the concept and explain its utility. See Christopher Holmes, "Problems and Opportunities in Polanyian Analysis Today," *Economy and Society* 41, no. 3 (2012): 468–84; Greta Krippner, Mark Granovetter, Fred Block, Nicole Biggart, Tom Beamish, Youtien Hsing, Gillian Hart et al., "Polanyi Symposium: A Conversation on Embeddedness,"

Socio-economic Review 2, no. 1 (2004): 109–35; Gareth Dale, "Lineages of Embeddedness: On the Antecedents and Successors of a Polanyian Concept," *American Journal of Economics and Sociology* 70, no. 2 (2011): 306–39; Kurtuluş Gemici, "Karl Polanyi and the Antinomies of Embeddedness," *Socio-economic Review* 6, no. 1 (2008): 5–33.

46. Polanyi, *The Great Transformation*, 205.
47. Ibid.
48. Ibid., 155.
49. Ibid.
50. Ibid., 156.
51. Ibid., 157.
52. Gerardo Quinones, Richard Heeks, and Brian Nicholson, "Embeddedness of Digital Start-Ups in Development Contexts: Field Experience from Latin America," *Information Technology for Development* 27, no. 2 (2021): 171–90; Sandbrook, "Polanyi and Post-neoliberalism in the Global South."
53. Michael Levien and Marcel Paret, "A Second 'Double Movement'? Polanyi and Shifting Global Opinions on Neoliberalism," *International Sociology* 27, no. 6 (2012): 724–44.
54. See, Ronaldo Munck, "The Resistible Rise of Market Fundamentalism: Rethinking Development Policy in an Unbalanced World," *Capital & Class* 35, no. 3 (2011): 491; Thomas A. Stewart, *Intellectual Capital: The New Wealth of Organization* (New York: Currency, 2010).
55. Fred Block and Margaret R. Somers, *The Power of Market Fundamentalism* (Cambridge, MA: Harvard University Press, 2014).
56. Polanyi, *The Great Transformation*, 157.
57. See Phillip McMichael, "World-Systems Analysis, Globalization, and Incorporated Comparison," *Journal of World-Systems Research* (2000): 668–89; Giovanni Arrighi, *The Long Twentieth Century. New and updated edition* (London: Verso, 2010); Silver and Arrighi, "Polanyi's 'Double Movement.'"
58. See Barry Eichengreen, "Hegemonic Stability Theories of the International Monetary System," *International Political Economy* (2002): 230–254; Isabelle Grunberg, "Exploring the 'Myth' of Hegemonic Stability," *International Organization* 44, no. 4 (1990): 431–477; Robert Gilpin, "The Theory of Hegemonic War," *The Journal of Interdisciplinary History* 18, no. 4 (1988): 591–613; Karen A. Rasler and William R. Thompson, "Global Wars, Public Debts, and the Long Cycle," *World Politics* 35, no. 4 (1983): 489–516.
59. See Michael Colaresi, "Shocks to the System: Great Power Rivalry and the Leadership Long Cycle," *Journal of Conflict Resolution* 45, no. 5 (2001): 569–93; William R. Thompson, "Polarity, the Long Cycle, and Global Power Warfare," *Journal of Conflict Resolution* 30, no.4 (1986): 587–615.
60. Silver and Arrighi, "Polanyi's 'Double Movement,'" 326.
61. John Agnew, "The New Global Economy: Time-Space Compression, Geopolitics, and Global Uneven Development," *Journal of World-Systems Research* (2001): 143.
62. Polanyi, *The Great Transformation*, 263–66.

63. Ibid., 266.

64. John W. Meyer, John Boli, George M. Thomas, and Francisco O. Ramirez, "World Society and the Nation-State," *American Journal of Sociology* 103, no. 1 (1997): 144–81.

Chapter 4

1. Joseph A. Schumpeter, *Business Cycles: A Theoretical, Historical, and Statistical Analysis of the Capitalist Process, Volumes I & II* (New York: McGraw-Hill Book Company, 1923), 170.

2. Ibid., v.

3. Nikolai D. Kondratieff and W. F. Stolper, "The Long Waves in Economic Life," *The Review of Economics and Statistics* 17, no. 6 (1935): 115.

4. Ibid., 304.

5. Ibid., 156.

6. Ibid., 137.

7. Ibid., 105

8. Ibid.

9. Ibid., 264.

10. Ibid., 276–278.

11. Ibid, 260.

12. Ibid, 310.

13. Schumpeter, *Business Cycles Vol. 2*, 639.

14. Ibid., 268–269.

15. Ibid., 293.

16. Ibid., 294.

17. Ibid., 698–700.

18. This is a common theme in World Systems Theory, Long Cycle Theory, and Hegemonic War Theory, each of which examines aspects of capitalist cycles, cycles of hegemonic power, and cycles of major world wars. See Arrighi, "Global Inequalities and the Legacy of Dependency Theory"; Terence K. Hopkins and Immanuel Maurice Wallerstein, *World-Systems Analysis: Theory and Methodology* 1 (Beverly Hills: Sage, Incorporated, 1982); Karen A. Rasler and William R. Thompson, "Global Wars, Public Debts, and the Long Cycle," *World Politics* 35 (July 1983): 489–516; Christopher Chase-Dunn and Joan Sokolovsky, "Interstate Systems, World Empires, and the Capitalist World Economy: A Response to Thompson," *International Studies Quarterly* 27 (Sept. 1983): 364–366; Raimo Vdyrynen, "Economic Cycles, Power Transitions, Political Management and Wars between Major Powers," *International Studies Quarterly* 27 (Dec. 1983): 389–418; George Modelski, *Long Cycles in World Politics* (Seattle: University of Washington Press, 1985); Robert Gilpin, *War and Change in World Politics* (Cambridge: Cambridge University Press, 1981); Jack S. Levy, "Theories of General War," *World Politics* 37, no. 3 (Apr. 1985): 344–74.

19. Fredric Jameson, "Culture and Finance Capital," *Critical Inquiry* 24, no. 1 (1997): 251.

20. Paul Bairoch and Richard Kozul-Wright, "Globalization Myths: Some Historical Reflections on Integration, Industrialization and Growth in World Economy," *UNCTAD Discussion Papers* 113 (1996).

21. Dani Rodrik, *The Globalization Paradox: Why Global Markets, States, and Democracy Can't Coexist* (Oxford and New York: Oxford University Press, 2011), 76.

22. Munck, "Globalization and Contestation: A Polanyian Problematic," 178.

23. Rodrik, *The Globalization Paradox*.

24. David Harvey, *The Condition of Postmodernity: An Enquiry into the Origins of Cultural Change* (Oxford: Blackwell, 1989), 239–240.

25. Michael W. Doyle, "Liberalism and World Politics," *American Political Science Review* 80, no. 4 (1986): 1152.

26. Glenda Sluga, *Internationalism in the Age of Nationalism* (Philadelphia: University of Pennsylvania Press, 2013), 16–17.

27. Giovanni Capoccia and R. Daniel Kelemen, "The Study of Critical Junctures: Theory, Narrative, and Counterfactuals in Historical Institutionalism," *World Politics* 59, no. 3 (2007): 343.

28. World Trade Organization, *World Trade Report 2013*, 49.

29. There are dissenting opinions on this. Thus, Paul Bairoch and Richard Kozul-Wright argue:

"Contrary to much conventional wisdom, the inter-war period was not one of stagnation but contained spurts of rapid growth. Indeed, the 1920s grew considerably faster than any previous decade, and taking a long perspective there was, in fact, very little difference in the annual growth rate in the globalization era, the period 1913–1950. It is also a myth that globalization tendencies were absent from the inter-war period. Although the average annual growth of trade in the 1920s was slower than in the previous epoch, it was actually faster than in the period 1870–1890 and trade grew very rapidly between 1924 and 1929. Indeed, by 1929 the share of trade in world output was close to its 1913 level, and actually peaked in some countries, most notably Japan. Also, between 1914 and 1938, the stock of FDI rose significantly, almost doubling from $14.3 billion to $26.4 billion... Without elaborating further on these trends, they do go some way to exposing the myth that the disintegration of the global economy can be explained simply by irrational political factors unleashed by the First World War and its aftermath. At the very least, the political economy of the inter-war period involved a complex intertwining of domestic and international economic forces." Paul Bairoch, and Richard Kozul-Wright. "Globalization Myths: Some Historical Reflections on Integration, Industrialization and Growth in the World Economy," in *Transnational Corporations and the Global Economy*, ed. Paul Bairoch and Richard Kozul-Wright (London: Palgrave Macmillan 1998), 50.

But even their trade numbers indicate that there was a general slowdown in trade in the interwar years. They show trade as a percentage of GDP: 1890 11%; 1913 12.9%; 1929 9.8%; 1938 6.2%; 1950 7.8%; 1970 10.2: 1992 14.3%s See table 1 in their original paper: Paul Bairoch and Richard Kozul-Wright, Globalization Myths: Some Historical

Reflections on Integration, Industrialization and Growth in the World Economy," Paper prepared for the WIDER Conference on Transnational Corporations and the Global Economy (Kings College, Cambridge (UK), Sept. 1995), 6.

30. Jeffry A. Frieden, *Global Capitalism: Its Fall and Rise in the Twentieth Century* (New York: W.W. Norton, 2006), 282.

31. Benjamin H Higgins, "Agriculture and War: A Comparison of Agricultural Conditions in the Napoleonic and World War Periods," *Agricultural History* 14, no. 1 (1940): 11.

32. John Boli and George M. Thomas, *Constructing World Culture: International Nongovernmental Organizations since 1875* (Stanford, CA: Stanford University Press, 1999), 22.

33. Douglas Kellner, "The Postmodern Turn: Positions, Problems, and Prospects," in *Frontiers of Social Theory: The New Syntheses*, ed. George Ritzer (New York: Columbia University Press, 1990), 286, 289.

34. There have been other studies that have sought to explain the simultaneity of the kinds of populist movements that swept across the globe in the early twenty-first century in terms of globalization. For example, in one of the more comprehensive analyses, Dani Rodrik (2021, 2018) has developed a conceptual framework to explain how globalization relates to populism. He argues that economic dislocations caused by globalization impact people's preferences for policies, shape politicians' platforms, and increase the salience of certain identity divisions. Rodrik's work touches on many of the points identified here, but it does not speak as directly to the relationship between nationalism and populism, nor to how today's movements relate to other forms of nationalism and populism. Therefore, the concept of *defensive nationalism* used here allows for greater elaboration of how and why such movements develop. See Dani Rodrik, "Why Does Globalization Fuel Populism? Economics, Culture, and the Rise of Right-Wing Populism," *Annual Review of Economics* 13 (2020): 133–70; Dani Rodrik, "Populism and the Economics of Globalization," *Journal of International Business Policy* 1, no. 1 (2018): 12–33.

35. Polanyi, *The Great Transformation*, 153.

36. Ibid., 159.

37. Ibid., 42–43.

38. Bairoch and Kozul-Wright, "Globalization Myths," 14.

39. James M. Gillies and Robert Cailliau, *How the Web Was Born: The Story of the World Wide Web* (Oxford: Oxford University Press, 2000), 2.

40. Ibid.

41. Roxana Radu, *Negotiating Internet Governance* (Oxford and New York: Oxford University Press, 2019), 44–45.

42. Paddy Scannell, "The Dialectic of Time and Television," *The ANNALS of the American Academy of Political and Social Science* 625, no. 1 (2009): 219–235.

43. Anuj Agarwal, "High Frequency Trading: Evolution and the Future," *Capgemini, London, UK* (2012): 4.

44. Maurice Obstfeld and Alan M. Taylor, "Globalization and Capital Markets," in *Globalization in Historical Perspective*, ed. Michael D. Bordo, Alan M. Taylor, and Jeffrey G. Williamson (Chicago: University of Chicago Press, 2003), 144.

Chapter 5

1. L. Welch Pogue, "The Next Ten Years in Air Transportation," *Proceedings of the Academy of Political Science* 21, no. 2 (1945): 23.
2. John Harold Clapham, *The Economic Development of France and Germany, 1815– 1914* (England: The University Press, 1923), 339.
3. Eric J Hobsbawm, *The Age of Capital 1848–1875* (London: Weidenfeld & Nicolson, 1975), 55.
4. Philip Bagwell and Peter Lyth, *Transport in Britain: From Canal Lock to Gridlock* (London and New York: Hambledon and London, 2002), 54.
5. In 1844, only 30 percent of the railway journeys were made by third-class passengers. By the 1870s that percentage had doubled. See Philip Bagwell and Peter Lyth, *Transport in Britain: from Canal Lock to Gridlock*, 58.
6. Clapham, *The Economic Development of France and Germany*, 339.
7. John F. Stover, *The Routledge Historical Atlas of the American Railroads*, ed. Mark C. Carnes (New York and London: Routledge, 1999), 38.
8. "ACROSS THE CONTINENT: From the Missouri to the Pacific Ocean by Rail. The Plains, the Great American Desert, the Rocky Mountains. One Hundred Hours from Omaha to San Francisco," *New York Times*, June 28, 1869, http://cprr.org/Museum/ Newspapers/New_York_Times/1869-06-28.html.
9. Binder, Frederick M., "Pennsylvania Coal and the Beginnings of American Steam Navigation," *The Pennsylvania Magazine of History and Biography* 83, no. 4 (1959): 424.
10. Ramon Knauerhase, "The Compound Steam Engine and Productivity Changes in the German Merchant Marine Fleet, 1871–1887," *The Journal of Economic History* 28, no. 3 (1968): 392.
11. World Trade Organization, *World Trade Report 2013: Factors Shaping the Future of World Trade* (2013), 46–47.
12. Luis Carlos Barragan, "The Egyptian Workers Who Were Erased from History," *Egyptian Streets*, Sept. 14, 2018. https://egyptianstreets.com/2018/09/14/the-egypt ian-workers-who-were-erased-from-history.
13. Alfred Dupont Chandler, Takashi Hikino, and Alfred D. Chandler, *Scale and Scope: The Dynamics of Industrial Capitalism* (Cambridge, MA; and London: The Belknap Press of Harvard University Press, 1994), 53.
14. World Trade Organization, *Factors Shaping the Future of World Trade*, 47.
15. Ibid.
16. Adam McKeown, "Global Migration, 1846–1940," *Journal of World History* (2004): 164.

17. Ibid., 157.

18. World Trade Organization, *Factors Shaping the Future of World Trade*, 48.

19. Robert Hoe, *A Short History of the Printing Press and of the Improvements in Printing Machinery from the Time of Gutenberg Up to the Present Day* (New York: R. Hoe, 1902), 32.

20. See "Graphic History," http://www.designhistory.org/BookHistory_pages/Letterpr ess.html.

21. A. J. Valente, "Changes in Print Paper during the 19th Century," Charleston Library Conference, 2012.

22. World Trade Organization, *Factors Shaping the Future of World Trade*, 47.

23. The United States Postal Service, "The Mailing Industry and the United States Postal Service: An Enduring Partnership," Smithsonian National Postal Museum, https://postalmuseum.si.edu/americasmailingindustry/United-States-Postal-Service.html.

24. Bessie Emrick Whitten, and David O. Whitten, *The Birth of Big Business in the United States, 1860–1914: Commercial, Extractive, and Industrial Enterprise* (Westport, CT: Praeger, 2006), 33.

25. Encyclopedia of Chicago, "Mail Order," http://www.encyclopedia.chicagohistory.org/pages/779.html.

26. Byron Lew and Bruce Cater, "The Telegraph, Co-ordination of Tramp Shipping, and Growth in World Trade, 1870–1910," *European Review of Economic History* 10, no. 2 (2006): 147.

27. Menahem Blondheim, *News over the Wires: The Telegraph and the Flow of Public Information in America, 1844–1897* (Cambridge, MA; and London: Harvard University Press, 1994), 15.

28. Christopher Hoag, "The Atlantic Telegraph Cable and Capital Market Information Flows," *The Journal of Economic History* 66, no. 2 (2006): 342.

29. Tom Standage, *The Victorian Internet: The Remarkable Story of the Telegraph and the Nineteenth Century's Online Pioneers* (New York: Berkeley Books, 1999), 101–102.

30. Morton Rothstein, "Centralizing Firms and Spreading Markets: The World of International Grain Traders, 1846–1914," *Business and Economic History* (1988): 106.

31. Standage, *The Victorian Internet*, 166–167.

32. Ibid., 165–167.

33. Lew and Cater, "The Telegraph, Co-ordination of Tramp Shipping, and Growth in World Trade," 149.

34. Craig Carey, "Breaking the News: Telegraphy and Yellow Journalism in the Spanish-American War," *American Periodicals* (2016): 135.

35. Chandler, Hikino, and Chandler, *Scale and Scope*, 62.

36. Standage, *The Victorian Internet*, 169.

37. David Hochfelder, "The Communications Revolution and Popular Culture," in *A Companion to 19th-Century America*, ed. William L. Barney (Malden, MA: and Oxford: Blackwell Publishers Ltd., 2001), 312–314.

38. Geoffrey Poitras, "Arbitrage: Historical Perspectives," *Encyclopedia of Quantitative Finance* (2010): 17.

39. Hochfelder, "The Communications Revolution and Popular Culture," 314.

40. A contemporary at the time describes the extent of *Credit Mobilier*'s activities: "In 1858, a contemporary described the scope of the operations of this new financial institution: the Society had erected the Western Railway Company by the buying-up and consolidation of several old Companies and by guaranteeing a million sterling of bonds required by the new Company. It had extended similar advantages to the Southern and Eastern Railway Companies. The operations on the Dole and Salins line had been suspended, and the Society had ensured the completion of the works by advances and by purchasing 16,000 bonds. To the Austrian Railway the Society had advanced three and a third millions sterling; it had become largely interested in the Ardennes lines; it undertook lines upon an extensive scale in the Pyrenean Department; it gave credit largely to two Swiss railways; it became mixed up with a railway in Spain; it undertook canals; it bought up all the omnibuses 'in Paris, and established a General Omnibus Association; it started a General Maritime Association, by purchasing sixty vessels, sailers and steamers: it bought up all the Gas Companies in Paris, and brought out a Central Gas Company; and considerable progress was made in buying up a Salt Works in the South of France.'" William Newmarch, "On the Recent History of the Credit Mobilier," *Journal of the Statistical Society of London* 21, no. 4 (Dec. 1858): 447–448.

41. Carlo Brambilla, "Assessing Convergence in European Investment Banking Patterns Until 1914," in *Convergence and Divergence of National Financial Systems: Evidence from the Gold Standards, 1871–1971*, ed. Anders Ögren and Patrice Baubeau (United Kingdom: Pickering & Chatto, 2014), 90.

42. Alexander Gerschenkron, *Economic Backwards in Historical Perspective: A Book Essays* (Cambridge, MA: Belknap Press of Harvard University Press, 1962), 13.

43. Gerschenkron, *Economic Backwards in Historical Perspective*, 13.

44. Steven I. Davis, *The Euro-Bank: Its Origins, Management and Outlook* (London: Palgrave Macmillan, 1980), 16.

45. Brambilla, "Assessing Convergence in European Investment Banking Patterns Until 1914," 90.

46. Polanyi refers to this as the emergence of "the self-regulating market."

47. Albert Fishlow, "Lessons from the Past: Capital Markets during the 19th Century and the Interwar Period," *International Organization* 39, no. 3 (1985): 383.

48. World Trade Organization, *Factors Shaping the Future of World Trade*, 50.

49. Jeffrey D. Sachs, Andrew Warner, Anders Åslund, and Stanley Fischer, "Economic Reform and the Process of Global *Integration*," *Brookings Papers on Economic Activity* 1995, no. 1 (1995): 47.

50. Sebastian Conrad, *Globalisation and the Nation in Imperial Germany* (Cambridge: Cambridge University Press, 2010), 51.

51. Sachs, Warner, Åslund, and Fischer, "Economic Reform and the Process of Global Integration," 7.

52. Guillaume Daudin, Matthias Morys, and Kevin O'Rourke, "Globalization, 1870–1914," *The Cambridge Economic History of Modern Europe* (2010), 6.

53. Karl Polanyi, *The Great Transformation* (Boston: Beacon, 1944), 15.

54. Leland H. Jenks, "Railroads as an Economic Force in American Development," *The Journal of Economic History* 4, no. 1 (1944): 13.

55. Standage, *The Victorian Internet*, 159.

56. Ibid., 163.

57. Glenda Sluga, *Internationalism in the Age of Nationalism* (Philadelphia: University of Pennsylvania Press, 2013), 14–15.

58. John A. Hobson, "The Ethics of Internationalism," *The International Journal of Ethics* 17, no. 1 (1906): 17.

59. John Maynard Keynes, *The Economic Consequences of the Peace* (New York: Harcourt, Brace and Howe, 1920), 11–12.

60. John Boli and George M. Thomas, eds., "INGOs and the Organization of World Culture," in *Globalization: Critical Concepts in Sociology*, ed. Roland Robertson and Kathleen E. White (London and New York: Routledge, 1999), 22.

61. Harald Fischer-Tiné, "Global Civil Society and the Forces of Empire: The Salvation Army, British Imperialism, and the 'Prehistory' of NGOs (ca. 1880–1920)," in *Competing Visions of World Order Global Moments and Movements, 1880s–1930s*, ed. Sebastian Conrad and Dominic Sachsenmaier (New York: Palgrave Macmillan, 2007), 30.

Chapter 6

1. L. Welch Pogue, "The Next Ten Years in Air Transportation," *Proceedings of the Academy of Political Science* 21, no. 2 (1945): 23.

2. Richard Gilbert and Anthony Perl, *Transport Revolutions Moving People and Freight Without Oil* (Philadelphia: New Society, 2010), 16.

3. David Oxley and C. Jain, "Global Air Passenger Markets: Riding Out Periods of Turbulence," *IATA The Travel & Tourism Competitiveness Report* (2015): 59.

4. Gerald N. Cook, "A Review of History, Structure, and Competition in the US Airline Industry," *Journal of Aviation/Aerospace Education & Research* 7, no. 1 (1996): 34.

5. World Trade Organization, *Factors Shaping the Future of World Trade*, 53.

6. Gilbert and Perl, *Transport Revolutions Moving People and Freight without Oil*, 16.

7. World Trade Organization, *Factors Shaping the Future of World Trade*, 53.

8. Ibid.

9. David Hummels, "Transportation Costs and International Trade in the Second Era of Globalization," *Journal of Economic Perspectives* 21, no. 3 (2007): 132–134.

10. Ibid., 52.

11. Marc Levinson, "Container Shipping and the Decline of New York, 1955–1975," *Business History Review* 80, no. 1 (2006): 49.

12. For the debate over the see Hummels; 2007; and Levinson, 2006.

13. David Hummels, "Have International Transportation Costs Declined," *Scientific and Technical Aerospace Reports* 45, no. 18 (2007): 5–6.

14. Marc Levinson, *The Box: How the Shipping Container Made the World Smaller and the World Economy Bigger* (Princeton, NJ; and Oxford: Princeton University Press, 2006), 14–15.

15. Ibid., 15.

16. Richard R. John, "Rendezvous with Information? Computers and Communications Networks in the United States," *Business History Review* 75, no. 1 (2001): 4.

17. Robin Chandler, "Creative Parallel Spaces in Science and Art: Knowledge in the Information Age," *The Journal of Arts Management, Law, and Society* 29, no. 3 (1999): 163–166.

18. R. R. John, "Rendezvous with Information? Computers and Communications Networks in the United States," 4.

19. Sheila C. Murphy, *How Television Invented New Media* (New Brunswick, NJ: Rutgers University Press, 2011), 48.

20. Ibid.

21. Ibid.

22. RS Components Pty Ltd, "How Did Semiconductors Change Our Lives," https://au.rs-online.com/web/generalDisplay.html?id=infozone&file=eletronics/how-did-semiconductors-change-our-lives.

23. Levinson, *The Box*, 3.

24. Ibid.

25. Thomas Marill and Lawrence G. Roberts, "Toward a Cooperative Network of Time-shared Computers," in Proceedings of the November 7–10, 1966, Fall Joint Computer Conference, 425–431.

26. Joseph C. R. Licklider, "Man-Computer Symbiosis." *IRE Transactions on Human Factors in Electronics* 1 (1960): 4–11.

27. Judy E. O'Neill, "The Role of ARPA in the Development of the ARPANET, 1961–1972," *IEEE Annals of the History of Computing* 17, no. 4 (1995): 76–81.

28. George A. Miller, and Joseph C. R. Licklider, "The Intelligibility of Interrupted Speech," *The Journal of the Acoustical Society of America* 22, no. 2 (1950): 167–173.

29. The interent has also been argued to have been the inheritor of an earlier technology, frequency hopping, the invention of which has been attributed to the glamorous Hollywood starlit Hedy Lamar. To help with the war effort during World War II, Lamar, who was a technological genius, researched ways to safely conduct submarine communications through radio transmissions. She and her partner patented a frequency-hopping technique for "secret radio transmission," but it was never practically implemented. However, there is some controversy over how original and useful Lamar's invention was. See Tony Rothman, "Random Paths to Frequency Hopping," *American Scientist*, Jan.–Feb. 2019, https://www.americanscientist.org/article/random-paths-to-frequency-hopping.

30. James M. Gillies and Robert Cailliau, *How the Web Was Born: The Story of the World Wide Web* (Oxford: Oxford University Press, 2000), 11.

31. Ibid., 1.

32. Ibid., 236.

33. Mark Handley and Jon Crowcroft, *The World Wide Web: Beneath the Surf* (London and New York: Routledge, 2015), vii.

34. Agence France Presse, "A 25-Year Timeline of the World Wide Web," *Insider*, Mar. 9, 2014, http://www.businessinsider.com/a-25-year-timeline-of-the-world-wide-web-2014-3.

35. To mark the occasion—and not miss an opportunity for publicity—the chairman of the AT&T ceremonially made the first phone call transmitted via satellite from his company's plant in Maine to US President Lyndon B. Johnson in the White House.

36. Laura Silver, "Smartphone Ownership Is Growing Rapidly Around the World, but Not Always Equally," *Pew Research Center*, Feb. 5, 2019, https://www.pewresearch.org/global/2019/02/05/smartphone-ownership-is-growing-rapidly-around-the-world-but-not-always-equally/.

37. Although large disparities in cell phone usage remains between the Global North and the Global South, as well as between the wealthy to poor in developing countries, communications access on the whole has increased spectacularly. According to World Bank data, it is estimated that at its height, in 2007: only 13 percent of the population in low- and middle-income countries had fixed telephone subscriptions, up from just under only 3.5 percent in 1995. By contrast, cell phone subscriptions increased from only 0.25 percent in 1995, to 102 percent in 2018! An indication of the rapid expansion of satellite usage is that whereas in 1966 only three countries—Canada, the Soviet Union, and the United States—had operational satellites, today the majority of countries across the globe have acquired them. As of July 2020, the Union of Concerned Scientists (UCSUSA) reported that the total number of satellites operating in orbit was 2,666. See Union of Concerned Scientist, "USC Satellite Database," published Dec. 8, 2005, updated Jan. 1, 2022, https://www.ucsusa.org/resources/satellite-database.

38. David Harvey, *The Condition of Postmodernity: An Enquiry into the Origins of Cultural Change* (United Kingdom: Wiley, 1989), 316.

39. World Trade Organization, *Factors Shaping the Future of World Trade*, 55.

40. Makeda Easter, "Remember When Amazon Only Sold Books?," *Los Angeles Times*, June 18, 2017, http://www.latimes.com/business/la-fi-amazon-history-20170618-htmlstory.html.

41. Ebay, "Our History," https://www.ebayinc.com/our-company/our-history/.

42. Anuj. Agarwal, "High Frequency Trading: Evolution and the Future," *Capgemini, London, UK* (2012): p. 4.

43. Harvey, *The Condition of Postmodernity*, 161.

44. World Trade Organization, *Factors Shaping the Future of World Trade*, 54.

45. Harvey, *The Condition of Postmodernity*, 161.

46. Ibid.

47. Ibid.

48. World Economic Forum, https://www.weforum.org/join-us/home.

49. World Trade Organization, "What We Stand For," https://www.wto.org/english/thewto_e/whatis_e/what_stand_for_e.htm.

50. Rupert Taylor, "Interpreting Global Civil Society," *Voluntas: International Journal of Voluntary and Nonprofit Organizations* 13, no. 4 (2002): 339.

51. Alexander Halavais, "National Borders on the World Wide Web," *New Media & Society* 2, no. 1 (2000): 7.

52. Ibid., 11.

53. Stephen Gill, "Globalizing Capital and Political Agency in the Twenty-first Century," in *Questioning Geopolitics: Political Projects in a Changing World-System*, ed. Georgi M. Derluguian and Scott L. Greer (Westport, CT; London: Greenwood Press, 2000), 15.

54. Helmut Anheier, Marlies Glasius, and Mary Kaldor, "Introducing Global Civil Society," *Global Civil Society 2001* (2001): 17.

55. Ronaldo Munck, "Global Civil Society: Myths and Prospects," *Voluntas: International Journal of Voluntary and Nonprofit Organizations* 13, no. 4 (2002): 349–361.

56. Taylor, "Interpreting Global Civil Society," 340–341.

57. Ibid., 340.

Chapter 7

1. Henry George, *Progress and Poverty an Inquiry into the Cause of Industrial Depressions and of Increase of Want with Increase of Wealth: The Remedy* (Kingsport Press, 1935), 8.

2. Paul Hayes, ed., *Themes in Modern European History 1890–1945* (London and New York: Routledge, 2002), 30.

3. Eric J. Hobsbawm, *The Age of Capital 1848–1875* (London: Weidenfeld & Nicolson, 1975), 231.

4. Vincent E. McHale and Eric A. Johnson, "Urbanization, Industrialization, and Crime in Imperial Germany: Part II," *Social Science History* 1, no. 2 (1977): 210.

5. Jesús Mirás Araujo, "Urbanization in Upheaval: Spanish Cities, Agents and Targets of a Slow Transformation," in *The Routledge Hispanic Studies Companion to Nineteenth-Century Spain*, ed. Elisa Martí-López (London and New York: Routledge, 2021), 218–234.

6. Hobsbawm, *The Age of Capital*, 167.

7. Adam McKeown, "Global Migration, 1846–1940," *Journal of World History* (2004): 155–189.

8. Hobsbawm, *The Age of Capital*, 229.

9. Adam McKeown, *Global Migration*, 157.

10. Fathali M. Moghaddam and Anthony J. Marsella, eds., *Understanding Terrorism: Psychosocial Roots, Consequences, and Interventions* (Washington, DC: American Psychological Association, 2004), 208.

11. Luigi De Rosa, "Urbanization and Industrialization in Italy (1861–1921)," *Journal of European Economic History* 17, no. 3 (1988): 477–478.

12. Ossi Kotavaara, Harri Antikainen, and Jarmo Rusanen, "Urbanization and Transportation in Finland, 1880–1970," *Journal of Interdisciplinary History* 42, no. 1 (2011): 92.

13. Hayes, ed., *Themes in Modern European History*, 30.

14. Hobsbawm, *The Age of Capital*, 206.

15. Ibid., 212.

16. Ibid., 207.

17. Ibid., 206.
18. Charles Kindleberger, "Group Behavior and International Trade," *Journal of Political Economy* 59, no. 1 (1951): 31.
19. Charles Kindleberger, *Manias, Panics and Crashes. A History of Financial Crises* (London: Macmillan, 1978).
20. O. V. Wells, "The Depression of 1873–79," *Agricultural History* 11, no. 3 (1937): 239.
21. Elmus Wicker, *The Banking Panics of the Great Depression* (New York: Cambridge University Press, 1996), 20.
22. Wells, "The Depression of 1873–79," 241.
23. H. Michell, "The Gold Standard in the Nineteenth Century," *Canadian Journal of Economics and Political Science/Revue* 17, no. 3 (1951): 375.
24. Donald Le Crone McMurry, *Coxey's Army: A Study of the Industrial Army Movement of 1894* (Boston: Little Brown, and Company, 1929), 3.
25. Herman C. Voeltz, "Coxey's Army in Oregon, 1894," *Oregon Historical Quarterly* 65, no. 3 (1964): 263.
26. Marc Levinson, *The Box: How the Shipping Container Made the World Smaller and the World Economy Bigger* (Princeton, NJ; and Oxford: Princeton University Press, 2006), 3.
27. See Arun Kundnani, "Where Do You Want to Go Today? The Rise of Information Capital," *Race & Class* 40, no. 2–3 (1999): 49; and Chia-Yu Hsu, Bo-Ruei Kao, Lin Li, and K. Robert Lai, "An Agent-Based Fuzzy Constraint-Directed Negotiation Model for Solving Supply Chain Planning and Scheduling Problems," *Applied Soft Computing* 48 (2016): 703–715.
28. Bernard Hoekman and Carlos A. Primo Braga, "Protection and Trade in Services: A Survey," *Open Economies Review* 8, no. 3 (1997): 286.
29. Robert Rowthorn and Ramana Ramaswamy, "Deindustrialization: Causes and Implications," Washington, DC: International Monetary Fund, 10, 1997, 2.
30. Robert Gilpin, *The Challenge of Global Capitalism: The World Economy in the 21st Century* (Princeton, NJ; and Oxford: Princeton University Press, 2018), 31–32.
31. Keith Eugene Maskus, *Intellectual Property Rights in the Global Economy* (Washington, DC: Institute for International Economics, 2000), 2.
32. Kundnani, "Where Do You Want to Go Today," 50.
33. Maskus, Intellectual Property Rights in the Global Economy, 2.
34. David Harvey, *The Condition of Postmodernity: An Enquiry into the Origins of Cultural Change* (United Kingdom: Wiley, 1989), 155.
35. Rowthorn and Ramaswamy, *Deindustrialization*, 2.
36. Harvey, *The Condition of Postmodernity*, 150.
37. Lloyd Rodwin and Hidehiko Sazanami, eds., *Industrial Change and Regional Economic Transformation: The Experience of Western Europe* (London: Routledge, 2017).
38. Ibid.
39. See John R. Walter, "US Bank Capital Regulation: History and Changes since the Financial Crisis," *Economic Quarterly* 1Q (2019): 1–40.
40. A financial derivative is a contract that *derives* its value from an underlying entity, such as an asset, index, or interest rate. They are used to shield investors

from potential risk. The more common derivatives are forwards, futures, options, and swaps.

41. Derivatives are one of the three main categories of financial instruments, the other two being equity (i.e., stocks or shares) and debt (i.e., bonds and mortgages).

42. Martin Neil Baily, Robert E. Litan, and Matthew S. Johnson, "The Origins of the Financial Crisis," *Initiative on Business and Public Policy at Brookings*, 2008, 8.

Chapter 8

1. For more on the history of fake news, see Julien Gorbach, "Not Your Grandpa's Hoax: A Comparative History of Fake News," *American Journalism* 35, no. 2 (2018): 236–49; Jonathan Albright, "Welcome to the Era of Fake News," *Media and Communication* 5, no. 2 (2017): 87–89; Robert Darnton, "The True History of Fake News," *The New York Review of Books*, 2017.

2. Mark Wahlgren Summers, *The Press Gang: Newspapers and Politics, 1865–1878* (Chapel Hill: University of North Carolina Press, 1994), 13.

3. Ronald J. Zboray and Mary Saracino Zboray, "The Changing Face of Publishing," in *The Oxford History of Popular Print Culture: Volume Six: US Popular Print Culture 1860–1920* (Oxford University Press, 2011): 30.

4. Matthew Rubery, "A Transatlantic Sensation: Stanley's Search for Livingstone and the Anglo," in *The Oxford History of Popular Print Culture Volume Six US Popular Print Culture 1860–1920*, ed. Christine Bold (Oxford and New York: Oxford University Press, 1860): 501–17.

5. Mary Vipond, *The Mass Media in Canada* (Toronto: James Lorimer & Company, 2000), 17.

6. Aled Jones, *Powers of the Press: Newspapers, Power and the Public in Nineteenth-Century England* (London and New York: Routledge, 2016), 24.

7. Richard Bach Jensen, *The Battle against Anarchist Terrorism: An International History, 1878–1934* (Cambridge: Cambridge University Press, 2014), 53.

8. Michael Schudson, "The Objectivity Norm in American Journalism," *Journalism* 2, no. 2 (2001): 149–70.

9. Summers, *The Press Gang*, 13.

10. Ibid., 10.

11. Theodore Peterson, *Magazines in the Twentieth Century* (Urbana: University of Illinois Press, 1956), 2.

12. Ibid.

13. Ibid.

14. Summers, *The Press Gang*, 10.

15. Frankie Hutton and Barbara Straus Reed, eds., *Outsiders in 19th-Century Press History: Multicultural Perspectives* (Bowling Green, KY: Bowling Green State University Popular Press, 1995), 3.

16. Zboray and Zboray, "Publishing between The Civil War," 34.

17. Schudson, "The Objectivity Norm in American Journalism," 156.
18. Jessica E. Jackson, "Sensationalism in the Newsroom: Its Yellow Beginnings, the Nineteenth Century Legal Transformation, and the Current Seizure of the American Press," *Notre Dame Journal of Law & Ethics & Public Policy* 19 (2005): 790.
19. Kevin Williams, *Read All About It! A History of the British Newspaper* (London; New York: Routledge, 2009), 139.
20. Anthony M. Nadler, *Making the News Popular: Mobilizing US News Audiences* (Champaign: University of Illinois Press, 2016) 38
21. Summers, *The Press Gang*, 14.
22. Robert E. Park, "The Natural History of the Newspaper," *American Journal of Sociology* 29, no. 3 (1923): 281, 283.
23. Summers, *The Press Gang*, 10.
24. Richard L Kaplan, *Politics and the American Press: The Rise of Objectivity, 1865–1920* (Cambridge: Cambridge University Press, 2002), 24, 27.
25. Maria Petrova, "Newspapers and Parties: How Advertising Revenues Created an Independent Press," *American Political Science Review* 105, no. 4 (2011): 793.
26. Julian Petley, *Film and Video Censorship in Modern Britain* (Edinburgh: Edinburgh University Press, 2011), 186.
27. Park, "The Natural History of the Newspaper," 286.
28. Ernest Gellner, "Introduction," in *Europe and The Rise of Capitalism*, ed. J. Baechler, J. A. Hall, and M. A. Mann (Oxford: Blackwell, 1988).
29. Jones, *Powers of the Press*.
30. John Steel and Marcel Broersma, "Redefining Journalism during the Period of the Mass Press 1880–1920: An Introduction," *Media History* 21, no. 3 (2015): 235–237.
31. Park, "The Natural History of The Newspaper," 286.
32. Richard L. Kaplan, "Yellow Journalism," *The International Encyclopedia of Communication* 11 (2008): 5369.
33. David W. Bulla and David B. Sachsman, "Introduction," in *Sensationalism: Murder, Mayhem, Mudslinging, Scandals, and Disasters in 19th-Century Reporting*, ed. David B. Sachsman, David W. Bulla, and David B. Sachsman (London and New York: Routledge, 2013).
34. Park, "The Natural History of The Newspaper," 287.
35. Ibid.
36. Ross Eaman, *Historical Dictionary of Journalism* (Lanham, MD: Scarecrow Press, 2009), 282.
37. Zboray and Zboray, "Publishing between The Civil War," 32.
38. Ibid.
39. Williams, *Read All About It!*, 127.
40. Ibid.
41. Ibid., 135.
42. In Europe, the concentration of media ownership was in large part driven by government policies. Although liberal reforms adopted across Europe after 1848 meant that outright censorship was no longer practiced, "'indirect' forms of press controls,

involving the requirement that publishers pay security bonds or 'caution money' and that newspapers pay special taxes. The caution money requirement was intended to ensure that only the relatively wealthy could publish newspapers, while the purpose of special press taxes was to ensure that only the relatively wealthy could buy them." See Robert Justin Goldstein, *Political Repression in 19th Century Europe* (New York: Taylor & Francis, 2013), 41.

43. Steel and Broersma, "Redefining Journalism during the Period of the Mass Press 1880–1920," 235.

44. Park, "The Natural History of The Newspaper," 285.

45. Ibid., 287.

46. Jones, *Powers of the Press*.

47. Hochfelder, "The Communications Revolution and Popular Culture," 314.

48. David Spencer, *The Yellow Journalism: The Press and America's Emergence as a World Power* (Evanston, IL: Northwestern University Press, 2007), 148–149.

49. Zboray and Zboray, "Publishing between The Civil War," 32.

50. Jones, *Powers of the Press*, 74.

51. Ibid.

52. Arthur A. Baumann, "The Functions and Future of The Press," *Fortnightly* 107, no. 640 (1920): 621.

53. Fredrick Lewis Allen 1931, http://gutenberg.net.au/ebooks05/0500831h.html, accessed July 25, 2021.

54. Roland T. Rust and Richard W. Oliver, "The Death of Advertising," *Journal of Advertising* 23, no. 4 (1994): 75.

55. Ibid., 74.

56. Ibid., 73.

57. Johanna E. Möller and M. Rimscha, "(De) centralization of the Global Informational Ecosystem," *Media and Communication* 5, no. 3 (2017): 38

58. Evangelos Pournaras, "Decentralization in Digital Societies—A Design Paradox," *arXiv:2001.01511* (2020): 8.

59. Félix Tréguer, "Gaps and Bumps in the Political History of the Internet," *Internet Policy Review* 6, no. 4 (2017): 4

60. Möller and Rimscha, "(De) centralization of the Global Informational Ecosystem," 40.

61. Maximilian Hösl, "Semantics of the Internet: A Political History," *Internet Histories* 3, no. 3–4 (2019): 285.

62. Cynthia Kroet, "'Post-Truth' Enters Oxford English Dictionary," *Politico*, June 27, 2017, https://www.politico.eu/article/post-truth-enters-oxford-english-dictionary/.

63. Eric Alterman, "Out of Print," *The New Yorker*, Mar. 24, 2008, https://www.newyorker.com/magazine/2008/03/31/out-of-print.

64. Isabella Simonetti, "Over 360 Newspapers Have Closed since Just Before the Start of the Pandemic," *New York Times*, June 29, 2022, https://www.nytimes.com/2022/06/29/business/media/local-newspapers-pandemic.html.

65. European Parliament, "Europe's Media in the Digital Decade," https://www.europarl.europa.eu/RegData/etudes/STUD/2021/690873/IPOL_STU(2021)690873_EN.pdf.

66. Eric Alterman, "Out of Print: The Death and Life of the American Newspaper," *The New Yorker*, Mar. 24, 2008, https://www.newyorker.com/magazine/2008/03/31/out-of-print.

67. Edelman Trust Barometer 2020, https://www.edelman.com/sites/g/files/aatuss191/files/2020-03/2020%20Edelman%20Trust%20Barometer%20Coronavirus%20Special%20Report_0.pdf.

68. Mattia Ferraresi, "As Europe Confronts Coronavirus, the Media Faces a Trust Test," *Nieman Reports*, Apr. 24, 2020, https://niemanreports.org/articles/a-trust-test-for-the-media-in-europe/.

69. Albright, "Welcome to The Era of Fake News," 87.

Chapter 9

1. John M. Merriman, *The Dynamite Club* (New Haven, CT; London: Yale University Press, 2016), XI.

2. Richard Bach Jensen, "Daggers, Rifles and Dynamite: Anarchist Terrorism in Nineteenth Century Europe," *Terrorism and Political Violence* 16, no. 1 (2004): 134.

3. Jensen, "Daggers, Rifles and Dynamite," 135.

4. Ibid., 134.

5. Richard Bach Jensen, "The International Anti-Anarchist Conference of 1898 and The Origins of Interpol," *Journal of Contemporary History* 16, no. 2 (1981): 324.

6. Jensen, "The International Anti-Anarchist Conference of 1898 and The Origins of Interpol," 324.

7. Jensen, *The Battle Against Anarchist Terrorism*, 238.

8. Beverly Gage, *The Day Wall Street Exploded: A Story of America in Its First Age of Terror* (New York: Oxford University Press, 2009), 44.

9. Ibid.

10. Emma Goldman, *Anarchism and Other Essays* (3rd rev. ed., New York: Mother Earth Publishing Association, 1917), https://www.lib.berkeley.edu/goldman/pdfs/EmmaGoldman_THEPSYCHOLOGYOFPOLITICALVIOLENCE.pdf, 7, 12.

11. Sara Kalm and Johannes Lindvall, "Immigration Policy and the Modern Welfare State, 1880–1920," *Journal of European Social Policy* 29, no. 4 (2019): 463–477.

12. Guillaume Daudin, Matthias Morys, and Kevin H. O'Rourke, "Europe and Globalization, 1870–1914," *Paris: OFCE* 17 (2008): 17.

13. Ashley S. Timmer and Jeffrey G. Williams, "Immigration Policy Prior to the 1930s: Labor Markets, Policy Interactions, and Globalization Backlash," *Population and Development Review* (1998): 744.

14. Richard Bach Jensen, *The Battle against Anarchist Terrorism: An International History, 1878–1934* (Cambridge: Cambridge University Press, 2014), 139–140.

15. Ibid., 247.

16. Ibid., 7.

17. Ibid., 7.

18. Frank Harris, *The Bomb, by Frank Harris* (New York (State): M. Kennerley, 1909), 230.
19. Ibid., 275–276.
20. Ibid.
21. Thomas Hegghammer, "Islamist Violence and Regime Stability in Saudi Arabia," *International Affairs* 84, no. 4 (2008): 703.
22. Hegghammer, "Islamist Violence and Regime Stability in Saudi Arabia," 706.
23. Tony Evans, "The Limits of Tolerance: Islam as Counter-Hegemony?," *Review of International Studies* 37, no. 4 (2011): 1761.
24. United Nations, *The Use of the Internet for Terrorist Purposes* (New York: United Nations Office on Drugs and Crime, 2012), 11.
25. Assaf Moghadam, *The Globalization of Martyrdom: Al Qaeda, Salafi Jihad, and The Diffusion of Suicide Attacks* (Baltimore: The John Hopkins University Press, 2008), 4.
26. Ibid., 38.
27. Ibid., 2.
28. Olivier Roy, "Al Qaeda in the West as a Youth Movement: The Power of a Narrative," *CEPS Policy Briefs* 1–12 (2008), 4.
29. Ibid., 6.
30. Ibid., 7.
31. Hania Zlotnik, "Trends of International Migration since 1965: What Existing Data Reveal," *International Migration* 37, no. 1 (1999).
32. Ibid., 24.
33. John Salt, and James Clarke, "International Migration in the UNECE Region: Patterns, Trends, Policies," *International Social Science Journal* 52, no. 165 (2000): 316.
34. Mathias Czaika and Hein De Haas, "The Globalization of Migration: Has the World Become More Migratory?," *International Migration Review* 48, no. 2 (2014): 285; Stephen Castles, "International Migration at the Beginning of the Twenty-First Century: Global Trends and Issues," *International Social Science Journal* 52, no. 165 (2000): 274.
35. Czaika and De Haas, "The Globalization of Migration," 285.
36. Hania Zlotnik, "Trends of International Migration since 1965: What Existing Data Reveal," *International Migration* 37, no. 1 (1999): 22.
37. Christine Ogan, Lars Willnat, Rosemary Pennington, and Manaf Bashir, "The Rise of Anti-Muslim Prejudice: Media and Islamophobia in Europe and the United States," *International Communication Gazette*, 76, no. 1 (2014): 27.
38. Michelle Mittelstadt, Burke Speaker, Doris Meissner, and Muzaffar Chishti, "Through the Prism of National Security: Major Immigration Policy and Program Changes in the Decade since 9/11," *Migration Policy Institute* 2 (2011): 1.
39. Terri A. Winnick, "Islamophobia: Social Distance, Avoidance, and Threat," *Sociological Spectrum* 39, no. 6 (2019): 359.
40. Ibid.
41. See Terri A. Winnick, "Islamophobia: Social Distance, Avoidance, and Threat"; Brian Robert Calfano, Paul A. Djupe, Daniel Cox, and Robert Jones, "Muslim Mistrust: The Resilience of Negative Public Attitudes after Complimentary Information," *Journal of Media and Religion* 15, no. 1 (2016): 29–42.

242 NOTES

42. Terri A. Winnick, "Islamophobia: Social Distance, Avoidance, and Threat," 359.

43. Danielle Lee Tomson, "The Rise of Sweden Democrats: Islam, Populism and the End of Swedish Exceptionalism," *Brookings*, Mar. 25, 2020. https://www.brookings.edu/research/the-rise-of-sweden-democrats-and-the-end-of-swedish-exceptionalism/.

44. Christina Schori Liang, "Europe for the Europeans," 21.

45. Monica Scislowska, "Poland Probes Mosque Attack, Far-Right 'Gallows' Protest," *AP News*, Nov. 27, 2017, https://apnews.com/article/7f31acb8461b4f5fb71325bb6efecfe3.

46. Angelique Chrisafis, "France's Headscarf War: 'It's an Attack on Freedom,'" *The Guardian*, July 22, 2013. https://www.theguardian.com/world/2013/jul/22/frances-headscarf-war-attack-on-freedom.

47. Hans-Georg Betz, "Mosques, Minarets, Burqas and Other Essential Threats: The Populist Right's Campaign against Islam in Western Europe," in *Right-Wing Populism in Europe: Politics and Discourse*, ed. Ruth Wodak, Majid KhosraviNik, and Brigitte Mral (London: Bloomsbury Academic, 2013), 72.

48. Ibid., 73.

49. Gabriela Baczynska, "Mosque Building Brings Islam Fears to Poland," *Reuters*, Apr. 1, 2010, https://www.reuters.com/article/us-poland-mosque/mosque-building-brings-islam-fears-to-poland-idUSTRE6302VN20100401.

Chapter 10

1. Guillaume Daudin, Matthias Morys, and Kevin O'Rourke, "Globalization, 1870–1914," *The Cambridge Economic History of Modern Europe* (2010): 9.

2. Herman C. Voeltz, "Coxey's Army in Oregon, 1894," *Oregon Historical Quarterly* 65, no. 3 (Sept. 1964): 263.

3. Ibid., 264.

4. Jeffrey Ostler, "Why the Populist Party Was Strong in Kansas and Nebraska but Weak in Iowa," *The Western Historical Quarterly* 23, no. 4 (1992): 453–454.

5. L. Frank Baum, *The Wonderful Wizard of Oz* (Oxford: Oxford University Press, 2008).

6. For more on this debate, see Ranjit S. Dighe, "The Fable of the Allegory: The Wizard of Oz in Economics: Comment," *The Journal of Economic Education* 38, no. 3 (2007): 318–324.

7. Hugh Rockoff argues: "On a general level the Wicked Witch of the East represents eastern business and financial interests, but in personal terms a populist would have had one figure in mind: Grover Cleveland. It was Cleveland who led the repeal of the Sherman Silver Purchase Act, and it was his progold forces that had been defeated at the 1896 convention, making it possible for America to vote for Bryan and free silver. But the American people, like the Munchkins, never understood the power that was theirs once the Wicked Witch was dead." Rockoff, Hugh, "'The Wizard of Oz' as a Monetary Allegory," *Journal of Political Economy* 98, no. 4 (1990): 746.

8. The history of the game Monopoly began in 1904, when a patent was granted to Elizabeth Maggie for "the Landlord's Game." This was the antecedent to the popular board game. Moreover, Maggie may have been a follower of Georgism, and she reputedly invented the game to teach people about monopolies and "Morganization." See Philip E. Orbanes, *Monopoly: The World's Most Famous Game—and How It Got That Way* (New York: Hachette Books, 2007).

9. See J. Bradford De Long, "JP Morgan and His Money Trust," *Wilson Quarterly* 16, no. 4 (1992): 16–30.

10. Henry Demarest Lloyd, *Lords of Industry* (United Kingdom: G.P. Putnam's sons, 1910): 3.

11. "The 'Omaha Platform' of the People's Party (1892)," *The American Yawp Reader*, https://www.americanyawp.com/reader/16-capital-and-labor/the-omaha-platform-of-the-peoples-party-1892/.

12. Henry George, *Progress and Poverty: An Inquiry into the Cause of Industrial Depressions The Remedy* (Kingsport Press, Inc., 1934).

13. Richard Franklin Bensel, *Passion and Preferences: William Jennings Bryan and the 1896 Democratic Convention* (Netherlands: Cambridge University Press, 2008), 1.

14. Kevin McDermott and Jeremy Agnew, *The Comintern: A History of International Communism from Lenin to Stalin* (London: Macmillan Press LTD, 1996), xviii.

15. Ibid., 8.

16. A. Smith, "The Land and Its People," 99.

17. Paul A. Fortier, "Gobineau and German Racism," *Comparative Literature* 19, no. 4 (1967): 341–350.

18. Constantin Frantz, *Der Untergang der alten Parteien und die Parteien der Zukunft* (Berlin: Niendorf, 1878), quoted in *The Rise of Political Anti-Semitism in Germany & Austria*, ed. Peter Pulzer (Cambridge, MA: Harvard University Press, 1988), 36.

19. Sebastian Conrad, *Globalisation and the Nation in Imperial Germany* (Cambridge: Cambridge University Press, 2010), 15.

20. Ibid.

21. Max Domarus and Adolf Hitler, *Hitler: Speeches and Proclamations 1932–1945: The Chronical of a Dictatorship: Voume. 2, The Years 1932 to 1934* (Mundelein, IL: BolchazyCarducci Publishers, 1990), 248.

22. António Costa Pinto, "Fascist Ideology Revisited: Zeev Sternhell and His Critics," *European History Quarterly* 16, no. 4 (1986): 471.

23. Mauro Marsella, "Enrico Corradini's Italian Nationalism: The 'Right Wing' of the Fascist Synthesis," *Journal of Political Ideologies* 9, no. 2 (2004): 206.

24. David D. Roberts, *The Syndicalist Tradition and Italian Fascism.* (United Kingdom: Manchester University Press, 1979), 120.

25. Robert Howse, "The World Trade Organization 20 Years on: Global Governance by Judiciary," *European Journal of International Law* 27, no. 1 (2016): 16.

26. Hopewell, *Breaking the WTO*, ix.

27. Ibid.

28. Bernt Hagtvet, "Right-Wing Extremism in Europe," *Journal of Peace Research* 31, no. 3 (1994): 241.

29. Manuel Funke and Christoph Trebesch, "Financial Crises and the Populist Right," *ifo DICE Report* 15, no. 4 (2017): 8.
30. Jon Henley, "Support for Eurosceptic Parties Doubles in Two Decades across EU," *The Guardian*, Mar. 2, 2020, https://www.theguardian.com/world/2020/mar/02/support-for-eurosceptic-parties-doubles-two-decades-across-eu.
31. Helena Smith, "Greek Leftist Leader Alexis Tsipras: 'It's a War between People and Capitalism,'" *The Guardian*, May 18, 2012, https://www.theguardian.com/world/2012/may/18/greek-leftist-leader-alexis-tsipras.
32. "READ: Jeremy Corbyn's 2017 Labour Conference," *PoliticsHome*, Sept. 27, 2017, https://www.politicshome.com/news/article/read-jeremy-corbyns-2017-labour-conference-speech.
33. "READ: Bernie Sanders' Speech at the Democratic Convention," *NPR*, July 25, 2016, https://www.npr.org/2016/07/25/487426056/read-bernie-sanders-prepared-remarks-at-the-dnc.
34. J. Lawrence Broz, Jeffry Frieden, and Stephen Weymouth, "Populism in Place: The Economic Geography of the Globalization Backlash," *International Organization* 75, no. 2 (2021): 464.
35. Dustin Voss, "The Political Economy of European Populism: Labour Market Dualisation and Protest Voting in Germany and Spain," *LEQS Paper* 132 (2018): 3.
36. National Front, http://www.nationalfront.org/ (since removed from the web).
37. Jefferson Chase, "AfD Cochair Petry Wants to Rehabilitate Controversial Term," *Deutsche Welle*, Sept. 11, 2016, https://www.dw.com/en/afd-co-chair-petry-wants-to-rehabilitate-controversial-term/a-19543222.
38. *Europe Now*, "The Rise of Nativism in Europe." By Jan Willem Duyvendak and Josip Kesic, Feb. 1, 2018, https://www.europenowjournal.org/2018/01/31/the-rise-of-nativism-in-europe/#_ftnref3.
39. Eric Thayer, "Transcript: Donald Trump's Victory Speech," *New York Times*, Nov. 9, 2016, https://www.nytimes.com/2016/11/10/us/politics/trump-speech-transcript.html.
40. Paul Bairoch, "European Trade Policy, 1815–1914," *The Cambridge Economic History of Europe* 8, no. 1 (1989): 160–80.
41. Harold James and Kevin H. O'Rourke, "Italy and the First Age of Globalization, 1861–1940," *Bank of Italy Economic History Working Paper* 16 (2011): 7.
42. Jeffrey D. Sachs, Andrew Warner, Anders Åslund, and Stanley Fischer, "Economic Reform and the Process of Global Integration," *Brookings Papers on Economic Activity* no. 1 (1995): 6.
43. Dani Rodrik, *The Globalization Paradox: Why Global Markets, States, and Democracy Can't Coexist* (Oxford and New York: Oxford University Press, 2011), 30.
44. Otto Pflanze, *Bismarck and the Development of Germany, Volume II: The Period of Consolidation, 1871–1880* (Germany: Princeton University Press, 2014), 7.
45. Ibid., 8.
46. See Alan John Percivale Taylor, *Bismarck: The Man and the Statesman* (New York: Vintage Books, 1967).

47. James C. Hunt, "Peasants, Grain Tariffs, and Meat Quotas: Imperial German Protectionism Reexamined," *Central European History* 7, no. 4 (Dec. 1974), 314.
48. James and O'Rourke, "Italy and the First Age of Globalization, 1861–1940," 8.
49. Stephen Broadberry and Kevin H O'Rourke, *The Cambridge Economic History of Modern Europe: Volume 2, 1870 to the Present* (Cambridge: Cambridge University Press, 2010), 26.
50. Kevin H. O'Rourke, "Tariffs and Growth in the Late 19th Century," *The Economic Journal* 110, no. 463 (2000): 458.
51. The Netherlands, Belgium, and Denmark did not impose tariffs on wheat. See Charles Kindleberger, "Group Behavior and International Trade," *Journal of Political Economy* 59, no. 1 (1951): 35.
52. David S. Wyman, *Paper Walls; America and the Refugee Crisis, 1938–1941* (Amherst: University of Massachusetts Press, 1968), 161.
53. Ibid., 163.
54. Marc-William Palen, "Protection, Federation and Union: The Global Impact of the McKinley Tariff Upon the British Empire, 1890–94," *The Journal of Imperial and Commonwealth History* 38, no. 3 (2010): 396.
55. Wyman, *Paper Walls*, 167.
56. Palen, "Protection, Federation and Union," 396.
57. Friedrich August Hayek, *The Road to Serfdom* (New York: Routledge, 1976).
58. Ayn Rand, *Atlas Shrugged* (New York: Penguin, 2005).
59. Kristen Hopewell, *Breaking the WTO: How Emerging Powers Disrupted the Neoliberal Project* (Palo Alto, CA: Stanford University Press, 2016), ix.
60. Ibid., 1.
61. Rodrik, *The Globalization Paradox*, 76.
62. Hopewell, *Breaking the WTO*, ix.
63. Robert Howse, "The World Trade Organization 20 Years On: Global Governance by Judiciary," *European Journal of International Law* 27, no. 1 (2016): 10.
64. Jeffry A. Frieden, *Global Capitalism: Its Fall and Rise in the Twentieth Century* (New York: W.W. Norton, 2006), 348, 351.
65. Serdar Altay, "Hegemony, Private Actors, and International Institutions: Transnational Corporations as the Agents of Transformation of the Trade Regime from GATT to the WTO" (PhD diss., University of Trento, 2012), 15.
66. Rodrik, *The Globalization Paradox*, 75.
67. Hopewell, *Breaking the WTO*, 11.
68. Frieden, *Global Capitalism*, 347.
69. Henry George, *Progress and Poverty*, 9.
70. Mary Elizabeth Lease, "Wall Street Owns the Country," *History Is a Weapon*, http://www.historyisaweapon.org/defcon1/marylease.html.
71. "The Omaha Platform: Launching the Populist Party," *The U.S. Survey Course on The Web*, http://historymatters.gmu.edu/d/5361/.
72. William Jennings Bryan, "Cross of Gold Speech," July 9, 1896. https://wwnorton.com/college/history/archive/reader/trial/directory/1890_1914/ch20_cross_of_gold.htm.

73. Ibid.
74. Megan Slack, "From the Archives: President Teddy Roosevelt's New Nationalism Speech," *The White House*, Dec. 6, 2011, https://obamawhitehouse.archives.gov/blog/2011/12/06/archives-president-teddy-roosevelts-new-nationalism-speech.
75. Gene Bernardini, "The Origins and Development of Racial Anti-Semitism in Fascist Italy," *The Journal of Modern History* 49, no. 3 (1977): 436.
76. Taken from Richard Wagner, "Prose Works. 3. The Theatre," trans. William Ashton Ellis (London: Routledge and Kegan Paul 1894), 79–100. Essay originally published in Richard Wagner, *Sämtliche Schriften und Dichtungen: Volume V* (Leipzig: Breikopf & Härtel: 1850), 66–85.
77. Houston Stewart Chamberlain, *The Foundations of the Nineteenth Century*, trans. *John Lees* (London: John Lane, 1911), 331.
78. Ben Macri, Vassar '99. "Anti-Semitism," 1896, http://projects.vassar.edu/1896/antisemitism.html.
79. Robert D. Johnston, "The Age of Reform: A Defense of Richard Hofstadter Fifty Years On," *The Journal of the Gilded Age and Progressive Era* 6, no. 2 (2007): 132.
80. Facundo Alvaredo, *The World Inequality Report* (Cambridge, MA: Harvard University Press, 2018), 182.
81. Alvaredo et al., *The World Inequality Report*, 182.
82. Kerry A. Dolan, ed., "The Definitive Ranking of the Wealthiest Americans in 2021," *Forbes*, https://www.forbes.com/forbes-400/.
83. "Bernie Sanders on Trade and U.S. Jobs," FEELTHEBERN.ORG, https://feelthebern.org/bernie-sanders-on-trade/.
84. Reuters Staff, "UK's Labour Vows Action on 'Tax and Wage Cheat' Multinationals," *Reuters*, Nov. 22, 2019, https://www.reuters.com/article/britain-election-labour/uks-labour-vows-action-on-tax-and-wage-cheat-multinationals-idUSL8N2824KM.
85. Reuters Staff, "Hollande: "Mon véritable adversaire, c'est le monde de la finance," *La Tribune*, Jan. 22, 2012, https://www.latribune.fr/actualites/economie/france/201201 22trib000679586/hollande-mon-veritable-adversaire-c-est-le-monde-de-la-finance.html.
86. Jeremy Corbyn, "Jeremy Corbyn Speech at Labour's Campaign Launch," *Labour*, May 9, 2017, https://labour.org.uk/press/jeremy-corbyn-speech-at-labours-campaign-launch/.
87. Adam Bienkov, "Jeremy Corbyn's General Election Campaign Launch Speech in Full," *Insider*, May 9, 2017, https://www.businessinsider.com/jeremy-corbyn-labour-party-general-election-campaign-launch-speech-in-full-2017-5.
88. "Transcript: Bernie Sanders's Full Speech at the 2016 DNC," *The Washington Post*, July 26, 2016, https://www.washingtonpost.com/news/post-politics/wp/2016/07/26/transcript-bernie-sanderss-full-speech-at-the-2016-dnc/.
89. William Echikson, "Viktor Orbán's Anti-Semitism Problem," *POLITICO*, May 13, 2019, https://www.politico.eu/article/viktor-orban-anti-semitism-problem-hungary-jews/.
90. Jason Horowitz, "Where Does Italy's Enfeebled Five Star Find Itself? At the Center of Power," *New York Times*, Aug. 22, 2019, https://www.nytimes.com/2019/08/22/world/europe/italy-politics-five-star-democratic-party.html.

91. Vona Gábor, "Az Agónia Elkezdődött és új Világrendnek Kell Épülnie," *Mandiner. hu*, May 6, 2013, https://mandiner.hu/cikk/20130506_vona_gabor_az_agonia_ elkezdodott_es_uj_vilagrendnek_kell_epulnie.

92. Eric Thayer, "Transcript: Donald Trump's Victory Speech," *New York Times*, Nov. 9, 2016, https://www.nytimes.com/2016/11/10/us/politics/trump-speech-transcr ipt.html.

93. Guardian Staff, "Donald Trump Calls Covid-19 'Kung Flu' at Tulsa Rally," *The Guardian*, June 20, 2020, https://www.theguardian.com/us-news/2020/jun/20/ trump-covid-19-kung-flu-racist-language.

94. "Top French Socialist and Anti-Racism Campaigner Faces Probe for Anti-Semitic Macron Tweet," *The Local*, Nov. 21, 2017, https://www.thelocal.fr/20171121/top-fre nch-socialist-and-anti-racism-campaigner; "Top French Socialist Booted from Party over Anti-Semitic Tweet," *The Times of Israel*, Nov. 22, 2017, https://www.timesofisr ael.com/top-french-socialist-booted-from-party-over-anti-semitic-tweet/.

Chapter 11

1. "The Omaha Platform: Launching the Populist Party," http://historymatters.gmu. edu/d/5361/.

2. Voeltz, "Coxey's Army in Oregon, 1894," 271.

3. Vladimir Il'ich Lenin, "Letter to the Secretary of the Socialist Propaganda League," https://www.marxists.org/archive/lenin/works/1915/nov/09.html.

4. Fortier, "Gobineau and German Racism," 346.

5. Steven E. Ascheim, "A Critical Introduction." In: Mosse, George L. The Crisis of German Ideology: Intellectual Origins of the Third Reich. (United States: University of Wisconsin Press, 2021), p. xiii.

6. Raul Cârstocea, "Anti-Semitism in Romania: Historical Legacies, Contemporary Challenges," *European Center for Minority Issues* (2014): 7.

7. I. Michael Aronson, "Russian Commissions on the Jewish Question in the 1880's," *East European Quarterly* 14, no. 1 (1980): 60.

8. Phillip Connor, "Number of Refugees to Europe Surges to Record 1.3 Million in 2015," *Pew Research Center*, Aug. 2, 2016, https://www.pewresearch.org/global/2016/ 08/02/number-of-refugees-to-europe-surges-to-record-1-3-million-in-2015/.

9. Funke and Trebesch, "Right-Wing Extremism in Europe," 7–8.

10. Danielle Lee Tomson, "The Rise of Sweden Democrats: Islam, Populism and the End of Swedish Exceptionalism," *Brookings*, Mar. 25, 2020, https://www.brookings.edu/ research/the-rise-of-sweden-democrats-and-the-end-of-swedish-exceptionalism/.

11. Krisztian Szabados, "The Particularities and Uniqueness of Hungary's Jobbik," in *The European Far Right: Historical and Contemporary Perspectives*, ed. *Giorgos Charalambous* (Norway: Peace Research Institute Oslo, 2, 2015), 53.

12. "Transcript: Donald Trump's Victory Speech," *New York Times*, Nov. 9, 2016, https:// www.nytimes.com/2016/11/10/us/politics/trump-speech-transcript.html.

13. Ibid., 50.

14. Ibid., 49.

15. Ibid.

16. Sue Reid, "Torn Apart by an Open Door for Migrants: Sweden Is Seen as Europe's Most Liberal Nation, but Violent Crime Is Soaring and the Far Right Is on the March, Reports SUE REID," *DailyMail.com*, Nov. 13, 2015, https://www.dailymail.co.uk/news/article-3317978/Torn-apart-open-door-migrants-Sweden-seen-Europe-s-liberal-nation-violent-crime-soaring-Far-Right-march-reports-SUE-REID.html.

17. "Reality Check: Is Malmo the 'Rape Capital' of Europe?," *BBC News*, Feb. 24, 2017, https://www.bbc.com/news/uk-politics-39056786.

18. Alexander Stille, "How Matteo Salvini Pulled Italy to the Far Right," *The Guardian*, Aug. 9, 2018, https://www.theguardian.com/news/2018/aug/09/how-matteo-salvini-pulled-italy-to-the-far-right.

19. David Duke quoted in Thomas Grumke, "Globalized Anti-Globalists—The Ideological Basis of the Internationalization of Right-Wing Extremism," in *The Extreme Right in Europe: Current Trends and Perspectives*, ed. Uwe Backes and Patrick Moreau (Oakville, CT: Vandenhoeck & Ruprecht, 2012), 325.

20. Formerly on their website, accessed in February 2019, which has been deleted.

21. Andreas Kemper, "AfD, Pegida and the New Right in Germany," *The European far Right: Historical and Contemporary Perspectives* (2015): 47.

22. Jan Willem Duyvendak and Josip Kesic, "The Rise of Nativism in Europe," *Europe Now*, Feb. 1, 2018, https://www.europenowjournal.org/2018/01/31/the-rise-of-nativism-in-europe/#_ftnref3.

23. Jason Wilson and Aaron Flanagon, "The Racist Replacement Theory Explained," *Hatewatch, Southern Poverty Law Center*, May 17, 2022, https://www.splcenter.org/hatewatch/2022/05/17/racist-great-replacement-conspiracy-theory-explained.

24. Gene Bernardini, "The Origins and Development of Racial Anti-Semitism in Fascist Italy," *The Journal of Modern History* 49, no. 3 (1977): 437.

25. Bridge Initiative Team, "Factsheet: Sweden Democrats," *Bridge*, May 14, 2020, https://bridge.georgetown.edu/research/factsheet-sweden-democrats/.

26. David Wearing, "Labour Has Slipped Rightwards on Immigration. That Needs to Change," *The Guardian*, July 25, 2017, https://www.theguardian.com/commentisfree/2017/jul/25/labour-immigration-jeremy-corbyn-attitudes.

27. Megan Apper, "Bernie Sanders on Immigration in 2007 Video: This Is a Bad Bill for American Workers," *BuzzFeed News*, Feb. 19, 2016, https://www.buzzfeednews.com/article/meganapper/bernie-sanders-on-immigration-in-2007-video-this-is-a-bad-bi.

28. Richard Orange, "Mette Frederiksen: The Anti-immigration Left Leader Set to Win Power in Denmark," *The Guardian*, May 11, 2019, https://www.theguardian.com/world/2019/may/11/denmark-election-matte-frederiksen-leftwing-immigration.

29. Pinto, "Fascist Ideology Revisited," 469.

30. David D. Roberts, *The Syndicalist Tradition and Italian Fascism* (Manchester: Manchester University Press, 1979), 75.

31. Zeëv Sternhell, "Fascism: Reflections on the Fate of Ideas in Twentieth-Century History," in *Reassessing Political Ideologies: The Durability of Dissent*, ed. Michael Freeden (London and New York: Routledge, 2001): 99.

32. A. Smith, "The Land and Its People," 88.

33. Pinto, "Fascist Ideology Revisited," 469–70.

34. Pulzer, *The Rise of Political Anti-Semitism in Germany & Austria*, 33.

35. Paul Lucardie, "Religious Parties in a Secular Society: The Dutch Paradox," in *Constellations of Value: European Perspectives on the Intersections of Religion, Politics and Society*, ed. Christoph Jedan (Berlin: LIT, 2013), 143.

36. Pinto, "Fascist Ideology Revisited: Zeev Sternhell and His Critics," 469.

37. George L. Mosse, *The Crisis of German Ideology: Intellectual Origins of the Third Reich* (Madison: University of Wisconsin Press, 2021), 8.

38. George L. Mosse, *The Crisis of German Ideology*, 9.

39. Zeev Sternhell, "How to Think about Fascism and Its Ideology," *Constellations* 15, no. 3 (2008): 281.

40. Pinto, "Fascist Ideology Revisited," 469.

41. Ibid., 471.

42. Marsella, "Enrico Corradini's Italian Nationalism," 205.

43. Joris Gijsenbergh, "Democracy's Various Defenders: The Struggle Against Political Extremism in the Netherlands, 1917–1940," in *Historical Perspectives on Democracies and their Adversaries*, ed. Joost Augusteijn, Constant Hijzen, and Mark Leon De Vries (Palgrave Macmillan, 2019), 69–98.

44. Richard Drake, "The Theory and Practice of Italian Nationalism, 1900–1906," *The Journal of Modern History* 53, no. 2 (1981): 218.

45. David D. Roberts, *The Syndicalist Tradition and Italian Fascism* (United Kingdom: Manchester University Press, 1979), 120.

46. See Pinto, "Fascist Ideology Revisited: Zeev Sternhell and His Critics."

47. Vona Gábor, "Az Agónia Elkezdődött és új Világrendnek Kell Épülnie," *Mandiner.hu*, May 6, 2013, https://mandiner.hu/cikk/20130506_vona_gabor_az_agonia_elkezdodott_es_uj_vilagrendnek_kell_epulnie; Thomas K. Grose, "Europe's Nationalists Target Climate Action," *U.S. News*, https://www.usnews.com/news/best-countries/articles/2019-05-08/europes-far-right-focuses-on-climate-change-instead-of-immigration.

48. Peter J. Hotez, "The Antiscience Movement Is Escalating, Going Global and Killing Thousands," *Scientific American*, Mar. 29, 2021, https://www.scientificamerican.com/article/the-antiscience-movement-is-escalating-going-global-and-killing-thousands/.

49. Andrew Jewett, "How Americans Came to Distrust Science," *Boston Review*, Dec. 8, 2020, https://bostonreview.net/articles/andrew-jewett-science-under-fire/.

50. Carla Montuori Fernandes et al., "The Denial of Science in the Antisystem Populist Rhetoric," *American Academic Scientific Research Journal for Engineering, Technology, and Sciences* 85, no. 1 (2022): 188.

51. Cristóbal Bellolio, "An Inquiry into Populism's Relation to Science," *Politics* (2022): 1.

52. Tom Nichols, *The Death of Expertise: The Campaign Against Established Knowledge and Why It Matters* (New York: Oxford University Press, 2017), 2.

53. Cristóbal Bellolio, "An Inquiry into Populism's Relation to Science," 5.

54. Kevin Freking, "Trump Tweets Words 'He Won'; Says Vote Rigged, Not Conceding," *Associated Press*, Nov. 16, 2020, https://apnews.com/article/donald-trump-tweets-he-won-not-conceding-9ce22e9dc90577f7365d150c151a91c7.

55. Krisztián Szabados, "Can We Win the War on Science? Understanding the Link between Political Populism and Anti-Science Politics," *Populism* 2, no. 2 (2019): 207–36.

56. Darren Loucaides, "In Italy, Five Star Movement's War on Journalism Is Picking Up Pace," *Columbia Journalism Review*, June 13, 2019, https://www.cjr.org/analysis/italy-five-star-movement.php.

57. Christopher Paul and Miriam Matthews, *The Russian "Firehose of Falsehood" Propaganda Model: Why It Might Work and Options to Counter It* (Santa Monica, CA: RAND Corporation, 2016), https://www.rand.org/pubs/perspectives/PE198.html.

58. Eric J. Oliver and Wendy M. Rahn, "Rise of the Trumpenvolk: Populism in the 2016 Election," *The ANNALS of the American Academy of Political and Social Science* 667, no. 1 (2016): 190.

59. Pulzer, *The Rise of Political Anti-Semitism in Germany & Austria*, 33.

60. Zeev Sternhell, Mario Sznajder, and Maia Ahseri, *The Birth of Fascist Ideology: From Cultural Rebellion to Political Revolution*, trans. David Maisel. (Princeton, NJ: Princeton University Press, 1994), 10.

61. Jason Sharlet, "'He's the Chosen One to Run America': Inside the Cult of Trump, His Rallies Are Church and He Is the Gospel," *Vanity Fair*, June 18, 2020, https://www.vanityfair.com/news/2020/06/inside-the-cult-of-trump-his-rallies-are-church-and-he-is-the-gospel.

62. George L. Mosse, *The Crisis of German Ideology: Intellectual Origins of the Third Reich* (Madison: University of Wisconsin Press, 2021), 9.

63. Aila Slisco, "One-Quarter of White Evangelicals Believe QAnon 'Storm' Is Coming to 'Restore Rightful Leaders,'" *Newsweek*, May 28, 2021, https://www.newsweek.com/one-quarter-white-evangelicals-believe-qanon-storm-coming-restore-rightful-leaders-1596086.

64. Jason Horowitz, "Hobbits and the Hard Right: How Fantasy Inspires Italy's Potential New Leader," *New York Times*, Sept. 21, 2022, https://www.nytimes.com/2022/09/21/world/europe/giorgia-meloni-lord-of-the-rings.html.

65. John Last, "How 'Hobbit Camps' Rebirthed Italian Fascism," *Atlas Obscura,* Oct. 3, 2017, https://www.atlasobscura.com/articles/hobbit-camps-fascism-italy.

66. Ibid.

67. Jason Horowitz, "Hobbits and the Hard Right."

68. Claudia Goldin, "The Work and Wages of Single Women, 1870 to 1920," *The Journal of Economic History* 40, no. 1 (1980): 81.

69. Ann Heilmann, *New Woman Fiction: Women Writing First-Wave Feminism* (Houndmills: Macmillan Press; New York: St. Martin's Press, 2000), 5.

70. Lucia Re, "Italians and the Invention of Race: The Poetics and Politics of Difference in the Struggle over Libya, 1890–1913," *California Italian Studies* 1, no. 1 (2010): 4.

71. Lauren Alex O'Hagan, "Contesting Women's Right to Vote: Anti-Suffrage Postcards in Edwardian Britain," *Visual Culture in Britain* 21, no. 3 (2020): 335.

72. Julia Christie-Robin, Belinda T. Orzada, and Dilia López-Gydosh, "From Bustles to Bloomers: Exploring the Bicycle's Influence on American Women's Fashion, 1880–1914," *The Journal of American Culture* 35, no. 4 (2012): 316.

73. Heilmann, *New Woman Fiction: Women Writing First-Wave Feminism*, 36.

74. Rafal Soborski, "National Populism and Fascism: Blood and Soil against Globalization," in *Ideology in a Global Age*, ed. Rafal Soborski (London: Palgrave Macmillan, 2013), 107–39.

75. Barry J. Balleck, *Hate Groups and Extremist Organizations in America: An Encyclopedia* (Santa Barbara, CA; Denver, CO: ABC-CLIO, 2019), 131.

76. Francis Fukuyama quoted in *The Washington Post*, "Authoritarianism Is Surging. Can Liberal Democracy Fight Back? Review of 'Liberalism and Its Discontents' by Francis Fukuyama and 'The Age of the Strongman' by Gideon Rachman," Review by Carlos Lozada, May 13, 2022, https://www.washingtonpost.com/outlook/2022/05/13/fukuyama-rachman/.

77. "Europe and Right-Wing Nationalism: A Country-by-Country Guide," *BBC*, Nov. 13, 2019, https://www.bbc.com/news/world-europe-36130006; Marc Santora, "Poland Election: Law and Justice Party Holds on to Power, Early Returns Show," *New York Times*, Oct. 13, 2019, https://www.nytimes.com/2019/10/13/world/europe/poland-election.html.

78. National Front, http://www.nationalfront.org/ (since removed from the Web).

79. Thomas Friedman, *The World Is flat* (New York: Farrar, Straus and Giroux, 2016).

Part V

1. The Coalition Forces that came together to rebuff Napoleon Bonaparte's attempt to expand French territory and colonize Europe were the United Kingdom, Austrian Empire, Kingdom of Prussia, Kingdom of Spain, Kingdom of Naples and Sicily, Kingdom of Sardinia, Dutch Republic, Russian Empire, the Ottoman Empire, Kingdom of Portugal, Kingdom of Sweden, and various Confederation of the Rhine and Italian states at differing times in the wars.

2. Kevin H. O'Rourke, "The Worldwide Economic Impact of the French Revolutionary and Napoleonic Wars, 1793–1815," *Journal of Global History* 1, no. 1 (2006): 123–49.

3. Karl Polanyi, *The Great Transformation: The Political and Economic Origins of Our Time* (Boston, MA: Beacon Press, 2001), 9.

4. Ibid.

5. Ibid., 8.

Chapter 12

1. Richard B. Elrod, "The Concert of Europe: A Fresh Look at an International System," *World Politics* 28 (1976): 159.

2. Ibid., 160.

3. Fredrich von Gentz quoted in Mark Mazower, *Governing the World: The History of an Idea, 1815 to the Present* (New York: Penguin, 2012), 4.

4. This includes "the Napoleonic Wars of 1800–1815. If we focus on wars between Polanyi's 'Great Powers'—the Austro-Sardinian War (1848–49), the Roman Republic War (1849), The War of Italian Unification (1859), The Seven Weeks War (1866), and the Franco-Prussian War (1970–71) amounted to a total of 17.7 months." Eric Royal Lybeck, "The Myth of the Hundred Years Peace: War in the Nineteenth Century," in *At War for Peace*, ed. Mohammadbagher Forough (Oxford: Inter-Disciplinary Press, 2010), 3. See also Richard J. Evans, *The Pursuit of Power: Europe 1815–1914* (New York: Penguin, 2016).

5. Eric Royal Lybeck, "The Myth of the Hundred Years Peace: War in the Nineteenth Century" (2010), 3. See also Evans, *The Pursuit of Power*, 3.

6. Kyle Lascurettes, "The Concert of Europe and Great Power Governance Today: What Can the Order of 19th-Century Europe Teach Policymakers about International Order in the 21st Century?," RAND National Defense Research Institute, Santa Monica, United States (RAND Corporation, 2017), 4.

7. Ibid., 4.

8. Lybeck, "The Myth of the Hundred Years Peace: War in the Nineteenth Century," 1.

9. Meredith Reid Sarkees, Frank Whelon Wayman, and J. David Singer, "Inter-State, Intra-State, and Extra-State Wars: A Comprehensive Look at Their Distribution over Time, 1816–1997," *International Studies Quarterly* 47, no. 1 (2003): 62.

10. David Harvey, *Condition of Postmodernity: An Inquiry into the Conditions of Cultural Change* (Hoboken: Blackwell Publishers, 1989), 264.

11. Kevin H. O'Rourke, "The Worldwide Economic Impact of the French Revolutionary and Napoleonic Wars, 1793–1815," *Journal of Global History* 1, no. 1 (2006): 148.

12. Benjamin H. Higgins, "Agriculture and War: A Comparison of Agricultural Conditions in the Napoleonic and World War Periods," *Agricultural History* 14, no. 1 (1940): 7.

13. O'Rourke, "The Worldwide Economic Impact of the French Revolutionary and Napoleonic Wars, 1793–1815," 5.

14. E. J. Hobsbawm, *The Age of Capital 1848–1875* (London: Little, Brown and Co., 1977), 49.

15. Mabel C. Buer, "The Trade Depression Following the Napoleonic Wars," *Economica* 2 (1921): 162.

16. Higgins, "Agriculture and War," 2.

17. Buer, "The Trade Depression Following the Napoleonic Wars," 160.

18. J. H. Clapham, "The Economic Condition of Europe After the Napoleonic War," *The Scientific Monthly* 11, no. 4 (1920): 322.

19. Higgins, "Agriculture and War," 9.

20. Joseph A Schumpeter, *Business Cycles: A Theoretical, Historical, and Statistical Analysis of the Capitalist Process*, Volume I (London: McGraw Hill Book Company, 1923), 267. Digital Library of India Item 2015.150123 https://archive.org/details/in.ernet.dli.2015.150123/mode/2up.

21. Higgins, "Agriculture and War," 9.

22. Schumpeter, *Business Cycles Vol. I*, 276.

23. Buer, "The Trade Depression Following the Napoleonic Wars," 169.

24. Hobsbawm, *The Age of Capital 1848–1875*, 45.

25. Ibid., 44.

26. Ibid., 45.

27. According to Buer: "it was estimated that between 1815–25, £36,000,000 was lent to France, £9,000,000 to the United States and £10,000,000 to Russia." At the same time, "in 1824–25 there were forty-one foreign and other trading ventures set up with nominal capitals to the amount of £32,840,000 on account of which upwards of £3,000,000 was actually paid. This makes a total of £8,000,000, a surprising one for that period and for an exhausted country." Buer, *The Trade Depression Following the Napoleonic Wars*, 167.

28. Charles Kindleberger, "The Rise of Free Trade in Western Europe, 1820–1875," in *The Rise of Free Trade*, ed. Cheryl Schonhardt-Bailey (New York: Taylor & Francis, 1997), 195.

29. Charles Kindleberger, "The Rise of Free Trade in Western Europe, 1820–1875," *The Journal of Economic History* 35, no. 1 (1975): 26.

30. Ibid., 31.

31. Ibid.

32. Hobsbawm, *The Age of Capital 1848–1875*, 49.

33. Polanyi, *The Great Transformation*, 202.

34. Christopher Kennedy, *The Evolution of Great World Cities: Urban Wealth and Economic Growth* (Canada: University of Toronto Press, 2011), 96.

35. Michael D. Bordo and Eugene N. White, "A Tale of Two Currencies: British and French Finance during the Napoleonic Wars," *The Journal of Economic History* 51, no. 2 (1991): 315.

36. Kennedy, *The Evolution of Great World Cities*, 96.

37. Ibid.

38. Ibid., 99.

39. Giovanni Arrighi, *The Long Twentieth Century. New and Updated Edition* (London: Verso, 2010), 267.

40. Ibid., 55.

41. Robert Latham, "History, Theory, and International Order: Some Lessons from the Nineteenth Century," *Review of International Studies* 23, no. 4 (1997): 426.

42. Michele Fratianni and Andreas Hauskrecht, "From the Gold Standard to a Bipolar Monetary System," *Open Economies Review* 9, no. 1 (1998): 621.

43. Arrighi, *The Long Twentieth Century*, 55.

44. Ibid., 56.

45. Polanyi, *The Great Transformation*, 32.

46. Luca Einaudi, *Money and Politics: European Monetary Unification and the International Gold Standard (1865–1873)* (Oxford: Oxford University Press on Demand, 2001), 21.

47. Maurice Obstfeld and Alan M. Taylor, "Globalization and Capital Markets," in *Globalization in Historical Perspective*, ed. Michael D. Bordo, Alan M. Taylor, and Jeffrey G. Williamson (Chicago: University of Chicago Press, 2003), 124.

48. Giulio M. Gallarotti, *The Anatomy of an International Monetary Regime: The Classical Gold Standard, 1880–1914*. (Oxford: Oxford University Press, 1995): 141.

49. Gallarotti, *The Anatomy of an International Monetary Regime*, 142.

50. Einaudi, *Money and Politics*, 20.

51. Ibid., 13.

52. Einaudi, *Money and Politics*, 37.

53. Ibid.

54. Ibid., 54–55.

55. See Bordo and White, "A Tale of Two Currencies"; Gallarotti, *The Anatomy of an International Monetary Regime*; Joseph S Nye, "The Changing Nature of World Power," *Political Science Quarterly* 105, no. 2 (1990): 177–92; Kindleberger, "The Rise of Free Trade."

56. Lord Stanley quoted in Einaudi, *Money and Politics*, 55.

57. Ibid., 189.

58. Ibid., 195.

59. Eric Helleiner, "Economic Nationalism as a Challenge to Economic Liberalism? Lessons from the 19th Century," *International Studies Quarterly* 46, no. 3 (2002): 313.

60. Ibid., 315.

61. Fredrick List quoted in Helleiner, "Economic Nationalism as a Challenge to Economic Liberalism?," 311–12.

62. Gallarotti, *The Anatomy of an International Monetary Regime*, 145.

63. World Trade Organization, *World Trade Report 2013: Factors Shaping the Future of World Trade*, 36.

64. Kennedy, *The Evolution of Great World Cities*, 97.

65. Dani Rodrik, *The Globalization Paradox: Democracy and the Future of the World Economy* (New York: WW Norton & Company, 2011), 25.

66. Ibid., 36.

67. Harold James and Kevin H O'Rourke, "Italy and the First Age of Globalization, 1861–1940," *Bank of Italy Economic History Working Paper*, no. 16 (2011): 13.

68. Rudiger Dornbusch and Jacob A Frenkel, "The Gold Standard Crisis of 1847," *Journal of International Economics* 16, no. 1–2 (1984): 2.

69. Mark Traugott, "The Mid-Nineteenth-Century Crisis in France and England," *Theory and Society* 12, no. 4 (1983): 457.

70. Ibid.

71. Harvey, *Condition of Postmodernity*, 262.

72. Ibid., 261–62.

73. J. S. Mill quoted in Dornbusch and Frenkel, "The Gold Standard Crisis of 1847," 2.

74. Brian S. Roper, *The History of Democracy: A Marxist Interpretation* (London: Pluto Press, 2013), 179.

75. Traugott, "The Mid-Nineteenth-Century Crisis," 457.

76. Ibid.

77. Ibid., 458.

78. Hobsbawm, *The Age of Capital*, 23.

79. Ibid.

80. Mike Rapport, "1848: European Revolutions," in *The Edinburgh Companion to the History of Democracy: From Pre-History to Future Possibilities*, ed. Benjamin Isakhan and Stephen Stockwell (Edinburgh: Edinburgh University Press, 2015), 282.

81. Hobsbawm, *The Age of Capital*, 39.

82. Rapport, "1848: European Revolutions," 286.

83. Hobsbawm, *The Age of Capital*, 50.

84. Ibid.

85. Ibid., 51.

Chapter 13

1. Maurice Obstfeld and Alan M. Taylor, *Global Capital Markets: Integration, Crisis, and Growth* (Cambridge: Cambridge University Press, 2005), 125.

2. Meredith Reid Sarkees, Frank Whelon Wayman, and J. David Singer, "Inter-state, Intra-state, and Extra-state wars: A Comprehensive Look at Their Distribution over Time, 1816–1997," *International Studies Quarterly* 47, no. 1 (2003): 62.

3. Jeffry A. Frieden, *Global Capitalism: Its Fall and Rise in the Twentieth Century* (WW Norton & Company, 2006), 282.

4. Frieden, *Global Capitalism*, 279, 347.

5. Ibid., 280–81.

6. Ibid., 288.

7. Ibid.

8. Ibid.

9. Andrew G. Terborgh, "The Post-War Rise of World Trade: Does the Bretton Woods System Deserve Credit?" *IDEAS Working Paper Series from RePEc* no. 78/03, 2003, p. 13.

10. Frieden, *Global Capitalism*, 289.

11. Ibid.

12. Arrighi, *The Long Twentieth Century*, 283.

13. Barry Eichengreen, *Exorbitant Privilege: The Rise and Fall of the Dollar and the Future of the International Monetary System.* (New York: Oxford University Press, 2010). 30.

14. A. D. Chandler, "The Competitive Performance of US Industrial Enterprises since the Second World War," *Business History Review* 68, no. 1 (1994): 3.

15. Ibid., 4.

16. Eichengreen, *Exorbitant Privilege*, 30.

17. Fratianni and Hauskrecht, "From the Gold Standard to a Bipolar Monetary System," 619.

18. Ibid., 5.

19. Ibid.

20. Kennedy, *The Evolution of Great World Cities*, 102.

21. Ibid.

22. Frieden, *Global Capitalism*, 293.
23. Geoffrey Jones, *Multinationals and Global Capitalism: From the Nineteenth to the Twenty First Century* (Oxford; New York: Oxford University Press, 2005).
24. Frieden, *Global Capitalism*, 283.
25. Chandler, "The Competitive Performance of US Industrial Enterprises since the Second World War," 51.
26. Ibid., 46.
27. Frieden, *Global Capitalism*, 296.
28. Obstfeld and Taylor, *Global Capital Markets*, 125.
29. Frieden, *Global Capitalism*, 291.
30. Ibid., 291–92.
31. William Glenn Gray, "Floating the System: Germany, the United States, and the Breakdown of Bretton Woods, 1969–1973," *Diplomatic History* 31, no. 2 (2007): 296.
32. See Frieden *Global Capitalism*; Arrighi, *The Long Twentieth Century*; John Gerard Ruggie, "International Regimes, Transactions and Change: Embedded Liberalism in the Postwar Economic Order," in *International Regimes*, ed. Stephen Krasner (Ithaca, NY: Cornell University Press, 1983).
33. Terborgh, "The Post-War Rise of World Trade," 23.
34. Kennedy, *The Evolution of Great World Cities*, 102.
35. Harvey, *Condition of Postmodernity*, 141.
36. Frieden, *Global Capitalism*, 345.
37. Gray, "Floating the System," 295.
38. Frieden, *Global Capitalism*, 342.
39. Obstfeld and Taylor, *Global Capital Markets*, 125.
40. Jeffry A Frieden, "Invested Interests: The Politics of National Economic Policies in a World of Global Finance," *International Organization* 45, no. 4 (1991): 346.
41. Gray, "Floating the System," 295.
42. Ibid., 434.
43. Harvey, *Condition of Postmodernity*, 141.
44. Arrighi, *The Long Twentieth Century*, 2.
45. Ibid., 287.
46. Ibid., 287.
47. Harvey, *Condition of Postmodernity*, 168.
48. Arrighi, *The Long Twentieth Century*, 72.
49. "The Reagan-Thatcher Revolution," *Deutsche Welle*, https://www.dw.com/en/the-reagan-thatcher-revolution/a-16732731.
50. John Lanchester, "Margaret Thatcher's Revolution," *The New Yorker*, July 29, 2013, https://www.newyorker.com/magazine/2013/08/05/1979-and-all-that.
51. Harvey, *Condition of Postmodernity*, 168.
52. Ibid., 170.

Conclusion

1. Henry George, *Progress and Poverty an Inquiry into the Cause of Industrial Depressions and of Increase of Want with Increase of Wealth: The Remedy* (Kingsport Press, 1935), 6.

2. Anthony M. Nadler, *Making the News Popular: Mobilizing U.S. News Audiences*, 114 (Champaign: University of Illinois Press, 2016), 39.

3. Julien Gorbach, "Not Your Grandpa's Hoax: A Comparative History of Fake News," *American Journalism* 35, no. 2 (2018): 248.

4. Jonathan Albright, "Welcome to the Era of Fake News," *Media and Communication* 5, no. 2 (2017): 87.

5. Peter Robins, ed., "On the Path to Day X: The Return of Germany's Far Right," *New York Times*, June 5, 2021, https://www.nytimes.com/2021/06/25/world/europe/germany-nazi-far-right.html.

6. "Germany Arrests 25 Suspected of Planning to Overthrow Government," *New York Times*, December 7, 2022, https://www.nytimes.com/2022/12/07/world/europe/germany-coup-arrests.html.

7. "Why Is There a Growing Far-Right Threat in Italy?," *TRTWorld*, June 29, 2021, https://www.trtworld.com/magazine/why-is-there-a-growing-far-right-threat-in-italy-47933.

8. "SUPO: Right-Wing Terrorism a Growing Threat in Finland," Mar. 23, 2021, https://www.helsinkitimes.fi/finland/news-in-brief/18916-supo-right-wing-terrorism-a-growing-threat-in-finland.html.

9. See Norman Angell, *Essays Towards Peace*, by Rationalist Peace Society; ed. John Mackinnon Robertson, p. ix. https://archive.org/details/essaystowardspea00ratiiala/page/74/mode/2up.

10. S. H. Swinny, "Rationalism and International Righteousness," in *Essays Towards Peace* (Watts, 1913), 78.

Bibliography

Journal Articles and Books

Agarwal, Anuj. "High Frequency Trading: Evolution and the Future." *Capgemini, London, UK* (2012): p. 20.

Agnew, John. "The New Global Economy: Time-Space Compression, Geopolitics, and Global Uneven Development." *Journal of World-Systems Research* (2001): pp. 133–154.

Albright, Jonathan, "Welcome to the Era of Fake News." *Media and Communication* 5, no. 2 (2017): pp. 87–89.

Allardyce, Gilbert. "What Fascism Is Not: Thoughts on the Deflation of a Concept." *The American Historical Review* 84, no. 2 (1979): pp. 367–388.

Altay, Serdar. "Hegemony, Private Actors, and International Institutions: Transnational Corporations as the agents of transformation of the trade regime from GATT to the WTO." (PhD dissertation, Trento, 2012).

Alvaredo, Facundo. "The World Inequality Report." In *The World Inequality Report* (Cambridge, MA: Harvard University Press, 2018).

Anbinder, Tyler. *Nativism and Slavery: The Northern Know Nothings and the Politics of the 1850's* (New York: Oxford University Press, 1992).

Anderson, Benedict R. O'G. (Benedict Richard O'Gorman). *Imagined Communities: Reflections on the Origin and Spread of Nationalism* (London; New York: Verso, 2006).

Anheier, Helmut, Marlies Glasius, and Mary Kaldor. "Introducing Global Civil Society." *Global Civil Society* (2001): pp. 3–22.

Araujo, Jesús Mirás. "Urbanization in Upheaval Spanish Cities, Agents and Targets of a Slow Transformation." In *The Routledge Hispanic Studies Companion to Nineteenth-Century Spain*, edited by Elisa Martí-López (London: Routledge, 2020), pp. 218–234.

Arendt, Hannah. *The Origins of Totalitarianism*. 1st ed. (New York: Harcourt, Brace, 1951).

Arrighi, Giovanni. "Global Inequalities and the Legacy of Dependency Theory." *Radical Philosophy Review* 5, no. 1/2 (2002a): pp. 75–85.

Arrighi, Giovanni. *The Long Twentieth Century: Money, Power, and the Origins of Our Times*. (London: Verso, 2002b).

Aronson, I. Michael. "Russian Commissions on the Jewish Question in the 1880's." *East European Quarterly* 14, no. 1 (1980): p. 60.

Atzmüller, Roland, Brigitte Aulenbacher, Ulrich Brand, Fabienne Décieux, Karin Fischer, and Birgit Sauer. *Capitalism in Transformation: Movements and Countermovements in the 21st Century* (Cheltenham, UK; Northampton, MA: Edward Elgar Publishing, 2019).

Aulenbacher, Brigitte, Richard Bärnthaler, and Andreas Novy. "Karl Polanyi, the Great Transformation, and Contemporary Capitalism." *Österreichische Zeitschrift Für Soziologie* 44, no. 2 (2019): pp. 105–113.

Bagwell, Philip and Peter J. Lyth. *Transport in Britain: From Canal Lock to Gridlock* (London: Hambledon and London, 2002).

Baily, Martin Neil, Robert E. Litan, and Matthew S. Johnson. "The Origins of the Financial Crisis." *Initiative on Business and Public Policy at Brookings*, November 2008.

Bairoch, Paul. "European Trade Policy, 1815–1914." *The Cambridge Economic History of Europe* 8, no. 1 (1989): pp. 160–180.

Bairoch, Paul and Richard Kozul-Wright. "Globalization Myths; Some Historical Reflections on Integration, Industrialization and Growth in World Economy." *UNCTAD Discussion Papers* no. 113 (1996), 37–68.

Balleck, Barry J. *Hate Groups and Extremist Organizations in America: An Encyclopedia* (Santa Barbara, CA; Denver, CO: ABC-CLIO, 2019).

Bärnthaler, Richard, Andreas Novy, and Basil Stadelmann. "A Polanyi-Inspired Perspective on Social-Ecological Transformations of Cities." *Journal of Urban Affairs* (2020): pp. 1–25. https://doi.org/10.1080/07352166.2020.1834404.

Baum, L. Frank. *The Wonderful Wizard of Oz* (Oxford: Oxford University Press, 2008).

Baumann, Arthur A. "The Functions and Future of the Press." *Fortnightly* 107, no. 640 (1920): pp. 620–627.

Becker, Karina and Klaus Dörre. "Völkisch Populism: A Polanyian-Type Movement?" In *Capitalism in Transformation: Movements and Countermovements in the 21st Century*, edited by Roland Atzmüller, Brigitte Aulenbacher, Ulrich Brand, Fabienne Décieux, Karin Fischer, and Birgit Sauer (Cheltenham, UK; Northampton, MA: Edward Elgar Publishing, 2019), pp. 152–168.

Bellolio, Cristóbal. "An Inquiry into Populism's Relation to Science." *Politics* (2022). https://doi.org/10.1177/02633957221109541.

Bensel, Richard Franklin. *Passion and Preferences: William Jennings Bryan and the 1896 Democratic Convention* (Cambridge: Cambridge University Press, 2008).

Berezin, Mabel. "Fascism and Populism: Are They Useful Categories for Comparative Sociological Analysis?" *Annual Review of Sociology* 45, no. 1 (2019): pp. 345–361.

Berman, Sheri. "The Causes of Populism in the West." *Annual Review of Political Science* 24 (2021): pp. 71–88.

Bernardini, Gene. "The Origins and Development of Racial Anti-Semitism in Fascist Italy." *The Journal of Modern History* 49, no. 3 (1977): pp. 431–453.

Betz, Hans-Georg. "Nativism Across Time and Space." *Swiss Political Science Review* 23, no. 4 (2017): pp. 335–353.

Betz, Hans-Georg. "Mosques, Minarets, Burqas and Other Essential Threats: The Populist Right's Campaign against Islam in Western Europe." In *Right-Wing Populism in Europe: Politics and Discourse*, edited by Ruth Wodak, Majid KhosraviNik, and Brigitte Mral (London: Bloomsbury Publishing Plc., 2013): pp. 71–88.

Bieling, Hans-Jürgen. "Aufstieg Des Rechtspopulismus Im Heutigen Europa–Umrisse Einer Gesellschaftstheoretischen Erklärung." *WSI Mitteilungen* 8, no. 2017 (2017): pp. 557–565.

Billig, Michael. *Banal Nationalism* (London: SAGE, 1995).

Blagojevic, Bojana. "Causes of Ethnic Conflict: A Conceptual Framework." *Journal of Global Change & Governance* 3, no. 1 (2010): pp. 1–25.

Block, Fred. "Polanyi's double movement and the reconstruction of critical theory." *Revue interventions économiques. Papers in political economy* 38 (2008).

Block, Fred and Margaret R. Somers. *The Power of Market Fundamentalism* (Cambridge, MA: Harvard University Press, 2014).

Blondheim, Menahem. *News Over the Wires: The Telegraph and the Flow of Public Information in America, 1844-1897* (Cambridge, MA; London: Harvard University Press, 1994).

Boli, John and George M. Thomas. "INGOs and the Organization of World Culture." In *Constructing World Culture: International Nongovernmental Organizations since 1875*, edited by John Boli & George M. Thomas (Stanford, CA: Stanford University Press, 1999), pp. 13-49.

Bonikowski, Bart. "Nationalism in Settled Times." *Annual Review of Sociology* 42, no. 1 (2016): pp. 427-449.

Bonikowski, Bart, Daphne Halikiopoulou, Eric Kaufmann, and Matthijs Rooduijn. "Populism and Nationalism in a Comparative Perspective: A Scholarly Exchange." *Nations and Nationalism* 25, no. 1 (2019): pp. 58-81.

Bordo, Michael D. and Eugene N. White. "A Tale of Two Currencies: British and French Finance during the Napoleonic Wars." *The Journal of Economic History* 51, no. 2 (1991): pp. 303-316.

Braga, Carlos Alberto Primo, Carsten Fink, and Claudia Paz Sepulveda. *Intellectual Property Rights and Economic Development*. World Bank Discussion Paper no. 412, 2000.

Brambilla, Carlo. "Assessing Convergence in European Investment Banking Patterns Until 1914." In *Convergence and Divergence of National Financial Systems: Evidence from the Gold Standards, 1871-1971*, edited by Anders Ögren & Patrice Baubeau (UK: Pickering & Chatto, 2014), pp. 89-108.

Breuilly, John. *The Oxford Handbook of the History of Nationalism*. 1st ed. (Oxford: Oxford University Press, 2013).

Broadberry, Stephen and Kevin O'Rourke H. *The Cambridge Economic History of Modern Europe: Volume 2, 1870 to the Present* (Cambridge: Cambridge University Press, 2010).

Broz, J. Lawrence, Jeffry Frieden, and Stephen Weymouth. "Populism in Place: The Economic Geography of the Globalization Backlash." *International Organization* 75, no. 2 (2021): pp. 464-494.

Broz, J. L., Jeffry Frieden, and Stephen Weymouth. "Populism in Place: The Economic Geography of the Globalization Backlash." *International Organization* 75, no. 2 (2021): pp. 464-494. doi:10.1017/S0020818320000314.

Brubaker, Rogers. *Citizenship and Nationhood in France and Germany* (Cambridge, MA: Harvard University Press, 1992).

Brubaker, Rogers. "Ethnicity, Race, and Nationalism." *Annual Review of Sociology* (2009): pp. 21-42.

Brubaker, Rogers. "The Manichean Myth: Rethinking the Distinction between 'Civic' and 'Ethnic' Nationalism." *Nation and National Identity: The European Experience in Perspective* (1999): pp. 55-71.

Brubaker, Rogers. "Migrations of Ethnic Unmixing in the 'New Europe'" *International Migration Review* 32, no. 4 (1998): pp. 1047-1065.

Brubaker, Rogers. "Populism and Nationalism." *Nations and Nationalism* 26, no. 1 (2020): pp. 44-66. doi:10.1111/nana.12522.

Buer, Mabel C. "The Trade Depression Following the Napoleonic Wars." *Economica*, no. 2 (1921): pp. 159-179.

Caiani, Manuela. "The Populist Parties and their Electoral Success: Different Causes Behind Different Populisms? The Case of the Five-Star Movement and the League." *Contemporary Italian Politics* 11, no. 3 (2019): pp. 236-250.

Cameron, Rondo E. *Banking in the Early Stages of Industrialization: A Study in Comparative Economic History* (New York: Oxford University Press, 1967).

Capoccia, Giovanni and R. Daniel Kelemen. "The Study of Critical Junctures: Theory, Narrative, and Counterfactuals in Historical Institutionalism." *World Politics* 59, no. 3 (2007): pp. 341–369.

Cârstocea, Raul. "Anti-Semitism in Romania: Historical Legacies, Contemporary Challenges." *European Center for Minority Issues* (2014): p. 7.

Cardoso, Fernando Henrique and Enzo Faletto. *Dependency and Development in Latin America* (Berkeley: University of California Press, 1979).

Carey, Craig. "Breaking the News. Telegraphy and Yellow Journalism in the Spanish-American War." *American Periodicals* (2016): pp. 130–148.

Cassis, Youssef, Giuseppe De Luca, and Massimo Florio. *Infrastructure Finance in Europe: Insights into the History of Water, Transport, and Telecommunications* (Oxford: Oxford University Press, 2016).

Castles, Stephen. "International Migration at the Beginning of the Twenty-First Century: Global Trends and Issues." *International Social Science Journal* 52, no. 165 (2000): pp. 269–281. doi:10.1111/1468-2451.00258.

Chamberlain, Houston Stewart. *The Foundations of The Nineteenth Century* (London: John Lane, 1913).

Chandler, Alfred D. and Bruce Mazlish. *Leviathans: Multinational Corporations and the New Global History* (Cambridge; New York: Cambridge University Press, 2005).

Chandler, Alfred Dupont, Takashi Hikino, and Alfred D. Chandler. *Scale and Scope: The Dynamics of Industrial Capitalism* (Cambridge, MA; London: The Belknap Press of Harvard University Press, 2009).

Chandler, Robin. "Creative Parallel Spaces in Science and Art: Knowledge in the Information Age." *The Journal of Arts Management, Law, and Society* 29, no. 3 (1999): pp. 163–176.

Chase-Dunn, Christopher and Joan Sokolovsky. "Interstate Systems, World Empires, and the Capitalist World Economy: A Response to Thompson." *International Studies Quarterly* 27 (Sept. 1983): pp. 364–366.

Christie-Robin, Julia, Belinda T. Orzada, and Dilia López-Gydosh. "From Bustles to Bloomers: Exploring the Bicycle's Influence on American Women's Fashion, 1880–1914." *The Journal of American Culture* 35, no. 4 (2012): pp. 315–331.

Clapham, J. H. "The Economic Condition of Europe After the Napoleonic War." *The Scientific Monthly* 11, no. 4 (1920): pp. 320–325.

Clapham, John Harold. *The Economic Development of France and Germany, 1815–1914* (England: The University Press, 1923).

Colaresi, Michael. "Shocks to the System: Great Power Rivalry and the Leadership Long Cycle." *Journal of Conflict Resolution* 45 no. 5 (2001): pp. 569–593.

Conrad, Sebastian. "'Nothing Is the Way It Should Be': Global Transformations of the Time Regime in the Nineteenth Century." *Modern Intellectual History* 15, no. 3 (2018): pp. 821–848.

Conrad, Sebastian. *Globalisation and the Nation in Imperial Germany* (Cambridge; New York: Cambridge University Press, 2010).

Conrad, Sebastian and Dominic Sachsenmaier. *Competing Visions of World Order: Global AU: And Movements, 1880s–1930s* (New York: Palgrave Macmillan, 2007).

Cook, Gerald N. "A Review of History, Structure, and Competition in the US Airline Industry." *Journal of Aviation/Aerospace Education & Research* 7, no. 1 (1996): p. 1.

Cox, Michael. "The Rise of Populism and the Crisis of Globalization: Brexit, Trump and Beyond." *Irish Studies in International Affairs* 28 (2017): pp. 9–17.

Crawford, Beverly and Ronnie D. Lipschutz. *The Myth of "Ethnic Conflict": Politics, Economics, and "Cultural" Violence* (University of California, 1998).

Cronin, Mike. *The Failure of British Fascism: The Far Right and the Fight for Political Recognition* (London: Macmillan Press, 1996).

Czaika, Mathias and Hein de Haas. "The Globalization of Migration: Has the World Become More Migratory?" *The International Migration Review* 48, no. 2 (2014): pp. 283–323. doi:10.1111/imre.12095.

Dale, Gareth. "Double Movements and Pendular Forces: Polanyian Perspectives on the Neoliberal Age." *Current Sociology* 60, no. 1 (2012): pp. 3–27.

Dale, Gareth. *Karl Polanyi: A Life on the Left* (New York: Columbia University Press, 2016). doi:10.7312/dale17608.

Dale, Gareth. "Karl Polanyi's the Great Transformation: Perverse Effects, Protectionism and Gemeinschaft." *Economy and Society* 37, no. 4 (2008): pp. 495–524.

Dale, Gareth. *Polanyi: The Limits of the Market* (Cambridge, Malden: Polity Books, 2013).

Dale, Gareth and Mathieu Desan. "Fascism." *Karl Polanyi's Political and Economic Thought: A Critical Guide* (2019): pp. 151–170.

Darnton, Robert. "The True History of Fake News." *The New York Review of Books*, February 2017.

Datta, Prabhat. "Secessionist Movements in North East India." *The Indian Journal of Political Science* 53, no. 4 (1992): pp. 536–558.

Daudin, Guillaume, Matthias Morys, and Kevin H. O'Rourke. "Europe and Globalization, 1870–1914." *IDEAS Working Paper Series from RePEc*, 2008.

Daudin, Guillaume, Matthias Morys, and Kevin O'Rourke. "Globalization, 1870–1914." *The Cambridge Economic History of Modern Europe* (2010): pp. 5–29.

Davidson, Theresa and Karlye Burson. "Keep Those Kids Out: Nativism and Attitudes toward Access to Public Education for the Children of Undocumented Immigrants." *Journal of Latinos and Education* 16, no. 1 (2017): pp. 41–50.

Davis, Steven I. *Euro-Bank: Its Origins, Management and Outlook* (Springer, 1980a).

Davis, Steven I. "Some Earlier Patterns in International Banking." In *The Euro-Bank: Its Origins, Management and Outlook* (New York: Wiley, 1980), pp. 7–25.

De Cleen, Benjamin and Yannis Stavrakakis. "How Should We Analyze the Connections between Populism and Nationalism: A Response to Rogers Brubaker." *Nations and Nationalism* 26, no. 2 (2020): pp. 314–322.

De Long, J. Bradford. "JP Morgan and His Money Trust." *Wilson Quarterly* 16, no. 4 (1992): pp. 16–30.

De Rosa, Luigi. "Urbanization and Industrialization in Italy (1861–1921)." *Journal of European Economic History* 17, no. 3 (1988): p. 467.

Dighe, Ranjit S. "The Fable of the Allegory: The Wizard of Oz in Economics: Comment." *The Journal of Economic Education*, 38 no. 3 (2007): pp. 318–324.

Domarus, Max and Adolf Hitler. *Hitler: Speeches and Proclamations, 1932–1945: The Chronicle of a Dictatorship*. Vol. 3 (Tauris, 1990). (Out of Print).

Dornbusch, Rudiger and Jacob A. Frenkel. "The Gold Standard Crisis of 1847." *Journal of International Economics* 16, no. 1–2 (1984): pp. 1–27.

Dörre, Klaus. "Take Back Control!" *Österreichische Zeitschrift Für Soziologie* 44, no. 2 (2019): pp. 225–243.

Doyle, Michael W. "Liberalism and World Politics." *American Political Science Review* 80, no. 4 (1986): pp. 1151–1169.

Drake, Richard. "The Theory and Practice of Italian Nationalism, 1900–1906." *The Journal of Modern History* 53, no. 2 (1981): p. 218.

Eatwell, Roger. "The Esoteric Ideology of the National Front in the 1980s." In *The Failure of British Fascism*, edited by Mike Cronin (London: Macmillan Press; New York: St. Martin's Press, 1996), pp. 99–117.

Edwards, Sebastian. "On Latin American Populism, and Its Echoes Around the World." *Journal of Economic Perspectives* 33, no. 4 (2019): pp. 76–99.

Eichengreen, Barry. *Exorbitant Privilege: The Rise and Fall of the Dollar and the Future of the International Monetary System* (Oxford; New York: Oxford University Press, 2011).

Eichengreen, Barry J. *The Populist Temptation: Economic Grievance and Political Reaction in the Modern Era* (New York: Oxford University Press, 2018).

Einaudi, Luca. *Money and Politics: European Monetary Unification and the International Gold Standard (1865–1873)* (Oxford; New York: Oxford University Press, 2001).

Elrod, Richard B. "The Concert of Europe: A Fresh Look at an International System." *World Politics* 28, no. 2 (1976): pp. 159–174.

Ernst, Nicole, Sven Engesser, Florin Büchel, Sina Blassnig, and Frank Esser. "Extreme Parties and Populism: An Analysis of Facebook and Twitter Across Six Countries." *Information, Communication & Society* 20, no. 9 (2017): pp. 1347–1364.

Evans, Richard J. *The Pursuit of Power: Europe 1815–1914* (Penguin, 2016).

Evans, Tony. "The Limits of Tolerance: Islam as Counter-Hegemony?" *Review of International Studies* 37, no. 4 (2011): pp. 1751–1773.

Fernandes, Carla Montuori, Luiz Ademir de Oliveira, Fernando de Resende Chaves, and Pedro Farnese. "The Denial of Science in the Antisystem Populist Rhetoric." *American Academic Scientific Research Journal for Engineering, Technology, and Sciences* 85, no. 1 (2022): pp. 1–13.

Fernandez, Lilia. "Nativism and Xenophobia." In *The Encyclopedia of Global Human Migration*, edited by Immanuel Ness (Hoboken, NJ: Wiley-Blackwell, 2013), pp. 1–7.

Fischer-Tiné, Harald. "Global Civil Society and the Forces of Empire: The Salvation Army, British Imperialism, and the 'Prehistory' of NGOs (Ca. 1880–1920)." In *Competing Visions of World Order*, edited by Sebastian Conrad and Dominic Sachsenmaier (New York: Palgrave Macmillan, 2007), pp. 29–67.

Fishlow, Albert. "Lessons from the Past: Capital Markets during the 19th Century and the Interwar Period." *International Organization* 39, no. 3 (1985): pp. 383–439.

Fortier, Paul A. "Gobineau and German Racism." *Comparative Literature* 19, no. 4 (1967): pp. 341–350.

Frantz, Constantin. *Der Untergang Der Alten Parteien Und Die Parteien Der Zukunft* Niendorf (Berlin, 1878).

Fratianni, Michele and Andreas Hauskrecht. "From the Gold Standard to a Bipolar Monetary System." *Open Economies Review* (/01/01, 1998): pp. 239–265.

Frieden, Jeffry. "The Fall and Rise of Global Capitalism." *New York: Norton* 16 (2006): pp. 7–8.

Frieden, Jeffry A. "Invested Interests: The Politics of National Economic Policies in a World of Global Finance." *International Organization* 45, no. 4 (1991): pp. 425–451.

Frieden, Jeffry A. *Global Capitalism: Its Fall and Rise in the Twentieth Century.* 1st ed. (New York: W.W. Norton, 2006).

Friedman, Thomas. *The World Is Flat* (New York: Farrar, Straus and Giroux, 2016).

Fuchs, Christian. *Nationalism on the Internet: Critical Theory and Ideology in the Age of Social Media and Fake News.* 1st ed. (Milton: Routledge, 2020).

Funke, Manuel and Christoph Trebesch. "Financial Crises and the Populist Right." *Ifo DICE Report* 15, no. 4 (2017): pp. 6–9.

Gage, Beverly. *The Day Wall Street Exploded: A Story of America in Its First Age of Terror* (Cary: Oxford University Press USA—OSO, 2009).

Gallarotti, Giulio M. and Giulio Gallarotti. *The Anatomy of an International Monetary Regime: The Classical Gold Standard, 1880–1914* (New York: Oxford University Press, 1995).

Gans, Carl. "Punctuated Equilibria and Political Science: A Neontological View." *Politics and the Life Sciences* 5, no. 2 (1987): pp. 220–227.

Gans, Chaim. *The Limits of Nationalism.* (Cambridge: Cambridge University Press, 2003). doi:10.1017/CBO9780511490231.

Gellner, Ernest. *Nations and Nationalism* (Ithaca, NY: Cornell University Press, 2006).

George, Henry. *Henry George's Progress and Poverty: An Abridgement of the Economic Principles* (New York (State): Harcourt, Brace and Company, 1924).

George, Henry. *Progress and Poverty: An Inquiry into the Cause of Industrial Depressions, and of Increase of Want with Increase of Wealth. The Remedy* (25th Anniversary edition, New York: Doubleday, Page, and Company, 1879).

Gerhardt, Uta. "The Use of Weberian Ideal-Type Methodology in Qualitative Data Interpretation: An Outline for Ideal-Type Analysis." *Bulletin of Sociological Methodology/Bulletin De Méthodologie Sociologique* 45, no. 1 (1994): pp. 74–126.

Gerschenkron, Alexander. *Economic Backwards in Historical Perspective: A Book Essays* (Cambridge, MA: Belknap Press of Harvard University Press, 1962a).

Gijsenbergh, Joris. "Democracy's Various Defenders: The Struggle Against Political Extremism in the Netherlands, 1917–1940." In *Historical Perspectives on Democracies and their Adversaries,* edited by Joost Augusteijn, Constant Hijzen, and Mark Leon De Vries (Palgrave Macmillan, 2019), pp. 69–98.

Gilbert, Richard and Anthony Perl. *Transport Revolutions Moving People and Freight without Oil* (Philadelphia, PA: New Society, 2010a).

Gilbert, Richard and Anthony Perl. "Transportation in the Post-Carbon World." *The Post Carbon Reader* (2010b): pp. 347–360.

Gill, Stephen. "Globalizing Capital and Political Agency in the Twenty-First Century." *Contributions in Economics and Economic History* (2000): pp. 15–32.

Gillies, James M. and Robert Cailliau. *How the Web was Born: The Story of the World Wide Web* (Oxford; New York: Oxford University Press, 2000).

Gilpin, Robert. *The Challenge of Global Capitalism: The World Economy in the 21st Century* (Princeton, NJ: Princeton University Press, 2018).

Gilpin, Robert. *War and Change in World Politics* (Cambridge: Cambridge University Press, 1981).

Gökalp, Ziya. *Turkish Nationalism and Western Civilization; Selected Essays* (New York: Columbia University Press, 1959).

Gorbach, Julien. "Not Your Grandpa's Hoax: A Comparative History of Fake News." *American Journalism* 35, no. 2 (2018): pp. 236–249.

Gray, William Glenn. "Floating the System: Germany, the United States, and the Breakdown of Bretton Woods, 1969–1973." *Diplomatic History* 31, no. 2 (2007): pp. 295–323.

Gregor, A. James. *Interpretations of Fascism* (New York: Routledge, 2017).

Grumke, Thomas. "Globalized Anti-Globalists: The Ideological Basis of the Internationalization of Right-Wing Extremism." In *Right-Wing Radicalism Today*, edited by Sabine Von Mering and Timothy Wyman Mccarty (Abingdon, Oxon: Routledge, 2013), pp. 27–35.

Grunberg, Isabelle. "Exploring the 'Myth' of Hegemonic Stability." *International Organization* 44 no. 4 (1990): pp. 431–477.

Guiso, Luigi, Helios Herrera, Massimo Morelli, and Tommaso Sonno. *Demand and Supply of Populism* (UK: Centre for Economic Policy Research London, 2017).

Habermas, Jürgen and Ciaran Cronin. "The European Nation-State: On the Past and Future of Sovereignty and Citizenship." *Public Culture* 10, no. 2 (1998): pp. 397–416. doi:10.1215/08992363-10-2-397.

Hagtvet, Bernt. "Right-Wing Extremism in Europe." *Journal of Peace Research* 31, no. 3 (1994): pp. 241–246.

Halavais, Alexander. "National Borders on the World Wide Web." *New Media & Society* 2, no. 1 (2000): pp. 7–28.

Halikiopoulou, Daphne and Tim Vlandas. "What Is New and What Is Nationalist about Europe's New Nationalism? Explaining the Rise of the Far Right in Europe." *Nations and Nationalism* 25, no. 2 (2019): pp. 409–434.

Hameleers, Michael and Rens Vliegenthart. "The Rise of a Populist Zeitgeist? A Content Analysis of Populist Media Coverage in Newspapers Published between 1990 and 2017." *Journalism Studies (London, England)* 21, no. 1 (2020): pp. 19–36. doi:10.1080/1461670X.2019.1620114.

Hammond, Bray. *Banks and Politics in America from the Revolution to the Civil War* (Princeton, NJ: Princeton University Press, 1991).

Handley, Mark and Jon Crowcroft. *The World Wide Web: Beneath the Surf* (London: Routledge, 2015).

Harris, Frank. 1855–1931. *The Bomb, by Frank Harris* (New York (State): M. Kennerley, 1909).

Harvey, David. "From Fordism to Flexible Accumulation." In *The Condition of Postmodernity: An Inquiry into the Conditions of Cultural Change* (Oxford; Cambridge, MAA: Blackwell, 1989), pp. 141–172.

Hayek, Friedrich August, *The Road to Serfdom*.(Routledge, 1976).

Hayes, Paul. *Themes in Modern European History 1890–1945* (London; New York: Routledge, 2002).

Hegghammer, Thomas. "Islamist Violence and Regime Stability in Saudi Arabia," *International Affairs* 84, no. 4 (2008): p. 703.

Heilmann, Ann. *New Woman Fiction: Women Writing First-Wave Feminism* (Houndmills. UK: Macmillan Press, 2000).

Helleiner, Eric. "Economic Nationalism as a Challenge to Economic Liberalism? Lessons from the 19th Century." *International Studies Quarterly* 46, no. 3 (2002): pp. 307–329.

Hicks, John D. *The Populist Revolt: A History of the Farmers' Alliance and the People's Party*. 2nd ed. (Minneapolis, MN: University of Minnesota Press, 1931).

Higgins, Benjamin. "The Economic War since 1918." In *War in the Twentieth Century*, edited by Willard Waller (New York: Dryden Press, 1940), pp. 135–191.

Higgins, Benjamin H. "Agriculture and War: A Comparison of Agricultural Conditions in the Napoleonic and World War Periods." *Agricultural History* 14, no. 1 (1940): pp. 1–12.

Higham, John. *Strangers in the Land Patterns of American Nativism, 1860–1925*. 2nd ed. (New Brunswick, NJ: Rutgers University Press, 2002).

Hoag, Christopher. "The Atlantic Telegraph Cable and Capital Market Information Flows." *The Journal of Economic History* 66, no. 2 (2006): pp. 342–353.

Hobsbawm, Eric. *The Age of Capital: 1845–1878* (New York: Scribner and Sons, 1975).

Hobson, John A. "The Ethics of Internationalism." *The International Journal of Ethics* 17, no. 1 (1906): pp. 16–28.

Hochfelder, David. "The Communications Revolution and Popular Culture." *A Companion to 19th-Century America* (2001): pp. 303–316.

Hoe, Robert. *A Short History of the Printing Press and of the Improvements in Printing Machinery from the Time of Gutenberg Up to the Present Day* (New York: R. Hoe, 1902).

Holmes, Christopher. *Polanyi in Times of Populism: Vision and Contradiction in the History of Economic Ideas* (London; New York: Routledge, Taylor & Francis Group, 2018).

Hopewell, Kristen. *Breaking the WTO: How Emerging Powers Disrupted the Neoliberal Project* (Palo Alto, CA: Stanford University Press, 2016).

Hopkin, Jonathan. *Anti-System Politics the Crisis of Market Liberalism in Rich Democracies* (New York: Oxford University Press, 2020).

Hopkins, Terence K. and Immanuel Maurice Wallerstein. *World-Systems Analysis: Theory and Methodology* (SAGE Publications, Inc., 1982).

Hösl, Maximilian. "Semantics of the Internet: A Political History." *Internet Histories* 3, no. 3–4 (2019): pp. 275–292.

Howard, Michael. "War and the Nation-State." *Daedalus* (1979): pp. 101–110.

Howse, Robert. "The World Trade Organization 20 Years On: Global Governance by Judiciary." *European Journal of International Law* 27, no. 1 (2016): pp. 9–77.

Hsu, Chia-Yu, Bo-Ruei Kao, Lin Li, and K. Robert Lai. "An Agent-Based Fuzzy Constraint-Directed Negotiation Model for Solving Supply Chain Planning and Scheduling Problems." *Applied Soft Computing* 48 (2016): pp. 703–715.

Hummels, D. "Have International Transportation Costs Declined." *Scientific and Technical Aerospace Reports* 45, no. 18 (2007).

Hummels, David. "Transportation Costs and International Trade in the Second Era of Globalization." *Journal of Economic Perspectives* 21, no. 3 (2007): pp. 131–154.

Hutton, Frankie and Barbara Straus Reed. *Outsiders in 19th-Century Press History: Multicultural Perspectives* (Bowling Green, OH: Bowling Green State University Popular Press, 1995).

Isakhan, Benjamin and Stephen Stockwell, eds. *The Edinburgh Companion to the History of Democracy: From Pre-History to Future Possibilities* (Edinburgh: Edinburgh University Press, 2015). https://www.jstor.org/stable/10.3366/j.ctt1g0b6rb.

Jackson, Jessica E. "Sensationalism in the Newsroom: Its Yellow Beginnings, the Nineteenth Century Legal Transformation, and the Current Seizure of the American Press." *Notre Dame Journal of Law Ethics & Public Policy* 19 (2005): p. 789.

James, Harold and Kevin H. O'Rourke. "Italy and the First Age of Globalization, 1861–1940." *Bank of Italy Economic History Working Paper* no. 16 (2011).

Jameson, Fredric. "Culture and Finance Capital." *Critical Inquiry* 24, no. 1 (1997): pp. 246–265.

Jenks, Leland H. "Railroads as an Economic Force in American Development." *The Journal of Economic History* 4, no. 1 (1944): pp. 1–20.

Jensen, Richard. "Daggers, Rifles and Dynamite: Anarchist Terrorism in Nineteenth Century Europe." *Terrorism and Political Violence* 16, no. 1 (2004): pp. 116–153.

Jensen, Richard Bach. *The Battle Against Anarchist Terrorism: An International History, 1878–1934* (Cambridge: Cambridge University Press, 2014).

Jensen, Richard Bach. "The International Anti-Anarchist Conference of 1898 and the Origins of Interpol." *Journal of Contemporary History* 16, no. 2 (1981): pp. 323–347.

Johanson, Katya and Hilary Glow. "Honour Bound in Australia: From Defensive Nationalism to Critical Nationalism." *National Identities* 11, no. 4 (2009): pp. 385–396.

John, Richard R. "Rendezvous with Information? Computers and Communications Networks in the United States." *Business History Review* 75, no. 1 (2001): pp. 1–13.

Johnston, Robert D. "The Age of Reform: A Defense of Richard Hofstadter Fifty Years On." *The Journal of the Gilded Age and Progressive Era* 6, no. 2 (2007): pp. 127–137.

Jones, Aled. *Powers of the Press: Newspapers, Power and the Public in Nineteenth Century England* (London: Routledge, 2016).

Jones, Geoffrey. *Multinationals and Global Capitalism: From the Nineteenth to the Twenty First Century* (Oxford; New York: Oxford University Press, 2005).

Judis, John B. *The Populist Explosion: How the Great Recession Transformed American and European Politics* (New York: Columbia Global Reports, 2016).

Kalm, Sara and Johannes Lindvall. "Immigration Policy and the Modern Welfare State, 1880–1920." *Journal of European Social Policy* 29, no. 4 (2019): pp. 463–477. doi:10.1177/0958928719831169.

Kaplan, Richard L. *Politics and the American Press: The Rise of Objectivity, 1865–1920* (Cambridge: Cambridge University Press, 2002).

Kaplan, Richard L. "Yellow Journalism." In *The International Encyclopedia of Communication*, edited by Wolfgang Donsbach (John Wiley & Sons: 2008).

Kaufmann, Eric. "Ethno-traditional Nationalism and the Challenge of Immigration." *Nations and Nationalism* 25, no. 2 (2019): pp. 435–448.

Kellner, Douglas. "The Postmodern Turn: Positions, Problems, and Prospects." In *Frontiers of Social Theory: The New Syntheses*, edited by George Ritzer (New York: Columbia University Press, 1990), pp. 255–286.

Kemper, Andreas. "AfD, Pegida and the New Right in Germany." *The European Far Right: Historical and Contemporary Perspectives* (2015): p. 43.

Kennedy, Christopher. *The Evolution of Great World Cities: Urban Wealth and Economic Growth* (Toronto: University of Toronto Press, 2011).

Keynes, John Maynard. *The Economic Consequences of the Peace* (New York: Harcourt, Brace and Howe, 1920).

Kindleberger, C. P. "The Rise of Free Trade in Western Europe, 1820–1875." *The Journal of Economic History* 35, no. 1 (1975): pp. 20–55. http://www.jstor.org/stable/2119154.

Kindleberger, Charles P. *Manias, Panics, and Crashes: a History of Financial Crises* (New York: Basic Books, 1978).

Kindleberger, Charles P. "Group Behavior and International Trade." *Journal of Political Economy* 59, no. 1 (1951): pp. 30–46.

Kindleberger, Charles P. "The Rise of Free Trade in Western Europe, 1820–1875." *The Journal of Economic History* 35, no. 1 (1975): pp. 20–55.

Kioupkiolis, Alexandros and Giorgos Katsambekis. "Radical Left Populism from the Margins to the Mainstream: A Comparison of Syriza and Podemos." In edited by Óscar García Agustín and Marco Briziarelli (London: Palgrave Macmillan, 2018), pp. 201–226.

Klein, Janet. "Conflict and Collaboration: Rethinking Kurdish-Armenian Relations in the Hamidian Period 1876–1909." *International Journal of Turkish Studies* 13, no. 1–2 (2007a): pp. 153–166.

Klein, Janet. "Kurdish Nationalists and Non-nationalist Kurdists: Rethinking Minority Nationalism and the Dissolution of the Ottoman Empire, 1908–1909." *Nations and Nationalism* 13, no. 1 (2007b): pp. 135–153.

Knauerhase, Ramon. "The Compound Steam Engine and Productivity Changes in the German Merchant Marine Fleet, 1871–1887." *The Journal of Economic History* 28, no. 3 (1968): pp. 390–403.

Kohn, Hans. "The Nature of Nationalism." *American Political Science Review* 33, no. 6 (1939): pp. 1001–1021.

Kondratieff, N. D. and W. F. Stolper. "The Long Waves in Economic Life." *The Review of Economics and Statistics* 17, no. 6 (1935): pp. 105–115. doi:10.2307/1928486. http://www.jstor.org/stable/1928486.

Konings, Martijn. *The Emotional Logic of Capitalism: What Progressives Have Missed* (Redwood City, CA: Stanford University Press, 2015).

Kotavaara, Ossi, Harri Antikainen, and Jarmo Rusanen. "Urbanization and Transportation in Finland, 1880–1970." *Journal of Interdisciplinary History* 42, no. 1 (2011): pp. 89–109.

Kuttner, Robert. *Can Democracy Survive Global Capitalism?* (WW Norton & Company, 2018).

Lascurettes, Kyle. *The Concert of Europe and Great Power Governance Today: What Can the Order of 19th-Century Europe Teach Policymakers about International Order in the 21st Century?* (Santa Monica, CA: RAND National Defense Research Institute, 2017).

Latham, Robert. "History, Theory, and International Order: Some Lessons from the Nineteenth Century." *Review of International Studies* 23, no. 4 (1997): pp. 419–443.

Levien, Michael and Marcel Paret. "A Second Double Movement? Polanyi and Shifting Global Opinions on Neoliberalism." *International Sociology* 27, no. 6 (2012): pp. 724–744.

Levinson, Marc. "Container Shipping and the Decline of New York, 1955–1975." *Business History Review* 80, no. 1 (2006a): pp. 49–80.

Levinson, Marc. *The Box: How the Shipping Container Made the World Smaller and the World Economy Bigger* (Princeton, NJ: Princeton University Press, 2006b).

Levy, Jack S. "Theories of General War." *World Politics* 37, no. 3 (Apr. 1985): pp. 344–374.

Lew, Byron and Bruce Cater. "The Telegraph, Co-Ordination of Tramp Shipping, and Growth in World Trade, 1870–1910." *European Review of Economic History* 10, no. 2 (2006): pp. 147–173.

Licklider, Joseph C. R. "Man-Computer Symbiosis." *IRE Transactions on Human Factors in Electronics* 1 (1960), pp. 4–11.

Lim, Sang Hun. "Look Up Rather Than Down: Karl Polanyi's Fascism and Radical Right-Wing 'Populism.'" *Current Sociology* (2021): 00113921211015715.

Lippard, Cameron D. "Racist Nativism in the 21st Century." *Sociology Compass* 5, no. 7 (2011): pp. 591–606.

Lloyd, Henry Demarest, *Lords of Industry*. (United Kingdom: G.P. Putnam's sons, 1910): p. 3.

Lucardie, Paul. "Religious Parties in a Secular Society: The Dutch Paradox," in *Constellations of Value: European Perspectives on the Intersections of Religion, Politics and Society*, edited by Christoph Jedan (Berlin: LIT, 2013), pp. 141–153.

Lucassen, Geertje and Marcel Lubbers. "Who Fears What? Explaining Far-Right-Wing Preference in Europe by Distinguishing Perceived Cultural and Economic Ethnic Threats." *Comparative Political Studies* 45, no. 5 (2012): pp. 547–574.

Lybeck, Eric Royal. "The Myth of the Hundred Years Peace: War in the Nineteenth Century." In *At War for Peace*, edited by Mohammadbaghe Forough (Oxford: Inter-Disciplinary Press, 2010), pp. 33–43.

Mackie, Nicola. "'Popularis' Ideology and Popular Politics at Rome in the First Century BC." *Rheinisches Museum Für Philologie* 135, no. H. 1 (1992): pp. 49–73.

Marill, Thomas and Lawrence G. Roberts. "Toward a Cooperative Network of Time-Shared Computers." In *Proceedings of the November 7–10, 1966, Fall Joint Computer Conference* (1966), pp. 425–431. https://doi.org/10.1145/1464291.1464336.

Marsella, Mauro. "Enrico Corradini's Italian Nationalism: The 'Right Wing'of the Fascist Synthesis." *Journal of Political Ideologies* 9, no. 2 (2004): pp. 203–224.

Martí-López, Elisa. *The Routledge Hispanic Studies Companion to Nineteenth Century Spain* (New York: Routledge, Taylor & Francis Group, 2021).

Maskus, Keith Eugene. *Intellectual Property Rights in the Global Economy* (Washington, DC: Institute for International Economics, 2000).

Mazower, Mark. *Governing the World: The History of an Idea, 1815 to the Present* (New York: Penguin, 2012).

Mazzini, Giuseppe. *The Duties of Man and Other Essays [by] Joseph Mazzini* (England: J.M. Dent & sons, ltd.; E.P. Dutton & co., inc., 1915).

McDermott, Kevin and Jeremy Agnew. *The Comintern: A History of International Communism from Lenin to Stalin* (Basingstoke: Macmillan International Higher Education, 1996).

McHale, Vincent E. and Eric A. Johnson. "Urbanization, Industrialization, and Crime in Imperial Germany: Part II." *Social Science History* 1, no. 2 (1977): pp. 210–247.

McKeown, Adam. "Global Migration, 1846–1940." *Journal of World History* (2004): pp. 155–189.

McMurry, Donald Le Crone, 1890. *Coxey's Army: A Study of the Industrial Army Movement of 1894* (Massachusetts: Little, Brown, and Company, 1929).

Meijers, Maurits. J. "Radical Right and Radical Left Euroscepticism. A Dynamic Phenomenon." *Notre Europe Policy Paper* 191 (April 7, 2017), 1–18.

Merriman, John M. *The Dynamite Club: How a Bombing in Fin-de-Siècle Paris Ignited the Age of Modern Terror* (New Haven, CT: Yale University Press, 2016).

Meyer, John W., John Boli, George M. Thomas, and Francisco O. Ramirez. "World Society and the Nation-State." *American Journal of Sociology* 103, no. 1 (1997): pp. 144–181.

Michell, H. "The Gold Standard in the Nineteenth Century." *Canadian Journal of Economics and Political Science/Revue Canadienne De Economiques Et Science Politique* 17, no. 3 (1951): pp. 369–376.

Miller, David. *On Nationality* (Oxford: Clarendon, 1997).

Miller, George A. and Joseph CR Licklider. "The Intelligibility of Interrupted Speech." *The Journal of the Acoustical Society of America* 22, no. 2 (1950): pp. 167–173.

Millett, Kris. "On the Meaning and Contemporary Significance of Fascism in the writings of Karl Polanyi." *Theory and Society* 50, no. 3 (2021): 463–487.

Milner, Helen V. "Voting for Populism in Europe: Globalization, Technological Change, and the Extreme Right." *Comparative Political Studies* 54, no. 13 (2021): pp. 2286–2320. doi:10.1177/0010414021997175.

Milner, Helen V. and Robert O. Keohane. "Internationalization and Domestic Politics: An Introduction." *Internationalization and Domestic Politics* (1996): pp. 3–24. https://www.migrationpolicy.org/research/through-prism-national-security-major-immigration-policy-and-program-changes-decade-911.

Mittelstadt, Michelle, Burke Speaker, Doris Meissner, and Muzaffar Chishti. "Through the Prism of National security: Major Immigration Policy and Program Changes in the Cecade since 9/11." *Migration Policy Institute* 2 (2011): p. 1.

Modelski, George, *Long Cycles in World Politics* (Seattle: University of Washington Press, 1985).

Moffitt, Benjamin. *The Global Rise of Populism: Performance, Political Style, and Representation.* 1st ed. (Palo Alto, CA: Stanford University Press, 2016).

Moghadam, Assaf. *The Globalization of Martyrdom: Al Qaeda, Salafi Jihad, and the Diffusion of Suicide Attacks* (Baltimore: The Johns Hopkins University Press, 2008).

Moghaddam, Fathali M. and Anthony J. Marsella. *Understanding Terrorism: Psychosocial Roots, Consequences, and Interventions* (Washington, DC: American Psychological Association, 2004).

Möller, Johanna E. and M. Rimscha. "(De) Centralization of the Global Informational Ecosystem." *Media and Communication* 5, no. 3 (2017): pp. 37–48.

Mosse, George L., *The Crisis of German Ideology: Intellectual Origins of the Third Reich.* (Madison: University of Wisconsin Press, 2021).

Mosse, George L. "Racism and Nationalism." *Nations and Nationalism* 1, no. 2 (1995): pp. 163–173.

Mouffe, Chantal. *For a Left Populism* (London: Verso, 2018).

Mudde, Cas. "An Ideational Approach." In *The Oxford Handbook of Populism*, edited by Cristóbal Rovira Kaltwasser, Paul Taggart, Paulina Ochoa Espejo, Pierre Ostiguy (Oxford: Oxford University Press, 2017), pp. 27–47.

Munck, Ronaldo. "Global Civil Society: Myths and Prospects." *Voluntas: International Journal of Voluntary and Nonprofit Organizations* 13, no. 4 (2002): pp. 349–361.

Munck, Ronaldo. "Globalization and Contestation: A Polanyian Problematic." *Globalizations* 3, no. 2 (2006): pp. 175–186.

Murphy, Sheila C. *How Television Invented New Media* (New Brunswick, NJ: Rutgers University Press, 2011).

Nadler, Anthony M. *Making the News Popular: Mobilizing U.S. News Audiences* (Urbana: University of Illinois Press, 2016).

Newth, George. "Populism and Nativism in Contemporary Regionalist and Nationalist Politics: A Minimalist Framework for Ideologically Opposed Parties." *Politics* (2021): pp. 1–22. https://doi.org/10.1177/0263395721995016.

Nichols, Tom, *The Death of Expertise: The Campaign Against Established Knowledge and Why It Matters* (Oxford University Press. 2017).

Novy, Andreas. "The Political Trilemma of Contemporary Social-Ecological Transformation–lessons from Karl Polanyi's the Great Transformation." *Globalizations* 19, no. 1 (2022): pp. 59–80.

Nye, Joseph S. "The Changing Nature of World Power." *Political Science Quarterly* 105, no. 2 (1990): pp. 177–192.

Obstfeld, Maurice, Jay C. Shambaugh, and Alan M. Taylor. "The Trilemma in History: Tradeoffs among Exchange Rates, Monetary Policies, and Capital Mobility." *Review of Economics and Statistics* 87, no. 3 (2005): pp. 423–438.

Obstfeld, Maurice and Alan M. Taylor. *Global Capital Markets: Integration, Crisis, and Growth* (Cambridge: Cambridge University Press, 2005).

Ogan, Christine, Lars Willnat, Rosemary Pennington, and Manaf Bashir. "The Rise of Anti-Muslim Prejudice: Media and Islamophobia in Europe and the United States." *International Communication Gazette*, 76, no. 1 (2014): p. 27.

O'Hagan, Lauren Alex. "Contesting Women's Right to Vote: Anti-Suffrage Postcards in Edwardian Britain." *Visual Culture in Britain* 21, no. 3 (2020): pp. 330–362.

O'Neill, Judy E. "The Role of ARPA in the Development of the ARPANET, 1961–1972." *IEEE Annals of the History of Computing* 17, no. 4 (1995): pp. 76–81.

Orbanes, Philip E., *Monopoly: The World's Most Famous Game—and How It Got That Way*. (New York: Hachette Books, 2007).

O'Rourke, Kevin H. "Tariffs and Growth in the Late 19th Century." *The Economic Journal* 110, no. 463 (2000): pp. 456–483.

O'Rourke, Kevin H. "The Worldwide Economic Impact of the French Revolutionary and Napoleonic Wars, 1793–1815." *Journal of Global History* 1, no. 1 (2006): pp. 123–149.

Osterhammel, Jürgen. "Nationalism and Globalization." In *The Oxford Handbook of the History of Nationalism*, edited by John Breuilly (Oxford: Oxford University Press, 2013), pp. 694–712.

Ostler, Jeffrey. "Why the Populist Party was Strong in Kansas and Nebraska but Weak in Iowa." *The Western Historical Quarterly* 23, no. 4 (1992): pp. 451–474.

Oxley, David and C. Jain. "Global Air Passenger Markets: Riding Out Periods of Turbulence." *IATA the Travel & Tourism Competitiveness Report* (2015): pp. 694–712.

Palen, Marc-William. "Protection, Federation and Union: The Global Impact of the McKinley Tariff upon the British Empire, 1890–94." *The Journal of Imperial and Commonwealth History* 38, no. 3 (2010): pp. 395–418.

Park, Robert E. "The Natural History of the Newspaper." *American Journal of Sociology* 29, no. 3 (1923): pp. 273–289.

Paxton, Robert O. "The Five Stages of Fascism." *The Journal of Modern History* 70, no. 1 (1998): pp. 1–23.

Paxton, Robert O. *The Anatomy of Fascism.* 1st ed. (New York: Knopf, 2004).

Payne, Stanley G. *Fascism: Comparison and Definition* (Madison: University of Wisconsin Press, 1983).

Payne, Stanley G. *History of Fascism, 1914–1945* (Madison: University of Wisconsin Press, 1996).

Petley, Julian. *Film and Video Censorship in Modern Britain* (Edinburgh: Edinburgh University Press, 2011).

Petrova, Maria. "Newspapers and Parties: How Advertising Revenues Created an Independent Press." *American Political Science Review* 105, no. 4 (2011): pp. 790–808.

Pinto, António Costa. "Fascist Ideology Revisited: Zeev Sternhell and His Critics." *European History Quarterly* 16, no. 4 (1986): pp. 465–483. doi:10.1177/026569148601600403.

Pogue, L. Welch. "The Next Ten Years in Air Transportation." *Proceedings of the Academy of Political Science* 21, no. 2 (1945): pp. 17–27.

Poitras, Geoffrey. "Arbitrage: Historical Perspectives." In *Encyclopedia of Quantitative Finance*, edited by Rama Cont (Chichester, West Sussex, England; Hoboken, NJ: Wiley, 2010), pp. 61–70.

Polanyi, Karl. *The Great Transformation: The Political and Economic Origins of Our Time* (Boston, MA: Beacon Press, 2001).

Pournaras, Evangelos. "Decentralization in Digital Societies—A Design Paradox." *arXiv Preprint arXiv:2001.01511* (2020): pp. 1–9. https://doi.org/10.48550/arXiv.2001.01511.

Pulzer, Peter G. J. and Peter Pulzer. *The Rise of Political Anti-Semitism in Germany & Austria* (Cambridge, MA: Harvard University Press, 1988).

Radu, Roxana. *Negotiating Internet Governance* (Oxford: Oxford University Press, 2019).

Rand, Ayn. *Atlas Shrugged* (New York: Penguin, 2005).

Rasler, Karen A., and William R. Thompson. "Global Wars, Public Debts, and the Long Cycle." *World Politics* 35, no. 4 (1983): pp. 489–516.

Re, Lucia. "Italians and the Invention of Race: The Poetics and Politics of Difference in the Struggle Over Libya, 1890–1913." *California Italian Studies* 1, no. 1 (2010), pp. 1–65.

Ernest Renan, "What Is a Nation? (Qu'est-Ce Qu'une Nation?, 1882)." In *What Is a Nation? And Other Political Writings*, translated by M. F. N. Giglioli (New York: Columbia University Press, 2018), 255. http://www.jstor.org/stable/10.7312/rena17430.15.

Ricardo, David. *On the Principles of Political Economy* (London: J. Murray, 1821).

Ritzer, George. *Frontiers of Social Theory: The New Syntheses* (New York: Columbia University Press, 1990).

Roberts, David D. *The Syndicalist Tradition and Italian Fascism* (Chapel Hill: University of North Carolina Press, 1979).

Robertson, J. M., and Rationalist Peace Society. *Essays towards Peace* (London: Watts, 1913).

Rockoff, Hugh. " 'The Wizard of Oz' as a Monetary allegory." *Journal of Political Economy* 98, no. 4 (1990): pp. 739–760.

Rodrik, Dani. *The Globalization Paradox: Democracy and the Future of the World Economy* (New York; London: WW Norton & Company, 2011a).

Rodrik, Dani. "Populism and the Economics of Globalization." *Journal of International Business Policy* 1, no. 1 (2018): pp. 12–33.

Rodrik, Dani. "What's Driving Populism?" *Project Syndicate*, July 2019, 9. http://www.bre sserpereira.org.br/terceiros/2020/janeiro/19.12-What-is-driving-populism.pdf.

Rodrik, Dani. "Why Does Globalization Fuel Populism? Economics, Culture, and the Rise of Right-Wing Populism." *Annual Review of Economics* 13, no. 1 (2021a): pp. 133–170.

Rodrik, Dani. *The Globalization Paradox: Why Global Markets, States, and Democracy can't Coexist* (Oxford; New York: Oxford University Press, 2011b).

Rodwin, Lloyd and Hidehiko Sazanami. *Industrial Change and Regional Economic Transformation: The Experience of Western Europe* (New York: Routledge, 2017).

Roeder, Philip G. "Liberalization and Ethnic Entrepreneurs in the Soviet Successor States." In *The Myth of "Ethnic Conflict": Politics, Economics and "Cultural" Violence*, edited by Beverly Crawford and Ronnie D. Lipschutz (eScholarship, University of California, 1998), 78–107.

Roper, Brian S. *The History of Democracy: A Marxist Interpretation* (London; New York: Pluto Press, 2013). https://www.jstor.org/stable/j.ctt183p7kp.

Rostow, Walt Whitman. "The Problem of Achieving and Maintaining a High Rate of Economic Growth: A Historian's View." *The American Economic Review* 50, no. 2 (1960): pp. 106–118.

Rothstein, Morton. "Centralizing Firms and Spreading Markets: The World of International Grain Traders, 1846–1914." *Business and Economic History* 17 (1988): pp. 103–113.

Rowthorn, Robert and Ramana Ramaswamy. *Deindustrialization: Causes and Implications* (Washington, DC: International Monetary Fund, 1997).

Roy, Olivier. "Al Qaeda in the West as a Youth Movement: The Power of a Narrative." *CEPS Policy Briefs* no. 1–12 (2008): pp. 1–8.

Rubery, Matthew. *Audiobooks, Literature, and Sound Studies* (Florence: Taylor & Francis Group, 2011).

Rubery, Matthew. "A Transatlantic Sensation: Stanley's Search for Livingstone and the Anglo." *American Press.in the Oxford History of Popular Print Culture Volume Six US Popular Print Culture* 1920 (1860): pp. 501–517.

Ruggie, John Gerard. "International Regimes, Transactions and Change: Embedded Liberalism in the Postwar Economic Order." In *International Regimes*, edited by Stephen Krasner (Ithaca, NY: Cornell University Press, 1983), pp. 195–232.

Rust, Roland T. and Richard W. Oliver. "The Death of Advertising." *Journal of Advertising* 23, no. 4 (1994): pp. 71–77.

Sachs, Jeffrey D., Andrew Warner, Anders Åslund, and Stanley Fischer. "Economic Reform and the Process of Global Integration." *Brookings Papers on Economic Activity* 1995, no. 1 (1995): pp. 1–118.

Sachsman, David B. *Sensationalism: Murder, Mayhem, Mudslinging, Scandals, and Disasters in 19th-Century Reporting* (London, New York: Routledge, 2017).

Salt, John, and James Clarke. "International Migration in the UNECE Region: Patterns, Trends, Policies." *International Social Science Journal* 52, no. 165 (2000): p. 316.

Sanchez, George J. "Face the Nation: Race, Immigration, and the Rise of Nativism in Late Twentieth Century America." *International Migration Review* 31, no. 4 (1997): pp. 1009–1030.

Sandbrook, Richard. "Polanyi's Double Movement and Capitalism Today." *Development and Change* 53, no. 3 (2022): pp. 647–675.

Sandbrook, Richard. "Karl Polanyi and the Formation of this Generation's New Left." *IPPR Progressive Review* 25, no. 1 (2018): pp. 76–103.

Sandbrook, Richard. "Polanyi and Post-Neoliberalism in the Global South: Dilemmas of Re-Embedding the Economy." *New Political Economy* 16, no. 4 (2011): pp. 415–443.

Sarkees, Meredith Reid, Frank Whelon Wayman, and J. David Singer. "Inter-State, Intra-State, and Extra-State Wars: A Comprehensive Look at their Distribution Over Time, 1816–1997." *International Studies Quarterly* 47, no. 1 (2003): pp. 49–70.

Scannell, Paddy. "The Dialectic of Time and Television." *The Annals of the American Academy of Political and Social Science* 625, no. 1 (2009): pp. 219–235.

Schudson, Michael. "The Objectivity Norm in American Journalism." *Journalism* 2, no. 2 (2001): pp. 149–170.

Schumpeter, Joseph A. *Business Cycles: A Theoretical, Historical, and Statistical Analysis of the Capitalist Process, Volumes I & II* (New York: McGraw-Hill book company, Inc, 1939).

Sheth, Jagdish N. and Barbara L. Gross. "Parallel Development of Marketing and Consumer Behavior: A Historical Perspective." *Historical Perspectives in Marketing* (1988): pp. 9–33.

Silver, Beverly J. and Giovanni Arrighi. "Polanyi's 'Double Movement': The Belle Époques of British and US Hegemony Compared." *Politics & Society* 31, no. 2 (2003): pp. 325–355.

Slobodian, Quinn. *Globalists: The End of Empire and the Birth of Neoliberalism* (Cambridge, MA: Harvard University Press, 2018).

Sluga, Glenda. *Internationalism in the Age of Nationalism* (Philadelphia: University of Pennsylvania Press, 2013).

Smith, Anthony. "'The Land and Its People': Reflections on Artistic Identification in an Age of Nations and Nationalism." *Nations and Nationalism* 19, no. 1 (2013): p. 87.

Soborski, Rafal. *Ideology in a Global Age: Continuity and Change* (New York: Palgrave Macmillan, 2013), pp. 107–139.

Spencer, David Ralph and Judith Spencer. *The Yellow Journalism: The Press and America's Emergence as a World Power* (Evanston, IL.: Northwestern University Press, 2007).

Spencer, Herbert. *The Proper Sphere of Government: A Reprint of a Series of Letters*, Originally published in *The Nonconformist* (London: W. Brittain, 1843).

Standage, Tom. *The Victorian Internet: The Remarkable Story of the Telegraph and the Nineteenth Century's Online Pioneers* (New York: Berkley Books, 1998).

Stanley, Jason. *How Fascism Works: The Politics of Us and Them* (New York: Random House, 2020.

Stavrakakis, Yannis and Giorgos Katsambekis. "Left-Wing Populism in the European Periphery: The Case of SYRIZA." *Journal of Political Ideologies* 19, no. 2 (2014): pp. 119–142.

Steel, John and Marcel Broersma. "Redefining Journalism during the Period of the Mass Press 1880–1920: An Introduction." *Media History* 21, no. 3 (2015): pp. 235–237.

Sternhell, Zeev. "How to Think about Fascism and its Ideology." *Constellations* 15, no. 3 (2008): pp. 280–290.

Sternhell, Zeëv. "Fascism." In *Reassessing Political Ideologies: The Durability of Dissent*, edited by Michael Freeden (London; New York: Routledge, 2001), p. 92.

Sternhell, Zeev, Mario Sznajder, and Maia Ashéri. *The Birth of Fascist Ideology: From Cultural Rebellion to Political Revolution* (Princeton, NJ: Princeton University Press, 1994).

Stewart, Thomas A. *Intellectual Capital: The New Wealth of Organization* (United Kingdom: Doubleday/Currency, 1997).

Stover, John F. *The Routledge Historical Atlas of the American Railroads* (New York; London: Routledge, 1999).

Summers, Mark Wahlgren. *The Press Gang: Newspapers and Politics, 1865–1878* (Chapel Hill: University of North Carolina Press, 1994).

Suny, Ronald. *The Revenge of the Past: Nationalism, Revolution, and the Collapse of the Soviet Union* (Stanford, CA: Stanford University Press, 1993).

Szabados, Krisztian, "The Particularities and Uniqueness of Hungary's Jobbik." In *The European Far Right: Historical and Contemporary Perspectives*, edited by Giorgos Charalambous (Norway: Peace Research Institute Oslo, 2, 2015), pp. 49–57.

Tamir, Yael. *Liberal Nationalism* (Princeton, NJ: Princeton University Press, 1993). doi:10.1515/9781400820849.

Taylor, Rupert. "Interpreting Global Civil Society." *Voluntas: International Journal of Voluntary and Nonprofit Organizations* 13, no. 4 (2002): pp. 339–347.

Tepper, Jonathan and Denise Hearn. "Big Companies Are Crushing Their Competition in the US, and It's Creating a Dangerous 'Fake Capitalism' That Hurts Workers and Consumers." *Insider (En Ligne), Mis En Ligne Le* 16 Janvier 2019, URL: https://www.businessinsider.com/monopolies-resulted-in-myth-of-capitalism-2019-1.

Terborgh, Andrew G. "The Post-War Rise of World Trade: Does the Bretton Woods System Deserve Credit?" *IDEAS Working Paper Series from RePEc* no. 78 (3), 2003.

Thomasberger, Claus and Michael Brie. "Karl Polanyi's Search for Freedom in a Complex Society." *Österreichische Zeitschrift Für Soziologie* 44, no. 2 (2019): pp. 169–182.

Thompson, William R., "Polarity, the Long Cycle, and Global Power Warfare." *Journal of Conflict Resolution* 30, no.4 (1986): pp. 587–615.

Timmer, Ashley S. and Jeffrey G. Williams. "Immigration Policy Prior to the 1930s: Labor Markets, Policy Interactions, and Globalization Backlash." *Population and Development Review* 24, no. 4 (1998): pp. 739–771.

Traugott, Mark. "The Mid-Nineteenth-Century Crisis in France and England." *Theory and Society* 12, no. 4 (1983): pp. 455–468.

Tréguer, Félix. "Gaps and Bumps in the Political History of the Internet." *Internet Policy Review* 6, no. 4 (2017): pp. 1–21.

Turcato, Davide. "Italian Anarchism as a Transnational Movement, 1885–1915." *International Review of Social History* 52, no. 3 (2007): pp. 407–444. doi:10.1017/S0020859007003057.

Valente, A. J. "Changes in Print Paper during the 19th Century." *Proceedings of Charleston Library Conference* (2012). http://dx.doi.org/10.5703/1288284314836.

Van Hauwaert, Steven M.b. "Thinking Outside the Box: The Political Process Model and Far Right Party Emergence." *Journal of Contemporary European Studies* 29, no. 1 (2021): pp. 84–98.

Vdyrynen, Raimo, "Economic Cycles, Power Transitions, Political Management and Wars between Major Powers," *International Studies Quarterly* 27, no. 4 (December 1983), 389–418.

Vipond, Mary. *The Mass Media in Canada* (James Lorimer & Company, 2000).

Voeltz, Herman C. "Coxey's Army in Oregon, 1894." *Oregon Historical Quarterly* 65, no. 3 (1964): pp. 263–295.

Voss, Dustin. "The Political Economy of European Populism: Labour Market Dualisation and Protest Voting in Germany and Spain." *LEQS Paper*, no. 132 (2018).

Wagner, Richard. *Judaism in Music (Das Judenthum in der Musik)*. Translated by William Ashton Ellis (Cincinnati, OH: Britons Publishing Company, 1966).

Wagner, Richard. *Sämtliche Schriften Und Dichtungen* (Breitkopf & Härtel, 1911).

Waldstreicher, David. *In the Midst of Perpetual Fetes: The Making of American Nationalism, 1776–1820* (Chapel Hill: University of North Carolina Press, 1997).

Walter, John R. "US Bank Capital Regulation: History and Changes since the Financial Crisis." *Economic Quarterly* 1Q (2019): 1–40.

Weber, Eugen. *Peasants into Frenchmen the Modernization of Rural France, 1870–1914* (Stanford, CA: Stanford University Press, 1976).

Wells, O. V. "The Depression of 1873–79." *Agricultural History* 11, no. 3 (1937): pp. 237–251.

Whitten, Bessie Emrick and David O. Whitten, *The Birth of Big Business in the United States, 1860–1914 : Commercial, Extractive, and Industrial Enterprise* (Westport, CT: Praeger, 2006).

Wicker, Elmus. *The Banking Panics of the Great Depression* (Cambridge; New York: Cambridge University Press, 2000).

Williams, Kevin. *Read All About It!: A History of the British Newspaper* (London; New York: Routledge, 2009).

Winnick, Terri A. "Islamophobia: Social Distance, Avoidance, and Threat." *Sociological Spectrum* 39, no. 6 (2019): p. 359.

World Trade Organization. "The Economics and Political Economy of International Trade Cooperation." In *World Trade Report 2007 Six Decades of Multilateral Trade Cooperation: What Have We Learnt?* (Switzerland: World Trade Organization, 2007), pp. 35–110.

Wyman, David S. *Paper Walls; America and the Refugee Crisis, 1938–1941* (Amherst: University of Massachusetts Press, 1968).

Zboray, Ronald J. and Mary Saracino Zboray. "The Changing Face of Publishing." In *The Oxford History of Popular Print Culture: Volume Six: US Popular Print Culture 1860–1920*, edited by Christine Bold (Oxford: Oxford University Press, 2011), pp. 23–42.

Žižek, Slavoj. "Against the Populist Temptation." *Critical Inquiry* 32, no. 3 (2006): pp. 551–574.

Zlotnik, Hania. "Trends of International Migration since 1965: What Existing Data Reveal." *International Migration* 37, no. 1 (1999): pp. 21–61.

News Articles and Online Sources

"ACROSS THE CONTINENT: From the Missouri to the Pacific Ocean by Rail. The Plains, the Great American Desert, the Rocky Mountains. One Hundred Hours from Omaha to San Francisco," *New York Times*, June 28, 1869. http://cprr.org/Museum/Newspap ers/New_York_Times/1869-06-28.html.

Agence France Presse, "A 25-Year Timeline of the World Wide Web," *Insider*, March 9, 2014. http://www.businessinsider.com/a-25-year-timeline-of-the-world-wide-web-2014-3.

Alterman, Eric, "Out of Print," *The New Yorker*, March 24, 2008. https://www.newyorker. com/magazine/2008/03/31/out-of-print.

Apper, Megan. "Bernie Sanders on Immigration in 2007 Video: This Is a Bad Bill for American Workers," *BuzzFeed News*, February 19, 2016. https:// www.buzzfeednews.com/article/meganapper/bernie-sanders-on-immigrat ion-in-2007-video-this-is-a-bad-bi.

Baczynska, Gabriela. "Mosque Building Brings Islam Fears to Poland," *Reuters*, April 1, 2010. https://www.reuters.com/article/us-poland-mosque/mosque-building-brings-islam-fears-to-poland-idUSTRE6302VN20100401.

Barragan, Luis Carlos. "The Egyptian Workers Who Were Erased from History," *Egyptian Streets*, September 14, 2018. https://egyptianstreets.com/2018/09/14/the-egyptian-workers-who-were-erased-from-history/.

Ben Macri, Vassar '99. "Anti-Semitism," 1896. http://projects.vassar.edu/1896/antisemit ism.html.

"Bernie Sanders on Trade and U.S. Jobs," FEELTHEBERN.ORG, https://feelthebern.org/ bernie-sanders-on-trade/.

Bienkov, Adam. "Jeremy Corbyn's General Election Campaign Lauch Speech in Full," *Insider*, May 9, 2017. https://www.businessinsider.com/jeremy-corbyn-labour-party-general-election-campaign-launch-speech-in-full-2017-5.

Bridge Initiative Team, "Factsheet: Sweden Democrats," *Bridge*, May 14, 2020. https://bri dge.georgetown.edu/research/factsheet-sweden-democrats/, accessed August 2, 2022.

Bryan, William Jennings. "Cross of Gold" Speech," July 9, 1896. https://wwnorton.com/ college/history/archive/reader/trial/directory/1890_1914/ch20_cross_of_gold.htm.

Chase, Jefferson. "AfD Cochair Petry Wants to Rehabilitate Controversial Term," *Deutsche Welle*, September 11, 2016. https://www.dw.com/en/afd-co-chair-petry-wants-to-rehabilitate-controversial-term/a-19543222.

Chrisafis, Angelique. "France's Headscarf War: 'It's an Attack on Freedom,'" *The Guardian*, July 22, 2013. https://www.theguardian.com/world/2013/jul/22/frances-headscarf-war-attack-on-freedom.

Cohen, Roger and Aurelien Breeden, "Pro-Macron Forces Expected to Prevail but Face Left-Wing Challenge," *New York Times*, June 12, 2022. https://www.nytimes.com/2022/ 06/12/world/europe/france-elections-macron.html?campaign_id=2&emc=edit_th_ 20220612&instance_id=63888&nl=todaysheadlines&regi_id=51583210&segment_ id=94977&user_id=13ff8d54cbf7af799d623a24b55951c7.

Connor, Phillip. "Number of Refugees to Europe Surges to Record 1.3 Million in 2015," Pew Research Center, August 2, 2016. https://www.pewresearch.org/global/2016/08/02/number-of-refugees-to-europe-surges-to-record-1-3-million-in-2015/.

Corbyn, Jeremy. "Jeremy Corbyn Speech at Labour's Campaign Launch," *Labour*, May 9, 2017. https://labour.org.uk/press/jeremy-corbyn-speech-at-labours-campaign-launch/.

"Coronavirus: Trump Stands by China Lab Origin Theory for Virus," *BBC News*, May 1, 2020. https://www.bbc.com/news/world-us-canada-52496098.

Democratic Audit UK, "Understanding the 'Rise' of the Radical Left in Europe: It's Not Just the Economy, Stupid," July 12, 2018. https://www.democraticaudit.com/2018/07/12/understanding-the-rise-of-the-radical-left-in-europe its not just-the-economy-stupid/.

Dolan, Kerry A., ed. "The Definitive Ranking of the Wealthiest Americans in 2021," *Forbes*. https://www.forbes.com/forbes-400/.

Duyvendak, Jan Willem and Josip Kesic. "The Rise of Nativism in Europe," *Europe Now*, February 1, 2018. https://www.europenowjournal.org/2018/01/31/the-rise-of-nativism-in-europe/#_ftnref3Guardian.

Easter, Makeda. "Remember When Amazon Only Sold Books?," *Los Angeles Times*, June 18, 2017. http://www.latimes.com/business/la-fi-amazon-history-20170618-htmlstory.html.

Ebay, "Our History," https://www.ebayinc.com/our-company/our-history/.

Echikson, William. "Viktor Orbán's Anti-Semitism Problem," *POLITICO*, May 13, 2019. https://www.politico.eu/article/viktor-orban-anti-semitism-problem-hungary-jews/.

Edelman Trust Barometer 2020, https://www.edelman.com/sites/g/files/aatuss191/files/2020-03/2020%20Edelman%20Trust%20Barometer%20Coronavirus%20Special%20Report_0.pdf.

"Europe and Right-Wing Nationalism: A Country-by-Country Guide," *BBC*, November 13, 2019. https://www.bbc.com/news/world-europe-36130006.

Le Gall, Arthur. "Europe's Media in the Digital Decade," European Parliament, Research for CULT Committee, Research for CULT Committee—Europe's media in the digital decade, European Parliament, Policy Department for Structural and Cohesion Policies (Brussels: May 2021). https://www.europarl.europa.eu/RegData/etudes/STUD/2021/690873/IPOL_STU(2021)690873_EN.pdf.

Feldstein, Martin. "Revolutionaries," Deutsche Welle, April 11, 2013. https://www.dw.com/en/the-reagan-thatcher-revolution/a-16732731.

Ferraresi, Mattia. "As Europe Confronts Coronavirus, the Media Faces a Trust Test," Nieman Reports, April 24. 2020. https://niemanreports.org/articles/a-trust-test-for-the-media-in-europe/.

Fredrick Lewis Allen 1931, http://gutenberg.net.au/eboks05/0500831h.html.

Freking, Kevin. "Trump Tweets Words 'He Won'; Says Vote Rigged, Not Conceding," *Associated Press*, November 16, 2020. https://apnews.com/article/donald-trump-tweets-he-won-not-conceding-9ce22e9dc90577f7365d150c151a91c7.

Fukuyama, Francis quoted in *The Washington Post*, "Authoritarianism Is Surging. Can Liberal Democracy Fight Back? Review of 'Liberalism and Its Discontents' by Francis Fukuyama and 'The Age of the Strongman' by Gideon Rachman," Review by Carlos Lozada, May 13, 2022. https://www.washingtonpost.com/outlook/2022/05/13/fukuyama-rachman/.

Fung, Brain. "FCC Repeals Decades-Old Rules Blocking Broadcast Media Mergers, Possibly Easing Way for Sinclair-Tribune Deal," *Washington Post*, November 16, 2017.

https://www.chicagotribune.com/business/ct-biz-fcc-media-merger-rule-20171116-story.html.

Gábor, Vona. "Az Agónia Elkezdődött és új Világrendnek Kell Épülnie," *Mandiner.hu*, May 6, 2013. https://mandiner.hu/cikk/20130506_vona_gabor_az_agonia_elkezdodott_es_uj_vilagrendnek_kell_epulnie.

Guardian Staff, "Donald Trump Calls Covid-19 'Kung Flu' at Tulsa Rally," *The Guardian*, June 20, 2020. https://www.theguardian.com/us-news/2020/jun/20/trump-covid-19-kung-flu-racist-language.

Global Opinions, "MeToo Is at a Crossroads in America. Around the World, It's Just Beginning," *The Washington Post*, May 8, 2020. https://www.washingtonpost.com/opinions/2020/05/08/metoo-around-the-world/.

Goldman, Emma. *Anarchism and Other Essays* (3rd revised edition, New York: Mother Earth Publishing Association, 1917), https://www.lib.berkeley.edu/goldman/pdfs/EmmaGoldman_THEPSYCHOLOGYOFPOLITICALVIOLENCE.pdf.

Graphic History, http://www.designhistory.org/BookHistory_pages/Letterpress.html, accessed January 14, 2023.

Grose, Thomas K. "Europe's Nationalists Target Climate Action," *U.S. News*, May 8, 2019. https://www.usnews.com/news/best-countries/articles/2019-05-08/europes-far-right-focuses-on-climate-change-instead-of-immigration.

Henley, Jon. "Support for Eurosceptic Parties Doubles in Two Decades across EU," *The Guardian*, March 2, 2020. https://www.theguardian.com/world/2020/mar/02/support-for-eurosceptic-parties-doubles-two-decades-across-eu, accessed July 20, 2021.

Horowitz, Jason. "Where Does Italy's Enfeebled Five Star Find Itself? At the Center of Power," *New York Times*, August 22, 2019. https://www.nytimes.com/2019/08/22/world/europe/italy-politics-five-star-democratic-party.html.

Hotez, Peter J. "The Antiscience Movement Is Escalating, Going Global and Killing Thousands," *Scientific American*, March 29, 2021. https://www.scientificamerican.com/article/the-antiscience-movement-is-escalating-going-global-and-killing-thousands/.

Jewett, Andrew. "How Americans Came to Distrust Science," *Boston Review*, December 8, 2020. https://bostonreview.net/articles/andrew-jewett-science-under-fire/.

Kroet, Cynthia. "'Post-Truth' Enters Oxford English Dictionary," *Politico*, June 27, 2017. https://www.politico.eu/article/post-truth-enters-oxford-english-dictionary/.

Lanchester, John. "Margaret Thatcher's Revolution," *The New Yorker*, July 29, 2013, https://www.newyorker.com/magazine/2013/08/05/1979-and-all-that.

Lenin, Vladimir Il'ich. "Letter to the Secretary of the Socialist Propaganda League," Marxist Internet Archive. *Lenin Collected Works*, Vol. 21 (Moscow: Progress Publishers, [197[4]]), pp. 423–428. https://www.marxists.org/archive/lenin/works/1915/nov/09.htm.

Loucaides, Darren. "In Italy, Five Star Movement's War on Journalism Is Picking Up Pace," *Columbia Journalism Review*, June 13, 2019. https://www.cjr.org/analysis/italy-five-star-movement.php.

Nagle, Angela. "The Left Case against Open Borders," *American Affairs* 2, no. 4 (2018). https://americanaffairsjournal.org/2018/11/the-left-case-against-open-borders/.

National Front, http://www.nationalfront.org/accessed April 11, 2018 (since removed from the web).

Orange, Richard. "Mette Frederiksen: The Anti-immigration Left Leader Set to Win Power in Denmark," *The Guardian*, May 11, 2019. https://www.theguardian.com/world/2019/may/11/denmark-election-matte-frederiksen-leftwing-immigration.

PoliticsHome staff, "READ: Jeremy Corbyn's 2017 Labour Conference," *PoliticsHome*, September 27, 2017. https://www.politicshome.com/news/article/read-jeremy-corb yns-2017-labour-conference-speech.

"READ: Bernie Sanders' Speech at the Democratic Convention," NPR, July 25, 2016. https://www.npr.org/2016/07/25/487426056/read-bernie-sanders-prepared-rema rks-at-the-dnc.

"Reality Check: Is Malmo the 'Rape Capital' of Europe?," *BBC News*, February 24, 2017. https://www.bbc.com/news/uk-politics-39056786.

Reid, Sue. "Torn Apart by an Open Door for Migrants: Sweden Is Seen as Europe's Most Liberal Bation, but Violent Crime Is Soaring and the Far Right Is on the March, Reports SUE REID," *DailyMail.com*, November 13, 2015. https://www.dailymail.co.uk/news/ article-3317978/Torn-apart-open-door-migrants-Sweden-seen-Europe-s-liberal-nat ion-violent-crime-soaring-Far-Right-march-reports-SUE-REID.html.

Reuters Staff, "Hollande: "Mom Véritable Adversaire, C'est le Monde de la Finance," *La Tribune*, January 22, 2012. https://www.latribune.fr/actualites/economie/france/ 20120122trib000679586/hollande-mon-veritable-adversaire-c-est-le-monde-de-la-finance.html.

Reuters Staff, "UK's Labour Vows Action on "Tax and Wage Cheat" Multinationals," *Reuters*, November 22, 2019. https://www.reuters.com/article/britain-election-labour/ uks-labour-vows-action-on-tax-and-wage-cheat-multinationals-idUSL8N2824KM.

Robins, Peter, ed. "On the Path to Day X: The Return of Germany's Far Right," *New York Times*, June 5, 2021. https://www.nytimes.com/2021/06/25/world/europe/germany-nazi-far-right.html.

Rothman,Tony. "Random Paths to Frequency Hopping," *American Scientist*, January–February, 2019. https://www.americanscientist.org/article/random-paths-to-freque ncy-hopping.

RS Components Pty Ltd, "How Did Semiconductors Change Our Lives," https://au.rs-online.com/web/generalDisplay.html?id=infozone&file=eletronics/how-did-semicon ductors-change-our-lives.

Santora, Marc. "Poland Election: Law and Justice Party Holds on to Power, Early Returns Show," *New York Times*, October 13, 2019. https://www.nytimes.com/2019/10/13/ world/europe/poland-election.html, accessed July 20, 2021.

Scislowska, Monica. "Poland Probes Mosque Attack, Far-Right 'Gallows' Protest," *AP News*, November 27, 2017. https://apnews.com/article/7f31acb8461b4f5fb71325bb6efecfc3.

Sharlet, Jason, ""He's the Chosen One to Run America": Inside the Cult of Trump, His Rallies Are Church and He is the Gospel," *Vanity Fair*, June 18, 2020. https://www.van ityfair.com/news/2020/06/inside-the-cult-of-trump-his-rallies-are-church-and-he-is-the-gospel.

Silver, Laura. "Smartphone Ownership Is Growing Rapidly Around the World, but Not Always Equally," Pew Research Center, February 5, 2019. https://www.pewresearch. org/global/2019/02/05/smartphone-ownership-is-growing-rapidly-around-the-world-but-not-always-equally/, accessed July 22, 2020 @ 2:39 pm.

Simonetti, Isabella. "Over 360 Newspapers Have Closed Since Just Before the Start of the Pandemic," *New York Times*, June 29, 2022. https://www.nytimes.com/2022/06/29/ business/media/local-newspapers-pandemic.html, accessed August 2, 2022.

Slack, Megan, "From the Archives: President Teddy Roosevelt's New Nationalism Speech," *The White House*, December 6, 2011. https://obamawhitehouse.archives.gov/blog/ 2011/12/06/archives-president-teddy-roosevelts-new-nationalism-speech.

Slisco, Aila "One-Quarter of White Evangelicals Believe QAnon 'Storm' Is Coming to 'Restore Rightful Leaders,'" *Newsweek*, May 28, 2021. https://www.newsweek.com/one-quarter-white-evangelicals-believe-qanon-storm-coming-restore-rightful-leaders-1596086.

Smith, Helena. "Greek Leftist Leader Alexis Tsipras: 'It's a War between People and Capitalism,'" *The Guardian*, May 18, 2012. https://www.theguardian.com/world/2012/may/18/greek-leftist-leader-alexis-tsipras.

Stille, Alexander. "How Matteo Salvini Pulled Italy to the Far Right," *The Guardian*, August 9, 2018. https://www.theguardian.com/news/2018/aug/09/how-matteo-salvini-pulled-italy-to-the-far-right.

"SUPO: Right-Wing Terrorism a Growing Threat in Finland," March 23, 2021. https://www.helsinkitimes.fi/finland/news-in-brief/18916-supo-right-wing-terrorism-a-growing-threat-in-finland.html.

Thayer, Eric. "Transcript: Donald Trump's Victory Speech," *New York Times*, November 9, 2016. https://www.nytimes.com/2016/11/10/us/politics/trump-speech-transcript.html.

"The Omaha Platform: Launching the Populist Party," *The World Almanac, 1893* (New York: 1893), pp. 83–85. Reprinted in George Brown Tindall, ed., *A Populist Reader, Selections from the Works of American Populist Leaders* (New York: Harper & Row, 1966), pp. 90–96. http://historymatters.gmu.edu/d/5361/.

"The 'Omaha Platform' of the People's Party (1892)," Edward McPherson, *A Handbook of Politics for 1892* (Washington, DC: James J. Chapman, 1892), pp. 269–271. https://www.americanyawp.com/reader/16-capital-and-labor/the-omaha-platform-of-the-peoples-party-1892/.

The United States Postal Service, "The Mailing Industry and the United States Postal Service: An Enduring Partnership," *Smithsonian National Postal Museum*, https://postalmuseum.si.edu/americasmailingindustry/United-States-Postal-Service.html.

Tomson, Danielle Lee. "The Rise of Sweden Democrats: Islam, Populism and the End of Swedish Exceptionalism," *Brookings*, March 25, 2020. https://www.brookings.edu/research/the-rise-of-sweden-democrats-and-the-end-of-swedish-exceptionalism/.

"Top French Socialist and Anti-Racism Campaigner Faces Probe for Anti-Semitic Macron Tweet," *The Local*, November 21, 2017. https://www.thelocal.fr/20171121/top-french-socialist-and-anti-racism-campaigner.

"Top French Socialist Booted from Party over Anti-Semitic Tweet," *The Times of Israel*, November 22, 2017. https://www.timesofisrael.com/top-french-socialist-booted-from-party-over-anti-semitic-tweet/.

"Transcript: Bernie Sanders's Full Speech at the 2016 DNC," *The Washington Post*, July 26, 2016. https://www.washingtonpost.com/news/post-politics/wp/2016/07/26/transcript-bernie-sanderss-full-speech-at-the-2016-dnc/.

"Transcript: Donald Trump's Victory Speech," *The New York Times*, November 9, 2016. https://www.nytimes.com/2016/11/10/us/politics/trump-speech-transcript.html.

Union of Concerned Scientist, "USC Satellite Database," published December 8, 2005, updated January 1, 2022. https://www.ucsusa.org/resources/satellite-database.

Washington Post Staff, "Transcript: Bernie Sanders's Full Speech at the 2016 DNC," *The Washington Post*, July 26, 2016. https://www.washingtonpost.com/news/post-politics/wp/2016/07/26/transcript-bernie-sanderss-full-speech-at-the-2016-dnc.

Wearing, David. "Labour Has Slipped Rightwards on Immigration. That Needs to Change," *The Guardian*, July 25, 2017. https://www.theguardian.com/commentisfree/2017/jul/25/labour-immigration-jeremy-corbyn-attitudes.

"Why Is There a Growing Far-Right Threat in Italy?," *TRTWorld*, June 29, 2021. https://www.trtworld.com/magazine/why-is-there-a-growing-far-right-threat-in-italy-47933.

Wilson, Jason and Aaron Flanagon, "The Racist Replacement Theory Explained," *Hatewatch, Southern Poverty Law Center*, May 17, 2022. https://www.splcenter.org/hatewatch/2022/05/17/racist-great-replacement-conspiracy-theory-explained.

Wilson, Mark R. "Mail Order," *Encyclopedia of Chicago*, 2005, http://www.encyclopedia.chicagohistory.org/pages/779.html.

World Economic Forum, https://www.weforum.org/

World Trade Organization, "What We Stand For," 2023, https://www.wto.org/english/thewto_e/whatis_e/what_stand_for_e.htm.

Index

For the benefit of digital users, indexed terms that span two pages (e.g., 52–53) may, on occasion, appear on only one of those pages.

Note: Tables and figures are indicated by *t* and *f* following the page number